Ending Stagnation

A New Economic Strategy for Britain

THE FINAL REPORT OF
THE ECONOMY 2030 INQUIRY

Acknowledgements

This book was produced with input from across the Resolution Foundation and Centre for Economic Performance research teams, and authored by Torsten Bell, Tom Clark, Emily Fry, Gavin Kelly and Greg Thwaites. We would like to thank in particular Camron Aref-Adib, Alex Beer, Tania Burchardt, Mike Brewer, Adam Corlett, Rui Costa, Swati Dhingra, Rebecca Hawkes, Lindsay Judge, Steve Machin, Jonathan Marshall, Charlie McCurdy, Henry Overman, Hannah Slaughter, James Smith, Lalitha Try, Anna Valero and David Willetts for their contributions to the content and arguments of the book. The book builds on Stagnation Nation: The Interim Report of the Economy 2030 Inquiry and is underpinned by the 70 reports written as part of this Inquiry. We are grateful to the authors of these reports and to all those who provided input into each of them through events, seminars and individual conversations. The leadership of the Commissioners and the guidance of the Advisory Group has been invaluable throughout this process, and we are grateful for all that both groups have brought to the work of The Economy 2030 Inquiry, as well as to the Nuffield Foundation for funding this ambitious project.

Citation

If you are using this document in your own writing, our preferred citation is: Resolution Foundation & Centre for Economic Performance, LSE, *Ending Stagnation: A New Economic Strategy for Britain,* Resolution Foundation, December 2023

Contents

Foreword

The UK has great strengths, but we are now a decade and a half into a period of stagnation. The combination of slow growth and high inequality is proving toxic for low- and middle-income Britain, with living standards under strain well before the cost of living crisis. The task facing the UK is to urgently embark on a new path.

This, the Final Report of The Economy 2030 Inquiry, sets out what a serious attempt to end Britain's relative decline looks like. Constraints and trade-offs are examined, and hard-headed choices made.

At its core is a strategy to reverse decades of under-investment, by private and public sectors alike, built on a realistic understanding of Britain's strengths. In place of nostalgia we must mobilise behind achievable versions of the future. The UK is a services superpower, an advantage to be built on in our great second cities. Good quality jobs must become the deliberate objective – rather than by-product – of our economic strategy, while our tax and benefit systems must fairly share rewards and sacrifice, as we target resilient public finances and rebuilt public services. Economic change must be faced and steered to support widely shared prosperity, as we wrestle with major shifts from Brexit to the net zero transition.

The Economy 2030 Inquiry is a collaboration between the Resolution Foundation and the Centre for Economic Performance at the London School of Economics, funded by the Nuffield Foundation. This Final Report is underpinned by the Inquiry's rigorous analysis, drawing on 70 reports, as well as extensive conversations with citizens and policy makers across the country. We thank all of those who have contributed to this work, and in particular our commissioners and staff for their commitment and engagement over the past two years.

Ending our stagnation will not be easy, but is essential for our shared prosperity, and it can be done. Now is the time for Britain to move beyond the dead-ends of boosterism and fatalism.

It is time for a new economic strategy for Britain.

Clive Cowdery & Minouche Shafik
Co-Chairs, The Economy 2030 Inquiry

Executive summary

Executive summary

The promise of shared prosperity is key to our social contract

Countries are bound together in a sense of shared endeavour by many things, from a common history to the collective provision of security for our homes, families and communities. But as traditional hierarchies have weakened and advanced economies become more diverse, the role of the state in delivering shared prosperity has become more central in underpinning social contracts. Rising wages, higher employment and the security of the welfare state have all helped deliver this in the past. Real wages nearly quadrupled, while state spending on healthcare as a share of the economy almost trebled, between the Second World War and the turn of the millennium.

But that progress, and the strength it gives to our society and democracy, should not be taken for granted. There are periods when the social contract comes under pressure; when a clear route to a better tomorrow is lacking, the improvements people expect dry up and some groups are left wondering whether the country works for them. Britain, as we outline in this final report of the Economy 2030 Inquiry, is in this undesirable position today.

That promise is under threat. The cost of living crisis is the immediate issue, but our ambitions must extend beyond getting through it

The early 2020s have been tumultuous years. Britain emerged from the pandemic straight into the cost of living crisis, and the highest inflation in four decades. Energy bills surged, food prices followed and now housing costs are on the rise. **Despite government support totalling £78 billion, hardship is everywhere to be seen: homelessness has hit record levels.** This is not the recovery from the pandemic anyone was hoping for.

But as pressing as today's issues are, policy makers must lift their sights to broader challenges to our shared prosperity. British households went into this crisis with low levels of financial resilience, and a sluggish living standards recovery is expected as we come out of it: **household incomes are not expected to reach their pre-cost of living crisis peak until 2027 at the earliest.**

This is the result of an economy defined by a decade and a half of stagnant incomes, and a generation and a half of high inequality, posing risks not only to our prosperity, but to our social fabric and democracy too. This makes the UK a stagnation nation.

Britain's huge strengths are not being harnessed: we are 15 years into relative economic decline

We were catching up with more-productive countries like France, Germany and the US during the 1990s and early 2000s. But that came to an end in the mid-2000s and our relative performance has been declining ever since, reflecting a productivity slowdown far surpassing those seen in similar economies. **Labour productivity grew by just 0.4 per cent a year in the UK in the 12 years following the financial crisis, half the rate of the 25 richest OECD countries (0.9 per cent).** The UK's productivity gap with France, Germany and the US has doubled since 2008 to 18 per cent, costing us £3,400 in lost output per person.

Claims that these measures of economic progress mean little for ordinary workers are common but painfully wide off the mark. Weak productivity growth has fed directly into flatlining wages and sluggish income growth: **real wages grew by an average of 33 per cent a decade from 1970 to 2007, but this fell to below zero in the 2010s.** In mid-2023 wages were back where they were during the financial crisis. **15 years of lost wage growth has cost the average worker £10,700 a year.**

Gaps between people and places are too high – the UK has the highest income inequality of any major European economy

While Britons have been living with stagnant wages for the last 15 years, high inequality has been a problem for more than twice as long. Having surged during the 1980s, and remained consistently high ever since, income inequality in the UK is higher than any other large European country. This is not a league table we should be aiming to top.

The persistence of high income inequality comes despite the success of the National Minimum Wage in reducing hourly wage inequality. Its stubborn grip reflects the top (largely men) having pulled away from the middle, benefit cuts, lower earners working shorter hours and housing costs rising for poorer households.

Income and productivity gaps between places both matter, and in the UK both are high and persistent. **Income per person in the richest local authority – Kensington** and Chelsea (£52,500) – was 4.5 times that of the poorest – Nottingham (£11,700) – in 2019.

Meanwhile, 80 per cent of the income variation between areas we see today is explained by the differences back in 1997. Productivity disparities are larger still, with that between the leading city and their other large counterparts being greater than in peer countries such as France; London is 41 per cent more productive than Manchester whereas Paris is only 26 per cent more productive than Lyon.

Low growth and high inequality are a toxic combination for low-to-middle income Britain and the young

The twin challenges that Britain faces – low growth and high inequality – are substantial issues on their own, but together they create a toxic combination.

Slow growth is always a problem, but even more so when lower-income households lack financial resilience: over one-in-four adults went into the pandemic saying they would not be able to manage on their savings for a month if their income stopped. Inequality seems to matter more when the economic music stops: **the share of the public citing poverty and inequality as one of the most important issues facing the country rose from 7 per cent in 2010 to 19 per cent pre-pandemic.**

This toxic combination is a disaster for low-to-middle income Britain and younger generations. We might like to think of ourselves as a country on a par with the likes of France and Germany, but we need to recognise that, except for those at the top, this is simply no longer true when it comes to living standards.

Middle-income Brits are now 20 per cent poorer than their peers in Germany and 9 per cent poorer than those in France. Worse, low-income households in the UK are now around 27 per cent poorer than their French and German counterparts. It's important to comprehend just how material these gaps are: the living standards of the lowest-income households in the UK are £4,300 lower than their French equivalents.

Meanwhile the young have seen generational pay progress grind to a halt and those born in the early 1980s were almost half as likely as their parents' generation to own their own home at 30. We cannot go on like this.

The great changes of the 2020s cannot be relied on to end stagnation

Countries can go through phases of relative stability, but the UK in the 2020s will not be such a country. Long-standing demographic and technological shifts will combine with Brexit, rising geopolitical tensions and the net zero transition. These will bring significant disruption for some, though not the radical reset for our economy or large job losses that many predict. Instead, rather than solving our stagnation, these challenges risk reinforcing it.

Brexit has already brought change, albeit not always in the form widely expected. Foreign direct investment has actually held up since the referendum, and three years into our new trading relationship it is not clear that exports to the EU have fallen disproportionately. Instead, the UK has suffered a broad-based fall in both openness and competitiveness. **By 2023, UK trade as a share of GDP was down 2.2 percentage points on pre-pandemic levels (compared to a rise of 0.5 percentage points across the rest of the G7).** This decline is focused on goods, with the UK losing market share across EU and non-EU markets, including the US, Canada, and Japan.

More change is to come as some sectors serving the EU market shrink and others grow as a result of less competition domestically. Fishing output will fall by 30 per cent, while food manufacturing could increase by more than 5 per cent. But these shifts will not lead to the benefits some hoped for: a manufacturing revival or a more regionally-balanced economy. UK manufacturing will change rather than grow, as high-productivity sectors like chemicals and electronics shrink even as lower-productivity food manufacturing expands. Wages in London, Wales and the North East will be hardest hit by the resulting decline in productivity which, across the country as a whole, means **workers will be £470 worse off by the end of the decade.**

Covid-19 caused huge disruption to our economy and our lives. But just as face masks no longer pile up in people's homes, so many of the economic shifts wrought by the pandemic have unwound. What remains is a shift to home working for higher earners **(the proportion working from home regularly surged during the pandemic, and remains high at 38 per cent of workers).** This undoubtedly makes life easier for many, but hardly lives up to excitable claims that Covid-19 would transform our economic geography or our productivity. Far from a global pandemic bringing big silver linings to our shores, its legacy includes the inflation surge we are still living through. And while the long-term impact of AI is highly uncertain, it's clear that the robots we were told would imminently take our jobs and raise our productivity have done neither.

The net zero transition brings many changes and some opportunities. But it is not a silver bullet

The net zero transition is crucial to the planet, and to making the UK a greener and healthier place to live. Our ability to navigate it is underpinned by a high degree of public consensus, but maintaining that requires clear sightedness about the opportunities, and disruption, it brings. The latter won't be in the form of large-scale job losses, with job change rather than destruction the norm. For example, **24 per cent of those working in emissions-intensive 'brown' jobs are large goods vehicle drivers – whose jobs will not disappear even as the vehicles they use become greener.**

Instead, major disruption risks hitting people as consumers, as our net zero commitments require significant investment in low-carbon infrastructure that has to be paid for before benefits from lower operating costs arrive. In the 2020s, this is principally about making our homes more energy efficient. Here there is a risk of outright failure to accelerate the transition, which has stalled after a **90 per cent fall in insulation installations since 2013.** In order to remain on track, the challenge facing policy makers will be to ensure the costs of insulating homes and installing heat pumps are fairly borne.

Low-income property owners are most exposed. **With the disposable income of poorer homeowners averaging £9,100, and the cost of insulating leaky homes over £8,000 per household, it is plain that the necessary investment isn't going to happen without major government intervention.** Current support – for example for heat pump installations – is available to any household irrespective of their financial means, which is affordable only because of very slow progress. The scale of the change to come means it will need to be targeted on the basis of both household income and wealth.

The concrete question of how these investments will be paid for should receive more attention than misplaced claims that net zero is a silver bullet that will hugely boost, or a catastrophe that will hold back, growth. The UK should learn from Joe Biden's Inflation Reduction Act, rather than pretending it can ignore or emulate it. There are new opportunities to be seized and green innovations to be exploited, but during the 2020s the main impact of the net zero transition on GDP will be to alter its composition, as we invest more but consume less, rather than change its level.

These changes do not provide the answers to the toxic combination of low growth and high inequality – but they provide the context within which any attempt to renew the country's path to economic success needs to be placed.

We cannot go on like this. Britain needs a new economic strategy

Relying on supposed silver linings or silver bullets is part of a wider problem: the belief that a policy shift in one area holds the answer to stagnation. It won't. Instead the task is to craft a new economic strategy, rebuilding the UK's route to shared economic success.

Why is a strategy needed? First, because the challenges are large and persistent. **Almost 9 million younger Brits have never worked in an economy that has sustained rising average wages.** Second, because those deep-rooted challenges and disruptions to come are inter-dependent. And third, because the financial crisis and Brexit have blown up major components of the UK's long-standing growth-model, which had itself been found wanting given the large and persistent gaps between people and places.

Some of the ingredients of a more comprehensive approach are visible, from the UK Government's focus on closing economic gaps between places, to the Labour Party's green investment plans, or the Welsh Government's prioritisation of social partnership. But the test for a broader economic strategy is that it combines: **goal orientation,** being clear about the problem a strategy is trying to solve; **clarity about context,** understanding the type of country we are and the opportunities and constraints this brings, without nostalgia about the past or wishful thinking about the future; **realism about trade-offs,** recognising the tensions that always exist; **policies of sufficient scale** to plausibly move the dial; and, finally, **staying power,** because change takes time and short-termism has been a key UK weakness for decades.

No one believes that Britain has such a strategy guiding policy and shaping private decisions today. There is a recognition, from the Prime Minister downwards, that we cannot continue as we are, but we are not on course towards setting any such strategy – indeed we are not serious about the task. Some argue we don't need growth at all because it won't translate into gains for ordinary households, ignoring the reality that a lack of growth is the cause of flatlining wages. More common is to recognise that growth is necessary, or that inequality is too high, but to be deeply unserious about what it might take to improve things. The realities of modern Britain are regularly ignored and the trade-offs between different objectives wished away. We are short-term to our core. Some seem to believe decline is inevitable, others that 'world beating' rhetoric automatically translates into 'world beating' reality. We need to move beyond both fatalism and boosterism.

Understanding your country is a prerequisite for making a success of it: we are a services superpower

Not being serious begins at the most fundamental level: failing to understand what Britain's 21st century economy actually looks like. Talk of the UK economy being narrowly built on banking is as common and misplaced as the claim that there is an easy route to turning ourselves into a German-style manufacturing superpower.

These lazy narratives obscure the reality that Britain is a broad-based services economy, built on successful musicians and architects as well as bankers. We're about ICT, education, culture and marketing, as well as finance (whose fraction of total exports fell from 12 per cent in 2009 to 9 per cent in 2022). No one celebrates it, but the UK is the second largest exporter of services in the world. And our services specialism does not lie behind our recent underperformance: on average, services-led economies tend to be richer than manufacturing-driven ones.

We have narrower, but important, manufacturing strengths too: aerospace and beverages stand out, while there are green technologies, from offshore wind to carbon capture, where specialisms can be built on. But the services-led nature of our economy is not going away, and our path to future prosperity lies in being a better version of Britain, not a British version of Germany. The things countries are good at are highly persistent: **of the top 10 products the UK was most specialised in back in 1989, seven were in our top 10 in 2019.** Even Brexit, the biggest shake-up to our economic place in the world in decades, will have little impact on the balance between goods and services – indeed the biggest risk is that it will change the quality, rather than the quantity, of British manufacturing. And not in a good way.

The UK needs to rethink and reorientate its approach on trade

EU membership provided Britain's trade strategy for the last half century. Post-Brexit a new one has yet to emerge, but it must if the shift of domestic manufacturing towards lower productivity activities is to be avoided, and the opportunities of growing global services trade seized.

The defensive priority now is securing EU market access for high-value-added manufacturing firms struggling to retain their place in European supply chains. Half-way houses, even joining the EU's Customs Union, will not address the fundamental issue faced by British manufacturers: the existence of the UK-EU border for goods. **Instead the objective should be a 'UK Protocol,' building on the current position of Northern Ireland to restore the lost benefits of being part of the EU's customs territory and the single market for goods.** This will not be easy, but it is essential to the future of some of our most successful manufacturing industries.

On services, trade policy must be more expansive in focus and innovative in approach. Here the UK is less dependent on the EU market – even before Brexit 63 per cent of services exports went outside the EU – and there is the potential to harness the UK's service specialism; global trade in the services Britain specialises in has tripled since 2005, growing twice as fast as trade in goods. Traditional, goods focused, free trade agreements have little to offer in this regard, so **the UK should pioneer new services trade agreements with the likes of Singapore, Australia, Canada, Switzerland and Japan.**

Turning around our second cities will boost national income and shrink regional gaps, but needs change on a scale not yet contemplated

Recognising the nature of our economy is not the same thing as welcoming all aspects of it, but a strategy which fails to understand the starting point is no strategy at all. A key challenge for a services-dominated economy is that exports and productive activity tend to be geographically concentrated. In the UK, that currently means in the capital, which accounts for 63 per cent of the UK's surplus in services trade. This holds back Britain's ability to take advantage of growing global markets.

While our current economic specialisation is consistent with future shared prosperity, our regional divides are not. Understanding the drivers of success in a services-led economy guides us to the best way of releasing the brake on its growth. High-value services thrive in large places with highly educated populations where many similar firms can co-locate: cities.

But far too few of our conurbations, all deeply scarred by deindustrialisation, have successfully made the transition to a services economy; all of England's biggest cities outside London have productivity levels below the national average. A strategy to turn this around is what an industrial strategy in a service-dominated economy looks like. This is not a strategy for the few: **the UK may be a 'green and pleasant land', but 69 per cent of the UK population live in cities or their hinterlands, compared to 56 per cent in France and just 40 per cent in Italy.**

At the heart of this problem are the UK's twin second cities: Greater Manchester and Birmingham. With populations of around 2.8 million each, their size means they must be centre stage not just for the sake of their own prosperity, but also for the sake of Britain's. They are too big to fail.

Closing their productivity gaps with London to those that Lyon and Toulouse have with Paris would narrow the UK's output gap to Germany by a fifth. But honesty about the scale of change required is essential. **It would require increasing each city's business capital stock by 15 to 20 per cent; over 160,000 additional high-skilled workers in each city; city centres expanding up or out; and billions of central government investment to expand transport networks.**

Ensuring more places can be at the cutting edge of the UK economy holds out the possibility of raising national growth and shrinking regional productivity gaps, reducing both national inequality and local poverty. Yet within-region inequality could widen – a richer Greater Manchester would have less poverty, but more higher earners too. Housebuilding must be expanded, because the goal is more successful cities, not clones of London with low earners facing exorbitant housing costs.

Residents are understandably ambivalent about higher local inequality, and the significant disruption involved in going for growth. This is why meaningful progress will not happen without bold and empowered local leadership able to manage the disruption involved, which in turn reinforces the case for genuine fiscal devolution.

The UK is a country living off its past, not investing in its future

Investing too little for one year is manageable, but doing so year after year is a recipe for relative decline. This is precisely what the UK has been doing and where it finds itself. **In the 40 years to 2022, total fixed investment in the UK averaged 19 per cent of GDP, the lowest in the G7.** Virtually all of the productivity gap with France is explained by French workers having more capital to work with.

Public sector investment is too low and too volatile

Although the majority of investment is in the private sector, public investment matters too. Here, the average OECD country invests nearly 50 per cent more than the UK and the results are everywhere to be seen: **UK hospitals have fewer beds than all but one OECD advanced economy and UK workers spend more time commuting than those in all but two.** Addressing this legacy requires a higher public investment future, as does a new challenge – the net zero transition.

Our public investment is not just too low, it is too volatile – the second-most volatile among advanced economies over the past 60 years. This prevents forward planning, raising the costs and challenges of getting investment done: even where public investment increases have been planned, £1 in every £6 allocated hasn't been spent.

This volatility reflects incentives for investment to be cut when belt tightening calls, as happened recently in the aftermath of the ill-fated mini-budget of September 2022. It is easier to cancel a bridge tomorrow than fire a nurse, or raise a tax, today. This short-termism is reinforced by a fiscal framework that treats investment spending identically to day-to-day spending, ignoring the value of assets on the public sector balance sheet. **The UK's fiscal rules should be reformed to banish feast and (more common) famines, in favour of sustained public investment of 3 per cent of GDP.** The Treasury should switch its focus to improving the quality, not fiddling with the quantity, of public investment.

Stability alone won't raise business investment – reforms must stoke firms' desire to invest and ability to get things built

British business has caught the same low investment disease as the British state, consistently lying in the relegation zone (bottom 10 per cent) of the OECD business investment league table. **If UK business investment had matched the average of France, Germany and the US since 2008 our GDP would be nearly 4 per cent higher today, boosting wages by around £1,250 a year.**

The sheer scale of political and economic instability hasn't helped. Since 2010 we have had Brexit, Liz Truss, nine Business Secretaries, four versions of the business department and almost annual changes to corporation tax. That last bit of policy instability should be ended by making the temporary full expensing of investment permanent. The stability and quality of policy could also be improved with a statutory National Growth Board, advising government and reporting to Parliament. But stability will not be enough, given that business investment fell during the politically and economically stable mid-2000s.

The UK stands out for low investment, but not low returns on investment when it does take place. So what constrains firms' desire or ability to realise those returns? For one thing, an unusual lack of pressure on British managers from above – via engaged owners – or below ¬– from empowered workers – to focus on long term growth¬. For another, the difficulty of getting anything built.

Ownership of British firms has become more remote, **with foreign ownership rising from 10 per cent in 1990 to over 55 per cent in 2020,** and extremely dispersed, as our pension funds – the overwhelmingly most important source of domestic capital and ownership – moved away from holding equities directly: only 2 per cent of their assets are now directly held UK equities. Diffuse owners, rationally for them but dangerously for Britain, do not incur the substantial costs of monitoring management, risking firms being run myopically with profitable investment foregone. **It is time for a major programme of pension fund consolidation: a far smaller number of far larger, and more active, pension funds is what UK PLC needs.**

In contrast to many European countries, the lack of 'owner voice' is matched by a lack of worker voice. This should change, with **worker representatives on the board of all larger UK firms, which research on Germany, Finland and Norway suggest would raise investment levels.** This would be a big change for British companies, but hardly an unimaginable one – a Conservative Prime Minister recently proposed this exact change.

Even if firms have the desire to invest, they also need the ability to do so – specifically the ability to get things built; in stark contrast to every other G7 economy, the UK has seen no increase in the amount of built-up land per capita since 1990. The cost of planning applications is five times higher in 2023 than 1990, and the outcomes far too unpredictable, also holding back housing and badly needed energy infrastructure. In future, businesses submitting applications consistent with local plans should be automatically approved.

While planning for housing should take place locally, subject to meeting nationally set housing targets, decision-making for business developments should be at a wider geographical level: it's time the benefits, not just the costs, of investment were recognised.

Claims that there are too many degrees distract us from the fact we need to invest more in skills, not less

When it comes to human capital, policy makers are distracted. They question whether we are doing too much education, despite the reality that the very growth sectors which the UK's future prosperity relies on are especially hungry for graduates. Fears of a brain drain from poorer communities are common. But in truth, young people from the most-deprived areas are two-and-a-half times less likely to leave their home area than their more affluent peers.

While the UK has a world-class university system and performs reasonably when it comes to school attainment at 16, provision after that for those not following an academic route is patchy at best, and a disgrace at worst. **Almost a third of young people are not undertaking any education by age 18 – compared to just one in five in France and Germany.** And only one in ten workers are qualified at sub-degree level (Level 4 and 5), half the share it should be given the make-up of the UK economy. Far too many young people peak at GCSE or A level equivalents in Britain, holding back future wages and careers.

Clearer non-academic routes, buttressed by increased student support, are needed. At the heart of these reforms should be **a new 'apprentice guarantee' for all qualified young people, with two thirds of the Apprenticeship Levy ringfenced for the under-25s** to reverse the trend of employers increasingly focusing on existing, older employees – apprenticeship starts for 19-24-year-olds have fallen by a third in the past decade.

Higher investment has to be paid for

In time, higher investment will create higher living standards, not to mention a greener economy. But only in time. A new economic strategy backing higher investment needs to confront the more immediate consequences with an unflinching eye: it requires higher savings (lower consumption) at home, or more borrowing from abroad. There are strong resilience arguments for higher investment to be accompanied by higher saving. The UK is a country that already borrows a lot – our current account deficit averaged 4 per cent of GDP over last decade – and a society where over two fifths of families had savings of less than one month's income when the pandemic hit. **The success of pension auto-enrolment should be built on, with a 50 per cent increase in minimum contribution rates.** But savings at the level of the economy as a whole do not just reflect the behaviour of households. The state also has an important role to play, too.

Investment and growth require a sustainable macroeconomic framework – we don't have one today

Economic, not just policy, stability underpins investment. Important guarantors of that are the ability to support the economy during downturns and keep the public finances on a sustainable path. **The repeated 'once-in-a lifetime' shocks of the past 15 years have seen public sector net debt rise from 36 to around 100 per cent of GDP** – an unprecedented peace-time rise. The lesson of those shocks is that both main parties' focus on debt falling slightly outside of recessions will not be enough in practice to avoid debt being on an upward trajectory.

A tighter fiscal policy will have to be run in good times. The best way to keep the requisite tightening manageable is to contain the pressure for the Treasury to spend big in bad times. The scope for the Bank of England to cut rates in a downturn should be increased by preparing for slightly negative interest rates (as seen in the likes of Denmark and Switzerland). And, **if we return to a low-interest rate world, the inflation target should also be raised from 2 to 3 per cent in coordination with other advanced economies.** Meanwhile, the Treasury needs to avoid being backed into providing hugely expensive universal programmes of support, such as the recent Energy Price Guarantee, due to the lack of more agile alternative options. Building a flexible payments infrastructure to target emergency support when needed would be an investment with high returns.

We must be as hard-headed about lower inequality as higher growth

Success for Britain does not look like becoming America. Despite being far richer, the past decade in the US has shown the dangers to democracy from being the most unequal advanced economy in the world. And **there is nothing economically or democratically sustainable about a UK status quo that saw almost 4 million people experience destitution in 2022.** We must be just as serious about reducing inequality as boosting growth.

But that is not where we are today. Some businesses think it's enough to talk about environmental, social and governance (ESG) issues, while each new crisis sees us patching up the welfare state rather than ensuring it is fit for purpose in the first place.

To make a serious dent in inequality, we need a two-pronged approach: good work must be a central objective of a new economic strategy, not a hoped-for by-product of it, while choices on tax and benefits ensure rewards and sacrifices are equitably shared.

Good jobs must be centre-stage, building on past successes as well as tackling stubborn weaknesses

Successes need to be built on, as well as entrenched problems addressed, in the world of work. The UK's high employment rate is a strength we should not take for granted: **the poorest half of households experienced two-thirds of the jobs growth in the decade after the financial crisis.** Further progress can be made. Reforms to the private pensions regime could nudge the better-off into working longer. **Universal Credit should be reformed and childcare support simplified to ensure work pays for mothers.** A priority must be made of helping the growing number who become sick or disabled remain attached to their current employer.

The minimum wage has seen the lowest earners consistently receive the fastest pay rises for over two decades, with particularly large gains for women and younger workers, and no material negative effect on employment. This is what a policy triumph looks like. **The current pace of minimum wage rises should be maintained, with a new ambition for the minimum wage to reach 73 per cent of median pay (£14 on current forecasts) by 2029.** Celebrating the success of the minimum wage must not, however, blind us to the total lack of progress elsewhere. A good work agenda must be more than a one-trick pony.

It is time to go beyond the minimum wage

As the minimum wage has ramped up this century, job satisfaction for lower earners has fallen. Too often, work does not offer them the security, flexibility or control that higher earners take for granted. Low earners are four times as likely as high earners to experience volatility in their hours or pay. Indefensibly, **half of shift workers in Britain receive less than a week's notice of their working schedules. Workers should have new rights to a contract enshrining minimum hours reflecting their usual work pattern, and two weeks' advance notice of**

shifts. Illness is bad for the financial, as well as physical, health for too many lower earners. **Statutory Sick Pay leaves many to live on just £44 if they are sick for a week, and should be reformed to pay 65 per cent of normal earnings.**

After raising the floor for workplace standards, we also need to enforce it. That is not a task taken seriously in a country that sees 334,000 employees paid less than the legal minimum. **We have too many enforcement agencies (six, overseen by seven government departments) with too few boots on the grounds (just 0.29 labour market inspectors per 10,000 workers),** putting the onus on workers to protect their own rights via employment tribunals – something the groups most at risk of having their rights breached are least likely to do. This system works for bad employers, but not their competitors who end up being undercut, nor their underpaid workers. Instead **we need a Single Enforcement Body, issuing meaningful fines and addressing systemic problems.**

Power and institutions matter in the labour market; not all problems can be addressed with national minimum standards. **Trade unions remain important but membership has declined from 52 to 22 per cent of the workforce since 1980.** Behind that decline lie not just structural changes, such as deindustrialisation. Legislative changes, that were meant to create a level playing field between employers and unions, have instead tilted the pitch against the latter. Antiquated restrictions, including unions having no right to enter workplaces and bans on online voting, should be lifted.

It is wishful thinking, though, to rely on a union renaissance or indeed a tight labour market to remedy poor conditions in the most problematic sectors. Here, institutional innovation is required, addressing industry specific problems that general employment law is too blunt a tool to crack. Learning from the experience of other flexible labour markets with well-established, or recently developed, sectoral bodies, from Ireland to New Zealand, **'Good Work Agreements' should bring together workers and employers to solve knotty problems about the quality of work in their industry, setting minimum standards or ways of working to be adopted sector-wide.** The first should be established in social care where a predominately female (77 per cent) workforce is often illegally underpaid, with warehousing and cleaning next in line.

Politicians' promises that every type of job will be available everywhere are very far from serious. But ensuring good jobs exist in every part of our country – particularly in the non-tradable sectors that provide largely for the domestic market, from care to hospitality – is a promise a new economic strategy can and must make.

High housing costs hold down living standards and push up inequality

The share of income families dedicate to housing has doubled since 1980. The rise has been largest for those on low incomes, whose home now costs them a third of their income. They increasingly rely on the private-rented sector, where costs are too high and quality too low.

Also too low is the number of homes in the UK. While the likes of France and Italy have seen big increases in the number of homes relative to inhabitants, the UK has made no progress. **The building of homes for social rent fell from over 40,000 homes a year in the 1990s, to just 8,000 a year over the past decade.** Higher standards in the private rented sector and higher housing supply are both needed – the 300,000 homes a year target included in the 2019 Conservative Manifesto and adopted by the Labour Party provides a good starting point, so long as they are focused in the areas of the country where housing costs are high or fast rising.

If Britain as a whole returns to steady growth, we should expect further increases in housing costs to follow. Of particular concern are those who may not benefit from that rising prosperity but nonetheless see their housing costs increase in response to it. Housing support in the benefit system exists precisely to protect them. Unfortunately, it has not been allowed to rise in line with rents since 2019. This is directly hitting poorer households, and also locking them out of those parts of the country where they might find better opportunities. **Relinking housing support to rent levels will lean against inequality and facilitate mobility. Reducing residential stamp duty would also help boost the latter.**

A decent society does not allow poorer people to fall ever further behind

We have an obligation to pensioners, and the 11 million people of working age for whom earnings make up less than half of their income, very often because of caring responsibilities or disabilities. So markets, however fair, and jobs, however good, cannot ensure that growth automatically boosts the living standards of the whole population. This is the job of the social security system, but it is not fulfilling that role today.

The UK has chosen a low level of basic income protection. Working-age benefits have for many decades risen only in line with prices, rather than keeping pace with (generally faster growing) earnings. In practice, we haven't even managed that recently – **benefit levels have failed to keep pace with prices in 10 of the past 15 years. Along with wider cuts since 2010, this has reduced incomes of poorest fifth by just under £3,000 a year.** As a result, over a quarter of households with a disabled adult are in poverty, as are more than two-fifths of families with three or more children (up from one-third in 2012-13), and inequality hasn't fallen despite the rising minimum wage and those progressive employment gains.

Looking ahead, rather than in the rear-view mirror, the current approach means disconnecting the living standards of poorer households from the rest of the population. Any economic strategy that claims to be serious about reducing inequality will need to change tack.

Ultimately social security benefits must grow in line with wages rather than prices. This is a big change, but the argument for it has already been won in countries such as New Zealand and Germany and here, too, on pensions. Concerns it will harm work incentives are overdone in the context of a fast-rising minimum wage; cutting out-of-work benefits is not the only way to improve work incentives. The costs are real, but over half of them can be covered by uprating pensions on the same basis as working age benefits, rather than via the 'triple lock'. This combined approach, along with fixing the most glaring holes in the safety net by abolishing two child limit, will cost 0.6 per cent GDP by 2039-40.

We need better, not just higher, taxes

Taxes are up, but their quality is not. **Having averaged 33 per cent of GDP in the first two decades of this century, the tax take is now on course to rise by over 4 per cent of GDP (£4,200 per household) by 2027-28.** The exact size of the state depends on political choices, but a new economic strategy must plan on higher taxes being here to stay. Higher debt interest costs and the state of public services point in that direction, before we even get to the pressures from our ageing population and the net zero transition. This is why politicians declaring their low-tax 'instincts' have raised taxes to their highest levels since the 1940s.

The growth and fairness penalties from our incoherent tax system are rising with the higher tax take. A new approach must recognise that **the burden cannot continue to fall disproportionately on employees, which means taxing income consistently whatever its source so that landlords pay the same taxes as their tenants and taxes on self-employed corporate lawyers are levelled up to those facing bankers.** This is an agenda that will push up unjustifiably low rates for some on higher incomes, while also cutting the highest marginal rates, including ending rates of 100 per cent facing some parents as their child benefit is taxed away

Wealth also needs to take more of the strain. **Household wealth has risen from three to over seven times national income since the 1980s, while poorly designed wealth taxes have not risen at all as a share of GDP.** Council tax cannot continue as a near-poll tax, only weakly linked to three-decades-old property values. An inheritance tax with fewer reliefs would be harder for the well advised to abuse and could halve tax rates for smaller estates.

Our tax system also needs to keep pace with the net zero transition. To ensure the burden of motoring taxes does not fall on poorer households yet to switch to electric vehicles, **a 6p per mile charge (equivalent to fuel duty) should be introduced for EVs.** By 2039-40 this policy will raise around 0.7 per cent of GDP. Combined with the broader package above, this amounts to a significant increase in revenues of 1.3 per cent of GDP by the end of the next decade. But importantly it will mean better, not just higher, taxes.

Economic change has slowed down – it must be embraced, and steered

The goal for a new economic strategy is not a somewhat richer, somewhat fairer, version of the UK's stagnant status quo, but a more enduring shift in direction. The pace of economic change, contrary to popular claims that it is speeding up, is slowing down; **the reallocation of labour between sectors is at its lowest level in over 90 years.** That matters: higher productivity sectors growing and lower productivity ones shrinking used to add 0.4 percentage points per year to growth in the pre-financial crisis decade.

The notion that it is somehow improper to take a view on the future shape of our economy, must be dispatched. Change must be steered, not with wishful thinking (the UK does not shape global technology developments) but via an understanding that even in a liberal market economy the government can and does shape outcomes.

This book sets out a strategy to grow higher-productivity tradable activity. For the UK, the size of these sectors servicing global demand is far from set in stone and small changes make a big difference: **halving the pace of decline in our share of global service exports between 2005 and 2018 would have meant an extra 585,000 people working in these growth-critical fields.**

It is easy to point at sectors it would be nice to grow, but a serious strategy must also wrestle with what should not expand. **Hospitality, accounting for over 60 per cent of employment growth across lower-paying sectors since 2008,** is a crucial employer, not to mention source of significant pleasure. Its size reflects in part a set of choices. The proportion of total consumption that hospitality represents is higher in the UK than anywhere else in Europe. Why? Because it is relatively cheap.

Improving pay and conditions for workers in this and other lower productivity sectors will over time change that. This is a feature, not a bug, of how improved labour market conditions can make Britain a fairer country; workers in lower income households benefit most from higher pay, while richer households, who spend a larger share of their budgets on face to face services, are most affected by the higher prices that follow.

Bad firms need to feel more competitive pressure

Shifting resources from low to high performing firms is much more important to raising national productivity than the current focus on supporting the 'long tail' of firms to improve. This type of dynamic change as some firms shrink and others grow has also slowed, and is directly discouraged by a tax system that favours small firms over large – encouraging some not to grow. Bad firms not only hold back the economy as a whole, but also the wages and wellbeing of those working in them. **Support should be focused on young, rather than small, firms, while competitive pressures should be fostered** via greater trade-openness and by pincering poor performers between higher investing competitors and rising labour standards.

Dynamic labour markets are about more than freedom to hire and fire

For good firms or higher productivity sectors to grow, workers need to move to them. But for too long we have assumed the UK's flexible labour regime, with the relative ease of hiring and firing, automatically engenders a truly dynamic labour market. It does not: **the proportion of workers switching job each quarter**

declined by 25 per cent between 2000 and 2019. This is not good news: workers' jobs typically enjoy pay growth 4 percentage points higher than individuals staying put. The missing ingredient is empowered workers, willing and able to take risks.

A key barrier for higher earners is a welfare state that offers them next to no income protection, so **new Unemployment Insurance should cover 65 per cent of previous wages for the first three months.** In contrast, lower earners receive greater income protection from the benefits system, but often risk losing informal security and flexibility over the hours they work when moving on. Stronger rights to security will mean taking a leap for a new job is more of a promise, and less of a threat.

Slow growth and high inequality are not inevitable. Britain has huge catch-up potential

Renewing the UK's economic strategy will be far from easy. Some might question how achievable a material increase in growth or reduction in inequality is for a relatively small and mature economy like the UK. But such fatalism misjudges the UK's room for improvement; we have a lot of catch-up potential.

Consider a set of similar comparator economies: Australia, Canada, France, Germany, and the Netherlands. We would long have considered them our peers and, though impressive, they are not the richest, or most equal, countries in the world. But all are now richer and more equal than Britain. We're 16 per cent poorer than these countries on average, suggesting catch-up potential that dwarfs the Office for Budget Responsibility's forecast of a 4 per cent hit from Brexit.

If Britain exploited its catch-up potential, closing its average income and inequality gaps with these peer economies, the typical household would be 25 per cent (£8,300) better off, with income gains of 37 per cent for the poorest households.

A better future for the UK does not need global growth to suddenly accelerate, or Britain to match American levels of productivity and Scandinavian levels of inequality. It just requires us to have the resolve to do what is necessary to converge with similar countries who, in the scheme of things, are not so very different to us. There is a lot to play for.

Moving the UK back into the pack is realistic – and transformative

The strategy outlined in this book could move us in that direction. **Over 15 years, improved physical and human capital might mean GDP being 7 per cent higher than currently expected. Wages would receive a 5 per cent boost,** sufficient to repair all of the damage done to UK pay levels relative to the G7 average between 2008 and 2022.

Raising growth alone would also raise inequality, with the top half seeing twice the income gains of the bottom half, but our reform agenda would shift the rewards decisively. Progressive wage growth, driven by a rising minimum wage, would raise living standards for middle income households in particular, while further employment gains would be concentrated at the bottom. When combined with our proposed tax and benefit reforms, the poorest households would see the fastest income gains of everyone. This is a new economic strategy capable of raising growth and cutting inequality.

Typical incomes before housing costs for the working-age population would rise by 11 per cent (almost £4,000) more than they otherwise would, sufficient to overtake France and halve the income gap with the Netherlands and Germany. **Relative poverty, rather than rising by 1.1 million as currently expected, would be cut by 1.3 million people.**

This would amount to a Britain back into the pack of peer economies, but with lots more work to do. And, with only 60 per cent of the eventual impact of higher business investment manifesting within the 15-year frame of our projections, this is an economic strategy whose impact would continue to build.

It is also a strategy to help resolve some of the big macroeconomic trade-offs facing the country. Faster growth, combined with the tax changes proposed, **would raise revenues to the tune of 3 per cent of GDP by the end of the 2030s.** That would provide useful resources to boost public investment, see to it that the debt burden is genuinely falling, and also support the rebuilding of public services.

Towards a fairer and more prosperous Britain

Ending stagnation is far from automatic, as Italy demonstrates. Disappointing economic outcomes, of the kind the UK has experienced, erode confidence that a better future is possible. Winners from the status quo may oppose change, be they older generations benefiting from the rise of wealth, younger ones confident of inheriting it, or richer households, relatively protected from the UK's relative decline by its high inequality.

But it is increasingly clear that there is a majority for change. It is middle income Brits, as well as just the poorest, who now find themselves far behind their peers in similar countries. It is not only millennials facing disappointment; **those in Generation X are entering their 50s and rightly wondering why their wages peaked in the 2000s.** Older voters care about the lives of younger relatives, and also the lack of growth that threatens the funding of the services that they rely on themselves. Many, comfortably off themselves, do not want to live in a nation where every town needs a food bank. **Today six in 10 Britons think the country is heading in the wrong direction, with far fewer – just 16 per cent – thinking it is on the right track.**

This book brings together an analysis of the key challenges facing the UK and the strengths that can be brought to bear in addressing them. It outlines the contours of an economic strategy that could provide a plausible path to ending stagnation, an agenda that builds on our strengths, invests in our future, delivers good jobs and fairly shares rewards and sacrifices. History teaches us that growth can speed up as well as slow down, and inequality can fall as well as rise. This stagnant chapter of British life has gone on long enough. It is time to turn the page.

A Stagnation Nation in 10 key facts

1. **Low growth:** Real wages grew by 33 per cent a decade from 1970 to 2007, but have flatlined since, costing the average worker £10,700 per year in lost wage growth.

2. **High inequality:** Income inequality in the UK is higher than any other large European country.

3. **The toxic combination:** Low growth and high inequality means typical households in Britain are 9 per cent poorer than their French counterparts, while our low-income families are 27 per cent poorer.

4. **Stalled progress:** 9 million young workers have never worked in an economy with sustained average wage rises, and millennials are half as likely to own a home, and twice as likely to rent privately, as their parents' generation.

5. **Talent wasted:** Almost a third of young people in the UK are not undertaking any education by age 18 – compared to just one in five in France and Germany.

6. **Gaping gaps:** Income per person in the richest local authority – Kensington and Chelsea (£52,500) – was over four times that of the poorest – Nottingham (£11,700) – in 2019.

7. **Bad work:** Half of shift workers in Britain receive less than a week's notice of their working hours or schedules.

8. **Flaky firms:** UK companies have invested 20 per cent less than those in the US, France and Germany since 2005, placing Britain in the bottom 10 per cent of OECD countries, and costing the economy 4 per cent of GDP.

9. **Taxes up:** Having averaged 33 per cent of GDP in the first two decades of this century, the tax take is now on course to rise over 4 percentage points by 2027-28: equivalent to £4,200 per household.

10. **The wrong track:** Six in ten Britons think the country is heading in the wrong direction, with far fewer – just one in six – thinking it is on the right track.

Ending Stagnation in 10 key steps

1. **A services superpower:** Britain must build on its strengths as the second biggest services exporter in the world, behind only the US, while protecting the place of its high value manufacturing in European supply chains.

2. **Our second cities are too big to fail:** Our cities should be centres for Britain's thriving high-value service industries. But instead, all England's biggest cities outside London have productivity levels below the national average.

3. **Investing in our future, not living off our past:** Public investment in the average OECD country is nearly 50 per cent higher than in the UK. Tackling this legacy, alongside the net zero transition, requires public investment to rise to 3 per cent of GDP.

4. **Pressure from above and below:** British managers too rarely invest for the long-term. Pressure for change should come from more engaged owners – a smaller number of far larger pensions funds – and from workers on boards.

5. **Good work in every town:** Despite the success of the minimum wage, a good work agenda cannot be a one-trick pony. Statutory Sick Pay can leave the ill on just £44 a week, while 900,000 workers miss out on paid holiday.

6. **Steering change:** Hospitality represents a higher share of consumption in the UK than anywhere else in Europe, because it is relatively cheap. Better pay for low earners in hospitality, paid for by higher prices that most affect better off households, will create a more equal UK.

7. **Recoupling everyone to rising prosperity:** Benefit levels have not kept pace with prices: cuts since 2010 have reduced the incomes of the poor by almost £3,000 a year. Shared prosperity means benefits rising with wages.

8. **Better, not just higher, taxes:** A rising tax burden should not just fall on earnings, but should be shouldered by other sources of income and wealth. Wealth has risen from three to over seven times national income since the 1980s.

9. **Resilient public and private finances:** Higher growth and higher taxes are needed to raise investment, rescue public services, and repair public finances. Higher investment should be funded by higher savings at home, not borrowing from abroad.

10. **Exploiting catch-up potential:** If the UK matched the average income and inequality of Australia, Canada, France, Germany and the Netherlands, the typical household would be £8,300 better off.

Introduction

We live in turbulent times

The early 2020s have not been easy years. Britain stepped straight out of the unprecedented shock delivered by Covid-19 into the cost of living crisis, triggered by surging energy prices. The first global pandemic in 100 years was followed by the highest inflation seen for four decades.

The UK's cost of living crisis has gone through several distinct phases, as the epicentre of the squeeze on households has moved from energy to food and then housing. Inflation had begun its long rise to over 11 per cent before Russia's invasion of Ukraine, but the conflict turbocharged price increases, including an unprecedented 54 per cent rise in household energy bills in April 2022.[1] By mid-2023 falling energy bills brought less relief than hoped, with the fastest food inflation since the 1970s seeing the cost of eating outstripping the cost of heating as the biggest pressure on family finances.[2]

The cost of living crisis has bitten deep and rightly been the priority for people and policy makers

Everyone is affected by surging prices, with millions cutting back on energy use, running down savings or taking on debt.[3] Wages in the early autumn of 2023 remain 2 per cent lower than they were two years prior.[4]

The Bank of England has spent 2023 wrestling with how to prevent high inflation from becoming embedded in the UK economy without sinking us into a recession. The largest series of interest rate rises in more than three decades has put more pressure on many families' finances: the nation's home owners will gradually face the consequences as they remortgage, with an average hit of £3,000 a year.[5]

---

1 House of Commons Library, Research Briefing: Domestic energy briefing, 06 June 2023.

2 T Bell, J Smith & L Try, Food for thought, Resolution Foundation, May 2023.

3 M Broome, K Handscomb & L Try, Hoping and Coping: How families were faring in March 2023, Resolution Foundation, April 2023.

4 In real (CPI-adjusted) terms, median monthly employee earnings in September 2023 were 1.9 per cent below their level in October 2021. Source: HMRC, Earnings and employment from Pay As You Earn Real Time Information, seasonally adjusted, October 2023, via ONS; ONS, Consumer Prices Index.

5 A Corlett, The Living Standards Outlook – Summer 2023 Update, Resolution Foundation, September 2023.

Meanwhile, private rents are up around 30 per cent between January 2021 and September 2023.[6]

While everyone has been affected by the cost of living crisis, they have not been affected equally. Low- and- middle income Britain spends a far greater proportion of their budgets on essentials – on the items whose prices have surged the most. [7] As a result, the poorest households faced inflation rates peaking up to 4 percentage points higher than those experienced by the top during this crisis.[8] As we heard in focus groups:[9]

> "It always seems to be the people on the lowest incomes, the people who are working class, that's having to struggle."

> Participant, Paisley focus group

The scale and impact of the surging cost of living resulted in governments across Europe stepping in to provide significant support. In the UK, this has come at a cost of £78 billion and rightly been increasingly focused on poorer households.[10] But in spite of this, hardship is everywhere to be seen.

The Trussell Trust – the largest food bank network – gave out over 3 million food parcels in 2022-23, up over a third on the previous year.[11] Despite such efforts, many are suffering: food insecurity has shot up to three times the levels seen pre-pandemic, and in spring 2023 one in five Britons were skipping meals or eating less.[12] Homelessness has reached a record high in both England and Scotland.[13]

---

6   HomeLet Rental Index, www.homelet.co.uk/homelet-rental-index, accessed 30th October 2023.

7   In 2019-20, food and energy made up 22 per cent of total spending for the lowest income households compared with 13 per cent for the richest households. Analysis of ONS, Living Costs and Food Survey.

8   T Bell, J Smith & L Try, Food for thought, Resolution Foundation, May 2023.

9   The quotes used throughout this book are from four reports: K Handscomb, L Judge & H Slaughter, Listen up: Individual experiences of work, consumption and society, Resolution Foundation, May 2022; L Judge & D Tomlinson, All over the place: Perspectives on local economic prosperity, Resolution Foundation, June 2022; L Murphy, Constrained choices: Understanding the prevalence of part-time work among low-paid workers in the UK, Resolution Foundation, November 2022; and T Burchardt, T Goatley & L Judge, Talking trade-offs: Deliberations on a higher-productivity future in the Birmingham and Greater Manchester urban areas, Resolution Foundation, November 2023.

10 For costings, See Chapter 3 of the OBR, Economic and fiscal outlook, March 2023; For the distribution of this support, see T Bell et al, We're going on a growth Hunt: Putting the 2023 Spring Budget in context, Resolution Foundation, March 2023.

11 The Trussell Trust, UK Factsheet - Emergency food parcel distribution in the UK: April 2022 - March 2023, April 2023

12 T Bell, J Smith and L Try, Food for thought, Resolution Foundation, May 2023.

13 DLUHC, Statutory homelessness in England: financial year 2022-23, October 2023; Scottish Government, Homelessness in Scotland: 2022-23, August 2023.

By the summer of 2023, wages were growing faster than prices again, but rising taxes and housing costs mean the recovery in living standards has a long way to go. As Figure 1 shows, household incomes are not expected to reach their pre-cost of living crisis peak until 2027 at the earliest.

Figure 1: lower for longer: income forecasts remain weak

Outturns and forecast for Real Household Disposable Income per person, in 2023 prices: UK

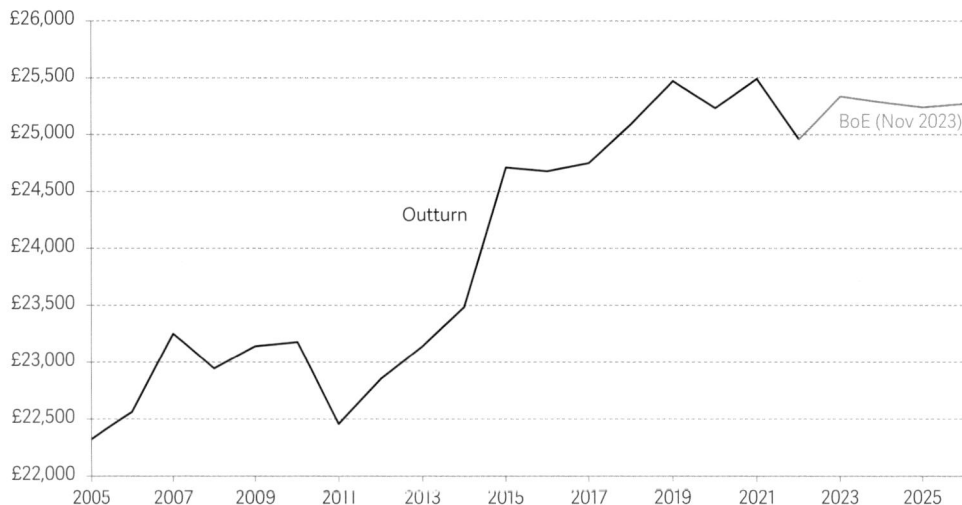

Notes: Includes non-profit institutions serving households (NPISH). The Bank of England line is constructed by combining its forecast for real post-tax household income growth with ONS projections for UK population growth.
Source: Analysis of ONS, National Accounts and National population projections; Bank of England, Monetary Policy Report, November 2023.

We must raise our sights beyond recovering from this latest crisis

Getting back to the levels of household incomes that we had in the middle of the pandemic cannot be the limit of our ambitions for the years ahead. We need to ask fundamental questions, including why quite so many Britons were sorely exposed during this crisis.

At root, there are two answers to that, both long predating the specific challenges of the last three years: a decade and a half of stagnant incomes – and a generation and a half of high inequality. Britain went into the pandemic and cost of living crisis with wages no higher than they were when we entered the financial crisis over a decade before,[14] and as the most unequal large economy in Europe.

14 ONS, Labour market statistics, September 2023.

The first purpose of this book is to get behind these sorts of grim facts and understand what it is about the workings of our economy that produces such disappointing results. The second is to set out how we can change things, with a road map for moving to a higher growth, fairer society: in short, a renewed economic strategy for Britain.

Over 15 disappointing years, the UK has bumped from crisis to crisis – sometimes improvising successfully, but with every new burst of turbulence adding to our problems and distracting attention from how deep they run. The result is a governing outlook that isn't focused on the fundamental failings that this book aims to fix.

Our motives go far beyond economics: part of the prize of ending stagnation is a healthier democracy. In a society that rightly cannot rely on traditional deference, the promise of widely shared prosperity is central to social cohesion. Not so long ago, the UK could point to tangible progress on living standards for most of its citizens: real wages nearly quadrupled between the Second World War and the millennium. With that sort of advance, it is possible to write a social contract that can bind increasingly diverse populations together. In its absence, unstable, divisive, and zero-sum forms of politics can rise. The affairs of a nation can easily be reduced to a grudge match and, in the worst case, alienation creates the conditions for backsliding from democracy. The UK has not reached that pass yet, but the lesson of history – and from around the world – is that complacency is never wise.[15]

So, as citizens as well as economists, we are determined to rebuild the UK's path to economic success. If the long years of stagnation have taught us anything, it is that this won't happen by accident, nor will it arise from visions of abstract utopias. A new approach must be rooted in an unflinching assessment of where we start from – our weaknesses as well as our strengths – with an unremitting focus on the real choices on offer.

Throughout, we draw on the detailed research carried out as part of The Economy 2030 Inquiry, a collaboration between the Resolution Foundation and the Centre for Economic Performance at the London School for Economics, funded by the Nuffield Foundation.[16] Our focus is a strategy for the UK economy as a whole. However, with increasingly devolved governance, this book should be of interest to (and indeed is informed by the work of) national and sub-regional administrations.

---

15 See, for example, M Wolf, The Crisis Of Democratic Capitalism, Allen Lane, 2023.

16 All research of The Economy 2030 Inquiry is available at www.economy2030.resolutionfoundation.org.

We proceed as follows:

- **Chapter 1** looks at the UK's toxic combination of low growth and high inequality, and the consequences for the living standards of low- and middle-income Britain.

- **Chapter 2** surveys the pressing challenges of this hour, including Brexit and the net zero transition, concluding that all of them matter, but none will shake Britain out of its present stagnation.

- **Chapter 3** makes the case that a renewal of our economic strategy is required, but not on offer. Approaches with clarity, direction and scale have remade economies in other times and places, and can do so again.

- **Chapter 4** identifies Britain's considerable strengths, and how we might build on them to drive growth.

- **Chapter 5** argues that a return to prosperity requires a fundamental shift: investing in our future, rather than living off our past.

- **Chapter 6** recognises the need to be as serious about getting inequality down as we are about getting growth up. The latter will translate into sorely needed pay rises, but this alone cannot deliver widely shared prosperity. A good jobs agenda is required.

- **Chapter 7** outlines a tax and benefit system that fairly shares reward and sacrifice, which must be centre stage.

- **Chapter 8** highlights that structural change, far from speeding up, has slowed down. Change must be embraced, but also steered to lastingly turn the tide on our stagnation era.

- **Chapter 9** wraps things up by considering the size of the prize, examining the scale of difference a strategy of this sort could make to the living standards of families across the UK.

Are we overstating the potential for policy makers to shift the dial on Britain's economic performance? Our aims are ambitious, but there is nothing inevitable about our current relative decline, just as there is no automatic reason why it should end. Within living memory, the UK has seen periods of significantly improved relative economic performance compared to similar countries. We should take heart, too, from the fact that many of Britain's underlying economic assets will only grow in relevance as we progress through the 21st century. And we have some political advantages that shouldn't be forgotten, including a degree of public consensus around some key issues, such as closing regional gaps and making progress towards net zero. The smartest politicians on all sides understand this.

The goal of securing a more prosperous and equal country is certainly challenging. But even in isolation well-crafted public policies can make a huge difference. Just think of the minimum wage, whose success over the past quarter of a century has gone far beyond anything imagined at its introduction. Britain, the low pay capital of Europe in the 1990s, stands on the brink of abolishing hourly low pay.[17] While the immediate impact of policies is often overstated, their longer-term, transformational potential – if part of a mutually reinforcing agenda for change – should not be underplayed.

Fatalism, as much as complacency, is the enemy of clear thought about the country's future. Realism, twinned with a sense of informed optimism about the potential power of policy, are preconditions for turning the page on stagnation, and writing a better next chapter for Britain.

---

17 Since the financial crisis, the median year-on-year wage growth across all workers has averaged approximately 2.6 per cent, whereas the equivalent growth for minimum-wage workers has been 4.5 per cent. For further discussion of pay growth and the impact of the minimum wage, see: N Cominetti et al., Low Pay Britain 2023: Improving Low-Paid Work through Higher Minimum Standards, Resolution Foundation, April 2023.

Chapter One

Starting from here

Chapter summary

- The UK has many strengths, from world-class universities and creative industries to high employment. But having grown more quickly than most advanced economies from the 1990s to the mid-2000s, the UK has been in relative decline ever since: the average productivity gap with France, Germany and the US doubled, to 18 per cent, between 2008 and 2022.

- Slow growth means flatlining wages: in mid-2023 wages were back where they were during the financial crisis, with the 15 years of lost wage growth costing the average worker £10,700 a year.

- Having surged during the 1980s, and remained consistently high ever since, income inequality in the UK was the highest of any large European country in 2019.

- Inequality between places is high and persistent too: all of England's biggest cities outside the capital have productivity levels lower than the UK average.

- This is stagnation: the toxic combination of low growth and high inequality is ruinous for low-to-middle income Britain. Middle-income Brits are now 20 per cent poorer than their peers in Germany and 9 per cent poorer than those in France. Worse, low-income UK households are now around 27 per cent poorer than their French and German counterparts – equivalent to £4,300 a year.

- The young have been particularly hard hit: 9 million younger Brits have never worked in an economy that has sustained rising average wages and today's young people are less than half as likely to own a home at age 30 as their parents' generation.

- Incomes have stagnated but wealth has grown: between the end of the 1980s and the start of the 2020s, the total value of household wealth in Britain has swollen from around three to nearly eight times GDP. Today's higher interest rates will reduce the scale, but not the fact of, this rise.

- Even as taxes rise, public services are struggling. The number of people waiting for NHS consultant treatment have more than doubled, from 3 million to 7.4 million, in the nine years after 2014.

The country wrestling with today's cost of living crisis, like the people, places, and firms experiencing it, has a history. Understanding where that history has left the UK is the purpose of this chapter. Alongside many strengths, it argues that the Britain of the 2020s risks being defined by the combination of sustained low growth and even more protracted high inequality. Each brings challenges, but a prolonged period of the two together condemns most of the population to stagnation. Shaking that off must be our top priority.

Britain has many advantages

In a global context, the UK is a privileged and prosperous nation. Having been one of the world's richest countries for centuries, our national incomes still average 6 per cent more than is typical for the advanced economies that make up the Organisation for Economic Cooperation and Development (OECD).[1]

The UK has many strengths. Our employment rate is high. Setting up a company is easy. Our population adopts technology swiftly. We have a long history of being relatively open to trade and Britain attracts far more than our share of foreign investment.[2] Finance is famously a forte, but many other sectors are hugely important too, with the globe-straddling English language also supporting all manner of cultural and educational exports.[3] Gaming and TV production have been growing fast. In the life sciences and pharmaceuticals, British firms are often at the cutting edge of innovation. They and many other industries benefit from the UK's world-class universities and research.[4] School standards generally exceed international averages.[5]

As a founding member of NATO and with a location just off the coast of western Europe, Britain can claim to be an island of relative stability and security in uncertain geopolitical times. Our geographical position may be insular, but it is not remote: our place and time zone afford natural integration into the dense North Atlantic systems of trade and travel. In the context of climate change, the UK is

---

1   Source: Analysis of OECD Incomes Distribution Database in 2019 prices, using OECD PPPs.

2   J De Lyon et al., Enduring strengths: Analysing the UK's current and potential economic strengths, and what they mean for its economic strategy, at the start of the decisive decade, Resolution Foundation, April 2022.

3   British Council, Global Perceptions Survey 2021, December 2021.

4   Department for Business, Energy & Industrial Strategy, International comparison of the UK Research Base, 2019: Accompanying note, July 2019.

5   According to the last cross national PISA study, 15-year olds in the UK rank above the OECD average in reading, maths and science, with the rating of maths improving since 2015. See: PISA results (2018) Country note: UK, OECD, December 2019.

less immediately vulnerable than many countries [6], and also benefits from natural potential to generate the renewable electricity that a greener world is going to need[7], as well as specialisms in key clean technologies.[8]

But we are in a period of relative decline

Recognition of the UK's enduring and underlying strengths must not inhibit an honest assessment of where we find ourselves today – deep into a period of relative decline. Britain's recovery from the pandemic is in line with European norms, but the longer-term picture is deeply unsettling. Looking back over the past 15 years reveals that Britain's economy in 2023 is 22 per cent smaller than it would have been had we continued on our pre-financial crisis trend.[9] Britain doesn't fare much better when looking to the future, with both the International Monetary Fund and the Bank of England pessimistic about the next few years.[10]

Such short-term predictions are particularly uncertain, but our recent experience of underperformance is painfully concrete. Yes, Britain is a secure member of the family of high-income nations, but it is a long way from the top of this group and the gap has been widening. To use a football analogy, we are not yet in immediate danger of relegation from the top division, but we are drifting further away from qualifying for the Champions League.

It is reasonable, albeit ambitious, to compare productivity in the UK with the US – the most productive large country in the world – along with the two most productive large European economies, France and Germany. Having stood at two-thirds of US productivity levels in 1970, all three European nations were gradually converging with America (see Figure 2). Within that cross-Atlantic story, the UK also gained ground on France and Germany during the 1990s and early 2000s. Sometime around the mid-2000s, however, the UK stopped catching up with anyone: its relative performance next to France, Germany and the US has been declining since.

---

6   www.gain.nd.edu/our-work/country-index, accessed 23 October 2023; D Eckstein, V Künzel & L Schäfer, Global Climate Risk Index 2021: Who suffers most from extreme weather events? Weather-related loss events in 2019 and 2000-2019, Germanwatch, January 2021.

7   Department for Business, Energy & Industrial Strategy, Energy white paper: Powering our net zero future, December 2020.

8   B Curran et al., Growing clean: Identifying and investing in sustainable growth opportunities across the UK, Resolution Foundation, May 2022

9   Source: ONS GDP quarterly national accounts, UK: April to June 2023, September 2023.

10 The Bank of England forecasts growth of 0.3 per cent in 2025. Bank of England Monetary Policy Report, August 2023. IMF, World Economic Outlook, October 2023 suggests the UK will grow 0.6 per cent in 2024 compared with 1.4 per cent for other advanced economies.

Figure 2: UK productivity has been falling behind the pack since the 2000s

Ratio of GDP per hour worked compared to the US, current PPP

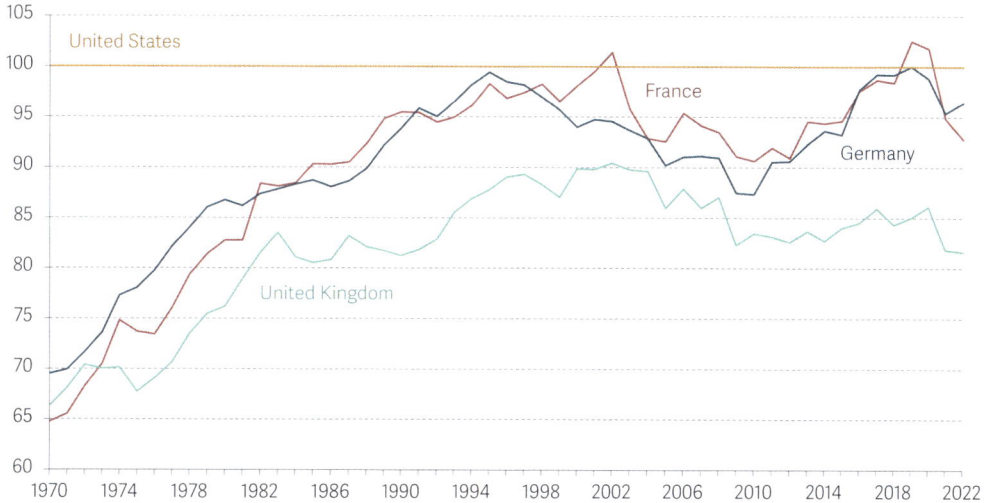

Notes: Data shown is two-year rolling averages. See R C Feenstra et al., The Next Generation of the Penn World Table, American Economic Review, 105(10), 3150-3182, 2015. Source: Analysis of OECD, Level of GDP per capita and productivity dataset.

While productivity growth slowed in most countries around or after the financial crisis, the British slowdown was exceptionally severe. In the 12 years following the crisis, labour productivity grew by only 0.4 per cent per year in the UK, less than half the average of 0.9 per cent among the 25 richest OECD countries. (There are a number of different ways in which economic progress can be compared across countries over time, as Box 1 explores.)

As a result, compared to the average of that in the US, France and Germany, the UK's productivity gap has widened by 9 percentage points since 2008 to stand at 18 per cent in 2022. To illustrate what this fall means, this 9-percentage point drop in relative productivity performance is worth £3,400 in lost output per person in the UK.

Box 1: The drivers of cross-country differences in living standards

How has the UK fared relative to comparator countries over time? Figure 3 sets out some basic aggregate indicators: total hours worked, the average productivity of those hours, and the way those two things combine in GDP per head.

Britons certainly haven't been shirking on the time spent working front: compared with 2006, we're working 11.3 per cent more hours overall. This has been largely driven by women, whose employment rate rose four times faster than that of men in the decade following the financial crisis – and particularly mothers who are part of a couple, whose average working hours (among those in work) increased by two hours per week over the same period.[11] That 11.3 per cent increase is significantly more than the OECD average (7.8 per cent) and well over double the French increase (4.3 per cent). Combined with employment changes, this means the total of hours worked elsewhere has sunk relative to the UK.

The consequences – even the meaning – of these extra British hours depends on why they are being worked, and how effectively. To the extent that they reflect more people having more opportunity to work then they are a good thing, and this is certainly partly the case since the financial crisis. Unfortunately, past research suggests that some of that extra toil in modern Britain also reflects people working more to maintain their incomes as hourly wages stagnate.[12]

The root of that wage stagnation and foregone leisure is the woeful trend in British labour productivity per hour that we examined in Figure 2. In every case, the comparators outperform Britain – with average OECD productivity rising by about 5.8 percentage points relative to the UK, and that of the US rising by 9.8 percentage points over these dozen years.

Finally, we can see how the changing hours and how productively they are used combines into GDP per head. We can see, for example, that the gap with Germany on this score (which was just 6 per cent at the time of the financial crisis) had risen

11 T Bell & L Gardiner, Feel poor, work more: Explaining the UK's record employment, Resolution Foundation, November 2019.

12 J P Pessoa & J Van Reenen, The UK Productivity and Jobs Puzzle: Does the Answer Lie in Wage Flexibility?, Economic Journal, 12, 2014.

by more than 6 percentage points to reach 12.2 per cent by 2019. The UK has deteriorated to similar extents when compared to the US and the OECD average. The comparison with France looks better, reflecting the extra work that Britons are doing compared to the French.

Figure 3: The UK's relative decline since the financial crisis needs to be considered across a range of metrics

Relative change in total hours worked, change in the gap in labour productivity per hour and GDP per capita, between the UK and selected advanced economies: 2007 to 2019

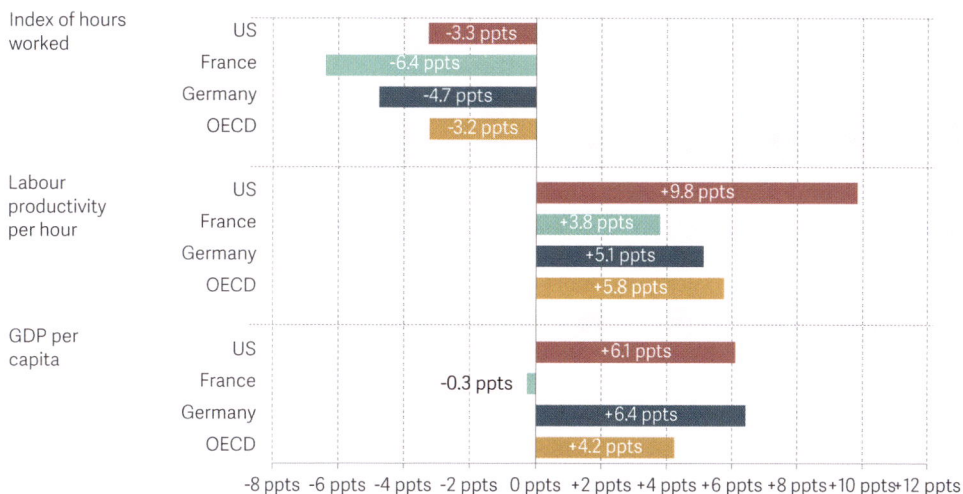

Notes: Total hours are expressed as an index = 100 in 2006. Pts are percentage point changes. Labour productivity is measured at constant 2015 PPPs. This is the correct measure to use when analysing relative growth rates, rather than relative levels. R C Feenstra et al., The Next Generation of the Penn World Table, American Economic Review, 105(10), 3150- 3182, 2015.
Source: Analysis of OECD, Level of GDP per capita and productivity dataset.

These productivity gaps are pervasive across different sectors of the UK economy: we are not less productive simply because we have, say, too little manufacturing.[13] Nor are they principally driven by Britain's skills base.[14] The UK scores well on

13 J Oliveira-Cunha et al., Business time: How ready are UK firms for the decisive decade?, Resolution Foundation, May 2021.
14 Although note that since the financial crisis the contribution of human capital accumulation – skilling up – to Britain's productivity growth fell slightly, while increasing in France and Germany.

aggregate measures of human capital,[15] although large issues persist, including its highly unequal distribution (which we return to in Chapters 5 and 6). This reflects a lack of intermediate level skills, very poor outcomes for those falling foul of binary English and maths exams at 16, and a significant class gap in higher education participation.[16]

What does materially help to explain the UK's productivity gap is the lack of physical and intangible capital available to British firms – and therefore British workers – to work with.[17] In the 40 years to 2022, total fixed investment in the UK averaged 19 per cent of GDP, the lowest in the G7 and some 3 percentage points below the G7 average of 22 per cent.[18] Britain's 'capital gap' – the amount of capital available per worker – explains almost all of our productivity gap with France.

Since the financial crisis, the UK's, already low, business investment rate – the part of GDP devoted by firms to building structures, buying machines and doing research and development – fell further, leaving Britain second last in a high-income OECD league table, ahead only of Greece.[19] Relatedly, the UK has also seen a significant slowdown in total factor productivity (TFP) growth following the financial crisis. However, while the UK's decline was larger than most, this drop was mirrored across advanced economies.[20]

No doubt, the precise causes of the UK's large and growing productivity gap with those economies at the global frontier will continue to be debated. But the consequences are already increasingly clear.

---

15 B Égert, C de La Maisonneuve & D Turner, A new macroeconomic measure of human capital exploiting PISA and PIAAC: Linking education policies to productivity, OECD Economics Department Working Papers, April 2022 and J Van Reenen & X Yang, Cracking the Productivity Code: A Comparative Analysis of UK's Labour Productivity, LSE, forthcoming.

16 S Machin, S McNally & J Ruiz-Valenzuela, Entry through the narrow door: The costs of just failing high stakes exams, Journal of Public Economics, 190, October 2020.

17 Intangible capital includes R&D, software, data and other innovative property. For more details, see: P Brandily et al., Beyond Boosterism: Realigning the policy ecosystem to unleash private investment for sustainable growth, Resolution Foundation, June 2023.

18 Source: Analysis of OECD Aggregate National Accounts.

19 Source: Analysis of OECD, GFCF database. Comparison to 'high income' OECD countries, specifically, Australia, Austria, Belgium, Canada, Denmark, Finland, France, Germany, Greece, Italy, Japan, Netherlands, New Zealand, Norway, Portugal, South Korea, Spain, Sweden, Switzerland, US.

20 P Goodridge and J Haskel, Accounting for the slowdown in UK innovation and productivity, The Productivity Institute, June 2022. TFP measures how well capital and labour in our economy are used, reflecting the likes of our knowledge base, network effects and spillovers. Of course, the new processes and ideas that TFP embodies are often implemented with new capital.

Relative decline has been catastrophic for wages and incomes

Productivity rises are the long-term driver of wage growth and recent British experience has underlined the connection between the two. The American experience over the last half century, during which the relationship between productivity growth and typical pay levels frayed, has led some to argue that the connection between growth and living standards has become unstuck. But as Box 2 explains, that has not been the case in the UK. More specifically, the recent absence of productivity growth has been a catastrophe for wages.

Box 2: Pay, productivity and a big Transatlantic divide

In competitive markets, a rational employer should seek to balance the output of the last worker that they hire with the wage paid. If this 'marginal' output exceeds the wage rate, then it makes sense to hire more staff; if the wage paid is higher than the value of extra output, then laying people off will boost profits. This reasoning points to a strong a priori connection between productivity and pay – indeed, for the marginal worker, it suggests the value of the two should be identical.

On a very long view, this theoretical link is reinforced by the 250 years of industrial history in which both output per worker and wages have increased by an order of magnitude. But in particular times and places the relationship can be less clear. If markets are less than competitive, then pay is not just determined by output, but also by power.[21] The typical worker might not feel the gains of rising productivity if at the same time the share of national income going to labour shrinks, or rising wage inequality, sees higher earners take a greater share of the pie. Both of these things have taken place over the last half-century in America, where – as Figure 4 shows – productivity has risen far faster than typical wages.

---

21 A Stansbury & L Summers, The Declining Worker Power Hypothesis: An explanation for the recent evolution of the American economy, NBER Working Paper, October 2020.

Figure 4: Median earnings have clearly decoupled from economic growth in the US

Indices of real-terms median pay and labour productivity, 1979=100: US

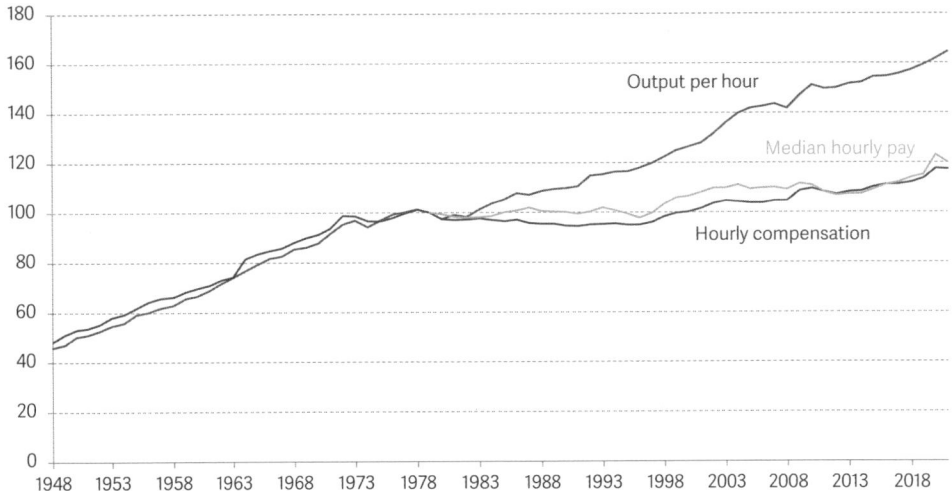

Notes: Data are for compensation (wages and benefits) of production/nonsupervisory workers in the private sector and net productivity of the total economy. Net productivity is the growth of output of goods and services less depreciation per hour worked. Source: The Economic Policy Institute's State of Working America Data Library.

But the tendency for British economists and politicians to focus on America should not lead us to conclude that the US experience is mirrored here. In Britain, when productivity rose, pay generally has too (as Figure 5 shows). Where some divergence has occurred in recent decades that largely reflects productivity filtering through as non-wage compensation (higher employer pension and national insurance payments), or higher import prices reducing the buying power of British workers.[22] For British, rather than American, workers, the real problem has arrived more recently – not from the breaking of the link between pay and productivity growth, but from the disappearance of the latter.

22 M Whittaker, Dead-end relationship?, Resolution Foundation, January 2020.

Figure 5: American-style decoupling has not taken place in the UK

Indices of real-terms median pay and labour productivity, 1980=100: UK

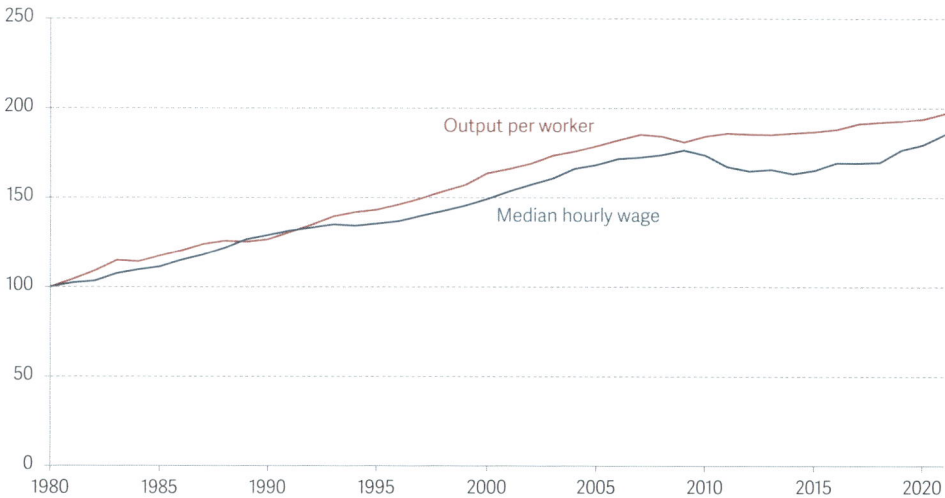

Source: Analysis of ONS, National Accounts; ONS, Annual Survey of Hours and Earnings; ONS, New Earnings Survey.

Any lingering doubts about the importance of British productivity for British wages should have been banished by the experience of the last 15 years: weak productivity growth has delivered an unprecedented stagnation in real wages, even before the highest inflation in four decades hit.[23] One year of slow wage growth is bad but manageable, but such a prolonged pay squeeze is ruinous. After a decade and a half of pay stagnation, in mid-2023 wages were back where they were before the financial crisis. Average weekly earnings that April stood at £497 in 2015 prices – £35 less than what workers were taking home in February 2008, 15 years earlier.[24] The cumulative effect of 15 wasted years is vast: £10,700 per worker per year (or £205 per week as shown in Figure 6) compared to a world in which pay had continued to grow at pre-financial crisis rates.[25]

---

23 N Oulton, The Productivity-Welfare Linkage: A Decomposition, ESCoE Discussion Paper 2022-07, March 2022.

24 ONS, Labour market statistics, June 2023, X09: Real average weekly earnings using consumer-price inflation (seasonally adjusted).

25 Source: Analysis of ONS, Average Weekly Earnings; and ONS, Consumer Prices Index including owner occupiers' housing costs. Assumes worker holidays are paid.

Figure 6: Average weekly earnings in 2023 are below their 2008 peak

Real average weekly earnings (regular pay), actual and pre-recession trend: GB

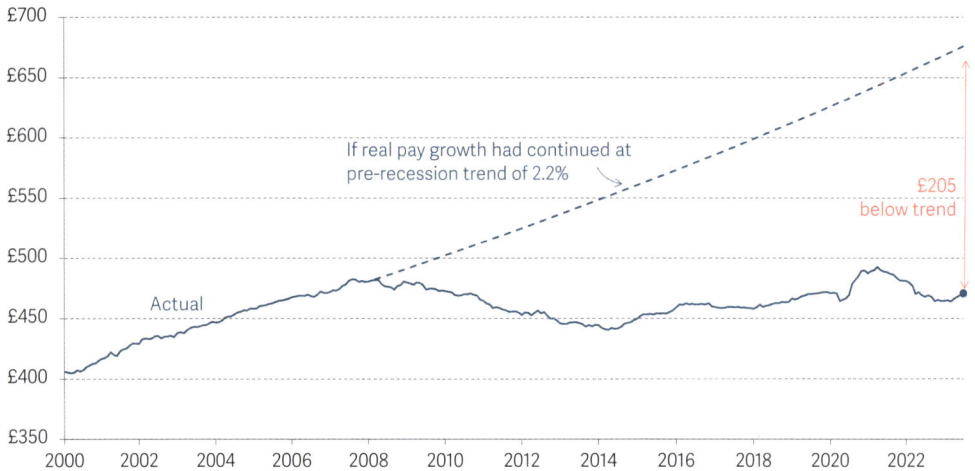

Notes: Adjusted to July 2023 prices using CPI. Pay is regular pay, i.e. excludes bonuses and arrears.
Source: Analysis of ONS, Labour market statistics.

This is an historical aberration. Real wages almost quadrupled between 1945 and 2000. From 1970 right up to 2007, wages were on average growing at a rate that would typically cash in at 33 per cent over a decade. That progress then ground to a halt, actually going into reverse at points in the 2010s and again more recently (see Figure 7).

This wage stagnation, inevitably, feeds through into real incomes, which is a wider measure of prosperity than pay. Here the jobs recovery of the 2010s softened the effect of the wage slowdown (the employment rate rose from around 70 per cent in the early 2010s to over 76 per cent at the dawn of the pandemic), but total income growth still slowed sharply. The discernible living standards progress of the 20th century, which saw people take their first foreign holidays or enjoy more meals out, has come to a stop.

Figure 7: Pay growth has been extraordinarily weak since the financial crisis

Rolling decadal growth rates of real wages, real GDP per capita, and real disposable income per capita: GB/UK

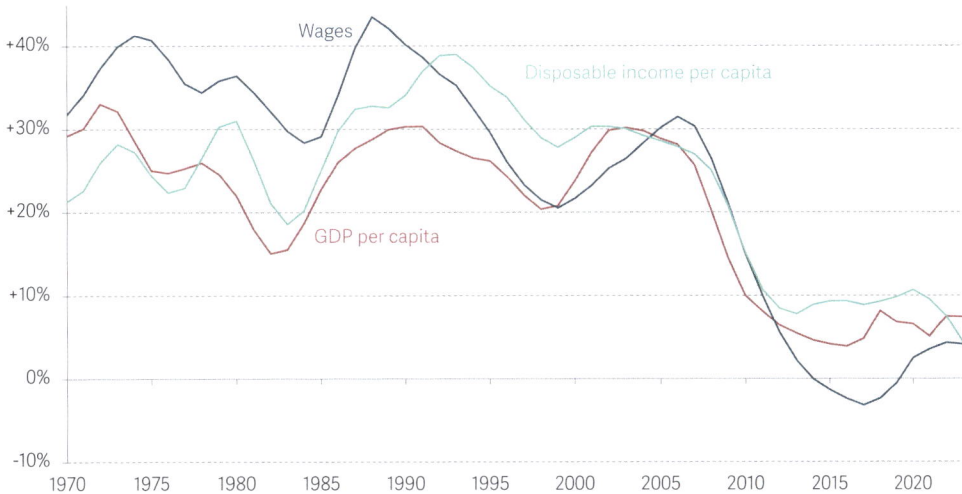

Notes: Rolling average of each variable in the three years centred on the date shown, compared to the three years centred on the date 10 years previous. For example, 2020 shows growth between 2009-2011 and 2019-2021. UK data for GDP and incomes, GB data for wages.
Source: Analysis of Bank of England, Millennium of Macroeconomic Data; OBR, Economic and Fiscal Outlook, March 2023; ONS, RHDI; ONS, UK resident population.

This is the toxic background to the current cost of living crisis, where double-digit inflation has meant a real income squeeze on a scale only usually seen during recessions. As Figure 8 shows, real incomes are on course to be lower in 2024-25 than in 2019-20, making this the worst Parliament on record for changes in living standards.[26]

---

26 This chart strips out pensioners, an important group, but one that is mostly protected from the vicissitudes of the labour market.

Figure 8: The worst Parliament on record for real household income growth?

Total real growth in median equivalised household disposable income per period for non-pensioners, after housing costs, by third of the income distribution: GB/UK

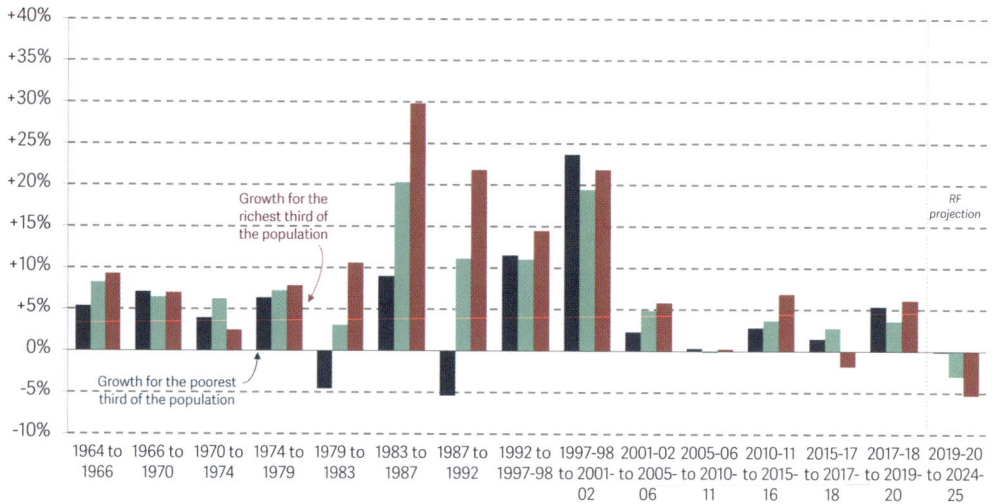

Notes: Projections taken from A Corlett, The Living Standards Outlook – Summer 2023 Update, September 2023. The chosen time periods correspond to the years of past general elections (plus 2024-25).
Source: Analysis of DWP & IFS, Households Below Average Income; and RF projection including use of the IPPR Tax Benefit Model, ONS data and OBR forecasts.

Weak income growth has been combined with stubborn inequality

Living with flatlining wages has been difficult for the past 15 years, but the UK has been living with high inequality for more than twice as long. The Gini coefficient for UK disposable household income (a summary statistic on a 0 to 100 scale, where 0 is defined as perfect equality and 100 where one plutocrat receives all the income) rose 10 points from 27 to 37 during the 1980s. This change was sufficient to transform the country from one with income gaps comparable with today's Scandinavia, to a mid-Atlantic society – with higher income inequality than any other large European country but lower than the vast income gaps of the US (Figure 9).

Figure 9: The UK is more unequal than all other large European countries

Gini coefficient for post-tax disposable income: selected OECD countries, 2019

Gini coefficent

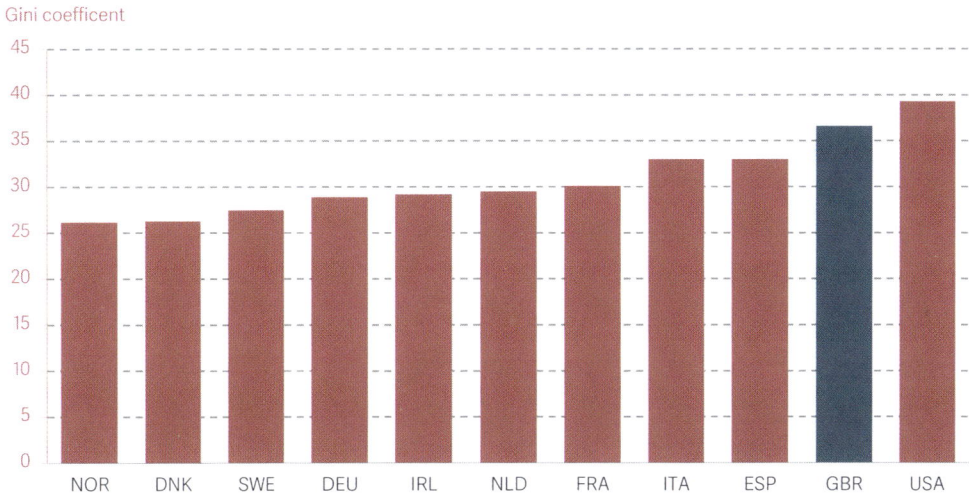

Notes: Data refers to the Gini (disposable income, post-taxes and transfers) which compares cumulative proportions of the population against cumulative proportions of income they receive, where 0 represents complete equality and 100 represents complete inequality.
Source: Analysis of OECD, Income Distribution data.

Since this big increase, headline British income inequality has remained broadly unchanged. But there has been a lot going on under the surface as some forces push incomes in a more equal direction and others the opposite.[27] On the positive side, recent employment growth has disproportionately benefited the less affluent,[28] while two decades of ramping up the National Minimum Wage has hugely reduced the gap between low and middling hourly wages.

Positive and progressive as these changes are, they have not been sufficient to reduce overall income inequality. Even as lower earners' wages have been rising, so have worrying signs about their job quality, as discussed in Box 3 and experienced by workers in some of our focus groups.

27 M Brewer & L Wren-Lewis, Accounting for Changes in Income Inequality: Decomposition Analyses for the UK, 1978–2008, Oxford Bulletin of Economics and Statistics, 78(3), August 2015.

28 S Clarke and N Cominetti, Setting the record straight: How record employment has changed the UK, Resolution Foundation, January 2019; J Cribb, R Joyce & T Wernham, Twenty-five years of income inequality in Britain: The role of wages, household earnings and redistribution, Institute for Fiscal Studies, March 2022.

"It seems to be all about how competitive we can be in this market that we're in, but they're just forgetting about the people on the ground that are actually generating this money. We just work at 150 miles an hour, and it just keeps going and going and going."

Participant, Solihull focus group

Box 3: Trends in the quality of work

Against the backdrop of Britain's wage stagnation, there has also been a relative deterioration in several aspects of lower earners' experience of work. Most employees are satisfied with their jobs, and there have been only limited falls in job satisfaction overall since the early 1990s among workers as a whole. But across a range of indicators – from job satisfaction, to workplace stress – the experience of work for low earners has declined. In the early 1990s, 76 per cent of the lowest earners were satisfied with their jobs but pre-pandemic this had dropped to 62 per cent, converging downwards towards the experience of higher earners (who consistently report the lowest level of job satisfaction).[29]

Most forms of job insecurity – such as short or zero-hours contracts – have remained stubbornly high among the low-paid, making it hard for them to know what they have coming in from one month to another, even as these forms of insecurity have fallen back among higher earners.[30]

Problems with the quality of jobs understandably lead workers to seek to minimise the time they spend in them. This is part of a wider pattern of lower earning men in particular working shorter hours, which means inequality in weekly earnings has not fallen as it has for hourly pay. This is one important obstacle in the way of an increased hourly pay floor translating into lower household income inequality.

---

29 Source: Analysis of British Household Panel Survey; UK Household Longitudinal Study, Understanding Society.

30 N Cominetti et al., Low Pay Britain 2022: Low pay and insecurity in the UK labour market, Resolution Foundation, May 2022.

Many other forces have worked to keep that overall income gap high:[31]

- The wage gap between the middle and top earners has remained stubbornly high.

- Patterns in the formation of households have evolved in ways that widen the income gap. The UK has both more two-earner and more no-earner households than many other countries.

- Poor households depend on state benefits for a large chunk of their income, and these have been subject to significant cuts during the 2010s. Typical incomes of the poorest fifth of the population were barely higher on the eve of the pandemic than they were in 2004-05, despite GDP per person growing by 12 per cent over this period.[32]

- Until very recently, falling interest rates have brought down housing costs for established home buyers (relatively richer people). In contrast, falls in home ownership and social renting among poorer households have seen them shift into the private rented sector, pushing up on their housing costs.[33]

- Income inequality between households can hide differences within them. The average working-age woman in the UK still earned 40 per cent less than her male counterpart in 2019. That gap is only about 13 percentage points, or 25 per cent, lower than it was 25 years ago.[34]

The toxic combination: weak growth and high inequality together

So far we have considered Britain's productivity problem and its high inequality separately. But it is their toxic combination that is so damaging, particularly to low- and middle-income Britain. While richer UK households have broadly equivalent incomes to their peers in comparable European economies, the same can no longer be said for the rest of the country, as Figure 10 illustrates.[35]

---

31 A Corlett, F Odamtten & L Try, The Living Standards Audit 2022, Resolution Foundation, July 2022.

32 Stagnation Nation, Resolution Foundation, July 2022.

33 D Tomlinson, Inequality street: Housing and the 2019 general election, Resolution Foundation, November 2019.

34 A Andrew, O Bandiera, M Costa-Dias, & C Landais, 'Women and men at work', IFS Deaton Review of Inequalities, December 2021.

35 The UK's comparatively poor income performance partly reflects relatively large rises in the UK price level. Over the same time period (2007 to 2018) the main UK measure of household incomes rose by 4 per cent, compared to the internationally comparable 2 per cent fall depicted here. Source: Analysis of IFS, Living standards, poverty and inequality in the UK, median household incomes before housing costs.

Figure 10: Richer UK households compare well – others do not

Incomes at the 10th, 50th and 90th percentiles of selected European countries: 2000-2022

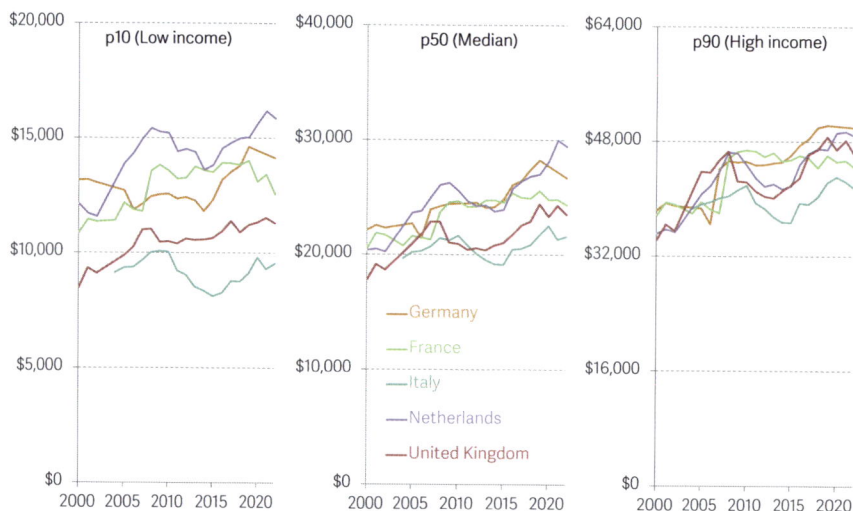

Notes: The chart uses current OECD PPPs. German data for 2020 and 2021 is not shown. UK data for 2022 is a Resolution Foundation nowcast.
Source: Eurostat, EU-SILC Distribution of income by quantiles; DWP, Households Below Average Income.

The incomes of middle Britain now sit below their equivalents in other Anglo-Saxon and Northern European countries (Figure 11). Specifically, they were 20 per cent lower than in Germany and fully 37 per cent lower than in Canada in 2019. But for low-income UK households the combined effects of low growth and high inequality are huge: they are now around 27 per cent poorer than their French and German counterparts – equivalent to £4,300 a year.

There is nothing resilient about an economy where the middle are this squeezed and the poor can barely stay afloat. Our introduction set out a few of the red flags: from reliance on food banks to markers of indebtedness. In the two years leading up to the pandemic, around one in four (26 per cent) of all adults said they would be unable to manage for a month on savings alone if their income stopped; so would nearly four in ten of those in the bottom two income deciles.[36]

36 Source: Analysis of ONS, Wealth and Assets survey.

Figure 11: Median household incomes in the UK are lower than in many advanced economies

10th percentile, median, and 90th percentile equivalised household net income relative to UK: selected OECD countries, 2018

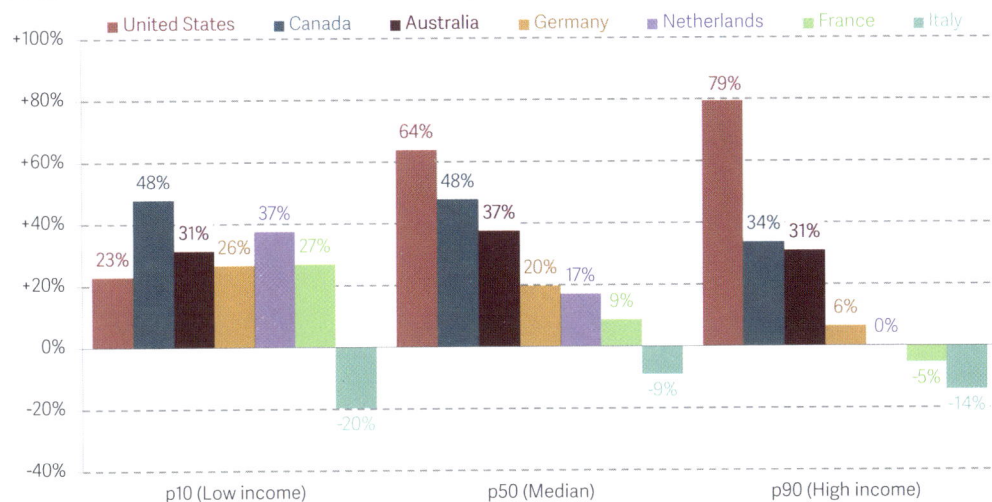

Notes: Difference between selected countries compared with UK p10, p50 and p90 household incomes using OECD PPPs for household final expenditure. International inequality comparisons are challenging because there are differences in survey coverage across countries and because of the difficulty in measuring prices across countries – both what components and weights of the price index should be, how to measure their relative levels, and how this interacts with things like housing tenure and how health and education are paid for. Correcting for some of these factors (such as imputed rents given that the income measure does not include imputed rental income) would improve the relative position of the UK.
Source: OECD Income Distribution Database; Eurostat, EU-SILC Distribution of income by quantiles; DWP, Households Below Average Income.

In our low-growth, high-inequality society poorer households have faced an immediate and intense struggle with the recent surge in the prices of essentials, from food to heating. The share of their budgets dedicated to such essentials had already risen from 51 per cent to almost 60 per cent between 2006 and 2019, as Figure 12 shows.[37] This left painfully little margin for adjustment when the cost

37 Source: Analysis of ONS, Living Costs and Food Survey.

of living crisis hit and recent price rises are translating into more people seeking debt advice.[38] Almost one in five report eating less or skipping meals,[39] while homelessness has reached record levels.[40]

Figure 12: The share of spending on 'essentials' has soared

Proportion of equivalised non-housing household consumption spent on 'essentials', by quintile of the working age equivalised net household income distribution: UK

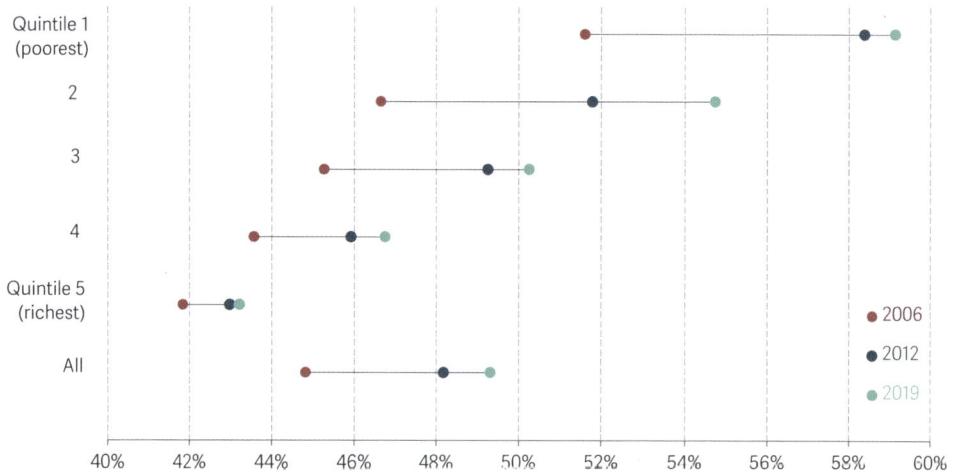

Notes: 'Essentials' covers food, fuel, clothing and transport. Distribution calculated on the basis of income after housing costs.
Source: Analysis of ONS, Living Costs and Food Survey.

In our focus groups, we heard about the day-to-day struggles of living on a low income.

> *"It's impossible actually to save if on a low income... I got paid on Friday and it was gone by Monday."*
>
> Participant, Sunderland focus group

38 Citizens Advice data shows a 16 per cent rise in the number of people seeking advice on fuel debt in September 2023 compared with the previous year. Citizens Advice, Advice Trends, September 2023.

39 T Bell, J Smith & L Try, Food for thought: The role of food prices in the cost of living crisis, Resolution Foundation, May 2023.

40 DLUHC, Statutory homelessness in England: financial year 2022-23, October 2023; Scottish Government, Homelessness in Scotland: 2022-23, August 2023.

The singular squeeze on lower-income families hits some parts of society harder than others. Particular groups are over-represented in the bottom income quartile, which contains 39 per cent of all single parents; 37 per cent of social renters; 45 per cent of adults in Bangladeshi households; and 42 per cent of adults in Pakistani households.[41]

People with a disability are also far more likely to be poor than the rest of the population: one in three (33 per cent) of adults in the lowest household income decile have a disability compared to just one in ten (9 per cent) of adults in the highest household income decile.[42] The toxic combination of low growth and inequality has huge implications for those people on the wrong side of any of the fault-lines of social injustice, be they created by race or health, gender or geography.

Stagnation has been particularly difficult for the young

The young have been particularly hard hit by the combination of slow growth and high inequality. Slow growth affects everyone's income gains, but maturing in harder times (when there are, for example, fewer promotion opportunities) can have a lasting impact, as people miss out on the career progression that tends to take place during our late 20s and 30s.[43] The cohort born in the 1980s, for example, has experienced lower levels of earnings than the 1970s cohort throughout their early thirties.

As a result, cohort-on-cohort improvements in household disposable income – something that would have been taken for granted throughout the second half of the 20th century – have also slowed or ground to a halt. The average income for those born in the early 1980s was almost £1,400 lower at 30 than those born 10 years previously [44]

Furthermore, the social mobility of younger generations is also held back by high inequality. There is strong international evidence regarding the link between mobility and income inequality.[45] In the UK, intergenerational social mobility was

41 Source: Analysis of DWP, Households Below Average Income, Income after housing costs in the three years to 2019.

42 O El Dessouky & C McCurdy, Costly differences: Living standards for working-age people with disabilities, Resolution Foundation, January 2023.

43 Some of this draws on: P Bourquin, M Brewer & T Wernham, Trends in income and wealth inequalities, IFS Deaton Review of Inequalities, forthcoming.

44 M Broome et al., An intergenerational audit for the UK: 2023, Resolution Foundation, November 2023.

45 M Corak, 'Income inequality, equality of opportunity, and intergenerational mobility', Journal of Economic Perspectives, 27(3), 2013. See also: M Brewer, What Do We Know and What Should We Do about Inequality?, SAGE Publishing, 2019.

lower for the cohort born in 1970 than it was for the one born in 1958 – that is to say, parental circumstances did more to shape the fortunes of youngsters who came of age in the (unequal) late 1980s than they had done for those maturing into the (relatively equal) 1970s.[46]

Figure 13: Home ownership rates are rising among younger people, but they still lag behind previous cohorts at the same age

Proportion of family units owning a home, by age of head of family unit and birth cohort: UK, 1961 to 2021-22

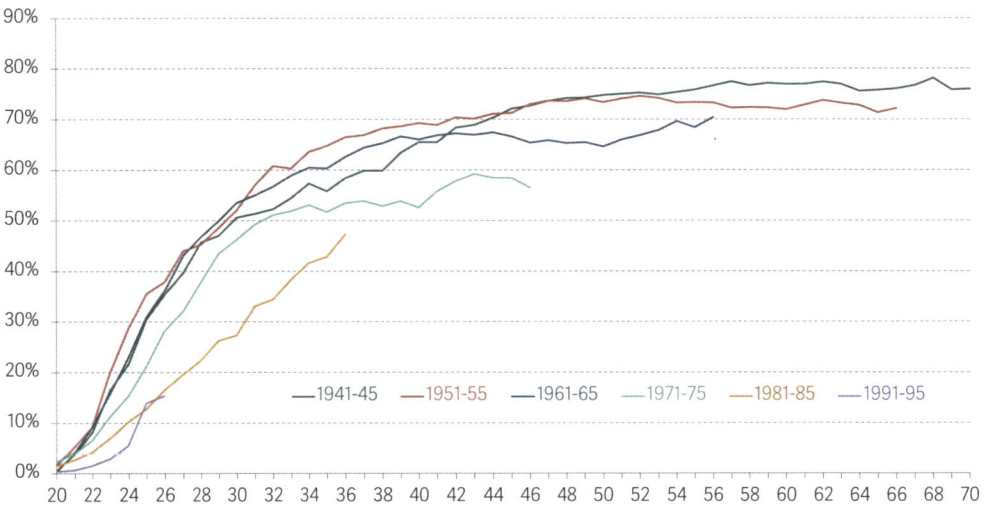

Notes: Figures for each cohort are derived from a weighted average of estimates by single year of age; cohorts are included if at least five birth years are present in the data.
Source: RF analysis of IFS, Households Below Average Income (1961-93); DWP, Labour Force Survey (1994-2016), Family Resources Survey (2017-18 to 2021-22).

In parallel, Britain's housing market has conspired against the young. Its winners tend to be concentrated among older generations: 12 per cent of people aged 60-64 own a second home (including buy-to-let properties).[47] By contrast, today's young people are less than half as likely to own a first home, and more than twice as likely to rent privately, compared to their parents' cohort. As Figure 13 shows,

46 Trends in intergenerational mobility are shown in: L Elliot Major & S Machin, Social Mobility and Its Enemies, Pelican, 2018. Trends in children's outcomes as they age are shown in: C Crawford, L Macmillan & A Vignoles, 'When and why do initially high-achieving poor children fall behind?', Oxford Review of Education, 43(1), 2017. See also: S Cattan et al., Early childhood and inequalities, IFS Deaton Review of Inequalities, June 2022.

47 Source: ONS, Wealth and Assets survey. Some of the gap between age groups will reflect life-cycle effects (e.g. older people are more likely to have been able to build up savings to purchase another property) not just cohort effects. But the wealth values of recent age cohorts have lagged behind older groups – for more see: K Henehan et al., An intergenerational audit for the UK 2021, Resolution Foundation, October 2021.

53 per cent of those born between 1961-1965 were home owners by the age of 30, compared to just 27 per cent for those born 1981-1985.[48]

The rise of wealth makes Britain feel less equal

These big shifts within the housing market in part reflect a wider trend that has helped some but not others navigate the impacts of stagnation: wages may have flatlined, but wealth has surged. Between the end of the 1980s and the start of the 2020s, the total value of household wealth in Britain has swollen from around three to more than seven times GDP.[49] Today's higher interest rates will reduce the scale, but not the fact of, this rise, which shapes how unequal Britain feels.[50]

With wealth inequality twice that of income, wealth rising relative to income in part explains why it can feel like Britain has become more unequal even though neither income or wealth inequality has recently risen.[51] It means wealth gaps between the have-lots and the have-nots increase: in 2006, the average wealth held by an adult in the wealthiest tenth of the population was £1 million more than an average adult in the middle of the distribution; by 2020 that gap increased to £1.4 million.[52] The UK's ethnicity wealth gap has also widened: the median wealth of people of Black ethnicity decreased from an already paltry 16 per cent of that held by their white counterparts in 2012 to 12 per cent in 2020. Bangladeshi households saw a similar decrease from 8 per cent to 4 per cent.[53] All of this dramatically affects how people experience the economy, meaning what you earn matters less and what you or your family own plays a bigger role.

---

48 M Broome et al., An intergenerational audit for the UK: 2023, Resolution Foundation, November 2023. See also: L Judge & J Leslie, Stakes and ladders: The costs and benefits of buying a first home over the generations, Resolution Foundation, June 2021. For further discussion of intergenerational inequality and home ownership, see: J Blanden, A Eyles & S Machin, Trends in intergenerational home ownership and wealth transmission, Centre for Economic Performance Discussion Paper, April 2021.

49 K Shah, Wealth on the eve of a crisis: Exploring the UK's pre-pandemic wealth distribution, Resolution Foundation, January 2022.

50 Higher interest rates push down on house prices as mortgages become more expensive and on the valuation of defined benefit pensions. For more detail, see: M Broome, I Mulheirn & S Pittaway, Peaked Interest?: What higher interest rates mean for the size and distribution of Britain's household wealth, Resolution Foundation, July 2023.

51 M Broome & J Leslie, Arrears fears: The distribution of UK household wealth and the impact on families, Resolution Foundation, July 2022. The share of wealth held by the richest tenth of families has hovered around 50 per cent since the start of the 1980s, and the top 1 per cent have consistently owned a little under a fifth of total wealth. For more on this, and why these are likely underestimates given the coverage of the surveys used to estimate these wealth shares, see: A Advani, G Bangham & J Leslie, The UK's wealth distribution and characteristics of high-wealth households, Fiscal Studies, October 2021.

52 Inflation adjusted figures. For more, see: M Broome et al., Peaked Interest?: What higher interest rates mean for the size and distribution of Britain's household wealth, Resolution Foundation, July 2023.

53 K Shah, Wealth on the eve of a crisis: Exploring the UK's pre-pandemic wealth distribution, Resolution Foundation, January 2022.

This wealth rise chiefly reflects rising values of existing assets, most obviously housing, rather than the creation of new ones via savings. This is good news for some: the rising prices of property and securities have delivered huge windfalls to those, particularly older households, who own them. But it has also 'locked out' those who start out without wealth, for example ramping up mortgage deposit requirements which have contributed to the fall in youth home ownership. In time wealth windfalls will be transferred down to today's younger cohorts, with the size of inheritances set to double over the next twenty years.[54] But inheritances often arrive late in life, and further reinforce the link between the living standards of younger cohorts and their parents' circumstances.[55] These unequal effects are already evident in the housing market, where the 'Bank of Mum and Dad' plays a large role.[56]

The growth of wealth can affect our politics, as well as who wins and loses living standards wise. All else equal, political incentives might be expected to shift towards protecting wealth built up in the past rather than prioritising growing incomes tomorrow – potentially locking in even more stagnation.[57]

Myriad inequalities between places are large and persistent

Limited social mobility and the rise of wealth are two related reasons why Britain might feel more unfair than stable (if high) income inequality levels suggest. Another is the extraordinarily uneven spread of productivity and income across different parts of the country. There is a lot of debate about just how exceptional these stark gaps are compared to those in other countries.[58] But there is no disputing their scale, nor public concern with them. Six in ten of the public see inequalities between areas as the "most serious" inequalities facing the country.[59]

---

54 J Leslie & K Shah, Intergenerational rapport fair?: Intergenerational wealth transfers and the effect on UK families, Resolution Foundation, February 2022.

55 P Bourquin, R Joyce & D Sturrock, Inheritances and inequality over the life cycle: What will they mean for younger generations?, Institute for Fiscal Studies, April 2021.

56 A home buyer with family help will typically snap up a property of a particular price when a decade younger than a buyer without that help. May Rostom, "Bomadland: How the Bank of Mum and Dad helps kids buy homes," Bank Underground blog, 25 July 2023.

57 A J Stewart, N McCarty & J J Bryson, Polarization under rising inequality and economic decline, Science Advances, 6(50), Dec 2020.

58 The coefficient of variation between metro areas' productivity is no higher in the UK than it is in Germany. For further discussion, see: P Brandily et al., Bridging the gap: What would it take to narrow the UK's productivity disparities?, Resolution Foundation, June 2022.

59 B Duffy et al, Attitudes to inequalities after Covid-19, The Policy Institute, Kings College, London, February 2021.

In 2019, income per person in the richest local authority – Kensington and Chelsea (£52,500) – was 4.5 times that of the poorest – Nottingham (£11,700). While different average wages have always been the main component of income disparities, an increasingly important role is played by investment income – its contribution to the total income gap between localities has doubled since 1997.[60] In Kensington and Chelsea, for example, average investment income per person has quintupled, while it has merely doubled across the country as a whole.

Productivity gaps grew with deindustrialisation in the later decades of the 20th century, and again in the first decade of the 21st as the likes of Milton Keynes and Swindon pulled ahead to become high-productivity areas (see Figure 14). Meanwhile, England's largest cities other than London continued to suffer from low productivity: indeed, what stands out as exceptional about our economic geography is that *all* of England's biggest cities outside the capital have productivity levels lower than the UK average.

Figure 14: Spatial disparities in productivity in the UK are large

Gross value added per job, by area: UK, 2019

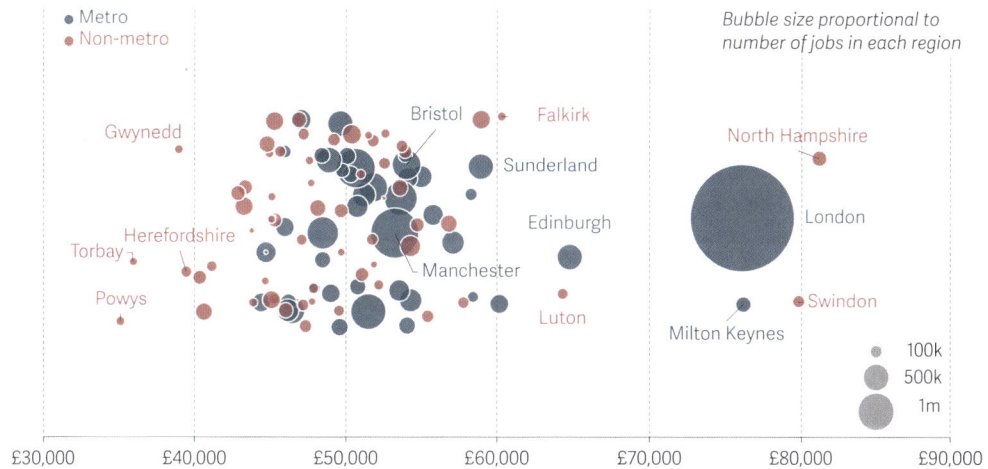

Notes: GVA per job in 2019, calculated as gross value added divided by number of jobs by workplace. Spatial units are a combination of OECD metro areas and NUTS3 for non-metro areas.

Source: Analysis of ONS, Subregional Productivity, July 2021.

60 Source: Analysis of ONS, Gross Disposable Household Income. For more detail on income gaps between places see: L Judge & C McCurdy, Income Outcomes: Assessing income gaps between places across the UK, Resolution Foundation, June 2022.

Regional gaps on both income and productivity are highly persistent over time. Many of today's under-performing post-industrial areas were the very industrial communities whose problems were chronicled by JB Priestly and George Orwell in the 1930s. Indeed, the plight of some of today's struggling communities – including South Wales and the West of Scotland – was officially recognised under the Special (Distressed) Areas Act of 1934. In more recent decades, we have the data to be more precise about the degree of persistence. The spatial differences in incomes we observe in 1997 still explain 80 per cent of the variation in the average local authority income per person in 2019. While employment gaps between areas have fallen, in other ways the gulf continues to deepen. Figure 15 shows that in the 15 years to 2019, while average incomes in London rose by 7 per cent, average incomes in Yorkshire and the Humber fell by 2 per cent.

Figure 15: Between 2004 and 2019, average incomes fell by 2 per cent in Yorkshire but rose by 7 per cent in London

Change in real income per capita (GDHI cash measure) between 2004-2019, and level of income per capita in 2004: UK nations and regions

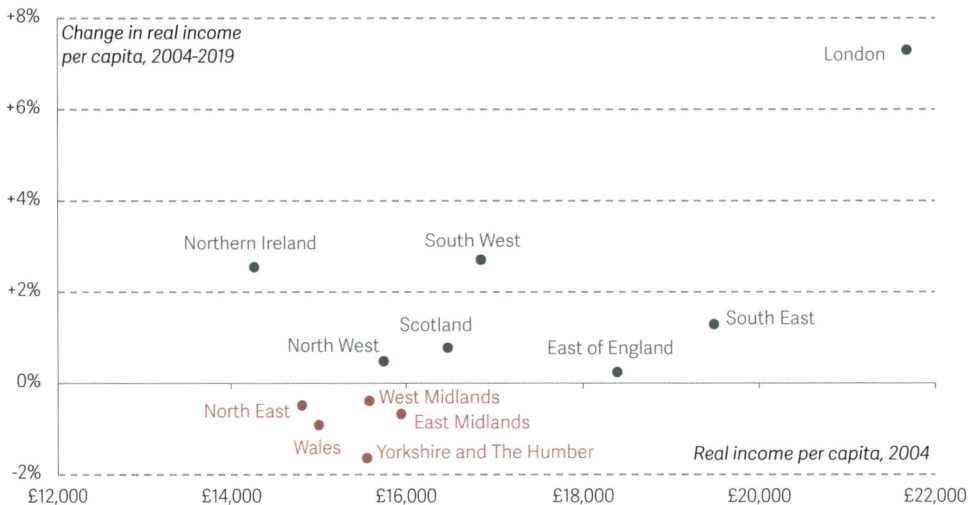

Notes: CPI-adjusted, 2020 prices.
Source: Analysis of ONS, Gross Disposable Household Income.

Britain's low growth and high inequality equates to stagnation.

The UK's slow growth and high inequality have, as we have shown, come together to leave families across the middle and lower reaches of the British income distribution with lower living standards than their peers in comparable countries. The public seems to sense the toxicity of this combination. Figure 16 reveals that concern about poverty and inequality, which was relatively muted during the years when inequality itself was rising, began to rocket once the big squeeze on average incomes took hold.

Figure 16: Public concern with poverty and inequality has increased since 2010

Proportion of respondents answering "poverty/inequality" to the question: "What do you see as the most/other important issues facing Britain today?"

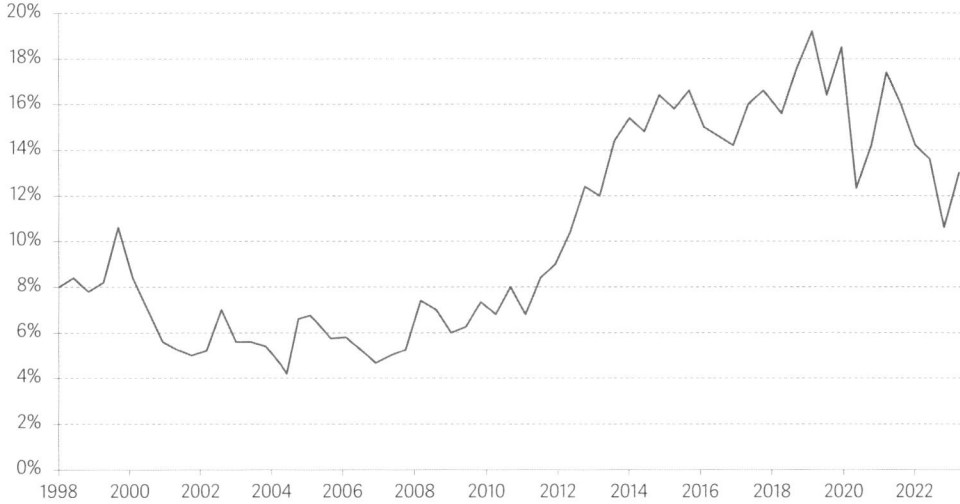

Notes: Data shown is five-month rolling averages, and a three-month rolling average for the final three months of data.
Source: Ipsos Issues Index.

This rising public concern is well-grounded. If sustained, this toxic combination poses serious risks not just to our economy, but to our society and democracy too. The slow-growth environment sharpens the consequences of inequality for middle class and poorer households, leaving them little wiggle room when bad times arrive. But the insidious consequences go way beyond the effect on the living standards of individual families. Stagnation left unaddressed risks a public mood of disillusionment, as promises of shared prosperity go unfulfilled. Younger workers are not seeing the progress their predecessors took for granted, as they are increasingly concentrated in lower-paying roles and seeing home ownership dreams delayed or dashed.[61]

61 K Henehan et al., An intergenerational audit for the UK: 2021, Resolution Foundation, October 2021.

Meanwhile older generations in particular face the consequences of stagnation for public services, which are struggling even as the tax burden rises. Despite taxes being on course to reach a 70-year high, the quality of public service provision is continuing to deteriorate on a range of metrics.[62] Perhaps the single greatest alarm is about the condition of the health service – whose longstanding frailties were made more acute during the pandemic. Figure 17 shows how the number of people waiting for consultant treatment following referral had more than doubled, from 3 million to 7.4 million, in the nine years after 2014.

Figure 17: NHS waiting lists have more than doubled since 2014

Total number of people waiting for NHS consultant treatment following referral: England

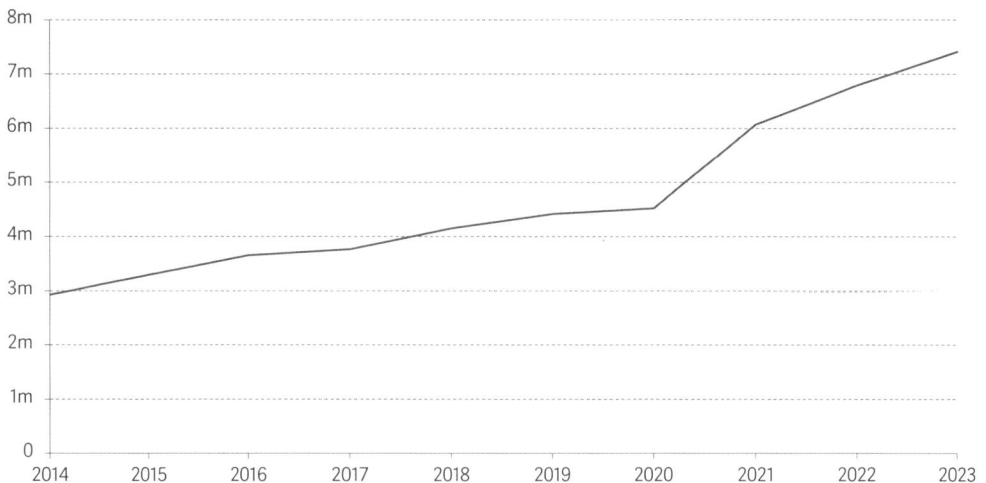

Notes: Mean number of people waiting each year. 2023 average includes January – July.
Source: NHS England and NHS Improvement, monthly RTT data collection.

Public concern about the health service may be particularly intense, but from unreliable trains to understaffed prisons and potentially unsafe school buildings, the sound of public services creaking is pervasive. Victims of crime are waiting record time for justice from the courts, reinforcing problems with public confidence in the police.[63] All this chimes with the dissatisfaction we heard in our focus groups:

---

62 T Bell et al., We're going on a growth Hunt, Resolution Foundation, March 2023.

63 Institute for Government, Performance Tracker 2022/23: Spring Update – Police, February 2023; and Performance Tracker 2022/23: Spring Update – Criminal Courts, February 2023.

"The police just haven't got the resources to deal with somebody that's dealing drugs... But it's just not the police that don't do things. It's then the courts that don't do anything."

Participant, Barnsley focus group

There is nothing automatic about escaping stagnation

None of this is a recipe for a strong society or healthy politics. Sadly, the experience of other countries doesn't suggest that escaping from stagnation is remotely automatic. Educated, affluent economies can stagnate for long periods – Italy has declined from being a GDP per capita peer of Germany in the 1980s to one of Spain today.[64] If politics fails to fix deep-rooted economic problems, those problems can spread to politics, in a dangerously self-reinforcing cycle. Wild oscillations in Rome, between governments led by populists and unelected technocrats, have come and gone without the underlying issues being fixed.

The two sides of stagnation can also make it harder for each of them to be addressed in isolation. High inequality makes the zero-sum politics of a stagnant economy more fraught. Relative positions matter far more when the gaps between them are so wide, and when any decline in position is much more likely to be associated with an absolute drop in living standards. At the same time, low growth leaves the government itself strapped for cash, reducing its scope to tackle inequality directly.

It is worth pausing on the fact that most people in the UK today have never lived in a country with inequality at the moderate level of the post-war age, when the top 10 per cent had less than three times the income share of the bottom 10 per cent. That gap widened into a five-fold differential by 1991, and has stayed high since.[65] About 25 million of us have only ever lived in that unequal country.[66] Meanwhile, some 8.8 million younger workers – around a quarter of people in employment today – have never worked in an economy with sustained average wage rises.[67]

The UK has endured a period of relative economic decline while remaining a highly unequal country. The two factors combining and persisting poses dangers not only to our incomes but to the fabric of the country, our politics and democracy.

---

64 L Codogno & G Galli, Lessons from Italy's economic decline, Resolution Foundation, November 2022.

65 Source: Analysis of DWP & IFS, Households Below Average Income, based on non-pensioners only.

66 Source: Analysis of ONS, Labour Force Survey.

67 Source: Analysis of ONS, Labour Force Survey. 8.8 million of those employed in 2022 were not yet 16 in 2007.

The great challenge for the 2020s must be to shake both problems off. The task is a daunting one, and made doubly so by the fact that it needs to be tackled amid a decade of major disruption, ranging from Brexit to the net zero transition to a changing geopolitical context and beyond. Some hope these forces for change could ultimately spur answers to the questions posed by this chapter. Others argue that the need to navigate these significant, specific disruptions will only make progress harder to achieve. What can be said for sure is that no serious strategy for the UK can ignore them – which is why the next chapter turns to the unavoidable disruptions confronting the country during the 2020s.

Chapter Two

Cool heads in torrid times

Chapter summary

- The 2020s has not been a stable decade so far, from the pandemic to the invasion of Ukraine. More disruption is to come as demographic and technological shifts combine with Brexit and the net zero transition. These will bring significant change for some, but not the radical reset for our economy many predict.

- Brexit has made Britain a less open economy; by 2023, UK trade as a share of GDP was down 2.2 percentage points on pre-pandemic levels (the rest of the G7 saw a 0.5 percentage points rise). The decline is goods focused, with market share lost not just with the EU but also the US, Canada, and Japan. Looking ahead, some sectors such as food manufacturing will grow, and others such as fishing will shrink. Rather than closing regional divides or reinvigorating manufacturing, by the end of the decade Brexit will see annual real wages £470 lower relative to if the UK was still in the EU.

- Britain needs to get serious about net zero: heat pumps need to be in our homes and electric vehicles on our streets. The transition promises a greener future and is unlikely to lead to large-scale job losses, but green growth will not catapult Britain out of stagnation. The priority is to find a fair way to fund the investment required, particularly in our homes: the cost of insulating a leaky home (£8,000) is far too high for poorer homeowners (average income £9,100).

- Britain's ageing is something that will need to be reckoned with, particularly as the 'demographic bulge' of baby boomers is tipping over into retirement. But for the next few years at least an influx of young adults born in the 2000s into the workforce is an offsetting force.

- While the eventual impact of AI is hugely uncertain, it's clear the robots we were promised would imminently take our jobs and raise our productivity have done neither.

- Most of the economic shifts wrought by the pandemic have unwound, except the shift to home-working (38 per cent of workers home-work regularly). This improves life for many, but does not live up to excitable claims that Covid-19 would transform our economic geography or productivity. Its main legacy is the inflation surge we are living through.

The 2020s: a decisive decade of change

Britain's economy may be stagnant, but the context within which attempts to redirect the country's path to economic success take place is far from unchanging. This decade has already seen the extraordinary disruption of the pandemic, followed by the invasion of Ukraine and now conflict in the Middle East. More is to come. The impacts of our radically changed trade regime post-Brexit will play out amid the challenges of new geopolitical realities, demography, technology and sustainability faced by so many advanced economies.

This chapter considers these shifts in turn, arguing that each is important but that prevalent, sometimes dominant, understandings of these changes – from assuming their main impact is widespread labour market disruption of the kind seen with deindustrialisation, to wishful thinking that sees any as a magic bullet to the UK's stagnation – do not provide a good guide for policy makers. Instead the task is to chart a course that takes account of them all, without imagining that any allows us to dissolve or transcend the underlying problems of lacklustre productivity and high inequality highlighted in Chapter 1.

Unstable times

Between the recovery of the early 1990s, and the financial crisis of 2008, economic life was calm; so calm it was labelled the era of NICE (non-inflationary continuous expansion). The subsequent 15 years, by contrast, have been dominated by disruption. The contrast between the steady growth and inflation of the pre-2008 world and the instability with which it was replaced is plain in Figure 18.

The proximate causes of the turbulence are familiar. After the recession of the financial crisis came austerity, the Euro crisis and then the vote to leave the EU. The latter triggered a slide in sterling, which settled at more than 12 per cent below its previous level.[1] Uncertainty rose, and business investment stagnated.[2] Then came Covid-19 and the brief but deep lockdown slump – the 10 per cent GDP fall in 2020 was the worst in a century – necessitating an unprecedented scale of government support. Many people's livelihoods were disrupted, with low-paid, young, and Black, Asian and minority ethnic workers most affected.[3] The main

---

1   S Dhingra et al., The Big Brexit: An assessment of the scale of change to come from Brexit, Resolution Foundation, June 2022.

2   J De Lyon et al., Trading places: Brexit and the path to longer-term improvements in living standards, Resolution Foundation, October 2021. P Brandily et al., Beyond Boosterism: Realigning the policy ecosystem to unleash private investment for sustainable growth, Resolution Foundation, June 2023.

3   M Brewer et al., Begin again? Assessing the permanent implications of Covid-19 for the UK's labour market, Resolution Foundation, November 2021.

change for higher earners, by contrast, was home working, as they built up extra savings from the lack of commuting or meals out.[4] Last but not least, the surge in European gas prices has made Britain, an energy importer, poorer. The pandemic put output on a more volatile path than seen in generations, but the years since have seen the same happen to prices, as discussed in the Introduction. Stable is not what the last 15 years have been.

Figure 18: Sustained economic stability has given way to turbulence

Peak and trough of CPI inflation and quarterly real GDP growth: UK

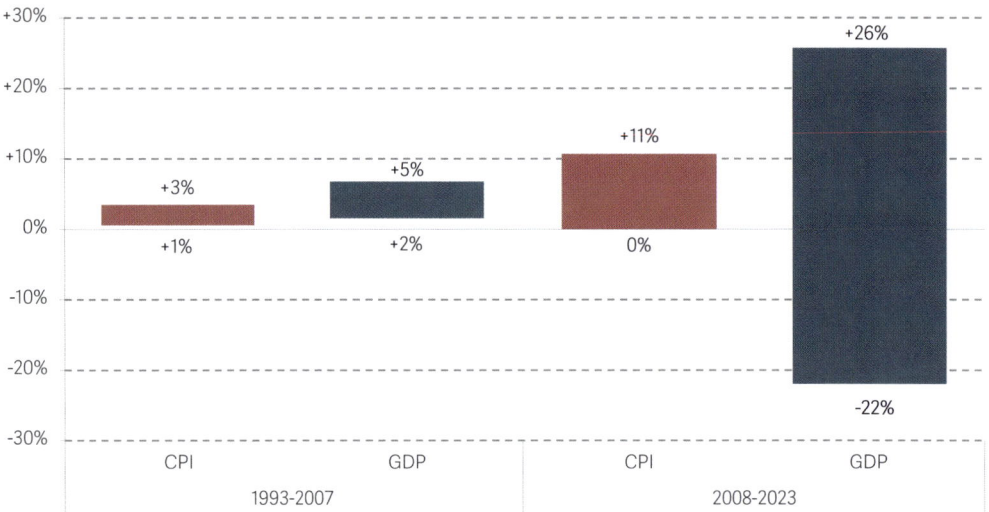

Source: Analysis of ONS, Consumer Prices; CPI, Historical Modelled Annual Rate; National accounts.

More change will come, the question is how to approach it

One certainty in the coming years is more disruption: the implications of Brexit for our trading relationships and our migration rules will continue to unfold; the net zero transition must accelerate; demographic and technological change will, of course, continue – and in some ways pick up pace. It is always a mistake to resist necessary change. It will come, and – as throughout economic history – it will create some jobs while displacing others, shifting the relative prices of particular

---

4   M Brewer, C McCurdy & H Slaughter, Begin again? Assessing the permanent implications of Covid-19 for the UK's labour market, Resolution Foundation, November 2021 & J Leslie & K Shah, (Wealth) gap year: The impact of the coronavirus crisis on UK household wealth, Resolution Foundation, July 2021.

goods and services, leaving both winners and losers. Understanding all this is essential to getting policy right and considering how these changes will (and won't) reshape the context for an economic strategy.

Denying or ignoring these changes is one danger, but not the only one. We will be led astray if we assume that all economic change manifests as a repeat of the deindustrialisation of the 1970s and the 1980s, with large, highly geographically concentrated job losses, or that a particular change would be a magic bullet to the UK's stagnation.[5] Both mistakes are visible in discussions of Brexit and of the net zero transition.[6]

The UK's fundamental problems are low growth and high inequality. But any economic strategy that doesn't grapple with the forces that will be pulsating through the economy in the coming years isn't a strategy at all. So let us now consider them in turn – and whether they look likely to reinforce, ameliorate or leave untouched our underlying stagnation.

Brexit is reshaping UK trade patterns – sometimes in unexpected ways

The UK is three years into a new economic era, defined by more potential freedom over domestic regulation and global trade relations, but also substantial trade barriers with the EU. The lack of wide-ranging tariffs shouldn't disguise the scale of the disruption: the new trade barriers have been estimated as equivalent to a 13 and 21 per cent increase in tariffs for our manufacturing and service sectors respectively,[7] similar in scale to the tariffs implemented during the China–US trade war but covering a much larger proportion of UK trade.

By any standards, this is a big change for the economy, after half a century of increasing alignment with the continental bloc. But it arrived somewhat falteringly. The Trade and Co-operation Agreement (TCA), which forms the basis of the UK's new relationship with the EU, came into force at the turn of 2020-21, four and a half years after the Brexit vote. Only then did the UK finally leave the customs union and the single market, while the full implementation of border checks lies ahead

5   J Muellbauer & D Soskice, The Thatcher Legacy: Lessons for the future of the UK economy, Resolution Foundation, November 2022.

6   See M Dathan, Staggering ten million jobs at in red wall seats at risk due to Government's carbon-neutral pledge, research reveals, The Sun, 5 January 2021; T Helm, 660,000 jobs at risk as UK's green investment lags, The Observer, 12 September 2021.

7   Unless otherwise stated the analysis in this section is drawn from S Dhingra et al., The Big Brexit: An assessment of the scale of change to come from Brexit, Resolution Foundation, June 2022.

rather than behind us.[8] Moreover, the effect of the changes was initially clouded in the statistical fog of the pandemic, which played havoc with global trade patterns.

But now the data is firming up, allowing us to assess the nature and scale of the TCA's initial impact. Discussions in advance focused on expected falls in goods and service exports to the EU, and on reduced foreign direct investment. The latter has not materialised[9] but the shift away from trade openness has been more broad-based than expected.

By 2023, Britain was the only major European country to have sustained a decline in trade openness even after global trade rebounded from the pandemic. UK trade (all imports and all exports added together) as a share of GDP was 2.2 percentage points below pre-pandemic levels (2019), compared to a rise in trade openness of 0.5 points for the G7 excluding the UK, including a 1.7 point rise in France with its similar trade profile.[10] A wider shift towards a less open and less competitive economy may be underway, with falling imports impacting customers and supply chains.[11]

Moreover, the initial effects have been much more marked for goods than services (a subject we return to in Chapter 4).[12] By the middle of 2023, goods imports and exports remained 12.1 and 14.7 per cent down respectively on Q1 2019, by far the most negative shift in the G7, with other members enjoying a surge in goods trade post-pandemic, as Figure 19 illustrates.[13] The UK is not only losing market share with EU partners, but also across three of its largest non-EU goods markets: the US, Canada, and Japan.[14] What has remained resilient is UK service trade,

8   Cabinet Office, The Border Target Operating Model: August 2023, September 2023. The UK Government has been phasing in border controls for goods imports from the EU from 2021, and has delayed certain checks several times due to concerns about their impact on the cost of living. The import checks that were delayed include health certification and sanitary and phytosanitary (SPS) checks on all agri-food products, physical SPS-checks on EU imports at designated Border Control Posts, and safety and security declarations.

9   UK FDI inflows as a share of EU-27 inflows actually stands above pre-Brexit levels, as it has generally been since the referendum. True, the UK's share of global FDI has dipped, but so has that across much of Europe: our share remains in line with that in Germany and France. Analysis of OECD, Foreign Direct Investment Statistics.

10 Source: Analysis of OECD National Accounts and ONS Trade Time Series Comparing 2019 with year ending Q2 2023

11 For example, food imports have been affected by Brexit as is discussed in: J D Bakker et al., Brexit and consumer food prices: May 2023 update, CEP, May 2023.

12 S Hale & E Fry, Open for Business?, Resolution Foundation, February 2023.

13 Source: Analysis of ONS Trade time series. Compares goods trade less precious metals Q1 2019 with Q2 2023 to exclude Covid-19 effects.

14 Source: Analysis of US Bureau of National Accounts; StatCan, and Statistics Bureau of Japan. Pre-Brexit refers to 2019, and is compared with full year of Q3 2022- Q2 2023.

reflecting strong global demand growth in areas of UK strengths, including intellectual property, business services – such as legal, advertising and consulting – and education services.

Figure 19: Closed for business after Brexit? UK trade has sunk relative to peers

Index of trade volumes (Q1 2019=100): G7 countries, with UK highlighted

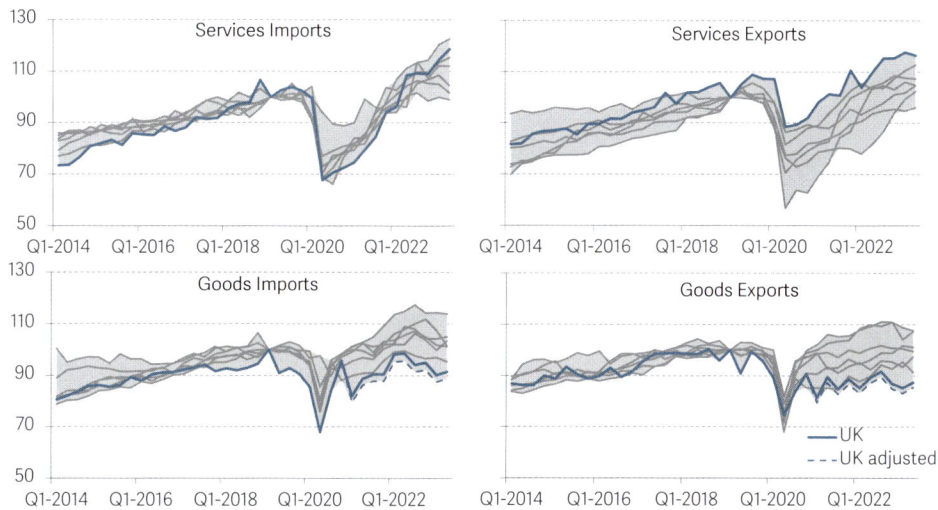

Notes: Range shows highest to lowest G7 country each quarter. Trade volumes are measured in national currency, chained volume estimates, national reference year, quarterly levels, seasonally adjusted. UK-EU goods trade flows are adjusted to account for measurement changes by using an uplift of 6 per cent for UK goods imports and 5 per cent for UK goods exports in line with the ONS, applied to the pre-2021 data, to adjust for the wider coverage of custom declarations data relative to the Intrastat survey.
Source: OECD, Quarterly National Accounts data and ONS, Trade Time Series.

These are still early days, and of course it takes years for capital and labour to adjust fully to a complex new regime. But LSE/Resolution Foundation modelling of the TCA's permanent effects allows us to consider the uneven ways in which the impact of a different trade relationship with the EU may unfold across the economy.[15] It highlights further falls in trade openness to come: by 2030 we expect

---

15 Modelling refers to results in Dhingra et al., The Big Brexit: An assessment of the scale of change to come from Brexit, Resolution Foundation, June 2022. Analysis uses CEP trade model from S Dhingra et al., The costs and benefits of leaving the EU: trade effects, Economic Policy 32(92), October 2017 with regionalised inputs from EUREGIO Regionalised Input Output Database and a dynamic adjustment using ONS, Labour Force Survey.

UK firms to export over 24 per cent less than if we had remained within the EU.[16] But as Figure 20 shows, this varies hugely by sector: agricultural exports are expected to fall by over 80 per cent in total (and by over 90 per cent to the EU).

Figure 20: Trade is set to decline due to Brexit – and crash in some sectors

Percentage change in total UK exports and imports, relative to remaining in EU: 2030

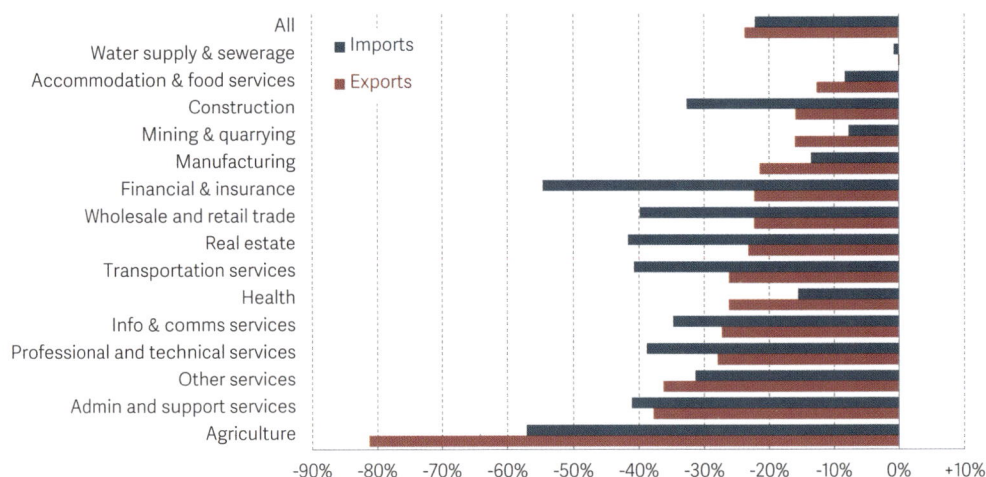

Source: Analysis uses CEP trade model from S Dhingra et al., The costs and benefits of leaving the EU: Trade effects, Economic Policy 32(92), October 2017, with regionalised inputs from EUREGIO Regionalised Input Output Database and a dynamic adjustment using ONS, Labour Force Survey.

Reduced trade openness will mean big changes for some sectors, but not the shape of the UK economy as a whole

Changes in trade will translate into big winners and losers within and between sectors when it comes to output, reflecting the differing opportunities to reorient to production for the domestic market. For example, that fall in agricultural exports doesn't mean British farms will soon all be out of business, because agricultural imports (far bigger than exports) are also set to more than halve.[17] Indeed, the total effect of the new trade barriers considered in isolation (note migration policy choices are also important, see Box 4) is to increase domestic agricultural output

---

16 14 per cent of this is due to the immediate new barriers introduced with the EU, and a further 9 per cent coming from forgone future EU integration.

17 Imports of food and live animals are three times as big as exports of this sector.

by as much as 20 per cent thanks to reduced competition from EU producers. In contrast, fishing (highly reliant on European customers) is expected to be one of the hardest-hit sectors, with output 30 per cent lower, as shown in Figure 21.

Box 4: Migration after Brexit

Trade shifts are just one consequence of Brexit. Another is the ability to fashion a migration policy to replace free movement within the EU. In the short run, net migration post-Brexit has been historically high, in particular due to humanitarian visas for those leaving Hong Kong and Ukraine, and an uptick in non-EU students. But even if the overall reduction many had expected has not yet materialised, UK immigration policy and patterns have changed with Brexit.[18] The fundamental policy choice made has been to shift away from EU free movement and towards more visas awarded with reference to skill and salary thresholds.[19] This should mean those coming to the UK to work are more qualified on average, and already means they are more likely to be non-EU citizens than when Britain was a member of the EU.[20] But whether this shift towards higher-skilled migration happens in practice will depend on how politicians respond to pressure from lower-paying sectors in particular to soften this approach either directly (by offering new or expanded routes for economic migrants) or indirectly (for example, via humanitarian or student visa routes).

The general economic effects of tighter rules on Europeans should play out gradually, with residency rights preserved for around 6 million established EU migrants.[21] But the new approach has some sectoral implications, particularly in industries previously dependent on a rapid turnover of lower-paid EU migrants. For example, the extent to which British farmers and food manufacturers can expand in response to reduced competitive pressure from imports will depend on their ability to find workers. Despite an expanded seasonal agricultural worker scheme, these sectors reported labour shortages in the years following Brexit, with

18 J Portes, Trade, Migration & Brexit, UK in a Changing Europe, October 2022.

19 Home Office, New immigration system: what you need to know, last updated August 2023.

20 K Henehan, If fewer workers migrate to Britain, our own will need greater mobility: Migration policy can complement an economic strategy, but it can't stand in for one, Resolution Foundation, February 2022.

21 Home Office, EU Settlement Scheme quarterly statistics, June 2023, August 2023.

widespread lobbying by these (generally lower productivity) sectors for more special treatment.[22] Sometimes automation might help, but sometimes – as in many agricultural picking roles – it will not.[23] This leaves policy makers to shape the size of these sectors in a renewed economic strategy.

Across the economy as a whole, claims that the unfolding post-Brexit changes on migration alone will drive a shift towards a high-wage economy are overdone, as indeed are opposing claims that a reduction in lower-skilled migration will have significant negative effects.[24]

More important for Britain's economy as a whole is the impact on manufacturing. For some, a potential benefit of the UK's exit from the EU is a partial reversal of the decline of manufacturing, with the hope that this will help narrow the UK's large regional divides. The argument rests on the idea that replacing membership of the single market (with its unique liberalisation of trade in services) with a free trade agreement with the EU (largely covering only goods trade) relatively favours those parts of the country that are manufacturing-heavy at the expense of London and the South East.[25]

Neither weak goods trade performance in recent years, nor our modelling, support this view. The main effect of the new trade regime is not to change the relative size of manufacturing in our economy, but to shift its nature. Some lower productivity manufacturing sectors will grow to service the domestic market (most notably food manufacturing), while other, higher productivity, sectors (including British successes like cars, chemicals and aviation) will shrink by a similar amount as our part in various deeply integrated EU supply chains diminishes over time (over half the UK's goods trade with EU countries is in intermediate inputs, rather than final goods). The average productivity of the parts of manufacturing that the TCA shrinks are much higher (£47 per hour) than the parts that it helps to grow (£37

---

22 House of Commons Environment, Food and Rural Affairs Committee, Labour shortages in the food and farming sector, March 2022.

23 K Henehan, If fewer workers migrate to Britain, our own will need greater mobility: Migration policy can complement an economic strategy, but it can't stand in for one, Resolution Foundation, February 2022.

24 K Henehan, Under new management: How immigration policy change will, and won't, affect the UK's path to becoming a high-wage, high-productivity economy, Resolution Foundation, February 2022. "We are not going back to the same old broken model with low wages, low growth, low skills and low productivity all of it enabled and assisted by uncontrolled immigration." Boris Johnson, Boris Johnson's keynote speech – We're getting on with the job, Conservative Party Conference, October 2021.

25 M Sandbu, Brexit and the future of UK capitalism, The Political Quarterly, April 2019.

per hour).[26] Already, the UK's exports of chemicals and transport have fallen much more than the average G7 country's following Brexit. This shift towards lower productivity activity is mirrored in service sectors.[27]

Figure 21: Brexit will slow growth – except in a few low-productivity sectors

Long-run change in UK gross output across sectors relative to a no-Brexit baseline

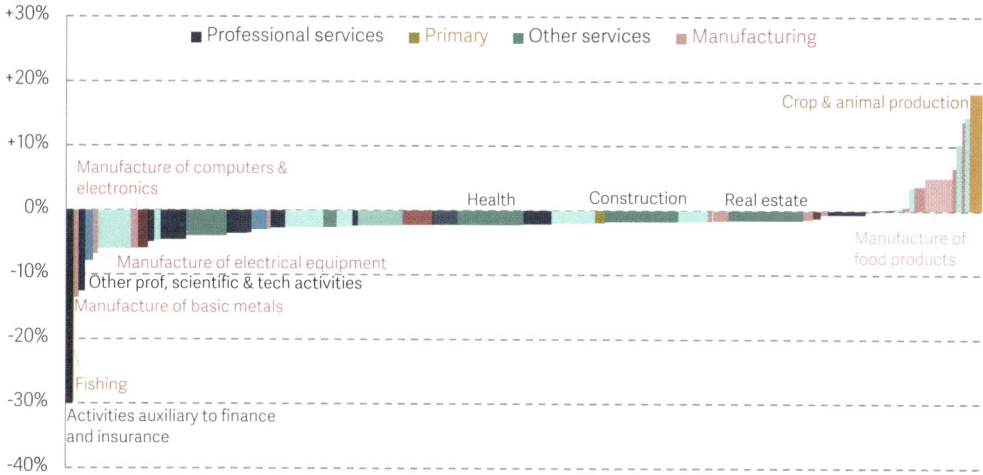

Notes: Width of bars represent the relative size of the sector.
Source: Analysis uses static CEP trade model from S Dhingra et al., The costs and benefits of leaving the EU: trade effects, Economic Policy 32(92), October 2017 with regionalised inputs from EUREGIO Regionalised Input Output Database.

Brexit's lasting effect is a headwind to tackling stagnation

These sectoral shifts mean a relatively small number of workers in the worst-hit sectors – for example, those 5,000 employed in fishing in 2019 – face increased uncertainty. These changes could be hugely significant in communities where these industries are concentrated and, if they lead to involuntary unemployment, both history and recent evidence warn us this can do lasting damage.[28]

---

26 S Dhingra et al., The Big Brexit: An assessment of the scale of change to come from Brexit, Resolution Foundation, June 2022.

27 Highly productive professional, scientific and technical activities and activities auxiliary to finance and insurance see the largest modelled falls in output, while transportation and repair services are the only services sectors set to rise.

28 Prolonged worklessness and depressed future pay are more common for those who leave work involuntarily than those who do not. N Cominetti et al., Changing jobs? Change in the UK labour market and the role of worker mobility, Resolution Foundation, January 2022.

However, for the labour market as a whole, the scale of change needs to be kept in perspective. The main effect of the rising trade barriers of Brexit will not be changing what jobs we do, but reducing our incomes. The total shift between sectors and regions will be small compared to that seen in previous decades, exactly because the nature of the UK economy is not set to shift fundamentally, as it did during deindustrialisation. Our modelling suggests less than 0.5 per cent of the workforce will move from their current region-sector as a result of Brexit. Moreover, this change is spread over many years, taking place incrementally, via firms' entry, exit and investment decisions.[29]

Lower wages rather than labour market churn is where the most material effects of Brexit will be felt. The direct impact of the new trade regime alone will depress long-run labour productivity by 1.3 per cent relative to what it would otherwise have been. The estimated impact on living standards is larger, with real wages 1.8 per cent lower – a loss of £470 per worker per year relative to staying in the EU. Above average real wage falls are expected in London, Wales and the North East, of £710, £550 and £510 respectively. Meanwhile, Northern Ireland's Protocol, which leaves it more closely aligned to the EU, insulates it from some of these changes, limiting the downward pressure on wages there to £230 per year. Sectorally, finance and insurance are set for the most significant real wage falls (£1,260 per year), with manufacturing wages also falling more than average (£650 per person per year relative to staying in the EU).

These income estimates focus solely on the direct effect of the change in the trade relationship with the EU. The Office for Budget Responsibility (OBR) takes account of wider impacts of the UK's exit from the EU – such as lower business investment and migration – in its judgement that the UK's long-run GDP will be 4 per cent lower than if we had not left the EU. It reached this broad judgement before Brexit was affected, and has seen little reason to alter it as the post-Brexit data comes in. Indeed, before the TCA was implemented, the OBR estimated that two-fifths of the 4 per cent impact had already occurred. [30]

29 S Dhingra et al., The Big Brexit: An assessment of the scale of change to come from Brexit, Resolution Foundation, June 2022.

30 Office for Budget Responsibility, How are our Brexit forecasting assumptions performing?, Economic and Fiscal Outlook, March 2023. Accessed 6 July 2023.

Far from giving the UK a different industrial structure, or closing regional divides, Brexit's role as a headwind to living standards growth should reinforce the urgency of Britain focusing on throwing off stagnation. Chapter 4 turns to how trade policy post-Brexit can play a part in doing so, recognising that Britain has chosen a new path outside the EU, just as wider trade-related geopolitical tensions have significantly risen, as Box 5 discusses.

Box 5: The new geopolitics

Heightened global tensions, particularly the strategic rivalry between the US and China, are directly impacting economic policy. While the Covid pandemic underscored the importance of resilient supply chains, geopolitical tensions have only risen since. Where would the West get its manufactured goods in the event of a Chinese invasion of Taiwan and a breakdown of trade relations?

Such concerns have led to a new focus on strengthening national capabilities, particularly in advanced manufacturing and key technologies.[31] These pressures apply in many Western countries and could accentuate so-called 'slowbalisation' or even the reversal of globalisation altogether.[32] As a medium-sized economy with distinctive comparative advantages it does not make sense for the UK to aim for a wide range of national capacities on its own: it is better to work with our international partners.

But there has already been a radical shift away from the UK having a very open market in corporate control to a restrictive regime set by the National Security and Investment Act 2021.[33] It lists seventeen key sectors and technologies where "Subject to certain criteria, you are legally required to tell the government about acquisitions of certain entities". The list mixes together key technologies and sectors, and indeed the responsibilities of entire government departments. Historically, selling UK assets to foreigners has been one of the ways Britain secures finance given our very low level of national savings – something that is arguably less sustainable in this changing geopolitical reality.

31 The White House, Remarks by National Security Advisor Jake Sullivan on Renewing American Economic Leadership at the Brookings Institution, April 2023.

32 IMF, Charting Globalization's Turn to Slowbalization After Global Financial Crisis, February 2023.

33 Cabinet Office, National Security and Investment Act 2021, November 2020.

Maintaining a consensus on the net zero transition requires clear thinking about the opportunities and challenges it brings

The transition to net zero is different from Brexit-driven change in many ways. Rather than a sudden shock with ongoing reverberations, it represents a large, long-term, and planned shift in the way that we power our economy. The UK's ability to achieve it is underpinned by a greater degree of public consensus on the issue than seen in many advanced economies.[34] Maintaining that, amid early signs that the political consensus on net zero has begun to fray, is far from automatic.[35] It requires combining a recognition of the necessity for decarbonisation with a nuanced understanding of the opportunities that it brings and the reality that, like every big economic change, it will create winners and losers, creating disruption that needs to be managed. The net zero transition is a big change, but is neither the economic disaster nor magic bullet that it is sometimes presented as.

For some, the net zero transition is more than a necessity or a situation to make the best of – they see it instead as the central means by which the UK raises growth and spreads good jobs.[36] It would obviously be nice if this were so: economic strategy could then be reduced to energetic action to avoid climate catastrophe. Others take the opposite view, characterising net zero as cratering rather than driving growth.[37]

The 'green growth' optimists are right about a great deal. They are right to argue that any new route to achieving sustainably stronger growth must have a commitment to net zero at its core.[38] They are right, too, that the transition will bring big benefits: not only helping avert climate disaster but improving air quality[39] and reducing our exposure to volatile energy costs.[40] They're right, again, to highlight the UK's innovative strengths that can be built upon to supply the growing global demand for clean technologies, goods and services.[41] They're even

34 J Marshall & A Valero, The Carbon Crunch: Turning Targets into delivery, Resolution Foundation, September 2021.

35 10 Downing Street, PM speech on Net Zero: 20 September 2023, September 2023.

36 H Horton & F Harvey, Stick with net zero targets for good of economy, businesses urge next PM, The Guardian, July 2022.

37 R Clark, The Government's absurd commitment to net zero is impoverishing the nation, The Telegraph, March 2022.

38 N Stern & A Valero, Innovation, growth and the transition to net-zero emissions, Research Policy 50(9), November 2021.

39 A Corlett & J Marshall, Shrinking footprints: The impacts of the net zero transition on households and consumption, Resolution Foundation, March 2022.

40 Department for Business, Energy & Industrial Strategy, British energy security strategy, April 2022.

41 B Curran et al., Growing clean: Identifying and investing in sustainable growth opportunities across the UK, Resolution Foundation, May 2022.

right to point out that weaker regional economies are likely to benefit most from the expansion of green technologies: while overall innovation is concentrated in the South East, the parts of the country with the highest proportion of green patents include Derbyshire, Nottinghamshire, Lincolnshire, Tees Valley, and Durham.[42]

But there are some that consider a green transition to be a magic bullet which will solve the UK's growth problems, and who downplay the many tricky, sometimes painful, balancing acts that it will involve. The net zero transition's main macroeconomic effect in the short term is neither to significantly increase or reduce the level of GDP, but to reallocate it away from consumption and towards investment as we focus resources on renewing our national infrastructure to underpin a net zero carbon economy.[43]

In some respects, the UK's transition to net zero is best thought of as an invest-to-save project, creating the infrastructure needed to allow us to heat our homes and travel without burning hydrocarbons.[44] The big upfront investments required will not be a major boost to growth (let alone consumption) in the short term, because it involves replacing large parts of our capital stock rather than adding to it. In the longer term that infrastructure should be cheaper to run – the shift to electric vehicles being one crucial case in point.[45] It is possible that in time, abundant, secure and cheap electricity generation could provide a major boost to growth.[46] But hoping that turns out to be the case is not the same thing as having an economic strategy that maximises our chances of escaping stagnation.

The net zero transition will change, rather than destroy, our jobs

What of jobs? Here again, opponents' claims that widespread job losses are on the cards, or supporters' promises that large numbers of new 'green jobs' will transform the labour market, are poor guides for policy makers. Changing our jobs, rather than creating or destroying them, looks set to be the dominant labour market impact of the net zero transition.

42 B Curran et al., Growing clean: Identifying and investing in sustainable growth opportunities across the UK, Resolution Foundation, May 2022.

43 J Pisani-Ferry & S Mahfouz, The economic implications of climate action, A Report to the French Prime Minister, November 2023.

44 Climate Change Committee, Sixth Carbon Budget, December 2020.

45 A Corlett & J Marshall, Shrinking footprints: The impacts of the net zero transition on households and consumption, Resolution Foundation, March 2022.

46 Department for Energy Security and Net Zero, Powering Up Britain: Energy Security Plan, March 2023.

Yes, it poses challenges for those in so-called 'brown jobs' in the emissions-intensive industries. But, while we estimate these comprise 4 per cent of UK employment (1.3 million people), nuance is required.[47] There is only an existential threat to a tiny minority of these posts, those which directly contribute to greenhouse emissions: the number of coal-mining operatives, for example, is likely to continue falling from the current level of 0.01 per cent of employment (2,700 workers).[48]

For far more brown jobs, transition will spell adjustment, rather than destruction. For energy-intensive manufacturing industries, the goal is for the likes of steel production to shift towards low-carbon methods rather than shut down. A huge chunk of all brown jobs – some 24 per cent of the total – are large goods vehicle drivers. They will still be needed: it's their vehicles that must change. Focusing on these kinds of changes is key, because while in the truckers' case it is manageable, in others there will be significant implications for reskilling. The 250,000 people working on the "maintenance and repair of motor vehicles" underline this reality,[49] since maintaining electric vehicles requires a different skill set.[50]

The transition should also be less disruptive to the UK labour market than that of other advanced economies, since we have relatively fewer workers in industry: it constituted just 18 per cent of UK employment in 2019, compared – for example – to 27 and 24 per cent respectively in Germany and Japan.[51]

But the coming labour market change extends way beyond emissions-intense sectors. A further 13 per cent of posts – 'green jobs' – can be identified as those that already involve significant green tasks (and are not particularly prevalent in emissions-intense sectors). Some green jobs, such as wind turbine engineers, are expected to grow this decade and beyond as the transition to an electrified power grid takes hold. Residents in Hull told us that they could see the expansion of this new industry (wind turbine production) happening before their eyes.

---

47 The analysis of green and brown jobs in this section is taken from: M Broome et al., Net zero jobs: The impact of the transition to net zero on the UK labour market, Resolution Foundation, June 2022.

48 Our analysis takes an occupational approach to classifying green jobs. Recent CCC analysis takes a sectoral approach and comes to similar conclusions. Only around 1 per cent of jobs are expected to be phased down or redirected due to the net zero transition.

49 ONS, Business Register and Employment Survey: Table 2, November 2021.

50 A Norman, A vehicle for change: Upskilling the UK's technicians to service and repair electric vehicles, The Social Market Foundation, December 2022.

51 Industry consists of mining and quarrying, manufacturing, construction, and public utilities (electricity, gas, and water). For more, see: The World Bank, Employment in industry (% of total employment) (modelled ILO estimate), accessed 2nd November 2023.

"[Siemens] are continuously building. Every time you go down there it seems to have got bigger and bigger."

Participant, Hull focus group

Here we have the enticing prospect of creating well-paid roles, including in industrial heartlands or places with natural features which are well-positioned to benefit from this shift. But, again, the overall scale of such job growth is not huge. Overall, this transition will mean significant changes for many workers, but this will mostly involve shifts in the tasks they undertake and the technology they use, rather than swift job losses or changes in the UK's employment structure.

The impact on consumers rather than workers is the more immediate challenge

The economic impact on living standards of decarbonisation go beyond the varied employment effects. There will be big effects on households as consumers – of home heating or transport. The investment costs associated with net zero are manageable (less than 1 per cent of GDP annually over the next 30 years), but they are substantial: £1.4 trillion by 2050. While major savings will eventually flow from the lower operating costs of low-carbon technologies (£1.1 trillion), these will materialise only gradually.[52] This raises pressing questions about who pays for upfront investments. Answering those in the wrong way could threaten not only the living standards of poorer households, but also the relative harmony with which climate change policy has until recently been discussed in the UK.

The 2020s will see the net zero transition move from the (relatively hidden) business of decarbonising electricity generation into the heart of day-to-day life: heat pumps need to be in our homes and electric vehicles on our streets. The UK Climate Change Committee's balanced path to net zero by 2050 will require emissions from surface transport and buildings to fall, from 2020 levels, by as much as 72 per cent and 48 per cent respectively by 2035.[53] The falling costs and rapid take-up of electric vehicles leave homes as the more difficult challenge. Over

---

52 J Marshall & A Valero, The Carbon Crunch: Turning Targets Into Delivery, Resolution Foundation, September 2021.

53 J Marshall & A Valero, The Carbon Crunch: Turning Targets Into Delivery, Resolution Foundation, September 2021.

the decade to 2032, the 'home front' of net zero will require a capital spend of £39 billion on efficiency measures (insulating walls and roofs) and £37 billion on clean heat,[54] with the required investment accelerating over the coming years to peak at £14 billion in 2028 (as Figure 22 shows).[55]

Figure 22: Investment in residential buildings needs to step up sharply

Annual additional capital investment in residential buildings: UK

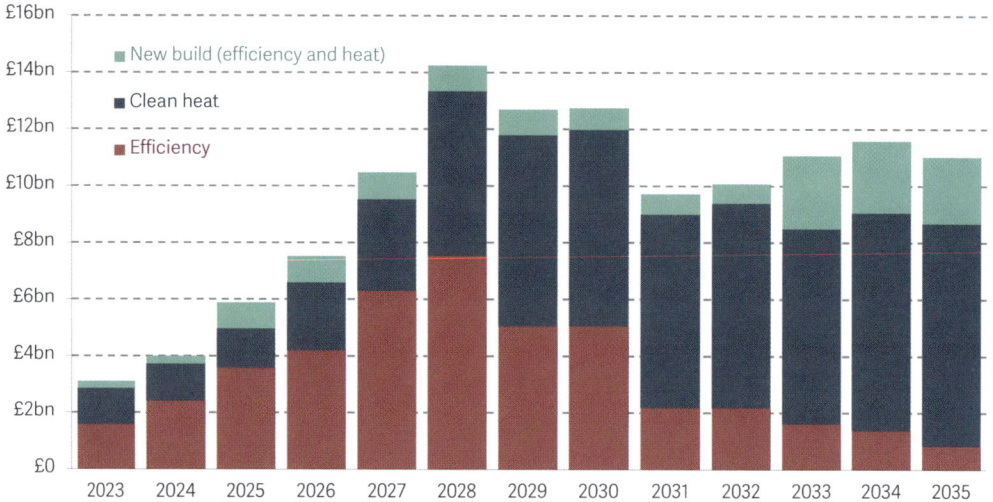

Source: Analysis of Climate Change Committee, Sixth Carbon Budget data.

Ramping up this scale of investment is hard even before you consider our recent record of failure: a 90 per cent fall in insulations since 2013, making the climb back up to the Government's ambition of 1 million home energy efficiency installations a year by 2030 particularly steep.[56] Box 6 below widens the frame for discussing the scale of the task that the UK faces in moving towards more sustainable heating sources. The UK is just as adrift on the test of how we heat our homes as we are on the test of how we avoid wasting that heat.

54 Climate Change Committee, Sixth Carbon Budget, December 2020.

55 These projections are in some respects optimistic, for example in assuming that there will be no waste of capital. The actual spend in the 2020s and 2030s may be higher.

56 See Table 10 in: Department for Business, Energy & Industrial Strategy, Net Zero Strategy: Build Back Greener, October 2021.

Box 6: Cold comfort: the home heating transition in Britain and elsewhere

Progress on decarbonising the UK's homes has been far too slow.[57] While Britain has made strides in greening its electricity supply, Figure 23 shows that only 6 per cent of the energy used to warm our flats and houses comes from green sources, against 75 per cent from gas. The sluggish take-up of heat pumps saw the UK install just 54,000 of them in 2021, against over 30 times as many gas boilers, almost 1.8 million of which were sold in the financial year 2020-21. That year, Germany and France installed three and ten times that number respectively.[58]

Figure 23: UK homes are largely heated by gas

Domestic heat supply by source, selected European countries: 2018

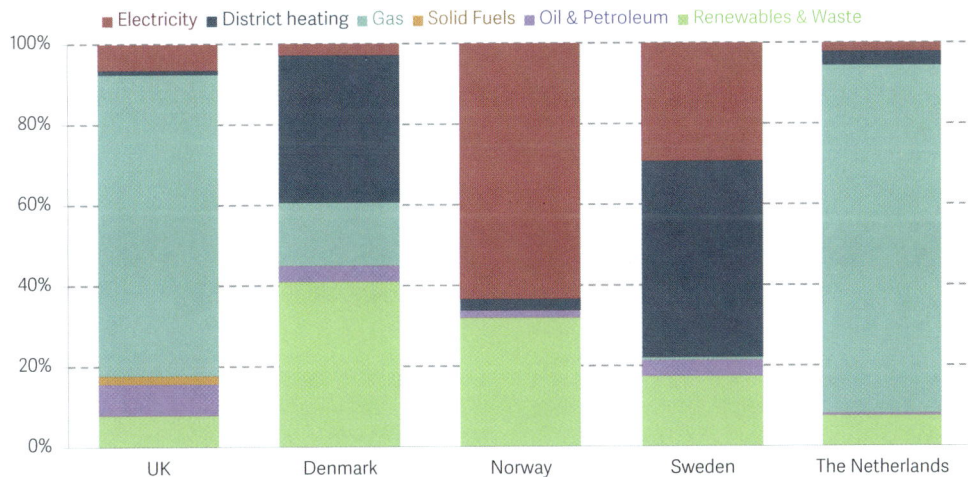

Source: Analysis of Eurostat.

Other countries, and our own history, hold lessons for how to transition at pace. Both the UK and the Netherlands made the original switch from coal to gas heating in under 15 years around the 1960s – and Figure 23 shows both remain very reliant on gas. By contrast

57 A Anis-Alavi et al., Hitting a brick wall: How the UK can upgrade its housing stock to reduce energy bills and cut carbon, Resolution Foundation, December 2022.

58 The evidence in this box draws on an externally commissioned essay as part of the Economy 2030 Inquiry: R Bruel & J Rosenow, The heat transition: Lessons from other Northern European countries on decarbonising heating, Resolution Foundation, January 2023.

Norway, Sweden and Denmark, initially spurred by the oil crisis of the 1970s and the hankering for 'energy independence', have now largely transitioned from fossil fuels to more sustainable heating sources. That motivation should also spur faster progress in the UK as we grapple with the consequences of our dependence on gas in the aftermath of the invasion of Ukraine.

The need to make progress is now urgent. Eight million buildings in England will need to switch to low carbon heating by 2035, which in many cases will require improvements to energy efficiency.[59] The most difficult change will be for lower-income home owners: owner-occupiers in the bottom fifth of the income distribution have an average income of around £9,100 a year, making the costs of overhauling home insulation and heating a significant challenge.[60] More broadly, the investments required to deliver net zero will come at a cost to consumption. But whose consumption is affected, and when, is down to decisions about how those investments are funded: individual self-funding, paying via energy bill levies, or general tax-funded subsidies will all have different consequences.

The fate of our whole transition could easily turn on such details. Recall how the sense of unfairness provoked by President Macron's hiking of fuel taxation inspired the *gilets jaunes*. That is just one telling example of how green policies can come unstuck.[61] In a Britain dogged by long-stagnant living standards, lack of regard for fair burden-sharing could be particularly liable to give rise to explosions. The bottom line? Sustainability without fairness could itself prove unsustainable, and disruption to patterns of consumption rather than employment are where the risks are highest.

In sum, the net zero transition must be an important part of a renewed economic strategy that moves us towards a more resilient, resource efficient and prosperous economy but – urgent imperative that it is – it comes with challenges. On its own, it is not, and must not be mistaken for, an alternative to that strategy.

---

59 National Infrastructure Commission, Second National Infrastructure Assessment, October 2023. The NIC estimates that overall public investment will need to increase by £10 billion per year to meet the challenges of the 2030s.

60 A Corlett & J Marshall, Shrinking footprints: The impacts of the net zero transition on households and consumption, Resolution Foundation, March 2022.

61 N Stern & A Valero, Innovation, growth and the transition to net-zero emissions, Research Policy 50(9), November 2021.

Technological shifts have not driven significant economic change in the recent past, but could in future

Technological change has been the one constant of economic life since the industrial revolution, as has demographic change for far longer (see Box 7). Think of the spinning jenny, the railway, the internal combustion engine, mains electricity, aviation, the Fordist assembly line, the container ship, the microprocessor, or the internet. Every one of the items on this (hopelessly incomplete) list has transformed some aspects of industrial life, destroying certain old trades and ways of life in the process.

More constant than technological change itself is the idea that it is always speeding up and driving ever more significant economic disruption. It's worth looking in the rear-view mirror, as well as ahead of us, to consider how useful this way of thinking is. In the long run, technical changes of the kinds mentioned have raised what we can collectively produce by an order of magnitude, and contributed to us living incomparably longer, richer and freer lives. Moreover, and in ways that have often been hard to foresee, the economy forged by these changes has always eventually created new opportunities for employment to replace the lost jobs – as today's near-record UK employment rate affirms.[62]

Box 7: Demographic change in the 2020s

It's hardly news that Britain is ageing. Despite some worrying recent trends, on a long view people are living longer.[63] Moreover, some of the more obvious economic effects are particularly pronounced in the 2020s as the 'demographic bulge' of baby boomers is tipping over into retirement.

Figure 24 summarises these trends, revealing that during the 2020s the UK population is expected to grow by 2.1 million (3.2 per cent) overall, while the number of older people (65 and above) is expected to increase by around 2.5 million (20 per cent).[64] This compares to an increase of 760,000 (or just 2 per cent) among those of working age. And at the same time, due to falling fertility rates, the numbers aged 15 or under is actually projected to shrink by 1.1 between million (9 per cent).

---

62 U Akcigit & J Van Reenen, The Economics of Creative Destruction: New Research on Themes from Aghion and Howitt, Harvard University Press, August 2023.

63 ONS, National life tables – life expectancy in the UK: 2018 to 2020, September 2021.

64 The analysis in this section is sourced from: M Broome, Big welcomes and long goodbyes: The impact of demographic change in the 2020s, Resolution Foundation, June 2022.

There are, however, a few twists on this familiar ageing story. For one thing, British society starts the 2020s a lot less elderly than many peer economies, including Japan, Italy and Germany.[65] Moreover, on the potential crunch of the ratio of pensioners to workers, OECD forecasts suggest that Britain will age less than similar societies like France and Germany during the next few years.[66]

In particular, thanks to the mini-baby boom of the early 2000s, the record 'life-cycle' flows out of the labour market will be balanced by exceptional 'flows in' during the next decade or so. While the number reaching state pension age is expected to surpass 800,000 in 2028 for the first time ever, the number of people turning 22 will exceed 900,000 in 2032 for the first time this century.

Figure 24: While pensioners proliferate, most age groups flatline

Historic and projected population estimates, by age group: UK

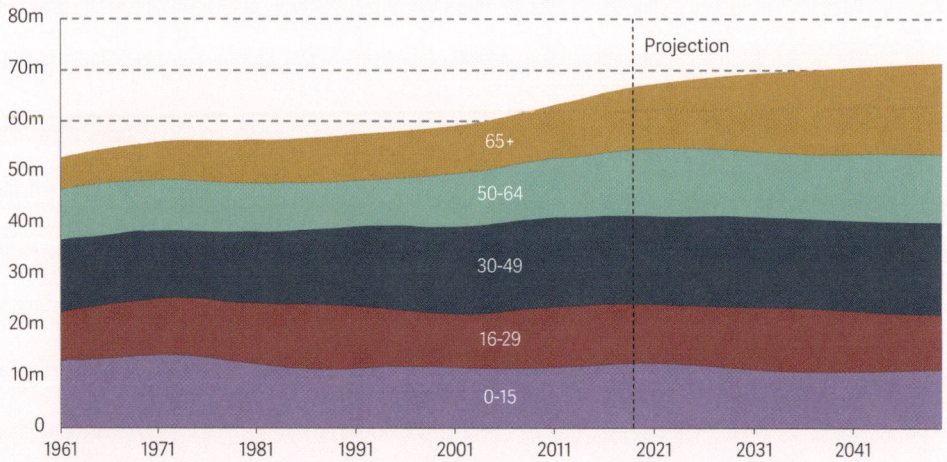

Source: ONS, Estimates of the population for the UK, England and Wales, Scotland and Northern Ireland: Mid-2020 edition, June 2021; ONS, National population projections: 2020-based, January 2022.

So what of the economics of these demographic changes? Often

the discussion of the impact of demographic shifts focuses purely

65 OECD, Elderly share of population, https://data.oecd.org/pop/elderly-population.htm#indicator-chart accessed 25 October.

66 OECD, Age ratio, https://data.oecd.org/pop/old-age-dependency-ratio.htm#indicator-chart, accessed 25 October.

on the fiscal implications of having more pensions to pay with fewer workers to tax. That is certainly a real challenge, but one already significantly mitigated by pension age increases.[67] Moreover, there are important broader economic effects that are too often overlooked. An older workforce may act as an impediment to growth if, for example, older workers are less mobile geographically, train less, or simply find it harder to adjust to new technologies. But at the same time, that fill-up of young workers over the 2020s must rank as a boon – and so, in relative terms, is the fact that we are less aged than many comparable countries. The UK's large flows in and out of the labour market may also facilitate economic change, allowing the structure of the economy to shift without individuals having to make moves to new roles or sectors (as discussed in Chapter 6).

An ageing population also changes the economy by shifting consumption patterns: younger and older people spend their money in different ways, and place different demands on public spending. We anticipate an older population to increase the total amount of spending on recreation and culture by 4.5 per cent and private healthcare by 6.7 per cent over the next decade. The latter will only make a relatively modest dent in a far bigger age-related rise in demand for – and employment of – health and social care workers predominantly funded via the public sector.

In sum, Britain's ageing is something that will need to be reckoned with, but is less significant than that of many other countries for the next few years at least, as an influx of young adults into the labour market is an important offsetting force.

But the long-term can be very long indeed, so it is worth looking more closely in the rear-view mirror to get more of a handle on what technological change has been doing to our jobs and wages in the recent past. The focus of rising alarm has been about the march of supposedly job-killing robots, but here the record of over-excited predictions of change make the case for keeping automation in perspective. One 2014 paper, which suggested that 35 per cent of UK jobs were at risk of automation by 2034, is typical of many prominent 2010s forecasts that robots would soon take all our jobs.[68] This striking claim was picked up by

67 Detail on State Pension age changes can be found in: D Thurley & R Keen, State Pension age review, House of Commons Library, August 2017.
68 Deloitte, Agiletown: The relentless march of technology and London's response, November 2014.

Monetary Policy Committee members and politicians, leading to a flurry of anxiety about automation-driven unemployment, with headlines such as "Robots have taken more than 60,000 jobs from British workers with 15 MILLION more to go".[69] But we're nearly halfway through the 20-year period in which automation was supposed to do for a third of all jobs, yet the employment structure is still pretty similar to 2014: neither mass change nor mass unemployment has come to pass. Indeed, in a world of stagnant productivity growth it's hard not to conclude the UK has had too few robots, rather than too many.[70]

As in other developed economies, technology has mostly exerted a powerful but more gradual effect: occupations that are more exposed such as machine operators and cashiers may not have seen mass layoffs, but they have seen lower employment growth.[71] The effect on wages is less clear, with some negative impact from robotic advancements but no negative wage relationship connected to software exposure.[72] Such correlations do not fully quantify the aggregate labour market effects of technology, because indirect effects (including higher productivity) are also important. For example, in recent years there has been a negative direct effect of new robotic technologies on manufacturing employment, and an offsetting positive indirect effect on services employment across local labour markets. Taken together, the adoption of automated robots wrought no significant aggregate change in employment across local labour markets between 1995 and 2019.

As ever however, the past is an imperfect guide to the future. Today, displacement concerns focus on the prospect of work previously considered as specialist being carried out by Artificial Intelligence. The swift progress of the likes of ChatGPT in particular has led to fears about what AI could soon mean for myriad jobs traditionally thought of as middle class or even professional – copy writing, coding, the writing of journalistic reports.

---

69 M Waghorn, Robots have taken more than 60,000 jobs from British workers – with 15 MILLION more to go, The Mirror, April 2018.

70 For example, see: International Federation of Robotics, World Robotics 2023 Report: Asia ahead of Europe and the Americas, September 2023.

71 R Costa & Y Yu, Adopt, adapt and improve: A brief look at the interplay between labour markets and technological change in the UK, Resolution Foundation, November 2022; OECD, What happened to jobs at high risk of automation?, January 2021.

72 For further discussion of wage polarisation, see: M Goos & A Manning, Lousy and lovely jobs: The rising polarization of work in Britain, The Review of Economics and Statistics, 89(1), February 2007; D Oesch, Occupational Change in Europe: How Technology and Education Transform the Job Structure, Oxford University Press, 2013; A Salvatori, The anatomy of job polarisation in the UK, Journal for Labour Market Research, 52(1), July 2018.

Predictions are often wrong – the best part of a decade after the first burst of concern about a supposedly imminent employment shock from driverless vehicles, there has still not been any great displacement. But we have seen AI recently move at a pace – and, potentially, into professional realms – that few would have anticipated a few years ago. Predictions of how this will affect work overall range from the catastrophic that up to half of employment is at risk, to the more bearable that it will augment jobs but not destroy them.[73] Some argue that these technologies will force inequality up, replacing routine white-collar work and possibly undermining hard-won worker power.[74] Other research suggests that lower skilled workers are poised to benefit the most from generative AI such as ChatGPT.[75] This leaves the specific issue of how it will impact work overall, best classified as 'radically uncertain.' That is to say, it is not merely risky on known probabilities, but unknowable in a way that rules out even envisaging some of the possible outcomes, and provides no sensible basis for attaching probabilities to any of them.

Given the uncertainty involved, no entirely reliable way of preparing is available, but broad principles are important to ensuring that our society is better-placed to adjust to the unexpected (a subject we return to in Chapter 6).[76] In particular, it is surely a good idea to run an economy that is broadly based, rather than unduly dependent on one or two industries; to run it with buoyant demand, so as to maximise the chances of any displaced workers finding alternative employment; and to avoid the great gulfs in fortune that it is terrifying to be on the wrong side of. Fear of change, after all, inspires nothing but the politics of sclerosis. All of which is to say that, if we could solve the problems of sluggish growth and high inequality identified in Chapter 1, we would also be far better placed to face the future with agility.

73 J Hayton, Organisational Adoption of Automation Technologies Literature Review, Institute for the Future of Work, August 2023.

74 S Bushwick, Unregulated AI Will Worsen Inequality, Warns Nobel-Winning Economist Joseph Stiglitz, Scientific American, August 2023.

75 For example, see: S Noy & W Zhang, Experimental Evidence on the Productivity Effects of Generative Artificial Intelligence, Working Paper, March 2023; E Brynjolfsson, D Li & L R Raymond, Generative AI at Work, NBER Working Paper, April 2023.

76 For example, see J Kay & M King, Radical Uncertainty: Decision-making for an unknowable future, Bridge Street Press, March 2020.

The lasting legacy of Covid-19 is hybrid working, but not economic transformation

Automation, of course, is far from the only form of technology that could disrupt the way we work. The ongoing communications revolution continues to affect how – and where – we work. The lockdowns introduced in the pandemic catalysed an acceleration, as workers in suddenly shuttered offices were forced to familiarise themselves with Zoom and Teams, and collectively discovered how much it was possible to do from home. There is evidence that at least some of the shift to home working is persisting – with a mix of in-office and work-from-home days now becoming standard for many middle and higher earners.[77] The proportion of those reporting they regularly worked from home increased from 5 to 10 per cent over the decade running up to the pandemic, but then surged and remained at an elevated 38 per cent of all workers in 2023 as shown in Figure 25.[78]

Figure 25: Working from home has persisted post-pandemic

Survey measures of prevalence of working from home: UK/GB

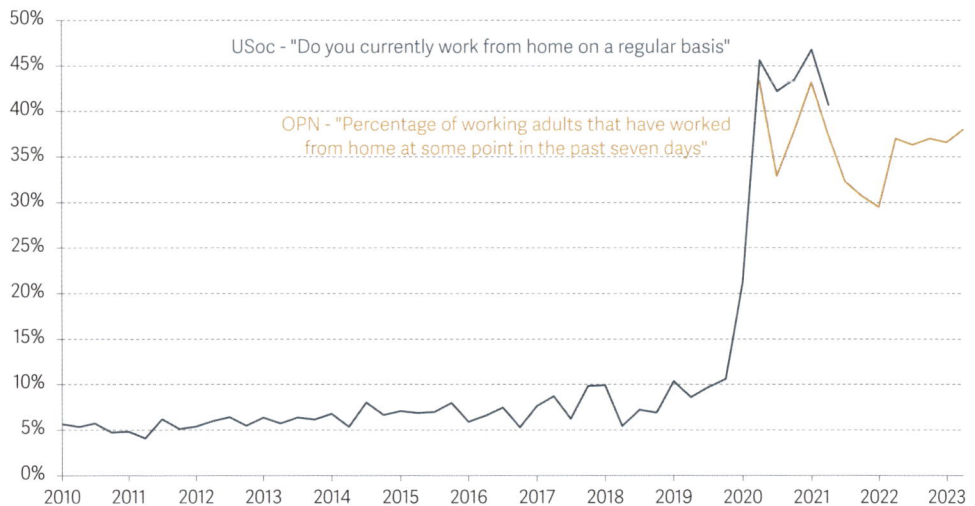

Source: Analysis of ONS, Opinions and Lifestyle Survey (OPN); Understanding Society (USoc).

---

77 J M Barrero, N Bloom & S J Davis, The Evolution of Work from Home, NBER Working Paper, September 2023.

78 M Brewer, J Leslie & L Try, Right where you left me? Analysis of the Covid-19 pandemic's impact on local economies in the UK, Resolution Foundation, June 2022.

This is a big shift, in which some have dared to hope they can spot answers to Britain's stagnation. Insofar as workers partially substitute their saved commuting time for longer working hours, that directly raises output.[79] Another boost to output (and inclusion) that hybrid working may have contributed to is the stronger post-pandemic shift towards full-time employment for mothers, as it eases the challenges of combining full-time work with parenting.[80]

Unfortunately, while hybrid working is a welcome development that can often raise well-being, the evidence it can provide a significant boost in productivity is weaker. While many workers report being more productive at home, research in the US has found that fully remote work leads to a 10 per cent lower productivity than fully in-person work.[81] Of those businesses adopting home working as a permanent part of their business model, fewer than half claim increased productivity is the aim, while 86 per cent of large businesses cite improved staff well-being as important.[82] Benefits going forward from longer-term dynamic improvements due to, for example, better matching of workers to jobs – particularly of college-educated parents with young children – are possible, but remain tentative and are unlikely to be the panacea for the child penalty faced by women in the labour force.[83]

What about inequality? Some dared to hope that Britain's stubborn regional gap might be aided by the shift towards home working as it widens the range of places in which skilled professionals can live. Some claimed this would see people earning London wages but living in Liverpool. But again, the evidence pointed to decidedly limited benefits on this count. As it is hybrid (rather than fully remote) work that is the new norm for higher earners, it generally facilitates longer commutes within region, rather than large numbers of people living in different regions from their employers. Shifts in the map of employment (accounting for dwindling office work and increased home working) were generally small.

The pandemic saw a shift playing out between inner and outer London, with work done estimated to have increased by 20 per cent in Lewisham but to have

---

79 N Bloom et al., Does working from home work? Evidence from a Chinese experiment, The Quarterly Journal of Economics, 130(1), February 2015.

80 M Brewer, C McCurdy & H Slaughter, Begin again? Assessing the permanent implications of Covid-19 for the UK's labour market, Resolution Foundation, November 2021.

81 J M Barrero, N Bloom & S J Davis, The Evolution of Work from Home, NBER Working Paper, September 2023.

82 J Leslie, Bouncebackability: The UK corporate sector's recovery from Covid-19, Resolution Foundation, June 2022.

83 For a discussion on the child penalty, see: H Kleven, C Landais & G Leite-Mariante, The Child Penalty Atlas, Working Paper, September 2023.

declined by a similar amount in Westminster. But across most of the country the shift in where work was done can be measured in a handful of percentage points either way.

Even when home working has meant a big shift towards more work being done in a local authority, it does not appear to have helped the lower earners living there (many hoped it would lead to more spending on local high streets). Haringey is a striking example, combining a big rise in working from home with an exceptionally large rise in those claiming unemployment benefits.[84]

Working from home brings benefits to people, saving on commuting time and simplifying busy lives. There are, however, as yet few signs that it will solve Britain's productivity problem – or indeed redraw its economic map.

Constants amid the change

John Maynard Keynes used to say that mathematics was less important for sound economics than a sense of proportion. That is especially true in a decade like the 2020s. Tumult abounds and poses many substantive challenges – but also a particular risk of distraction from our underlying challenges.

We've reviewed the big specific changes confronting the British economy in the 2020s: the continuing convulsions created by technology and the evolution of our demographics; the demands of the green transition created by this hour of environmental danger and the need for energy security; and the UK-specific issues as we enter a new relationship with a giant trading bloc next door. No strategy can claim to be serious without tackling all of the issues. But nor, as we have seen, should any of the change they bring be viewed as an alternative to a strategy. The new frictions on trade created by Brexit, whatever its other benefits, will only add to the UK's productivity problem, just as some aspects of the net zero transition could, if badly handled, put further pressure on stagnant living standards.

We can and should look for opportunities to harness inevitable changes to make Britain more prosperous and fairer, which is the focus of Chapter 8. What we must not do, however, is be distracted, thinking we can take our eye off those core problems of stagnation or be lulled into believing that they will be addressed as a by-product of managing the disruptions of the 2020s. Instead, we must confront them head on, with a strategy designed for that purpose. The next chapter sets out the criteria for a serious strategy of that type.

---

84 M Brewer et al., Right where you left me? Analysis of the Covid-19 pandemic's impact on local economies in the UK, Resolution Foundation, June 2022.

Chapter Three

Getting serious

Chapter summary

- No single policy shift holds the answer to ending stagnation. Instead the task is to build a new economic strategy to tackle low growth and high inequality.

- As well as being clear about its objectives, an effective strategy would start from the reality of our existing economy, be clear about trade-offs we face, be backed up by policies capable of moving the dial, and have staying power.

- Elements of a way forward have been proposed, from the UK Government's focus on closing economic gaps between places, to the Labour Party's green investment plans, or the Welsh Government's prioritisation of social partnership. And we can learn from our own past and from countries that have renewed their economic strategies: for example Germany after reunification.

- But we are not on course to build a new economic strategy. Partly because it is hard and partly because it is far from clear that policy makers are serious about doing so.

- Some argue we don't need growth because it won't translate into gains for ordinary households, ignoring the reality that a lack of growth is the cause of flatlining wages. More common is to recognise that growth is necessary, or that inequality is too high, but to be deeply unserious about what it might take to change things. A manufacturing jobs revival is promised, with no engagement with the reality of declines in such jobs across the advanced world. Half of the debate about Brexit denies its costs, while the other half denies its reality.

- There is a recognition, from the Prime Minister downward, that we cannot continue as we are, but there is nothing automatic about escaping stagnation. Italy provides a warning. As late as 2000, Italy's GDP per capita was in line with that of Germany and significantly ahead of the UK, but in recent years Italy's productivity has actually been falling. By 2019, Italian GDP per capita had fallen to 17 per cent below Germany's and was on a par with Spain's, having been 22 per cent higher in 2000.

The previous chapters argued that the twin giants holding back British living standards are low growth and high inequality, and that the fight against them must wrestle with – but not be distracted by – the significant disruption the 2020s has in store. We now turn to how we should respond. The scale of the challenge posed by stagnation, laid bare in Chapter 1, means that tweaks to individual policies are insufficient. Instead, the UK must forge a comprehensive new economic strategy. This will not involve government dictating, still less doing, everything itself, but consist of clarity about the broad direction in which Britain needs to go and the commitment to make all policy arrows point in that direction for year after year.

We focus on the challenge for the UK as a whole, although the analysis has major implications for devolved nations and regions, who play important roles in supporting growth, reducing inequality and blazing a different trail.

The UK requires a new economic strategy

The longer we live as a stagnation nation, the grimmer the consequences for our living standards. Real typical household income growth is on track to be just 6 per cent over the full 20 years up to 2025-26 – a barely discernible crawl of progress, overwhelmed by the many big bumps along the way.[1] If, in contrast, incomes had continued to rise at the more traditional rate of 2 per cent annually, they would have increased by almost 50 per cent in this time.[2] Grim, too, are the consequences of being a stagnation nation for the state: revenues stand still without meaningful growth, and in our ageing society, merely maintaining existing levels of public service provision requires a higher tax burden. In practice, it can often feel like standards are slipping even as taxes rise. More broadly, stagnation holds back the country as a whole: in the decades ahead, our place in the world and even the quality of our democracy may be at risk if we cannot change course.

Some suggest specific policy shifts that can unlock a brighter future. The former Prime Minister Boris Johnson talked of lower migration as being the key to a new high-wage economy,[3] while others view significant change on housing (be that planning liberalisation or a land value tax) as a magic bullet.[4]

1   A Corlett, The Living Standards Outlook – Summer 2023 Update, Resolution Foundation, September 2023.
2   Calculated based on income projections as published in: T Bell et al., Inflation Nation: Putting Spring Statement 2022 in context, Resolution Foundation, March 2022.
3   Conservatives, Boris Johnson's keynote speech – We're getting on with the job, 6 October 2021.
4   S Bowman, J Myers & B Southwood, The housing theory of everything, Works in progress, September 2021.

There may be occasions when a single shift can address the major challenges facing a nation. This is the case when reversing a macroeconomic policy is a precondition of progress, as with Britain's withdrawal from the Gold Standard in 1931 and arguably also with the 1992 devaluation. But even in these cases additional policies were also important in turning things round, including a new inflation-targeting regime in the second case, and greatly reduced interest rates in both.

More fundamentally, the decade of the 2020s is not one of those times when progress is blocked by a single overwhelming obstacle. A wider strategic reset is required for at least three reasons.

First, the challenges that the UK faces are huge. A tweak to the benefits system will not end a situation where low-income Brits are 27 per cent poorer than their French equivalents and 33 per cent poorer than their German ones (as shown in Chapter 1). However vital, investing in specific new green technologies will not on its own raise woeful growth to an adequate rate. The problem of our cities makes the point. All of England's biggest cities apart from London currently have productivity levels below the national average. Closing this chasm requires change on a scale not currently contemplated: reducing Greater Manchester's productivity gap with London to 20 per cent (from 35 per cent) would require a £30 billion boost to aggregate business capital and an increase to its graduate workforce of as many as 180,000 workers. [5]

Second, as we have shown, our challenges and changes interlock – not just low growth and high inequality themselves, but also the demographic, technological and environmental changes to come. The future of the UK's automotive industry will be shaped by post-Brexit trade policy as much as our domestic approach to net zero. There are, of course, always interdependencies for policy makers to consider when it comes to the public finances. But with significant demands for higher investment at a time of higher public debt, the unavoidable reality that money spent on one priority can't be spent on an alternative could become a source of controversy, redoubling the argument for a fully integrated strategy.

Third, major planks of what had long passed as Britain's economic strategy have just been upended in recent times. Financial services were long seen as our most important 'comparative advantage,' but far less so after the financial crisis. And

---

5   This would entail increasing Greater Manchester's business capital by 15 per cent. For more discussion, see Chapter 4 and: P Brandily et al., A tale of two cities (part 2): A plausible strategy for productivity growth in Greater Manchester and beyond, Resolution Foundation, September 2023.

for half a century, the UK has prioritised open access to a large, integrated and continent-wide home market. Brexit changes that.

The ingredients

What are the key characteristics of a serious strategy? We suggest five principal requirements.

1. *Clear objectives:* a strategy must be clear about the problem it is trying to solve, which in our context means the stagnation driven by those two underlying problems of low growth and high inequality. The corresponding prize is stronger, sustainable and inclusive growth.

2. *Clarity about context:* good strategies don't start with a blank sheet – they must be alert to the status quo, though not beholden to it. They move from a hard-headed assessment of the country's strengths and weaknesses to a clear understanding of the resulting constraints and opportunities. They deal with the world as it is, so have no room for wishful or nostalgic thinking.

    In the present context, this will involve careful judgements about which structures of the UK economy run so deep that they will be very hard to shift anything other than gradually, and distinguish them from features that are more malleable. The path dependency here will be powerful but there will also be long-established economic patterns – whether in production, consumption or distribution – that are susceptible to concerted policy action. Our commitment to the net zero transition, for instance, inevitably means that some parts of our economy will have to function very differently in the future. We must also be realistic about what domestic policy can do in a rich but medium-sized and fairly open economy. Many key variables – whether commodity and energy prices, the technological frontier, or long-term interest rates – are set at the global level. And, as recent years have underlined, they are subject to global shocks and shifts in geopolitics.

3. *Realism about trade-offs:* recognition of the real options on offer, and their costs as well as their benefits, is what distinguishes a strategy from a wish list. There are often tricky balances to strike even between competing objectives within the strategy, as for example, when 'agglomeration effects' create a tension between raising average productivity and more geographically balanced output.

A lot of the dilemmas boil down to decisions over scarce resources. Sometimes these crystallise in the public finances: tax versus spend, or one spending priority versus another. But sometimes the choice is about resource allocation across the economy as a whole. For example, all those extra workers that will undertake home retrofitting as implied by Government plans must come from somewhere: where? Likewise, boosting investment must, at least in the short run, mean lower consumption or higher net imports and hence foreign borrowing: which? Then there are deeper dilemmas of political economy, such as the right balance to strike between cross-border economic integration and national policy autonomy.

The job of a strategy isn't necessary to resolve all such trade-offs in a binary fashion – in a democracy, the task of politics is often to manage tensions that are longstanding features of societies or economies. But the job is to expose them, and thereby reveal the true choices on offer. Moreover, by setting out the assorted balancing acts that public policy is saddled with, an economic strategy can ensure that objectives that matter for general prosperity but don't naturally attach to any particular vocal lobby – such as the diffuse benefits to all of us from existing companies facing at least the possibility of forceful competition – aren't allowed to drop out of mind. By providing a coherent framework for balancing judgments, it can also avoid the need to relitigate the nature (or even the existence) of trade-offs between different objectives every time an individual decision is made.

4. **Sufficient scale:** having set out clear objectives, a strategy must be backed by policies of a scale commensurate with the ambition of the desired outcome. In some times and places, a collection of relatively minor adjustments may suffice. But the diagnoses set out in the previous chapters suggest that, to have the necessary impact, an integrated and high-voltage response will be required for Britain today.

5. **Staying power**: strategies play out over time – they can only be effective when they persist. Unfortunately, one of the problems of policy making in the UK has been policy and institutional short-termism: this has been a feature of the British model over much of the 20th century.[6] It still afflicts us, as evidenced, for example, by the hopelessly short lifespan of the recently axed Industrial

---

6   N Crafts, Adapting Well to New Circumstances? UK Experience in Changing Times, Resolution Foundation, November 2022.

Strategy Council or the debacle of HS2 (see Box 8).[7] Stability is a special challenge in the face of shocks such as AI and climate that lack obvious precedents and introduce radical uncertainty, for which the only preparation is to be predictably flexible.[8] Staying power is easier in some times and places than others. In many successful countries, the political system and broader institutional settlements help. Simplistic calls to 'take the politics out' of big decisions that are bound to inspire divergent reactions are naïve. But building institutions that can reinforce, rather than undermine, a long view is possible: the UK's National Infrastructure Commission is one useful example. Ensuring the early involvement of a broad group of stakeholders can also go some way to ensuring more constituencies of interest feel like insiders, reducing the pressure for the regular policy swerves that can otherwise flow from turbulent, winner-takes-all politics.

Box 8: Lessons from HS2

The painful saga of the UK's largest current infrastructure project, HS2, underlines how far we have slid off track in approaching even the biggest economic decisions in a strategic manner. However one weighs the prospective benefits against the gargantuan costs of the scheme, the last couple of years – during which the Leeds leg of the scheme was amputated, the final link into London Euston indefinitely suspended, and then the second phase of the project connecting to Manchester axed entirely – has been utterly shambolic. As things stand Britain looks set to have spent tens of billions on a high-speed railway that only connects Birmingham to west London, an outcome nobody would ever have designed.[9] These rapid policy shifts do more than demonstrate the lack of a clear national strategy, they illustrate the dangers for industries and places of the absence of such a strategy.

7   The Industrial Strategy Council was launched in November 2018 and abolished in March 2021: M Kleinman, Kwarteng axes star-studded Industrial Strategy Council with hint at BEIS rebranding, Sky News, March 2021.

8   N Stern & A Valero, Innovation, growth and the transition to net-zero emissions, Research Policy, Volume 50, Issue 9, November 2021, 104293, ISSN 0048-7333, https://doi.org/10.1016/j.respol.2021.104293.

9   S Taaffe-Maguire, HS2 explained: What is the route now, what are the costs and why is the Manchester leg being axed?, Sky News, October 2023.

As the National Infrastructure Commission notes, the abrupt scrapping of the second phase of HS2 "leaves a major gap in the UK's rail strategy around which a number of cities have based their economic growth plans."[10]

Strategic resets have been pulled off before

In light of what passes for our current economic policy discussion, it might feel like our criteria for a serious strategy are simply beyond reach. Certainly, other countries have demonstrated that decades can pass without a serious strategy in place. And there is no blueprint from another time or place that we can replicate wholesale. But recent history, both here and elsewhere, offers lessons to be learned: our "Navigating Economic Change" essay series, commissioned as part of the Economy 2030 Inquiry, fleshes them out in detail.[11]

The German experience after reunification is a prime example of a big shock being managed in a strategic fashion. On average, the equivalent of more than £74 billion was spent on reunification every year between 1990 and 2018.[12] With cross-party consensus on doing 'whatever it takes', social security and pension entitlements were near-immediately harmonised. There was also huge backing for public infrastructure in East Germany, alongside the modernisation of an antiquated industrial capital stock focused particularly on manufacturing. The result? Despite stubborn challenges in East–West migration and an Eastern lag in knowledge-based sectors, both the productivity and the income gap between the former two Germanies shrank dramatically. A close reading (see Box 9) reveals lessons from what went wrong as well as right, but the main moral of the story is that sustained and well-resourced strategic direction can achieve an awful lot.

---

10 National Infrastructure Commission, Second National Infrastructure Assessment, October 2023.

11 The full set of essays is available on the Resolution Foundation website: Navigating Economic Change: Lessons from abroad and history.

12 K Enenkel & F Rösel, German Reunification: Lessons from the German approach to closing regional economic divides, Navigating Economic Change, The Economy 2030 Inquiry, December 2022.

Box 9: The broadly successful strategy of German reunification[13]

Within months of the fall of the Berlin wall in 1989, Germany embarked on a reunification that rapidly transformed the Communist East into a democratic market economy. Cross-party support unlocked vast funding – equivalent in largesse to the UK's furlough scheme but for every year over the last 30 years. Trillions were spent over the decades, with impressive results in narrowing the once-vast gap in living standards between East and West seen in Figure 26. Where average wages in the East used to be just half (51 per cent) those of the West, they are now 83 per cent, and the gap on incomes and GDP per head has closed in similar fashion. Life expectancy at 65, which used to be decidedly shorter, has completely equalised. Industry capital per worker in the East now actually exceeds the West. On the flipside, there has been demographic divergence, with a falling net 1.7 million people moving from East to West Germany between 1989 and 2019. The effect of this, together with a falling birth rate in the East, is evident in the relative fall in its population density.[14]

All of this is, first and foremost, a demonstration of what can be done when serious resources are deployed in a sustained way towards a strategic ambition. But not everything has gone right. The UK should take a cautionary look at the German experience in supporting legacy jobs in manufacturing in less urban areas, which sometimes came at the expense of growth in higher-value, knowledge-based activities and the role of large cities. One possible consequence of seeking to shore up the old over the new is evident in one last indicator in the chart: a marked decline in support for mainstream parties in the East. Where communities struggle to see the future, rising average incomes don't automatically translate into political contentment.

---

13 The evidence in this box draws on an externally commissioned essay as part of the Economy 2030 Inquiry: K Enenkel & F Rösel, German Reunification: Lessons from the German approach to closing regional economic divides, Navigating Economic Change, The Economy 2030 Inquiry, December 2022.

14 C Bangel et al., The Millions Who Left, Zeit Online, May 2019.

Figure 26: One nation politics – how reunification closed the German divide

Various metrics in East Germany as a share of the West German score

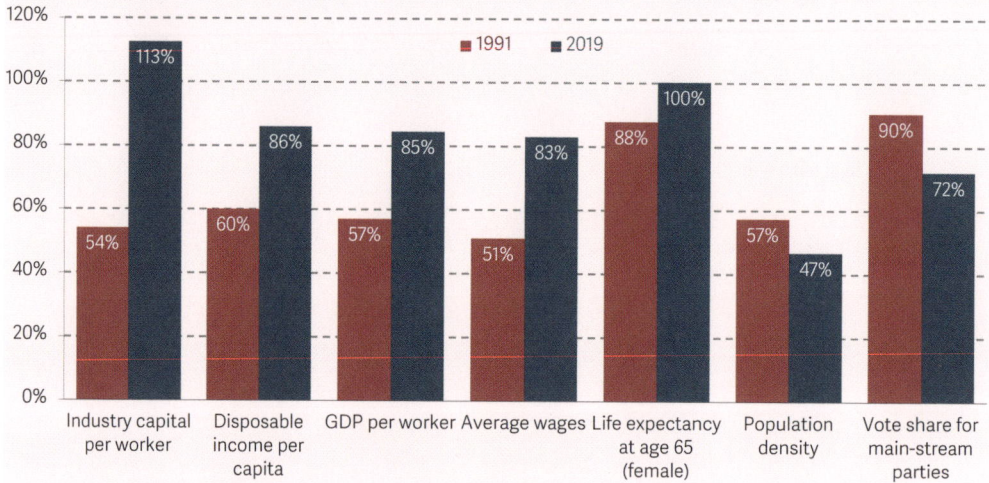

Notes: Life expectancy: without Berlin; Population density: East Berlin is part of East Germany and West Berlin part of West Germany; Capital stock: 2018, GDP per worker: 1992, Population density: 2017, Vote for mainstream parties: 1990 and 2017. Average wages calculated as total wages divided by total number of workers.
Source: Volkswirtschaftliche Gesamtrechnungen der Länder, Anlagevermögen in den Ländern der Bundesrepublik Deutschland 1991 bis 2018; Volkswirtschaftliche Gesamtrechnungen der Länder, Entstehung, Verteilung und Verwendung des Bruttoinlandsprodukts in den Ländern der Bundesrepublik Deutschland; Volkswirtschaftliche Gesamtrechnungen der Länder, Bruttoinlandsprodukt, Bruttowertschöpfung in den kreisfreien Städten und Landkreisen der Bundesrepublik Deutschland 1992 und 1994 bis 2019; Bundesagentur fuer Arbeit, Arbeitsmarktstatistik; Volkswirtschaftliche Gesamtrechnungen der Länder, Bruttoinlandsprodukt, Bruttowertschöpfung in den Ländern der Bundesrepublik Deutschland 1991 bis 2020, Reihe 1, Länderergebnisse Band 1 Destatis, Bevölkerung: Kreise, Stichtag.

New Zealand is another country that experienced a major shock, which struck when the UK joined the European Economic Community in 1973, significantly reducing the nation's access to what had been its largest export market. With the energy upheavals of the 1970s hitting as well, trade patterns shifted and the sectoral mix of the economy inescapably had to change, too. And it did. Initially, though, there was little strategy involved, but rather a period of instability and repeated crises. Next – from the 1980s – came a drive to recast the whole country's model (see Box 10), through deep market liberalisation, a floating exchange rate, public service reform and a new macroeconomic regime. Things were moving, but there was also a major shift in the balance of power away from workers, as union coverage plunged and inequality soared.[15] Arguably, much of New Zealand politics and public policy in more recent times can be seen as attempts to pick up the pieces after decades that ushered in change, but forgot about fairness.

Box 10: Shocks, shifts and inequality: the New Zealand story[16]

After being one of the world's most prosperous countries in the 1900s, New Zealand's relative performance slipped from the First World War right through until the 1980s. Various price and energy shocks in the 1960s and 70s were compounded by a loss of access to its major trading partner when the UK joined the European Community.

Figure 27: The Antipodean shift – how New Zealand reallocated

Percentage point change in each industry's share of gross value added: 1986-87 to 2020-21

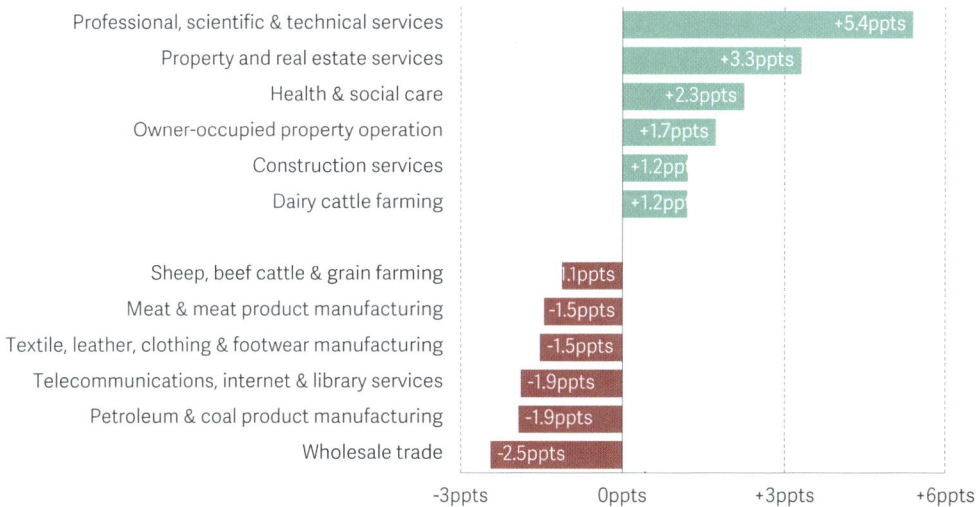

Source: Analysis of Stats NZ, Table SNE048AA.

A strategic response was eventually settled on in the form of deep liberalisation between 1984 and 1991. Subsidies were removed from almost every sector, and international trade was opened up via free trade

---

15 C Ball & J Creedy, Inequality in New Zealand 1983/84 to 2013/14, New Zealand Treasury, June 2015.

16 The evidence in this box draws on an externally commissioned essay as part of the Economy 2030 Inquiry: A Grimes, New Zealand: Lessons on economic reform from a distant relative, Navigating Economic Change, The Economy 2030 Inquiry, September 2023.

agreements with a host of East Asian countries. By the mid-1990s, as previously protected sectors were flushed out, change was palpable. Between 1987 and 2020 the economy saw a significant restructuring, with (Figure 27) marked growth in higher-paying, knowledge-intensive professional industries. Three other sectors that boomed were closely related to property, reflecting strong internal migration and increased housing demand, particularly in the cities. There were also huge reallocations within agriculture, particularly towards dairy farming.

Did it work? There were vast improvements in average incomes, but also rocketing inequality. Efforts to tackle entrenched educational disadvantage were short-lived and ineffective. In an unbalanced housing market, price growth far outpaced incomes leaving New Zealand one of the least affordable OECD countries.[17]

This was most acutely felt in Auckland, the most populous area.[18] While the original free market drive had distinctly bipartisan lineage, having begun under the fourth Labour government, by the late 2010s, Jacinda Ardern's government was signalling the need for another change of direction, with more of an emphasis on active social policy and poverty reduction. A hankering for greater security in specific low-paid sectors – like cleaning and hospitality – spurred Wellington to set up 'Fair Pay Agreements,' which bring together unions and employer associations to drive up labour standards in particular industries.[19] While the recent defeat of that Labour government means that specific elements of the Ardern agenda look vulnerable, the new government may feel the need to address questions about security in other ways.

What about lessons closer to home? During recent history, the country has in fact pursued identifiable economic strategies. The most consequential recent example was under the Thatcher government, where strident approach to industrial relations, determined anti-inflation policies, a shakeout of old industries

---

17 OECD, Better life index, accessed 12 July 2023.

18 W Cox, 2023 Demographia International Housing Affordability, March 2023.

19 For a fuller discussion of New Zealand's FPAs see Box 3 in C McCurdy, H Slaughter & G Kelly, Putting good work on the table: Reforming labour market institutions to improve pay and conditions, Resolution Foundation, September 2023.

and a growing private service economy all combined with a mutually-reinforcing dynamic. We'll return to this case study in Chapter 8. But Thatcher's was not the first strategy in post-war Britain.

Harold Wilson's Government came to power in 1964 committed to achieving faster economic growth which, in his view, relied on a reorientation of industrial and social policy. The core objective was the rapid expansion of rising industries and the reallocation of skilled labour towards them. This shift required the existence of 'social infrastructure' to smooth the path for transitioning workers. Low welfare benefits at a flat rate were an impediment to better-paid, skilled workers embracing change. The task was to "ease the transition from job to job which must be made if the country is to achieve the redeployment of manpower which it so urgently needs".[20] The necessary social infrastructure, as Wilson saw it, included a shift towards earnings-related unemployment benefits, plus compensation for layoffs (under the Statutory Redundancy Pay Act, 1966), Industrial Training Boards, expanded universities, the launch of the Open University and a new polytechnic system. Did it work? Perhaps – there was a 44 per cent rise in labour reallocation between industrial sectors in the decade following 1968 compared to the one that went before, a dynamism surpassing all the preceding peacetime decades of the 20th century.[21] And of course, this was achieved without the mass unemployment and social division that accompanied the economic upheavals of the 1980s.

But there were flaws in the implementation, including benefit calculations of such baffling complexity that few workers understood what they were entitled to, or noticed when the Thatcher government unwound the reforms just over a decade later. The strategy, then, ultimately lacked staying power. More immediately, it was at least overshadowed and arguably overwhelmed by the doomed attempt to ward off the 1967 devaluation, and the austere macroeconomics that followed in its wake. While there is useful food for thought in the Wilson experience, it is also a reminder that it's hard to plan for the future unless you can make your way through the present.

---

20 G Kelly, Preparing for a decade of economic change: Lessons from the era of White Heat, Resolution Foundation, July 2021.

21 T Bell et al., The UK's decisive decade: The launch report of The Economy 2030 Inquiry, Resolution Foundation May 2021.

Talking strategically, acting sporadically

Turning back to that present, while few would claim that the UK has a clearly established economic strategy, it is good news that at least the question of the future direction of our economy – and the need to revitalise growth – is being debated.

Politicians in both the main parties are beginning to talk about stagnation:

> *"If we cannot accelerate growth, people will begin to lose faith in the moral and material case for free markets... So, the question we face today is urgent and it is consequential: How do we accelerate growth?"*[22]

> Rishi Sunak

> *"We are now in the worst of all possible worlds, with inflation high... and growth low...– in other words, there is stagflation... Growth has stagnated, not just this year but over the last 12 years."*[23]

> Rachel Reeves

The ideas and commitments currently being developed may not add up to a comprehensive approach, but some of them could become useful planks of a new overarching strategy. There is much to build on, including from different political parties and devolved governments. Examples include:

- **Investment:** Both main parties have recognised that low overall investment is a key factor holding the UK back,[24] and agree the state has direct role in fixing this, including by providing a more stable macroeconomic environment.[25] The Government has ramped up public sector net investment in recent years, albeit with cuts now pencilled in.[26]

---

22 R Sunak, Chancellor Rishi Sunak's Mais Lecture 2022, February 2022.
23 R Reeves, Speech in House of Commons debate: Achieving economic growth, May 2022.
24 R Sunak, Chancellor Rishi Sunak's Mais Lecture 2022, February 2022.
25 See K Starmer, Speech at the BCC Global Annual Conference 2023, May 2023.
26 See F Odamtten & J Smith,Cutting the cuts, Resolution Foundation, March 2023.

- **Net zero:** The UK generally has an unusual, and welcome, cross-party consensus on eliminating greenhouse emissions by 2050 – a target enshrined in law, and supported by a strong mechanism for accountability in the Climate Change Committee.[27]

- **Closing regional gaps:** There is now near universal awareness that the scale of Britain's regional gaps requires attention. In 2022, the government published a White Paper on 'Levelling Up,'[28] and later that same year the Labour Party also recognised that changes of governance would be needed to address geographical inequalities.[29] However, the ambitions of both can fall short on clarity or realism.[30]

- **Home nations:** The UK's unique structure of four sovereign nations, each with their own culture, history and governance provides an opportunity for experimentation and cross-pollination on policy, economic leadership and indeed strategy itself. The Scottish Government recently published its 10-year economic strategy,[31] fusing a focus on the net zero transition, and ambitions for a 'wellbeing economy' with substantial reductions in poverty.[32] Meanwhile, the Welsh Parliament has passed legislation that seeks to increase the involvement of employer and worker representatives in the decisions made by public bodies, including the establishment of a Social Partnership Council.[33]

- **Science:** the UK ranks first among the G7 in citation impact and produces 14 per cent of the world's most highly cited publications.[34] The Government has identified this as one source of comparative advantage, talks of cementing the UK's status as a 'science superpower,'[35] and intends to increase public R&D funding by 25 per cent (in real terms) between 2022-23 and 2024-25.[36]

---

27 Prime Minister Rishi Sunak has recently delayed some key net zero deadlines, including the ban on sales of new internal combustion engine cars, but was keen to reiterate his commitment to the headline net zero targets. See Sunak, R., PM speech on Net Zero, September 2023.

28 Department for Levelling Up, Housing and Communities, Levelling up the United Kingdom, February 2022.

29 Labour Party, A New Britain: Renewing Our Democracy and Rebuilding Our Economy, December 2022.

30 E Shearer, Will the levelling up missions help reduce regional inequality?, Institute for Government, March 2022.

31 Scottish Government, Scotland's National Strategy for Economic Transformation, March 2022.

32 Legislation.gov.uk, Child Poverty (Scotland) Act 2017.

33 Government of Wales, Social Partnership and Public Procurement (Wales) Act, September 2023.

34 Department for Business, Energy & Industrial Strategy, International comparison of the UK research base, 2019: Accompanying note, July 2019.

35 J Madingley & P Vallance, The UK as a science and technology superpower, Council for Science and Technology, June 2021.

36 HM Treasury, Autumn Budget and Spending Review 2021, October 2021.

- **Trade after Brexit:** Departure from the EU, and lack of any imminent trade deal with the US, has seen the UK Government seek to affect a 'tilt' towards the Indo-Pacific. Geographical distance is an issue, but there are several countries in the region (prominently India) with which trade costs are currently high and where there should be scope to trade more, particularly in services that the UK specialises in.[37]

While the initiatives under each of these headings are potentially significant, they are not cohesively joined up. More fundamentally, the UK has not thought systematically about its economic strategy, or the lack of one, since the financial crisis. Austerity was the focus of governments for much of the 2010s, and while individual elements of the pre-financial crisis approach have, increasingly, been challenged or entirely altered as the last 15 years have ground on, there has been no overarching rethink. Crisis management – much of it necessary, some of it creative – has instead been the order of the day. Such innovation in policy as we have seen has tended to come in the form of improvisation in the face of those crises, rather than via new strategic thinking. From bank nationalisation amid the great financial storm to furlough at the start of the pandemic, British institutions have shown they can sometimes act with impressive agility, speed and imagination. Sadly, the same seriousness of purpose mustered amid emergencies has not been found when it comes to longer-term questions of charting a viable path towards enduring prosperity.

Ultimately, the UK is not on course to rebuild its economic strategy because we are not serious about doing so

The UK is not on course to renew its economic strategy because we are collectively not serious about doing so. While broad-based rhetorical commitments to raise growth and reduce inequality are increasingly heard, we are not remotely hard-headed enough about the nature, scale, and consistency of the action required to make a material difference. Nor is our politics serious about grappling with the constraints that follow from the nature of our domestic economy or our place as a wealthy, but medium-sized, part of the global economy.

---

37   S Hale, A presage to India: Assessing the UK's new Indo-Pacific trade focus, Resolution Foundation, January 2022.

Some even say that we don't need growth, going as far as to claim that it won't translate into gains for ordinary households, even as it is painfully clear that the lack of productivity growth has driven our post-financial crisis wage stagnation.[38]

The far more common approach, though, is to want growth but not be serious about how to achieve it. Politicians often talk as if they will reorient the UK's economy towards goods, driving a manufacturing jobs revival. But this wishes away the generations-long, inexorable decline in such jobs across the advanced world: the logical corollary of the extraordinary productivity of high-end manufacturing is that it doesn't need so many workers to get the same output.[39] Too often debate about the future of our economy is unmoored from its reality.

The discussion often unmoors from reality in different ways around Brexit. Some stick their heads in the sand, denying the various negative effects on doing business, even as they become manifest. Others who warned against these Brexit costs, are now reluctant to engage with the political and legal facts of our departure, because that means accepting this is unlikely to change over the medium term. Then there's migration: some claim that either ramping it up, or clamping down on it, will solve our ills, despite there being little evidence for either proposition.[40] Meanwhile, many experts and officials spent much of the past decade fretting that robots would "take our jobs," even as the business investment needed for technological advancement flatlined. Indeed, much of our public discourse carries on as if Britain's problem is accelerating flux – at a time when the rate of structural industrial change is at its lowest since at least the 1930s.[41]

We are equally lacking in seriousness when it comes to tackling inequality. The basic fact of large gaps between people and places is (mostly) recognised, but correspondingly substantial responses are rarely proposed. Councils are busy bidding for small sums of central government investment, when making a meaningful dent in the shortfall in the capital stock of our underperforming cities would require far larger stream of finance, sustained for decades.[42] Discussions of 'inclusive prosperity' too often collapse into firms committing to corporate social

---

38 M Whittaker, Dead-end relationship? Exploring the link between productivity and workers' living standards, Resolution Foundation, January 2020. N Oulton, The Productivity-Welfare Linkage: A Decomposition, ESCoE Discussion Paper 2022-07, March 2022.

39 George Osborne promised a "march of the makers" in his 2011 Budget, 23 Mar 2011.

40 K Henehan, Under new management: How immigration policy change will, and won't, affect the UK's path to becoming a high-wage, high-productivity economy, Resolution Foundation, February 2022.

41 N Cominetti et al., Changing jobs?: Change in the UK labour market and the role of worker mobility, Resolution Foundation, May 2021.

42 P Brandily et al., Bridging the gap: What would it take to narrow the UK's productivity disparities, Resolution Foundation, June 2022.

responsibility or 'ESG' (environmental, social, and governance) agendas, while back in the real world it is perfectly legal for workers to have shifts cancelled with no notice. When it comes to raising taxes, we turn to National Insurance precisely because it isn't called a tax – even though we know it only falls on flatlining wages, as opposed to (often more buoyant) incomes of other types.

A strategy must take a long-term view, but the UK today is characterised by the sort of short-termism that saw us cut home insulation measures by 90 per cent in the early 2010s – even as we recommitted to a net zero future.[43] We don't join the dots, and we don't ensure policies are pushing in the same direction. In short, we don't do strategy.

Getting serious about doing so requires hard graft in government, even in tranquil times. Thorny decisions might be pondered in the safety of think-tanks and universities, but are far tougher to deal with amid the frenzied demands of governing and politics – let alone in a period of seemingly continual crisis. There is nothing automatic about the UK escaping from stagnation, despite that status quo being economically dismal, and – quite possibly – democratically dangerous. Italy's recent experience confirms this.

There is nothing automatic about escaping stagnation, but the price of failing to do so is high

Just as important as the lessons from the conscious shifts to new economic strategies covered above, are the stark warnings from countries that have answered underlying weaknesses with nothing but drift. Italy stands out here. Not so long ago, it was viewed as an affluent, high-skilled European economy – in fact, during the 1970s and early 1980s Italy became far richer than the UK, matching German output levels as Figure 28 shows. Aspects of its model, such as its vibrant networks of export-oriented artisanal firms, were held up as a system of industrial organisation that others should emulate.[44] As late as 2000, Italy's GDP per capita was broadly in line with that of Germany and significantly ahead of the UK.

43 S Cran-McGreehin, Households are paying the price for slow progress on insulating homes, Energy & Climate Intelligence Unit, January 2022.

44 M Piore & C Sabel, The Second Industrial Divide: Possibilities for Prosperity, Basic Books, 1984.

Figure 28: The UK's, or any country's, place in the world is not fixed

GDP per capita, US dollars, 2015 prices: Germany, UK, Italy and Spain

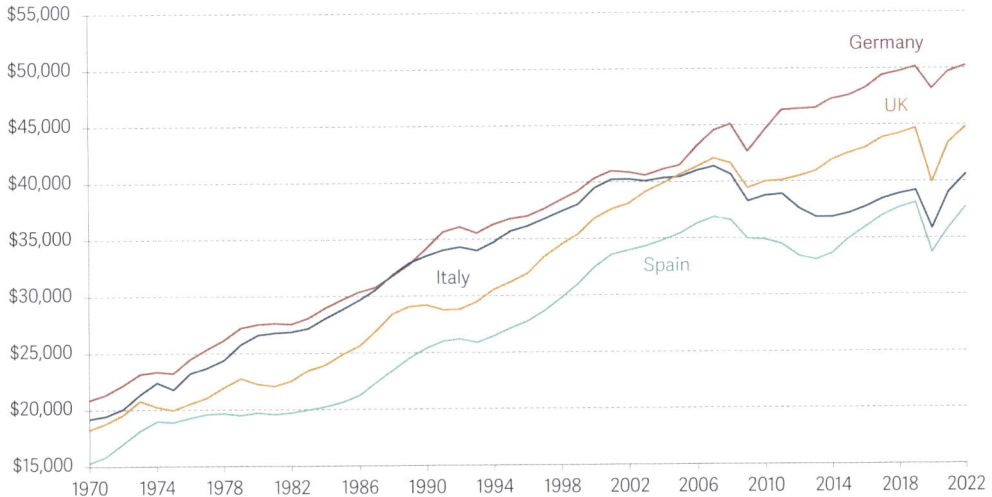

Notes: Purchasing Power Parities used to present data in comparable terms.
Source: Analysis of OECD, Level of GDP per capita and productivity.

Yet remarkably, in light of continuing advancement in science and technology, on the most general measure of productivity the country has spent the last four decades not moving forward, but instead slipping back (Box 11). By 2019, Italy's GDP per capita had fallen 17 per cent below Germany's. Such sustained economic underperformance can transform a country's economic place in the world, and the living standards of its population. Italy's GDP per capita is now on a par with Spain's, having been 22 per cent higher in 2000.

Box 11: Italy's productivity decline[45]

Italy is haunted by nearly half a century of stasis and decline and offers a stark warning to stagnant Britain. Since the 'Italian miracle' of the 1950s and 60s, the trend of Total Factor Productivity (TPP) – that is,

the rate at which the economy as whole converts inputs like capital and labour into outputs – has been abysmal. Sometimes considered a measure of overall 'know-how', TFP generally advances with scientific

---

45 The evidence in this box draws on an externally commissioned essay as part of the Economy 2030 Inquiry: L Codogno & G Galli, Lessons from Italy's economic decline, Navigating Economic Change, The Economy 2030 Inquiry, November 2022.

knowledge and technology, as it has continued to do in most European countries. But in Italy, it stagnated since the later 1970s and has more recently declined outright – falling by a staggering 13.7 percentage points between 1998 and 2019 (Figure 29).

Figure 29: Italy's slide has lasted nearly half a century

Total Factor Productivity: UK and Italy (Index, 1970 = 100)

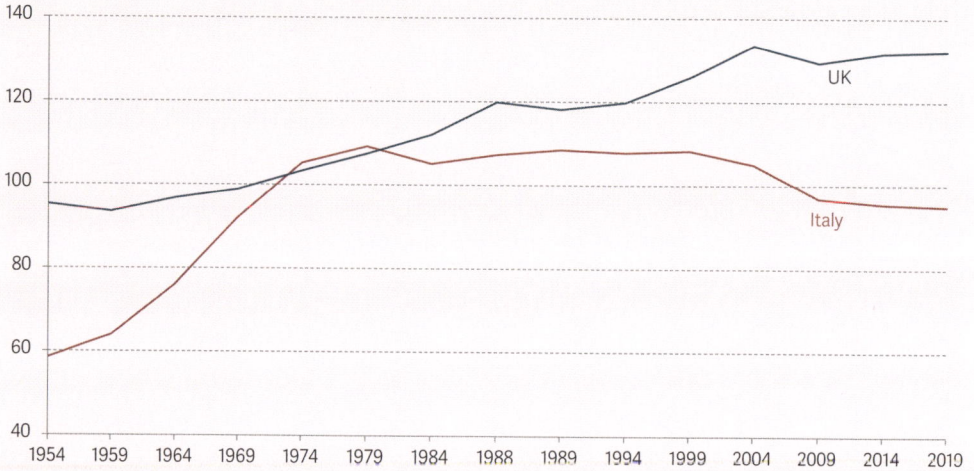

Source: Analysis of University of Groningen, Penn World Tables.

Multiple reinforcing factors appear to be responsible: the large proportion of unproductive small firms; a lack of business dynamism; poor innovation systems; inadequate workplace skills; and repeated concerns over fiscal sustainability.

Then there is political instability. Emergency governments, often dominated by 'technocrats', have become an almost routine response to recurrent financial crises. Backlashes have followed, with populist parties of various stripes thriving, which makes it even more difficult to embark on reform or strategic decisions to turn the country around. Italy is as a salutary example of how hard stagnation can be to shift once it becomes entrenched.

This should serve as a warning for the UK. What matters is whether we take that warning as a spur to action rather than an acceptance of defeat. The rest of this volume is tasked with what that action should be, outlining a strategy for taming the twin giants of low growth and inequality highlighted from the start. It is a strategy ambitious enough to take them both on, one that meets the demanding criteria delineated at the start of this chapter, and one that offers the UK a route to economic success in the world as we find it, not the world as we might like it to be. So, let us now turn our minds towards the integrated policies and institutional reforms that, taken together, can guide Britain through the 2020s and beyond – towards a richer, fairer and greener future.

Chapter Four

Building on Britain's strengths

Chapter summary

- The UK is a broad-based services superpower, the second-largest services exporter in the world with successful musicians and architects as well as bankers. This is not the cause of our slow growth: services-led economies are on average higher-income than goods specialists.

- The nature of the UK economy will not change anytime soon: of the top 10 products the UK was most specialised in back in 1989, seven were in our top 10 in 2019.

- We have narrower, but important, manufacturing strengths that should be built on, including in green industries from offshore wind to carbon capture.

- A post-Brexit trade policy must aim to protect the place of the UK's high value manufacturing in European supply chains, while seizing the opportunities for faster growing global services trade: global trade in the services Britain specialises in has tripled since 2005, growing twice as fast as trade in goods.

- A serious economic strategy must recognise the crucial role played by every part in our economy, factoring in the overwhelming importance of everyday services, from hairdressers to the high street, for 11 million jobs.

- While our current economic specialisation is consistent with future prosperity, our regional divides are not. The UK's most plausible route to raising national income and closing regional gaps is our big cities outside London succeeding: Britain's 'twin second cities', Birmingham and Greater Manchester, might have populations of 2.8 million people each, but their productivity lags behind the UK average. The country as a whole is poorer as a result.

- This would require change on a scale not currently being contemplated: reducing Birmingham and Greater Manchester's productivity gap with London in line with those of Toulouse and Lyon with Paris respectively could require increasing each cities' business capital stock by 15 to 20 per cent and population by over 160,000 graduates each.

- The disruption involved means meaningful progress will not happen without bold and empowered local leadership able to manage the disruption involved. This reinforces the case for genuine fiscal devolution.

The UK has a growth problem. It is a problem with profound implications for the living standards of the British people, as the preceding chapters have made clear. Despite those high stakes, it is not clear it is a problem we are serious about addressing, with nostalgia, short-termism and wishful thinking all holding us back.

This chapter turns to what a hard-headed attempt to address the problem would look like. Its argument is that we must understand the nature of our economy – its strengths as well as weaknesses – if we are to make a success of it. We must stop living off our past and invest in our future across public and private sectors, while contending with the macroeconomic consequences of these changes. Get it right and we can harness our strengths to set the UK on a path to a more sustainable, prosperous future.

The UK is a broad-based services superpower

The foundation of a renewed economic strategy is clarity about what kind of economy it relates to. We must resist the immediate temptation to look for inspiration overseas and instead take as our starting point the reality of the British economy at home: successful strategies are not written on blank slates. Only by fully knowing our economy can we get a better view of the real, and sometimes difficult, choices on offer – costs, benefits and broader consequences – and thereby clarify the right priorities for public policy. Too often that clarity is missing, with the common caricature that our economy is narrowly built on banking as misplaced as claims that there is an easy route to becoming a German-style manufacturing powerhouse.

What marks the UK out is the depth and breadth of its strength in services, which make up four-fifths of the economy, and specifically our tradable services (those that can be sold to other UK regions, or overseas, and are generally higher productivity). Over the past two decades, these services have grown to make up 45 per cent of our economy and to employ around 28 per cent of our workforce (8 million workers).[1] Although politicians rarely boast about it, the UK is the second-largest exporter of services in the world: in 2022, £7 out of every £100 spent buying traded services internationally was spent buying services from the UK.

The UK's comparative advantages in services trade stretches far beyond finance – whose proportion of total exports fell from 12 per cent in 2009 to 9 per cent in 2022 – to information and communications, cultural, and intellectual property services

---

1   Source: Analysis of ONS, Regional gross value added (balanced) by industry: all ITL regions, April 2023, and ONS, Labour Force Statistics, April 2023 & B Broadbent et al., The Brexit vote, productivity growth and macroeconomic adjustments in the United Kingdom, Bank of England, August 2019.

(the creative industries are a rising British strength highlighted in Box 12).[2] When combined with more concentrated, but very important, manufacturing strengths, our overall degree of export specialisation is typical for a country of our size and level of development. The UK may be a service-led economy but it is far from a finance-dominated, one-trick pony.

Box 12: Film and the creative industries

The legacy of Shakespeare lives on – at the very least as a British export. Britain is the fourth most specialized country in personal, cultural and recreational services among advanced economies, and outperforms peers in several creative and artistic endeavours. This is big business: the creative industries accounted for 6 per cent of the UK economy in 2022, and have grown faster than the UK economy overall since 2011.[3] The creative industries are estimated to represent service exports worth £41.4 billion in 2020 (14.2 per cent of UK service exports), alongside £8.9 billion of goods exports.[4] British film, video and television production have doubled in size since 2000. In 2022 alone, more than 200 movies and many more TV shows were made in the UK. These include both domestic productions such as Happy Valley, which also bring in overseas royalties, and inward investment-driven global shows produced here, including blockbusters such as Barbie, and TV shows such as The Lord of the Rings: Rings of Power.[5]

The UK's creative strengths can be traced to cultural openness, high-quality creative education and the role that public service broadcasting (via both the BBC and Channel 4) has in shaping the market. Although London is an important centre for the industry, South West Greater Manchester, Glasgow, Cardiff and the Vale of Glamorgan, Bristol and Oxfordshire have all seen fast growth in the film and TV sectors this millennium.[6]

---

2   Source: Analysis of ONS, UK trade time series, October 2023; ONS, UK trade in services: service type by partner country, July 2023.

3   Department for Digital, Culture, Media and Sport, DCMS Economic Estimates: Monthly GVA (to December 2022), February 2023.

4   Department for Digital, Culture, Media and Sport, Economic Estimates: Trade for DCMS Sectors and the Digital Sector, 2021, August 2023.

5   British Film Institute, Official 2022 statistics reveal a record £6.27 billion film and high-end television production spend in the UK, February 2023.

6   ONS, Regional gross value added (balanced) by industry: all ITL regions, April 2023.

The UK's services specialism can form the bedrock of a growth strategy and is certainly not a barrier to it

The underlying nature of the British economy is neither the cause of our recent relative decline nor a barrier to future growth. Our sectoral mix does not explain our productivity gap with peer economies and on average, services specialist nations are richer than their manufacturing focused peers.[7] Changing patterns of trade and geopolitics also point to advantages from UK specialisms. The UK is less exposed economically than, say, Germany, which struggles with the economic implications of its past dependence on Russian gas, alongside the implications for its domestic industrial base of rising tensions between the US and China that are manufacturing focused.

Global trade is growing particularly quickly in areas that the UK specialises in and, as a medium-sized economy, there is a lot to play for in terms of our share of such trade. Figure 30 dives beneath these aggregates, with a host of information about what Britain sells to the world, and where the potential for growth lies. The vertical axis uses a measure called 'revealed comparative advantage' to identify our strengths (a positive number indicates a particular good or service constitutes a larger share of UK than global exports). The horizontal axis looks at recent growth in global trade in each product, while the size of the circles reveals how important they are for global trade as a whole. Bigger circles in the top-right quadrant are potential growth engines, containing sectors of established British strength in large and fast-growing global markets.

Insurance and pensions, personal, cultural and recreational services are all revealed as areas of established British strength where there is a growing global demand. Perhaps most promising of all is the 'other business services' category. This covers fields including law, accounting, consulting, advertising, technical and scientific services, all areas in which the UK punches above its weight.

---

7   J De Lyon et al., Enduring strengths: Analysing the UK's current and potential economic strengths, and what they mean for its economic strategy, at the start of the decisive decade, Resolution Foundation, April 2022.

Figure 30: A service superpower on the world stage

Revealed UK comparative advantage (vertical axis) and 10-year annualised growth in global export value by product category (horizontal axis) for 2019

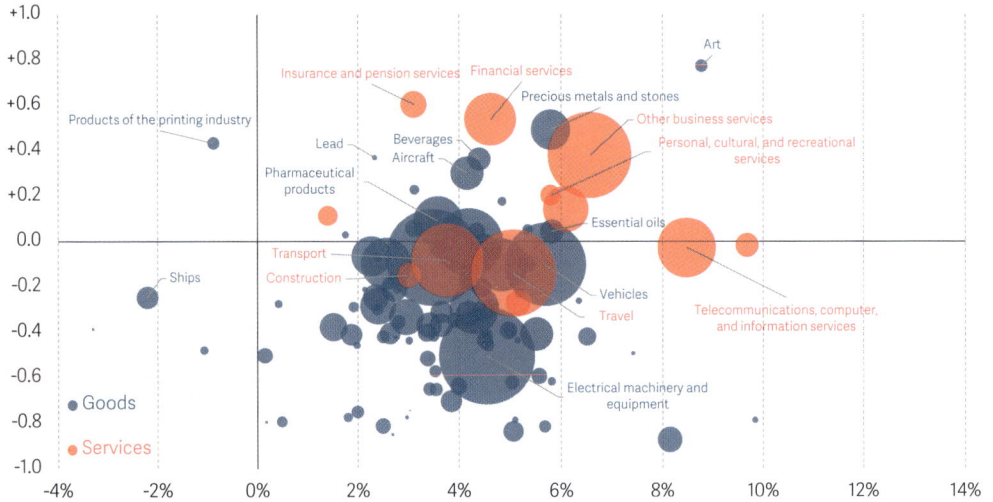

Notes: The horizontal axis measures compound annual growth rates of export volumes between 2009 and 2019. The vertical axis shows Revealed Comparative Advantage in 2019. RCA is a measure of a country's specialisation in exporting a specific product, which is calculated by comparing the share of a country's total exports in a specific good or service to the share of the same good or service in all global exports. The size of the bubbles corresponds to each product's share in world trade in 2019.
Source: Analysis of Harvard Growth Lab, Atlas of Economic Complexity (HS version) and OECD-WTO, Balanced Trade in Services.

There is another crucial British specialism that isn't directly visible on the chart: education. This substantial export (worth £22 billion in 2022)[8] is subsumed within the giant bubble labelled "travel", but in isolation would rank as another comparative advantage. More than 600,000 international students were enrolled at UK universities in 2020/21[9], while the UK, home to less than 1 per cent of the world's population, accounts for 14 per cent of the most highly cited academic publications.[10]

---

8   Source: Analysis of ONS, UK trade in services: service type by partner country, August 2023.

9   Department for International Trade & Department for Education, International Education Strategy: 2022 update, May 2022.

10 Department for Business, Energy and Industrial Strategy, International comparison of the UK research base, July 2019.

The UK must value its important, but narrower, manufacturing strengths without pretending widespread reindustrialisation is on the cards

As well as a significant source of export earnings, our educational strengths have a positive feedback effect on other parts of the economy – not least manufacturing – supporting our strengths in high-tech fields from robotics to medical technology.[11] Recognising that the UK's economy is, and will remain, services-led does not mean giving up on manufacturing: it is not an either/or. The UK's manufacturing strengths are often highly complementary with related services.

As Figure 30 spells out, there are several goods industries that are nationally strong and globally growing – for example, aircraft and beverages. Pharmaceuticals, a far larger sector, draws on the UK's strong life sciences base, but our comparative advantage in this area is relatively modest following declines in the late 2010s.

More generally, manufacturing may constitute only 10 per cent of our economy but it is crucial to many places, underpinning livelihoods and providing the only plausible route to highly productive activity. In Derby and East Cheshire, for example, manufacturing makes up over a quarter of total output, thanks to highly productive transport and chemical industries respectively.[12] In these areas, local prosperity will substantially depend on the ability to develop these strengths.

Future areas of manufacturing strength are likely to be closely aligned to existing capabilities, with our analysis highlighting opportunities clustered in the chemicals and machinery categories, including the production of medical equipment. Britain can also build on specialisms in 'clean' technologies, with the UK among the top 10 exporters of 'green products' overall and having strengths in tidal stream, offshore wind, nuclear energy and carbon capture and storage technologies.[13] But the UK ranks only fifteenth globally in terms of its overall clean-tech specialisation, with South Korea and Japan producing around four times as many clean patents per

---

11 J De Lyon et al., Enduring strengths: Analysing the UK's current and potential economic strengths, and what they mean for its economic strategy, at the start of the decisive decade, Resolution Foundation, April 2022.

12 Source: Analysis of ONS, Regional gross value added (balanced) by industry: all ITL regions, April 2023.

13 B Curran et al., Growing clean: Identifying and investing in sustainable growth opportunities across the UK, Resolution Foundation, May 2022.

100,000 workers as the UK.[14] That is good news for the planet but when it comes to the British economy, it reinforces the fact that our approach to manufacturing must be to support innovation,[15] seize opportunities based on current or latent strengths, and help existing industries (such as steel) navigate decarbonisation.[16] But we cannot place more weight on the green sector than it can plausibly bear as the primary source of growth or good jobs.

Claims that manufacturing can be a main driver of high quality, high-paying jobs growth are overdone. The entirety of manufacturing now accounts for just 8 per cent of employment in the UK (see Figure 31) and not one OECD country has seen a material rise in their manufacturing share of employment this millennium.[17]

Figure 31: Manufacturing isn't likely to drive employment growth in Britain this century

Manufacturing employment as a share of total employment (blue line) and manufacturing output as a share of total output (red line), 2015 prices: selected economies, 1990 - 2019

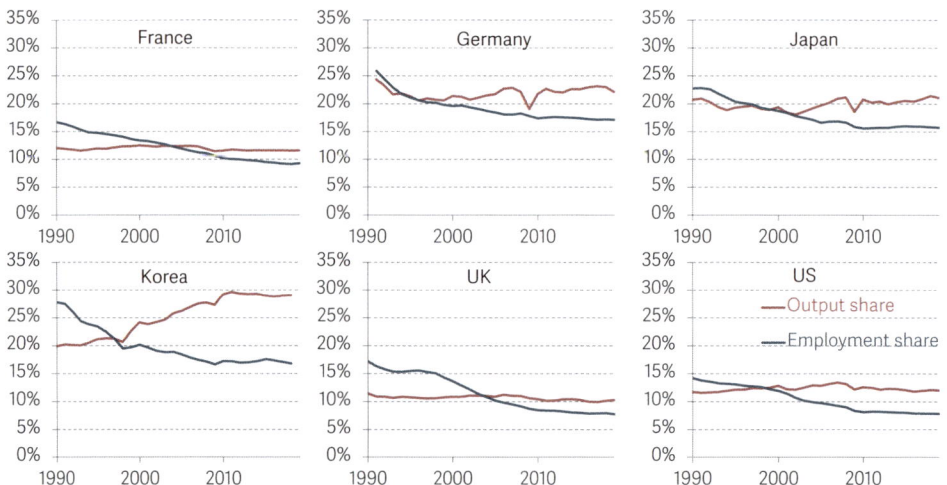

Source: Analysis of OECD, STAN Industrial Analysis 2020 ed.

14 Revealed technological advantage (RTA) is an analogue of RCA, but calculated using data on international patenting activity across categories of technology classes. Analysis of Worldwide Patent Statistical Database (PATSTAT Global) published by the European Patent Office (EPO), 2021. Based on patenting during 2015-2018.

15 Some good news for British firms is that innovation spending is far stronger in the UK than previously thought. Unlike other areas of business investment, data reveals that Britain outperforms the OECD average on R&D investment as a share of GDP (2.9 vs 2.7 per cent), although still lags countries like the US and Germany. Source: OECD Research and Development Statistics, which includes revised UK data submitted by the ONS in February 2023.

16 Successfully decarbonising existing sectors is as important for our future economy as innovative green strengths. For more, see: UKRI, Enabling Net Zero: A Plan for UK Industrial Cluster Decarbonisation, October 2023.

17 Source: Analysis of OECD, STAN Industrial Analysis 2020 ed.

Proposals for a renewed economic strategy focused on attempting a widespread reindustrialisation (as some leading politicians, at least rhetorically, propose) is highly unlikely to be successful.[18] It ignores over 100 years of history, and the reality that national specialisations are persistent: of the top 10 products in which the UK was most specialised in 1989, seven were also in our top 10 in 2019.[19] Advanced economies rarely see transformations in their competitive specialisms, reflecting the roles of accumulated knowledge, capital, institutions, experienced labour, and path dependency in foreign market shares in competing globally in the high-value-added sectors that are central to maintaining our living standards. Even as highly consequential a change as Brexit will not fundamentally alter our industrial structure, as Chapter 2 showed.

Those arguing otherwise should be clear that attempting to transform the UK, with its modestly-sized home market and equally modest capital stock compared to countries such as Germany and South Korea, into a manufacturing-heavy economy would require impossibly huge investments that would lower consumption for decades with far from guaranteed success.

If we are to succeed, it will be as a better version of Britain, not a British version of Germany or the US as we outline in Box 13. The task is to embrace and build on our enduring strengths, while ensuring more people and places enjoy the benefits from such an approach.

Box 13: Lessons from Biden's Inflation Reduction Act

How should Britain respond to President Biden's Inflation Reduction Act and its $400 billion of green subsidies?[20] The Government and many economic liberals' main reaction is to wish this protectionism wasn't happening, while in contrast corporates and campaigners have

---

18 George Osborne promised a "march of the makers" in 2011, HM Treasury, 2011 Budget: Britain open for business, March 2011; J Elgot, Labour vows to reverse decline in UK manufacturing, The Guardian, February 2022.

19 Source: Analysis of Harvard Growth Lab, Atlas of Economic Complexity (SITC version). For more, see: J De Lyon et al., Enduring strengths: Analysing the UK's current and potential economic strengths, and what they mean for its economic strategy, at the start of the decisive decade, Resolution Foundation, April 2022.

20 The Inflation Reduction Act was signed into law by President Biden in August 2022. While the headline figure of support is $369 billion, this is uncapped and therefore support provided could be upwards of $1 trillion, for example, see: J Bistline et al., Economic Implications of the Climate provisions of the Inflation Reduction Act, NBER Working Paper Number 31267, May 2023. The support is made up mainly of investment and production tax credits over a 10-year horizon, and also direct expenditures. More on the IRA can be found in P Brandily et al., Beyond Boosterism: Realigning the policy ecosystem to unleash private investment for sustainable growth, Resolution Foundation, June 2023.

argued that the UK should be doing exactly the same thing.[21] Neither offers a useful guide, but there are important lessons for those considering the UK's economic strategy.

First, recognise that the US approach is here to stay. It reflects both geopolitics, principally the heating up of competition with China, and domestic politics, as Biden tries to decarbonise the US while keeping Trump out of office. The EU has also followed suit.[22]

Second, given this reality the UK will need to be active in supporting green growth industries, but should do so with the full knowledge that Britain is not the US. Our home market is five times smaller than the EU's and seven times smaller than the US's – something that plays a bigger role in deciding what gets produced where in a more protectionist world. Rather than showing blanket support for anything called a green industry, the task is to prioritise those green technologies in which economies of scale are smaller, where supply chain security demands it or where the UK has current or potential comparative advantage.

Third, Britain should think about consumption. A cheaper transition to net zero thanks to production subsidies by US and EU taxpayers should be welcomed, not least where it might also lead to more resilient supply chains. A diversified solar manufacturing capacity, currently dominated by China, has its merits, even if those solar panels aren't produced in the UK.

In sum, Biden's plan is not something for the UK to ignore or simply copy. But it does provide an example for what ambitious, strategic economic thinking looks like in action.

This discussion of which sectors are likely to bear the biggest burden in terms of the UK's future growth has focused on tradable services and goods. This reflects the fact that tradable industries are around 14 per cent more productive than

21 Institute of Directors, The UK needs its own Inflation Reduction Act, March 2023.
22 European Commission, The Green Deal Industrial Plan: Putting Europe's net-zero industry in the lead, accessed 5th November 2023.

non-tradable industries, a gap that is only likely to grow.[23] However, non-tradable services (sometimes referred to as the 'everyday economy') should be centre stage in a renewal of the UK's economic strategy, even if not as the central engine of productivity growth, as Box 14 sets out.

Box 14: Non-tradable services

The UK's strengths across a range of advanced service industries and high-value manufacturing are complemented by a huge 'everyday economy' of restaurants, hairdressers and public services.[24] These are the non-tradable services that shape our high streets and define much of how we interact with the world on a day-to-day basis, and which account for one third of the UK's economic output. Crucially, private non-tradeable services (including retail, bars and restaurants, and care) account for a whopping 10.8 million jobs, 34 per cent of the total workforce and so must be centre stage in any economic strategy with the objective of providing good work, a major theme of Chapter 6.[25]

In addition, there are desirable ways to raise productivity in lower-paying non-tradable sectors, including via personalisation, better management practices and more widespread use of 'employment friendly technologies'.[26] But there are also dangers of focusing productivity-raising efforts here. Not only can such gains be hard to realise, they can be undesirable – for example, by reducing face-to-face contact in social care, or delivering lower hospitality prices for higher earners at the price of intensified work for lower earners. We should pause before prioritising this approach to raising productivity. The proportion of workers who say their job requires that they work "very hard" is already high, having increased from 30 per cent in the early 1990s to 46 per cent pre-pandemic, with

---

23 These two categories inevitably hide a huge amount of productivity variation within sectors and there are some kinds of non-tradables – such as health and education – that help to make the whole economy more productive, as well as being valuable in their own right. The figures on employment and productivity in the tradable and non-tradable sectors are taken from B Broadbent et al., The Brexit vote, productivity growth and macroeconomic adjustments in the United Kingdom, Bank of England, November 2020.

24 R Reeves, The everyday economy, March 2018.

25 B Broadbent et al., The Brexit vote, productivity growth and macroeconomic adjustments in the United Kingdom, Bank of England, August 2019. N Cominetti et al., Low Pay Britain 2023: Improving Low-Paid Work through Higher Minimum Standards, Resolution Foundation, April 2023.

26 D Rodrik, An Industrial Policy for Good Jobs, The Hamilton Project, September 2022.

the biggest increases among the lowest paid.[27] At the economic strategy level the key tasks are to increase the employment share of tradable sectors (raising aggregate productivity given they are on average more productive), while improving the quality of work (and productivity where consistent with that) in non-tradable sectors.

The goal of clarity about the nature of the UK economy is not an academic one, but exists to provide a hard-headed underpinning to consistent choices across the full range of policy domains. The task is to give Britain greater capacity to produce, and ability to sell, high-value services, while defending our manufacturing strengths. To see how this approach to economic strategy translates into policy choices we now turn to what it means for the UK's trade strategy. Not least because it's high time Britain got one.

Britain needs a trade strategy

Britain has not had a trade strategy for a very long time because for half a century, EU membership effectively provided one. Post-Brexit, we are still waiting for one to emerge. The understandable tactical priority has been to minimise the reduced trade-openness of the UK economy by rapidly signing fairly standardised free trade agreements (FTAs) with as many countries as possible, protecting firms' market access and the range, quality and prices of products enjoyed by consumers. The final Brexit deal of 2020, the Trade and Cooperation Agreement (TCA), is itself most importantly an FTA with the EU, albeit one with some 'deep' provisions. 'Rollover' FTA agreements were also struck with the vast majority of countries that had pre-existing EU agreements, alongside new FTAs focusing on an Indo-Pacific tilt (deals with Australia and New Zealand, alongside joining the Comprehensive and Progressive Agreement for Trans-Pacific Partnership).

But this tactical approach has now run out of road. Only two major trade partners, China and the US, have not yet agreed a comprehensive FTA with the UK. While they are important (representing 23 per cent of UK trade) neither is likely to agree a deal anytime soon, given rising geopolitical tensions and domestic political pressures.[28] More fundamentally, traditional 'free trade' agreements' almost exclusively focus on barriers facing goods trade, and do little to liberalise in the ways that matter most for a services superpower: the increase in goods trade

---

27 K Shah & D Tomlinson, Work experiences: Changes in the subjective experience of work, Resolution Foundation, September 2021.

28 Source: Analysis of ONS, UK total trade: all countries, seasonally adjusted, July 2023.

flowing from such deals are estimated to average between 54 and 97 per cent compared to just 5 to 17 per cent for financial services.[29]

So a new trade strategy is needed, one with clear objectives grounded in the UK's wider economic strategy. It needs to recognise the context and constraints within which we operate; reflect, rather than ignore, trade-offs; and be highly integrated with domestic policy. Its twin objectives should be:

- a 'defensive' objective on goods: prioritising EU market access for high-value-added manufacturing firms struggling to retain their place in European supply chains; and,

- an 'expansive' objective on services: seeking to ensure the UK benefits from the growth in global services trade, which is particularly strong in areas of British specialism.

The higher-productivity parts of British manufacturing are most at risk post-Brexit

UK goods trade is where the initial impact of Brexit has been most visible and where the longer-term implications may be most significant. The volume of goods trade was down 10.5 per cent on pre-TCA levels by the middle of 2023, while services trade has not seen a similar hit.[30] The longer-term impact of goods-trade frictions with the EU is to shift the nature of UK manufacturing, as discussed in Chapter 2. Higher-productivity areas, such as chemicals or transport manufacturing, will shrink, as they rely on being part of integrated European supply chains to achieve the economies of scale necessary to be competitive. In contrast, low-productivity (for example food) manufacturing for domestic consumption will grow in the face of reduced competitive pressure. There are hard lessons here from the lack of import competition for British manufacturers in the decades following the Second World War, which contributed to their relatively sluggish productivity growth.[31] A serious strategy for manufacturing to contribute to growth in a country the size of the UK looks outward, instead of turning in.

---

29 Source: Analysis of DBT, Services trade modelling working paper; OECD, STRI, Measuring services liberalisation and commitments in the GATS and RTAs; and ECB Working Paper Series, Global trade in final goods and intermediate inputs: impact of FTAs and reduced 'Border Effects'.

30 ONS, UK trade time series, October 2023. Volume of exports in goods less precious metals and fuels calculated comparing first half of 2019 with the first half of 2023. Volume of services exports had risen by 14 per cent comparing H1 2019 with H1 2023.

31 N Crafts, Adapting well to new circumstances: UK Experience in Changing Times, Resolution Foundation, November 2022.

The defensive priority now is to be clear eyed about what it would take to prevent this structural shift, and the loss of high-quality firms and jobs that it implies. No one should pretend it will be easy. Small improvements to the status quo such as government promises of a seamless digital border, Labour's plan to negotiate light-touch Sanitary and Phytosanitary checks (regarding food safety, animal and plant health), or even the UK joining the EU's Customs Union, will not address the fundamental issue faced by British manufacturers: the existence of the UK-EU border for goods. Ultimately, frictionless flow for goods between the UK and EU is the essential condition for maintaining or growing the UK's role in European supply chains.[32] And trade agreements beyond Europe cannot compensate for its absence because, for physical goods in particular, the pull of trade 'gravity' towards markets we are closer to is hard to defy.[33]

Thus the objective of the UK's trade strategy should be to restore the lost benefits of being part of the EU's customs territory and the single market for goods through a 'UK Protocol', building on the agreement that Northern Ireland has. This is not the same thing as re-entering the single market as a whole, with its implications for services and the free movement of people, still less rejoining the EU.[34] But it would involve negotiating alignment with Brussels in respect of goods, as regards both customs and standards.

The prize is big: a UK Protocol could boost our GDP by as much as 1 to 2 per cent.[35] Achieving it would be far from easy, in terms of domestic politics or diplomacy, due to EU qualms about dividing the 'four freedoms' (goods, services, capital and people). But it isn't unimaginable. UK politicians will in time understand that most of the regulatory freedom foregone is notional, given existing TCA 'level-playing-field' commitments, while the costs of the status quo are anything but notional for some of our most successful manufacturing industries. For its part, the British public is substantially less interested in what the Government agrees on regulatory alignment than it is about free movement of people.[36]

---

32 S Bhalotia et al., Trading Up: The role of the post-Brexit trade approach in the UK's economic strategy, Resolution Foundation, June 2023.

33 For example, see: T Chaney, The Gravity Equation in International Trade: An Explanation, NBER Working Paper, August 2013; J E Anderson, A Theoretical Foundation for the Gravity Equation, American Economic Review, 69(1): 106–16. 1979.

34 A UK Protocol would also remove the complicated demands still involved in separately managing Northern Ireland-Great Britain trade flows after the Windsor Framework.

35 Source: Analysis uses CEP trade model from S Dhingra et al., The costs and benefits of leaving the EU: trade effects, Economic Policy 32(92), October 2017 with regionalised inputs from EUREGIO Regionalised Input Output Database and ONS, Nominal output per hour by industry (2019).

36 British Social Attitudes, Wave 38, Immigration, October 2021.

And while Brussels is not open to a UK Protocol-like arrangement at present, a trade strategy is not just about what is on the table right now. Moreover, a UK Protocol reflects not only what the EU agreed in the Northern Ireland Protocol but what was offered during Theresa May's premiership.[37] There are also obvious gains for the EU in removing the challenges around the Northern Ireland border and from regaining frictionless access to British goods markets. So such an arrangement may be feasible in future if, and only if, a UK Government resolves to keep its eyes on that prize.

On services, trade policy must be more expansive in focus and innovative in approach

While global goods trade has doubled since 2005, services trade has expanded faster. Moreover, global trade in the services in which Britain is strong is up by more again, almost tripling as Figure 32 shows. Looking ahead, the tilt to services in world trade is set to continue: global services exports are expected to grow from 25 per cent to 28 per cent of total exports by 2035.[38]

These patterns of global trade growth mean the UK's specialisations can and should be harnessed as part of an attempt to turn around the country's dire growth performance. And here there is scope for the UK to put its new trade policy freedoms to work beyond Europe. The UK is relatively less dependent on the EU market for services – even before Brexit 63 per cent of services exports went outside the EU, compared to just 52 per cent of goods exports.[39]

There is more scope for liberalisation of service trade too, given the focus of existing FTAs on barriers to goods trade. This also highlights the challenge for UK trade policy, which will need to innovate in its content and method. The UK should develop a new framework for services trade agreements (STAs), focusing on digital agreements, bolstering the ability of suppliers to move across borders, and recognising equivalence, where it exists, between regulatory regimes and professional qualifications.

---

37 A Seeley et al., The UK's EU Withdrawal Agreement, House of Commons Library, July 2019.

38 UK Government, Global Trade Outlook, February 2023.

39 2019 figures. Source: Analysis of ONS, International Trade Time Series, August 2023.

Figure 32: Britain's stronger services are outpacing global trade trends

Index of global exports of goods, services, and services with UK Revealed Comparative Advantage (2005 = 100)

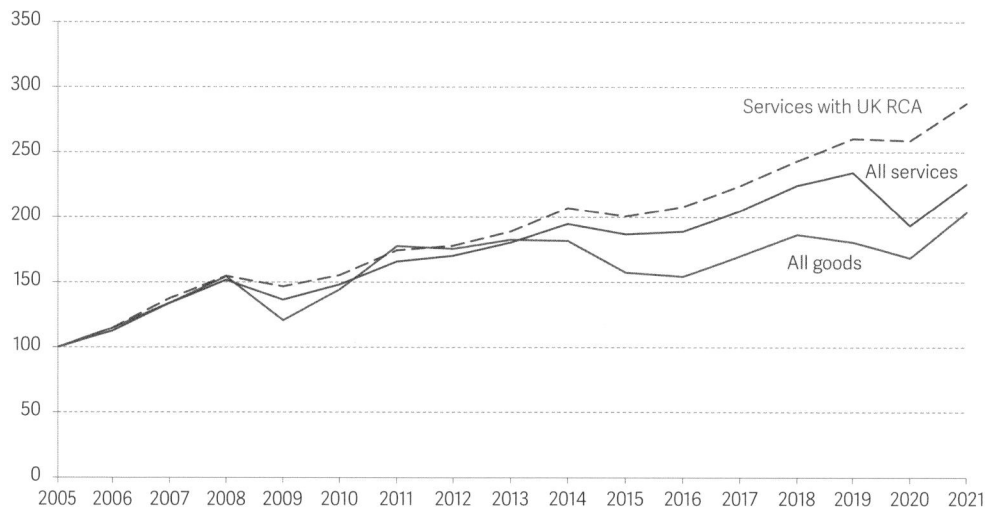

Notes: Services with UK RCA includes the sectors where the UK has a revealed comparative advantage in 2019 which includes Government goods and services, Charges for the use of intellectual property, personal, cultural, and recreational services, Other business services, financial services, insurance and pension services.
Source: Analysis of Harvard Growth Lab, Atlas of Economic Complexity (HS version) and OECD-WTO, Balanced Trade in Services.

Not only will the subject matter differ from traditional FTAs, but the process for agreeing them will change too, with a greater role for regulators rather than traditional tariff-focused trade negotiators. Models for this approach include the UK-Australia trade deal, which launched a 24-month inter-regulator dialogue on overcoming market barriers, and the Bank of England's current attempt to negotiate an ambitious UK-Swiss financial services agreement. Identifying partners suitable for STAs would redirect UK trade policy towards higher-income countries the UK already has FTAs with, including Singapore, Australia, Canada, Switzerland and Japan (alongside prioritising discussions with the EU on the recognition of UK professional qualifications and a renewed data adequacy arrangement). The UK is also an attractive services liberalisation partner for these countries, representing a disproportionately significant market.[40]

40 The UK accounts for between 4 and 7 per cent of their services exports, more than double what its share of global GDP would lead you to expect.

Reaping the benefits of service trade liberalisation in the form of a bigger and more productive tradable service sector requires more than new trade agreements – the UK must also have greater capacity for such activity. That capacity is constrained by the large, and increasing, concentration of service trade in London. Such trade in the capital grew 45 per cent between 2016 and 2021, in contrast to no growth across the rest of the UK.[41] We next turn to a plausible route to addressing this capacity constraint.

The UK's service specialism poses economic geography challenges, but offers solutions too

Recognising the nature of our economy is not the same thing as welcoming all aspects of it or ignoring the challenges it brings. An economic strategy that fails to understand it is no strategy at all. One key challenge to highlight is that tradable services tend to be geographically focused. While goods exports are spread across areas with very different wage levels, services exports are more concentrated in highly productive areas.[42] In the UK that currently means in London and the South East. Partly as a result, the UK's economic spatial disparities are large: in 2019, London produced £76,000 of value added per job, more than twice that in Powys and Torbay. The disparities are also persistent. Over the last 20 years, few areas of the UK have seen a large change in their relative position when it comes to GVA per worker. This matters for living standards, with 80 per cent of today's variation in incomes across local authorities predicted by the pattern in 1997.[43]

So while the starting point for a serious economic strategy should be to accept path dependency in our industrial structure, it must confront it on economic geography. Our current economic specialisation is consistent with future prosperity, but our regional gaps are not – as politicians of both main parties have noted, the UK is like a jumbo jet running mostly on one engine (London and the South East). Luckily the services-led nature of our economy suggests a plausible route to both greater capacity for services and overcoming our regional productivity divides. High-value services industries thrive when similar firms co-locate in large places with highly educated populations: cities.

---

41 ONS, Subnational trade time series, June 2023.

42 Source: Analysis of ONS, International trade in services by subnational areas of the UK and ONS, UK regional trade in goods statistics disaggregated by smaller geographical areas; J De Lyon et al., Trading Places: Brexit and the path to longer-term improvements in living standards, The Resolution Foundation, October 2021.

43 L Judge & C McCurdy, Income outcomes: Assessing income gaps between places across the UK, Resolution Foundation, June 2022.

Our large regional productivity gaps fundamentally reflect our failure to ensure that enough of our big cities, all deeply scarred by deindustrialisation, successfully transitioned to contribute to our national success in new ways (something we have seen happen in many cities once written off as Rust Belts around the world, as Box 15 sets out). London alone accounts for 63 per cent of the UK's surplus in services trade and, aside from Edinburgh, the UK does not have any highly productive mid-sized metro areas (see Figure 33).[44]

Figure 33: The UK's large cities are further behind the capital than in France

Gross value added (GVA) per worker by country and area: 2018

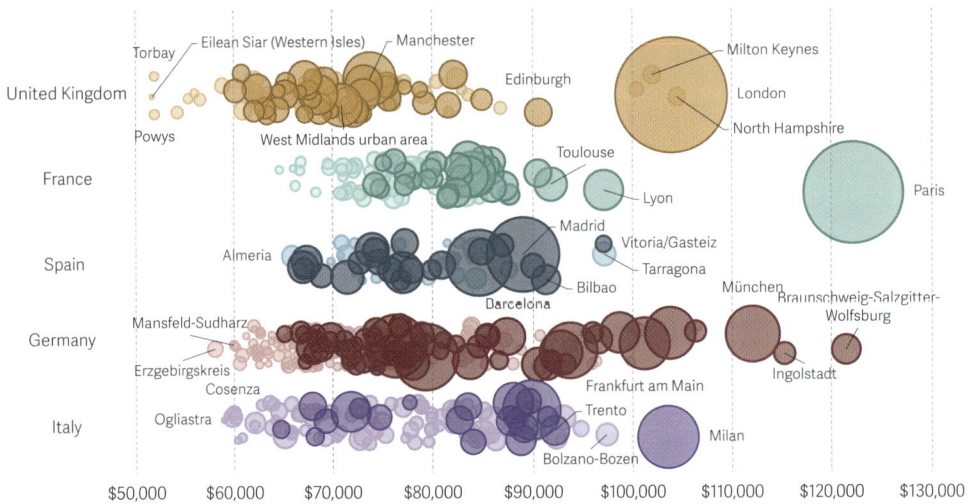

Notes: PPP adjusted. Spatial units are a combination of OECD metro regions and NUTS3 for non-metro regions. Metro areas are shown in darker bubbles in the figure. Bubbles are proportional to the number of workers in each region. Gross value added (GVA) is the value of a unit's outputs less the value of inputs used in the production process to produce the outputs.
Source: Analysis of OECD, Regional Economy Database.

The popular focus on the lower productivity gaps between places in Germany offers little guide for the UK, with its more even spread of output reflecting a manufacturing-dominated economy. But France, also a services-led economy, has more productive second cities relative to the UK: Lyon is 21 per cent less productive than Paris, whereas Manchester is 31 per cent less productive than

44 Source: Analysis of ONS, International trade in services by subnational areas of the UK: 2018, September 2020.

London.[45] France, therefore, offers a plausible prospect should the UK pursue a growth strategy that builds from our strengths, and recognises the constraints (such as the concentration of some productive services in large cities), and the opportunities (it need not concentrate just in the capital) that follow.

Box 15: Post-industrial revolution – three cities that turned things around[46]

Deindustrialisation has hit all the UK's large cities, but also many cities worldwide. The UK could learn a lot from places that suffered equally severe shake-outs, but eventually alighted on a more successful response.

Lille is in the heart of France's largest former coal-mining and textiles region. While its struggles are far from over, the city has risen to be France's third-largest service centre, with unemployment now comparable to the national average and a population that is growing again.[47] Over 30 years, there has been a strategic focus on building a competitive economy but also an attractive place to live, with deep investment to turn brownfield sites into green spaces and housing. It has fully exploited its strategic position on the Eurostar, between Brussels, London and Paris.

Pittsburgh in the US state of Pennsylvania saw its heavy industry collapse in the 1970s. But from the 1980s, the 'Pittsburgh model' – combining strong mayoral leadership, a business voice and community purpose – begun to turn things round. Federal, state and mayoral investment improved inner-city areas for families and businesses: for example, by building transport infrastructure and promoting a green environment. Industrial-university partnerships have also helped the city retain graduates and diversify employment opportunities. Pittsburgh now ranks second out of major US urban areas for increases in its share of knowledge, professional and creative

---

45 P Brandily et al., A tale of two cities (part 2): A plausible strategy for productivity growth in Greater Manchester and beyond, Resolution Foundation, September 2023. We choose Lyon and Paris as a sensible benchmark here for a number of reasons. First, France is a comparable economy to the UK when it comes to overall size as well as specialism in high-value-added service activities. Second, Lyon is not dissimilar in size nor rank to Greater Manchester.

46 The evidence in Box 15 draws on an externally commissioned essay as part of the Economy 2030 Inquiry: S Frick et al., Lessons from successful 'turnaround' cities for the UK, Navigating Economic Change, The Economy 2030 Inquiry, May 2023.

47 S Frick, Turnaround Cities: French Case Study Insights from Lille, Discussion Paper, Blavatnik School of Government, University of Oxford, February 2023.

workers, and tenth in the crucial measure of increasing its share of college graduates.[48]

Bilbao, in the Basque country of Spain, was built on steel and coal, a shaky foundation for 21st-century prosperity. However, over the past four decades the Basque government, which enjoys significant autonomy,[49] has combined support for existing industries with the promotion of knowledge-intensive sectors that complement them. This 'cluster' strategy has involved promoting R&D activities within existing firms, while establishing non-profit technology centres to supplement that R&D effort and facilitate knowledge transfers. Cultural life and the lived environment have also been a great focus, with the city's Guggenheim museum being the most prominent result.

Britain's twin second cities are too big to fail

The productivity of many of our largest cities lags behind the UK average, bucking the global trend for bigger urban areas to be more productive.[50] The country as a whole is poorer as a result. At the heart of this problem are the UK's 'twin second cities': Greater Manchester and Birmingham. With populations of around 2.8 million each, both easily rank among the biggest 30 cities in Europe. Yet Birmingham is 14 per cent less productive than the UK overall, and has an employment rate 5 per cent below the national average, while even Greater Manchester, widely regarded as an economic success story, has productivity 12 per cent below the UK average.[51]

Their size and central role in their regional economies means they must be centre stage not just in their own economic strategies, but in Britain's. They should not be the limit of our ambition, given the potential of other cities such as Leeds and Bristol – ideally, every region would have a powerful city engine. But we need to start somewhere because no strategy can realistically hope to apply the same energy and resource to all of our big cities at once. Instead it must have priorities: Greater Manchester and Birmingham should be ours.

48 R Florida et al., Heartland of talent: How heartland metropolitans are changing the map of talent in the US, Heartland Forward, February 2022.

49 For example, including revenue-raising powers.

50 Analysis of OECD, Regional Economy Database.

51 Source: Analysis and facts that follow are from the following pair of papers unless otherwise stated: P Brandily et al., A tale of two cities (part 1): A plausible strategy for productivity growth in Birmingham and beyond, Resolution Foundation, September 2023; P Brandily et al., A tale of two cities (part 2): A plausible strategy for productivity growth in Greater Manchester and beyond, Resolution Foundation, September 2023.

Their sheer scale justifies this prioritisation. Simplistically, it means if they are not contributing to nationwide growth, they are almost certainly holding it back. They are too big to fail. But more importantly that scale means they should also be uniquely well placed to play host to tradeable service firms, which tend to cluster in big city centres with large pools of skilled labour to draw upon.

This is not a strategy for the few: overall, 69 per cent of Britons live in cities or their hinterlands, compared to 56 per cent in France and 40 per cent in Italy. Claims that boosting cities will come at the cost of struggling counties or towns nearby are also wrong-headed.[52] Buckinghamshire has the same average income as London despite productivity being £20,000 per job lower, because it is near the capital. On productivity too, cities and their wider regions have a shared destiny: proximity to the giant, humming capital partly explains why productivity is so high in what might otherwise be sleepy North Hampshire. Over and above these regional effects, our cities should be contributing to, rather than drags on, the public finances, supporting the funding of public services for the UK as a whole.

Closing Greater Manchester and Birmingham's productivity gaps to London to those that Lyon and Toulouse have with Paris respectively would increase total GVA by almost £20 billion a year. This 1 per cent boost to national productivity would narrow the UK's GVA per worker gap to Germany by 20 per cent, and to Australia by 32 per cent. When it comes to making a success of the UK's largest cities, we really are all in this together, with this focus providing a plausible route to boosting national growth, closing regional productivity gaps and driving up local living standards too.

No one should underestimate the scale of change involved

Despite the consensus emerging about addressing Britain's regional gaps, sometimes described as 'levelling up', there have been few serious policy shifts. Welcome commitments, such as to increase public R&D spending outside the Greater South East by 40 per cent between 2021-22 and 2030, are combined with deeply unserious approaches.[53] Allocating small pots of cash to improve local areas via competitive bidding regimes is a ludicrous way to finance local

---

52 P Swinney, Does 'trickle out' work? How cities help their surrounding towns, Centre for Cities, September 2023.

53 DLUHC, Levelling Up the UK, 2022.

government. A striking 18 per cent of all revenue grants and 30 per cent of all capital grants for local authorities are wound up every year, making long-term planning difficult.[54]

The creation of nine Metro Mayoralties and their rising profile locally and nationally are real progress, with recently announced 'Trailblazer' devolution deals for Greater Manchester and the West Midlands increasing those city regions' flexibility over spending priorities.[55] But the centrepiece of the Government's promise to support economic activity in the twin second cities, the project to build a high-speed train line (HS2) connecting the city centres of England's three largest cities, has collapsed and may now run from Birmingham to the outskirts of London. This is not what a serious economic strategy looks like.[56]

Honesty about the scale of change required is badly needed. Modelling suggests reducing Birmingham and Greater Manchester's productivity gap with London into line with those of Toulouse and Lyon with Paris respectively could require increasing each cities' business capital stock by 15 to 20 per cent and population by over 160,000 high-skilled workers each (to facilitate an increase in the cities' graduate shares, which is particularly weak in Birmingham).[57]

Greater higher education participation and upskilling of residents would both be welcome, but a higher-skilled workforce will require a bigger population, by means of inflows of graduates from elsewhere and a reduced 'brain drain' to the South East of students from both cities' highly rated universities.[58] As one Mancunian spelt out:

> "There are a lot of graduates that would like to stay here but they can't really. They need to move down to London, at least to get that initial experience. So, if we had more of that here, that would be amazing."

> Participant, Greater Manchester deliberative workshop

54 A Breach & S Bridgett, Centralisation Nation: How a broken system of local government harms the British economy, Resolution Foundation & Centre for Cities, September 2022.

55 DLUHC, Greater Manchester Combined Authority Trailblazer deeper devolution deal, March 2023.

56 The Rt Hon Rishi Sunak MP, What the plan to launch Network North means for you, October 2023.

57 Specifically, these reports model an increase of 165,000 graduates in Birmingham and 180,0000 graduates in Greater Manchester.

58 H Overman & X Xiaowei, 'Spatial disparities across labour markets' in the Deaton Review of Inequality, February 2022.

Our second cities can prosper if we recognise the different roles that different parts of the cities play

Clarity is needed about the nature, not just the scale, of change. Local economic strategies tend to be sector focused, but the task in this case is one of place. In the 21st century, successful large cities that make effective use of investment and human capital do not all look the same but have specific features, with different parts of cities playing distinct roles (in the same way that different places fulfil different roles in the national economy). They provide locations – usually including but not limited to the city centre – where large volumes of high-value activity from a wide range of sectors can cluster, underpinned by access to a deep pool of skilled labour in the wider city region, which provides attractive places to live and fast connections to those productive areas.

Figure 34: Graduate premiums have been falling in West Midlands Combined Authority (WMCA) and Greater Manchester

Graduate hourly pay premium compared to workers with A-levels, for selected areas

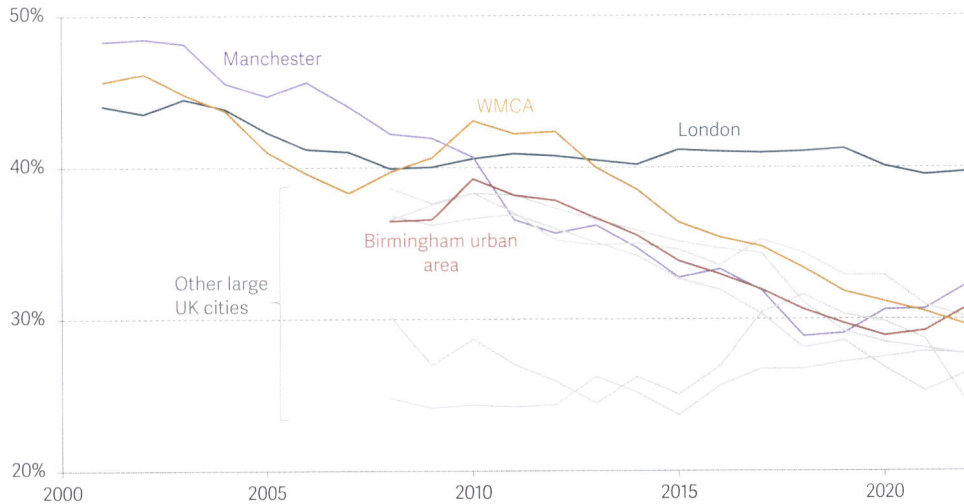

Notes: Chart shows the five-year moving average of within-period estimates of the coefficients on having a degree versus having A-level qualifications in a standard Mincerian wage equation. Regressions also include age and gender. Approach is based on that used in: A Stansbury, D Turner & E Balls, Tackling the UK's regional economic inequality: Binding constraints and avenues for policy intervention, 2023. Other cities shown in grey are Liverpool, Bristol, Leeds, Cardiff, Glasgow, Sheffield and Newcastle. Source: Analysis of ONS, Labour Force Survey and Annual Population Survey.

Change means tough decisions about how land is best used

But Birmingham and Greater Manchester do not function in this way today. Although graduates in these cities still earn a wage premium compared to those without degrees, this has been falling in recent decades (see Figure 34). Over the past two decades, Manchester and Birmingham's graduate wage premium has fallen from above that of London to around three-quarters of its figure despite no observable difference in the quality of graduates.[59]

Combined with limp investment returns in both cities, this suggests the cities don't merely have too few graduates but that they are not currently able to grow or attract enough highly productive firms to make good use of those they already have. Ensuring these cities can increase our national capacity for more high-productivity service activity requires concerted action to change this.

The good news is that both city centres are already performing their key role, hosting the most productive activity in the city – a worker in central Birmingham produces 27 per cent more than one based elsewhere in the city. Similarly, close to a half of workers in central Greater Manchester work in highly productive knowledge-intensive services compared to one-fifth across the city. But the city centres are simply too small to make the cities as a whole prosperous, serving as the base for just one-in-eight workers in Manchester and one-in-nine workers in Birmingham. Contrast that with almost three-in-ten workers in Glasgow. The important shift to hybrid, rather than fully remote, working has changed how often people are in the office but not where those offices are. We estimate that central Birmingham needs an additional 165 hectares of office space, and it certainly has scope to build up – its low-rise city centre is just 3.3 storeys high on average, compared to 5.4 in central Manchester, which will need to build out (including on the 5 per cent of land near the centre being used for storage and warehousing) and prioritise office space over housing and retail activity in the city centre.

An effective city centre requires more than office space: firms will only locate there if there is a deep pool of skilled labour within reasonable commuting distance. The populations of both cities are ardent car-users: nearly seven-in-ten commutes are made by private vehicle and one Mancunian spelt out why:

---

59 While there are no observable differences, some unobservable characteristics can explain some of these changes. For more, see: H Overman & X Xu, Spatial disparities across labour markets, IFS Deaton Review of Inequalities, February 2022.

"Driving is 10x more convenient – public transport is just not good enough. Dirty, crowded, not reliable, expensive."

Participant, Greater Manchester deliberative workshop

Some US cities manage to be productive while relying on cars for access to the city centre. But they look nothing like Birmingham or Greater Manchester – aping them would require bulldozing large swathes of the city for more roads and doubling the space given to car parks. In addition, congestion and air pollution are already worse in Birmingham and Manchester than in US cities like Portland and Denver.[60] If our second cities are to be effectively bigger with higher-performing centres there is no alternative to developing their public transport networks. Currently half of Birmingham's highly skilled workers cannot reach the central employment district within 45 minutes, and even after the significant investments in recent years, that figure is 40 per cent in Greater Manchester. Improvements to bus services and doubling expansion plans for the two cities' tram networks would be a good place to start, at a cost of around £10 billion,[61] enabling 145,000 more graduates to access the city centres within 45 minutes in one fell swoop.[62]

Cities that grow their economies and populations but not their housing stocks get into real trouble. Existing owners of property end up reaping many of the rewards of improved productivity, while existing residents see their income gains wiped out by fast rising rents.[63] To be consistent with the population growth noted above, 116,000 more homes would be needed in Birmingham and 126,000 more across Greater Manchester. This requires a step change in house-building – doubling the building rate across Birmingham, for example – but is essential if the benefits of these cities' prosperity are to be widely shared. If only half of the additional homes needed are built, around 30 per cent of the total gains to the typical household from these cities becoming higher-productivity could be wiped out. Progress will not be achieved without significant government investment – a £4 billion grant would be required to maintain both cities' share of social housing at current levels.

---

60 Source: Analysis of IQAir, City ranking based on annual average PM2.5 concentration.

61 A total of £2.2 billion has already been allocated to Greater Manchester and Birmingham from the City Region Sustainable Transport Settlement and if the second tranche is allocated in much the same way, these two cities could expect a further £3.4 billion between them. However, that leaves an estimated shortfall of £2.8 billion to £3.3 billion.

62 145,000 is the total amount of graduates who would be able to access their respective city centres in Greater Manchester (52,000 graduates) and Birmingham Urban Area (93,000 graduates).

63 C Hilber, The Economic Implications of House Price Capitalization: A Synthesis, Real Estate Economics, Vol 45, Issue 2, December 2015.

A new era of city growth will require national investment and empowered local leadership

Can all this be done? Birmingham City Council's brush with effective 'bankruptcy' in 2023 painfully underlines the scale of the challenge.[64] But drawing fatalistic conclusions shows a lack of imagination or memory. Large cities in advanced economies drive, rather than hold back, national growth. And as recently as the 1960s, national government was so worried about Birmingham's economy being too strong that they legislated to stifle development there for the sake of balance.[65] In contrast some look at Greater Manchester, the regeneration of Salford Quays, towers rising in the city centre, a Metrolink stretching from the airport to Rochdale, and think 'job done'. But complaints that the city centre has benefitted from too much development risk complacency when there is much further still to go – at the current rate of progress it will take 90 years to meet the goal of closing Greater Manchester's productivity gap with London to that between Paris and Lyon.

So the task is to navigate fatalism and complacency, with city growth strategies for the long term. Re-kitting these cities properly is not just in residents' interests but in Britain's. Indeed it is what a hard-headed industrial strategy in a service-dominated economy looks like.[66] But we need to be hard-headed too about what this will, and will not, achieve. Successfully closing productivity gaps between cities does not, and should not, mean every city becoming like London: they will specialise in different sectors and remain very different in size, culture and housing costs. However, ensuring more places are part of the cutting edge of the UK economy holds out the possibility of raising national growth and shrinking regional productivity gaps, increasing incomes in poorer regions while reducing national inequality and local poverty. Yet within-region inequality in productivity and incomes would likely widen – a richer Greater Manchester with the extra homes its success requires has less poverty, but more higher earners too.

---

64 S Madden, 'Bankrupt' Birmingham City Council approves finance plan, BBC, September 2023.

65 See: Statement by Minister of the State at the Board of Trade, George Darling, as he extends controls and restricts, among other things, the development of offices in Birmingham: Hansard, 3 November 1965 vol 718 cc1163-91.

66 R Juhász, N Lane & D Rodrik, The New Economics of Industrial Policy, Annual Review of Economics, August 2023.

That higher inequality at the local level and the significant disruption needed to shift to a higher-productivity equilibrium are things that residents are understandably ambivalent about:[67]

> *"Too much too quick will just change the areas completely and gentrify everywhere and push a lot of people out."*
>
> Participant, Birmingham deliberative workshop

This is why meaningful progress will not happen without empowered local leadership, able to embrace the disruption involved because they have the ability to shape it, and significant investment from central government, requiring national politicians to concentrate their efforts.

The former does not exist today – responsibility for economic leadership has been increasingly devolved to our major cities yet not the means to make it a reality. That would require fiscal devolution. If city leaders had control over local taxes they would have the means to sustain a growth strategy without constant recourse to central government and the incentive to do so, with growth resulting in higher tax revenues rather than reductions in grants from central government as we see today.[68]

The starting point for fiscal devolution, initially to the West Midlands, Greater Manchester and London but then to other areas, would be control over the level and nature of council tax, as the largest component of local government finances.[69] But it cannot finish there, given that council tax revenues do not rise or fall materially with the ebb and flow of local economic growth. Mayors should also have control over the design of business rates, and should be assigned 100 per cent of their revenues, plus a substantial share of local income tax receipts so that taxpayers and service users in the city meaningfully benefit from their growing cities. Just as we saw with progressive waves of fiscal devolution to Scotland and Wales, this can be achieved on a revenue-neutral basis, meaning neither HM Treasury nor other local authorities need pay the price. Full devolution of council tax, business rates and – for Greater Manchester and Birmingham – a fifth of all

---

67 T Burchardt, T Goatley & L Judge, Talking trade-offs: Deliberations on a higher-productivity future in the Birmingham and Greater Manchester urban areas, Resolution Foundation, November 2023.

68 A Breach, S Bridgett & O Vera, In Place of Centralisation: A Devolution Deal for London, Greater Manchester, and the West Midlands, Resolution Foundation, November 2023.

69 In 2019/20 (the last year before emergency Covid-19 funding), local authorities in England received 22 per cent of their funding from government grants, 52 per cent from council tax, and 27 per cent from retained business rates. For more, see: G Atkins & S Hoddinott, Local government funding in England: How local government is funded in England and how it has changed since 2010, March 2020.

local income tax revenues would be matched with cuts of around 60 per cent in central government grants in our twin second cities.[70] In time, as fiscal devolution is extended to other areas and local growth trajectories diverge, there will be tension in combining those stronger incentives with the redistribution required to ensure poorer areas can deliver crucial services. But this is a tension many other less centralised countries have navigated successfully and so should the UK.

Productivity in 21st Century Britain will continue to be unevenly distributed across the country, but the status of the places in which we live and the standard of their public realm should not be. Our qualitative research showed consistent concerns from people about the state of town centres, the quality and availability of public services and the capacity of local government to deliver the basics. The share of people thinking their local area has deteriorated in the preceding two years rose from 18 per cent in 2010-11 to 26 per cent in 2019-20.[71] Tackling this sense of decline is essential to delivering on a social contract that promises you will gain from the national economy wherever you live. Too often that promise has not been met: council revenues per person fell by 30 per cent between 2009 and 2019 in the most-deprived places, compared to 15 per cent in the least-deprived places.[72]

Fiscal devolution will give local leaders the scope to raise their own resources to invest in their cities' futures, but as we have shown central government investment will be needed if the transport networks needed to underpin growth and housebuilding needed to ensure that growth is inclusive are to happen. And a core objective of rewiring our great cities is to enable them and their surrounding regions to attract far larger quantities of private investment. This is just one part of a wider shift that must sit at the centre of a renewed economic strategy: moving Britain from being a country living off its past to one investing in its future. It is to this higher-investment future that the next chapter turns.

70 In London a much smaller share of income tax would need to be shared with City Hall to ensure revenue neutrality. A Breach, S Bridgett & O Vera, In Place of Centralisation: A Devolution Deal for London, Greater Manchester, and the West Midlands, Resolution Foundation, November 2023.

71 Department for Digital, Culture, Media & Sport, Community Life Survey 2020/21, July 2021.

72 T Harris, L Hodge & D Phillips, English local government funding: Trends and challenges in 2019 and beyond, Institute for Fiscal Studies, November 2019.

Chapter Five

Investing in Britain's future

Chapter summary

- Investing too little for one year is manageable, but doing so year after year is a recipe for decline. This is what the UK has been doing: in the 40 years to 2019, total investment in the UK averaged 19 per cent of GDP, the lowest in the G7.

- Public sector investment is too low: the average OECD country invests nearly 50 per cent more than the UK. It is also too volatile, cut whenever belt tightening calls. The UK's fiscal rules should be reformed to banish feast and (more common) famines, with sustained public investment of 3 per cent of GDP.

- British business has caught the same low investment disease: if they had matched the average investment levels of France, Germany and the US since 2008 our GDP would be nearly 4 per cent higher today, boosting wages by £1,250 a year.

- Where Britain stands out is the unusual lack of pressure on managers from above – via engaged owners – or below ¬– from empowered workers – to invest for long term growth¬. A smaller number of larger, and more active, pension funds is what UK PLC needs, along with worker representatives on large firms' boards.

- Firms also need the ability to get things built: in stark contrast to every other G7 economy, the UK has seen no increase in the amount of built-up land per capita since 1990.

- Higher investment will need to be paid for, largely through higher savings given the UK already borrows a lot from abroad and saves to little: over two fifths of families had savings of less than one month's income when the pandemic hit.

- A tighter fiscal policy in good times is required, along with more room for the Bank of England to cut interest rates in bad, if public debt is to stop rising: the past 15 years have seen it increase from 36 to around 100 per cent of GDP – an unprecedented peace-time rise.

Many of the challenges that the UK is wrestling with have parallels elsewhere: low productivity growth in Italy or high inequality in the US. But when it comes to low investment, the UK is in a league of its own. The consequences are that British workers have less kit to work with, worse infrastructure to rely on and fewer ideas to implement, and fewer British firms are able to compete. This translates into lower productivity and holds back wage growth. It underpins stagnation.

The UK is a low-investment nation

Investing too little for one year is manageable, but doing so year after year is a recipe for relative decline. This is precisely what the UK has been doing and where it finds itself. In the 40 years to 2022, total fixed investment in the UK averaged just 19 per cent of GDP as shown in Figure 35, the lowest in the G7.[1] Output per hour worked has grown by less than half a per cent per year since 2005, half the rate of the OECD as a whole, and weak capital growth is an important contributing factor.

Figure 35: Taking the low road: Britain's investment lags the global pack

Gross fixed capital formation as a proportion of GDP: selected Advanced Economies

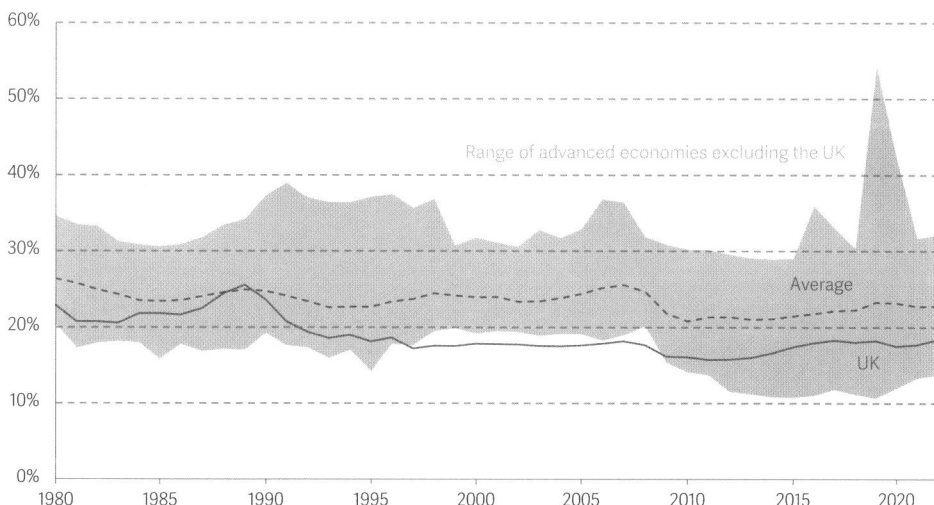

Notes: Where data is available, the swathe includes Australia, Austria, Belgium, Canada, Czech Republic, Denmark, Estonia, Finland, France, Germany, Greece, Iceland, Ireland, Israel, Italy, Japan, Korea, Latvia, Lithuania, Luxembourg, Netherlands, New Zealand, Norway, Portugal, Slovak Republic, Slovenia, Spain, Sweden, Switzerland and US. Data is unavailable before 1990 for Czech Republic and Slovenia, before 1992 for Slovak Republic, before 1993 for Estonia, before 1995 for Latvia and Lithuania, and in 2022 for US.
Source: Analysis of OECD, Aggregate National Accounts.

1   Source: Analysis of OECD data. This is calculated as simple averages of the ratio of total gross fixed capital formation (GFCF) to GDP, in current prices.

In the past, some have pointed to low investment levels as a natural feature of the UK economic strategy, or even a strength. Low domestic investment might have made sense when the UK was the most advanced economy in the world with a huge capital stock relative to its competitors. But this argument lacks any punch when the UK hasn't been at the productivity frontier for over a century.

More recently, arguments have been made that Britain's low investment reflects an impressively efficient sweating of its asset base – a justification, for example, for low investment in utilities before and after privatisation – or that it is merely an automatic corollary of being a service-led economy.[2] But no one would use the word efficient to describe the UK's energy or water networks today, and our industrial mix does not explain our lower investment levels. Virtually all of the UK's substantial productivity gap with France, which has a similar industrial mix, can be accounted for by French workers having over 40 per cent more capital to work with.[3]

Rather than being distracted by popular worries about too much investment in robots that will take our jobs, UK policy debates should focus on the danger of too little investment, in automation and almost everything else.[4] There is no plausible route to the UK ending this period of stagnation that does not involve turning around our dire investment performance. The question is how.

UK public investment is too low and too volatile

Although the majority of investment is made in the private sector, public investment matters too. It accounts for a fifth of total investment in the UK and dominates in some critical sectors – from transport infrastructure to health – and in poorer places.[5]

In OECD advanced economies, the average amount of public sector investment is 3.7 per cent of GDP a year, nearly 50 per cent more than in the UK. And our low public investment norm is persistent: we have been in the weakest third of OECD

2   M Starks, Watt's the plan? Renewing utilities regulation for the net zero era, Resolution Foundation, November 2023.

3   The productivity gap with the US can be partly explained by poor management practices; just 11 per cent of UK firms are as well-managed as the best quarter of US firms. This is covered in detail in: J Oliveira Cunha et al., Business time: How ready are UK firms for the decisive decade?, Resolution Foundation, November 2021.

4   S Farrell, UK economy has "too few robots", warn MPs, The Guardian, September 2019

5   F Odamtten & J Smith, Cutting the cuts: How the public sector can play its part in ending the UK's low-investment, Resolution Foundation March 2023.

countries for three in every four years this century. Had OECD average levels of public investment prevailed over the past two decades, we would have invested around £500 billion more.[6]

The results can be seen all around us. UK hospitals have fewer beds per capita than all but one of the OECD advanced economies, and fewer MRI machines than all but four. Our economy is held back by poor transport links and traffic congestion: UK workers spend more time commuting than those in all but two OECD countries. Addressing this legacy of low public investment requires a sustained step change, but so does a new challenge – the net zero transition. The National Infrastructure Commission has estimated it will require new public investment of between £3 and £12 billion each year merely to fund the transition to heat pumps by the end of the decade.[7]

But UK public investment is not just too low, it is far too volatile – the second-most volatile among advanced economies over the past 60 years.[8] Volatility compounds the under-investment problem, making it difficult for finance managers to plan ahead with confidence. This has led to persistent underspends: even where public investment increases have been planned, government has failed to spend £1 in every £6 allocated. Public investment feasts and famines also make maintaining supply chains hard, driving higher costs when public investment is ramped up.[9]

In large part this reflects incentives for policy makers to cut investment when belt tightening is needed: public investment has been reduced by 20 per cent on average during periods of consolidation.[10] To the Government's credit, public investment had been on the increase in the early 2020s to levels not sustained since the 1970s. But they have not been sustained this time either, with investment spending reduced in the aftermath of Liz Truss' mini-budget (by around £20 billion by 2027-28 relative to public investment remaining constant as a share of GDP).[11]

Politicians always have strong incentives to cut investment spending. Amid a budgetary crunch, it is easier to cancel a bridge tomorrow than fire a nurse, or

---

6   F Odamtten & J Smith, Cutting the cuts: How the public sector can play its part in ending the UK's low-investment, Resolution Foundation March 2023.

7   National Infrastructure Commission, Second National Infrastructure Assessment, October 2023. The NIC estimates that overall public investment will need to increase by £10 billion per year to meet the challenges of the 2030s.

8   IMF data, among the group of advanced economies the IMF provides comparable data for.

9   Capital spending plans: how much will actually be spent? Box 3.2 in OBR, Economic and fiscal outlook, March 2020.

10 F Odamtten & J Smith, Cutting the cuts: How the public sector can play its part in ending the UK's low-investment, Resolution Foundation March 2023.

11 Office for Budget Responsibility, Economic and fiscal outlook, November 2022.

raise a tax, today. This short-termism is reinforced by a fiscal framework that treats investment spending identically to day-to-day spending, while ignoring the value of assets on the public sector balance sheet. Britain's highly centralised state means these incentives to cut investment can easily be translated into action.[12] The result is that the Treasury uses public investment for something entirely inappropriate: fine-tuning fiscal policy. Volatile and low public investment follows.

It's time for our fiscal framework to lean into, rather than against, investment

Britain needs to become a normal investor – public investment of 3 per cent of GDP would step us up to the OECD average. Sustaining higher investment requires rewiring our fiscal framework to lean against rather than reinforce short-termism, including having fiscal rules distinguishing between current and investment spending. Today's target for total borrowing, which includes investment spending, not to exceed 3 per cent of GDP should be replaced with a target for tax revenues to cover day-to-day spending (a current budget balance rule). Ideally the target to see net debt falling – a fiscal rule that only considers the cost of investment – would also be replaced with one to see net worth improving, which also accounts for the value of the asset acquired. It would be unthinkable for a well-run company not to take this more rounded view of its balance sheet.[13]

We also need to make public investment plans stick. As things stand, Treasury ministers announce (and vary) headline public investment plans at whim with no meaningful parliamentary approval.[14] These roles need to be flipped. A Public Investment Act at the start of each parliament should enshrine the total investment planned for a period running at least a year into the following parliament.[15] This would free the Treasury up to focus on improving the quality, rather than fiddling with the quantity, of public investment.

---

12 In other major European economies between 50 and 75 per cent of public investment is done by subnational government.

13 This would not preclude an active focus on the overall debt interest bill, which remains important to fiscal sustainability, but would materially reduce the temptation for the Treasury to cut investment. It would also improve wider incentives, including removing the enticement to use fire sales of public assets to cut debt levels even where they represent poor value for money.

14 The Commons merely rubber-stamps budgets for each financial year when it is far too late to change them.

15 While ministers would propose that level, parliament should receive independent advice from the National Infrastructure Commission on its implications.

Box 16: Implications of high interest rates for public investment

The recent and swift arrival of higher interest rates does nothing to diminish the need for a future of higher public investment, but it does raise its cost and complicate how it is achieved. Low levels of public investment has meant significant rationing, with many projects with substantially positive returns not going ahead.[16] On this basis higher interest rates, while reducing those returns, are unlikely to fundamentally challenge the value for money of marginal investment projects whose returns will remain positive. But rising interest rates should provide a sharp reminder of the need for far better transparency over the business and strategic case for projects, with much wider publishing of cost-benefit analyses.[17] This is what it means to have the Treasury spending more of its effort improving the quality of public investment, rather than cutting the quantity of it. And at margins, higher rates will mean more public investment spending being financed by tax, rather than by borrowing. This is particularly true in the context of public investment that is highly desirable but does not have large financial returns, such as installing heat pumps in private households. So while higher interest rates should not prevent a sustained move to higher public investment, they do complicate it, given the direct impact on the wider balancing act between tax rises and the pressing need to renew public services. This reinforces how costly it has been not investing in an era of lower rates.

Public investment, far from crowding out, generally complements – and encourages – private investment.[18] So raising it is a necessary, but far from sufficient, condition for a renaissance in business investment. Such a renaissance is badly needed.

16 F Odamtten & J Smith, Cutting the cuts: How the public sector can play its part in ending the UK's low-investment, Resolution Foundation March 2023.

17 A Bailey et al., Euston we have a problem: Is Britain ready for an infrastructure revolution?, Resolution Foundation, March 2020.

18 Economists find strong evidence that increasing public investment does also boost private investment. For a meta-study on the size of those effects, see: P R D Bom & J Ligthart, What have we learned from three decades of research on the productivity of public capital?, Journal of Economic Surveys, 28, December 2014.

British business can make returns but does not invest. Basic stability would help

British business under-invests year in, year out. For almost all of the past two decades, the UK has been in the relegation zone (bottom 10 per cent) of the OECD business investment league table. This reflects business investment falling in the early 2000s as a share of GDP, falling further during the financial crisis, flatlining after 2016, and only starting to show signs of growth post-pandemic.[19] If UK business investment had matched the average of France, Germany and the US since 2008 – with 2 per cent of GDP additional investment each year – our GDP would be nearly 4 per cent higher today, boosting wages by around £1,250 a year.[20]

The sheer level of recent economic and political instability in Britain, from Brexit to Liz Truss' short tenure in Downing Street, has obviously not encouraged investment. Lower-level instability since 2010 has included nine Business Secretaries, four versions of the businesses department, and too many industrial strategies or growth plans to count. Corporation tax has changed almost annually.

That last bit of policy instability should be brought to an end by making the temporary full expensing of investment in plant and machinery permanent.[21] Government should also exempt new structures and improvements from the calculation of business rates, ending a major disincentive to commercial construction or improvements. These tax changes could eventually increase business capital, and GDP, sufficiently to ensure they do not have large permanent costs.[22]

More broadly, stronger institutions would also help underpin policy stability and quality. A National Growth Board should build upon the previous Industrial Strategy Council but with a broader remit and a statutory footing, avoiding a repeat of the Council's experience of being arbitrarily ditched. With powers analogous to the Climate Change Committee – advising government and reporting

---

19 ONS, Gross fixed capital formation – by sector and asset, September 2023; ONS, GDP in chained volume measures – real-time database, September 2023. 2019 prices.

20 P Brandily et al., Beyond Boosterism: Realigning the policy ecosystem to unleash private investment for sustainable growth, Resolution Foundation, June 2023

21 The types of investment that qualify should also be expanded to all business capital – something particularly important in a service economy relying on less traditional forms of investment. This could be funded by tightening the limits on tax deductibility of interest, reducing the tax system's bias towards debt financing. The current policy is outlined in HMRC, Capital allowances: full expensing for companies investing in plant and machinery from 1 April 2023 until 31 March 2026, March 2023. See also: IFS Green Budget 2023, October 2023.

22 P Brandily et al., Beyond Boosterism: Realigning the policy ecosystem to unleash private investment for sustainable growth, Resolution Foundation, June 2023.

to parliament on the UK's growth trajectory and strategy – it would underpin greater focus on and co-ordination of policy frameworks, holding ministers to their word on whether policies' design and implementation actively support investment and productivity growth.[23]

A period of political and policy stability will help. But too much faith is placed in stability alone – by technocrats and today's political leaders promising to do better than their predecessors on this front. To understand why, recall that the structural fall in business investment happened not around the time of the Brexit vote, but during the early 2000s – a period of political calm and the stable economic environment of the NICE (non-inflationary continuous expansion) decade.[24]

Reassuringly this failure is not because investment in the UK doesn't pay. In fact, returns on capital in the UK have if anything been relatively high (see Figure 36), suggesting worthwhile investments are not being pursued.

Figure 36: UK returns are high, and can't explain weak investment

Aggregate return on investment, market sector excluding agriculture, by country: 1995-2019

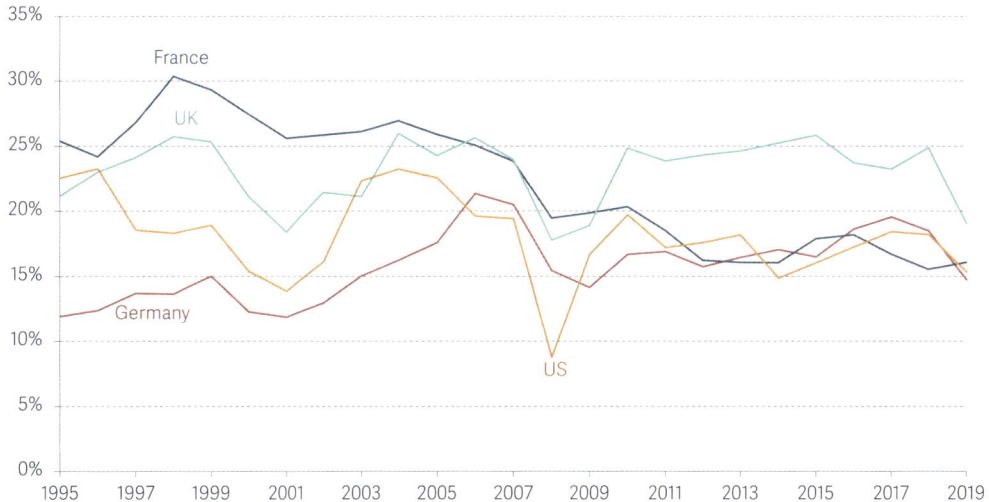

Notes: Aggregate rate of return is calculated as gross value added less depreciation and labour compensation costs as a proportion of total capital.
Source: Analysis of EUKLEMS, 2023 Release.

---

23 For more detailed recommendations on a new productivity institution in the UK, including the role of business and worker representatives see: A Valero and B van Ark, A new UK policy institution for growth and productivity: a blueprint, Productivity Agenda Chapter 10, The Productivity Institute; and CEP – POID discussion paper, November 2023.

24 M King, Speech given by Mervyn King, Governor of the Bank of England, October 2003.

So the question is why firms are constrained in their desire or ability to undertake worthwhile investment opportunities. There is little sign of a widespread problem with access to finance in the aggregate, but while Britain does not stand out for low returns on investment, it stands out in other ways that hold clues to the UK's low investment trap.

Box 17: Who pays for investment in regulated sectors?

Although we have set out specific challenges preventing the public and private sectors from investing, there isn't a hard line between the two. The UK's largely privatised but highly regulated utilities – like water and electricity – showcase how public and private sectors are intertwined in some of our most capital-intensive industries in particular.[25] Post-privatisation in the 1980s and 1990s, the broad approach has been for regulators to hold the ring, regulating prices that offer investors a reasonable rate of return on investment while controlling costs for consumers. This is relatively straightforward for regulators balancing costs and returns of investment for small system upgrades and maintenance. But several of these sectors are entering a high investment phase as critical infrastructure is upgraded or replaced, not least as we decarbonise our energy sector.

Government and regulators face tough choices about the level, nature and financing of investment. Front and centre is the decision about how investment is paid for: should that come from loading more onto household bills (tough, especially for poorer households, following a bout of high inflation), or from public sector investment (tough if returns are privately held and given competing pressures on public spending). The balance of private and public investment in these regulated sectors will have huge consequences for how much is invested in Britain, and who pays for it.

The UK now has a network of regulators whose considerable powers can be deployed to support a higher-investment economic strategy. To ensure clarity of purpose and avoid drift, government should ensure each of these key sectors has

---

25 The evidence in Box 17 draws on M Starks, Watt's the plan? Renewing utilities regulation for the net zero era, Resolution Foundation, November 2023.

a new overall system operator, with responsibility for making specific plans for investment and clearing the path for implementation. This is the approach which the Government is taking to boost the capacity of the National Grid with the new Future Systems Operator.

We need to focus on firms' desire to invest with pressure from above and from below

Rising interest rates are biting across borders, and bad taxes are found in many countries. Bad managers are, however, an area in which Britain stands out – only a small proportion of UK firms are as well managed as the best 25 per cent of US firms.[26] This matters for reasons beyond investment.[27] But well-managed firms make better investment decisions, being demonstrably better at forecasting the growth of the aggregate economy and of their own firm.[28]

More importantly, leaders of large British firms stand out internationally for the extraordinary latitude they enjoy. They are not exposed to the pressures that managers elsewhere face from above – via engaged owners – or below – from empowered workers – to focus on long-term growth. A renewed economic strategy must combine reforms that encourage proactive owners and proactive workers, squeezing investment-wary managers into raising their game.[29]

The ownership of UK-listed firms has become more remote – with foreign ownership of UK public firms rising from just over 10 per cent in 1990 to over 55 per cent in 2020 – and extremely dispersed.[30] The UK stands out in the OECD for having one of the lowest proportion of firms with 'blockholder' shareholders, big enough to have an incentive and the ability to influence firm decisions, as shown in Figure 37.

---

26 Management practises rank low internationally compared to other developed economies. Just 11 per cent of firms are better managed than the top quintile of US firms compared with more than 18 per cent of German firms. Source: Analysis of World Management Survey public data, https://worldmanagementsurvey.org, accessed 19 October 2023.

27 D Scur et al., The World Management Survey at 18: lessons and the way forward, Oxford Review of Economic Policy, 2021.

28 N Bloom et al., Do well managed firms make better forecasts?, POID Working Paper, January 2022. T Goodman et al., Management Forecast Quality and Capital Investment Decisions, The Accounting Review, 2014 demonstrates how better forecasts are linked to better investment decisions.

29 P Brandily et al., Beyond Boosterism: Realigning the policy ecosystem to unleash private investment for sustainable growth, Resolution Foundation, June 2023.

30 Analysis of ONS, Ownership of UK quoted shares 2020. There is substantial evidence that foreign-controlled firms are often highly productive and can bring know-how and skills to the host economies. See, for example, G Awano, Foreign direct investment and labour productivity, a micro-data perspective: 2012 to 2015, ONS, 2017; N Bloom et al., Americans Do IT Better: US Multinationals and the Productivity Miracle, American Economic Review, 2012; and J Haskel et al., Does Inward Foreign Direct Investment Boost the Productivity of Domestic Firms?, Review of Economics and Statistics, 2007.

Figure 37: British management lacks pressure from above

Proportion of listed companies that have a controlling shareholder, by country: 2012

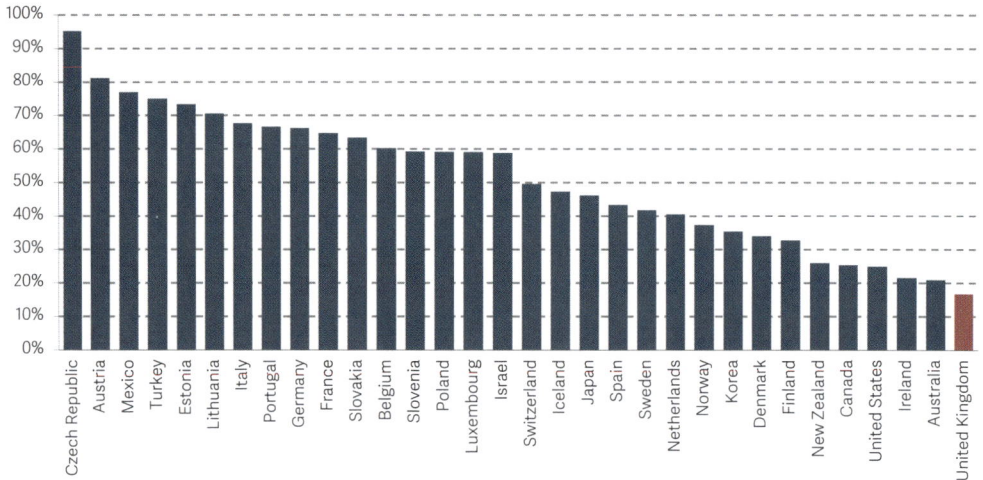

Notes: Controlled firms identified using a Shapely-Shubik algorithm to identify owners that have enough votes to change a vote decision. The algorithm has been adjusted to allow for owners in the same corporation to act in unison. A firm is classified as controlled if its Shapley-Shubik power index is 75 per cent or greater.
Source: G Aminadav & E Papaioannou, Corporate control around the world, The Journal of Finance 2020.

This is ultimately a story about pension funds – the only plausible source of large, long-term, domestic capital, and therefore ownership, in the UK. Structural and regulatory changes have weakened the central role of pension funds as engaged owners of UK firms over recent decades, with the closure of most private defined benefit (DB) schemes (such as final salary pensions), and a switch to defined contribution (DC) schemes. The large, legacy DB schemes have moved away from holding more rewarding but riskier UK equities in favour of safe assets such as bonds. Conversely, DC schemes are fast-growing owners of corporate Britain, but they are fragmented and almost exclusively invest passively through pooled investments such as stock market trackers. Only 2 per cent of the assets of our DC and DB pension funds are now directly held UK equities.[31]

It is this pension landscape that must be reformed to tackle Britain's disengaged ownership problem. While it is rational for small, fragmented shareholders not to incur the substantial costs of monitoring the management of the firms they own,

31 Analysis of UBS, Pension Fund Indicators and Pension Protection Fund, Purple Book 2022.

this is a significant collective action problem that puts firms in danger of being run myopically and profitable investment foregone. To underpin more concentrated ownership, we should reform three strands of the pension landscape: DB, DC and the Local Government Pension Schemes (LGPS). The common objective would be to produce a system that directly holds more UK equities (listed and unlisted) via a smaller number of far larger pension funds, which have the incentive and means to take an active interest in their holdings. This will also give them the scale to invest in unlisted high growth firms and infrastructure projects in the UK. Specifically, we propose:[32]

- legislating to facilitate the entry of DB schemes into 'superfunds' and extend the remit of the Pension Protection Fund (which absorbs DB funds when an employer becomes insolvent) to provide a state-backed consolidation option for solvent pension schemes – something the PPF itself has expressed interest in;[33]

- accelerating the consolidation of DC schemes, requiring funds to carry out stringent value-for-money tests and mandating funds that fail them to close, with a target of there being fewer than 250 DC funds by the end of the decade, just over 10 per cent of the number of schemes that exist today; and,

- pooling the £300bn of LGPS assets, currently split between 86 local pension funds in England alone, into one consolidated fund, which would have similar in-house scale and expertise as the large Canadian and Dutch pension funds.[34]

The UK stands out even more internationally when we recognise that the lack of 'owner voice' is matched by a lack of worker voice, so that pressure from below for managers to invest for the long term is unable to compensate for the lack of such pressure from above. Many European countries take a different approach, with some adopting two-tier board systems, with a supervisory board composed of representatives of shareholders and workers who together select and monitor executives.[35] This recognises that workers, particularly if they develop firm-specific skills, have as much interest in the long-term fortunes of their firm as

32 The government already favours pension fund consolidation, but our focus on securing more concentrated ownership, rather than just the provision of finance, points towards a more comprehensive approach being required. HM Treasury, Chancellor Jeremy Hunt's Mansion House speech, July 2023.

33 Josephine Cumbo, "Pension Protection Fund pushes for new remit to boost UK investment," Financial Times, 5 September 2023.

34 P Brandily et al., Beyond Boosterism: Realigning the policy ecosystem to unleash private investment for sustainable growth, Resolution Foundation, June 2023.

35 https://www.worker-participation.eu/National-Industrial-Relations/Countries, Accessed: October 2023.

shareholders, even substantial ones. Their representation on corporate boards can support a focus on longer-term value creation within businesses. Research on the experiences of Germany, Finland and Norway suggests that workers having board roles has positive effects on investment levels and productivity (and contrary to some expectations, a negligible effect on wages).[36] To increase the pressure on managers to invest for the long term from below as well as above, we propose the mandatory inclusion of worker representatives at the board level for all larger UK firms (both listed and unlisted) with more than 200 employees. This would be a big change for British corporate governance, but not an unimaginable one – a Conservative Prime Minister proposed this exact change in the recent past.[37]

A prerequisite for higher investment is that firms have the ability to build

Firms need the ability to invest along with the desire to. Even in a service-led economy like the UK that means the chance to build, with structures making up around half of business investment, and much of the rest needing a structure to house it.[38] But building things is not something the UK does much of. While we have relatively liberal product and labour markets, the same is not true for land.[39]

The UK has actually seen no increase in the amount of built-up land per capita since 1990, and if anything, a fall this century. This is in stark contrast to every other G7 economy, which not only have higher levels of built-up land per head, but have seen substantial increases decade on decade. As with the lack of block shareholders, this is the kind of UK exceptionalism that underpins our status as a low-investment nation. The physical constraints of a crowded island cannot explain this: as Figure 38 reveals, denser countries such as the Netherlands and Japan are seeing built-up per land per person go forward rather than back.[40]

36 See: S Jäger, B Schoefer & J Heining, Labor in the Boardroom, The Quarterly Journal of Economics, 2021. J Harju, S Jäger & B Schoefer, Voice at work, National Bureau of Economic Research, 2021 See also a study that focuses on worker outcomes in Norway: C Blandhol et al., Do employees benefit from worker representation on corporate boards?, National Bureau of Economic Research, WP 28269, 2020.

37 R Moss, Theresa May promises worker representatives on boards, Personnel Today, July 2016.

38 P Brandily et al., Beyond Boosterism: Realigning the policy ecosystem to unleash private investment for sustainable growth, Resolution Foundation, June 2023.

39 P Cheshire & C Hilber, Office Space Supply Restrictions in Britain: The Political Economy of Market Revenge, The Economic Journal, Vol 118 Issue 529, May 2008.

40 The UK ranks sixth in population per square km (after South Korea, the Netherlands, Israel, Belgium, and Japan) and fifth in the share of land being already built-up (behind the Netherlands, Belgium, Germany and Japan).

Figure 38: Britain hasn't been building

Square meters of built-up land per capita, by country: 1975-2014

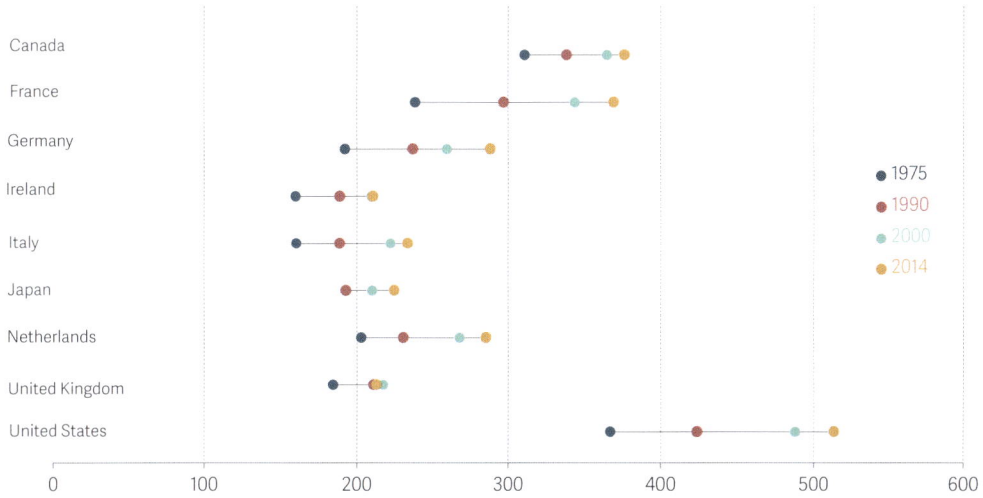

Source: Analysis of OECD, Built-up area and built-up area change in countries and regions.

The overall lack of British development is not because we protect more of our green and pleasant land: countries like Germany and the Netherlands have far more of their land protected on environmental grounds than the UK.[41] Instead, navigating our planning system is simply too difficult and too expensive. The cost of planning applications is five times more in 2023 than it was in 1990, and the outcomes far too unpredictable.[42] This holds back business investment, but also provides a major barrier to badly needed housing and net zero infrastructure (as Box 18 explains).

---

41 According to OECD statistics on protected areas, 35 per cent of the UK's land is protected, compared with 48 per cent in Germany and 45 per cent in the Netherlands. See: OECD (2023), Protected areas (indicator).

42 LPDF, Small builders, big burdens: How changes in planning have impacted on SME house builders, September 2023.

Box 18: Planning barriers in the way of net zero

Decarbonising transport, buildings and industry is necessary for achieving net zero but will place strains on the UK's electricity infrastructure. By 2035, the Government projects a 60 per cent increase in electricity demand.[43] This requires not only building thousands of wind turbines and solar panels but overhauling and hugely expanding the electricity network. The speed of infrastructure construction will need to far exceed what has been achieved historically. Recent National Grid research found that "five times the amount of new electricity transmission infrastructure will need to be delivered in the next seven years than has been built in the past 30 years".[44]

Yet planning restrictions have held back investment, for example in onshore wind turbines. Planning bottlenecks also hold back investment in grid connections, despite specific planning rules that apply to Nationally Significant Infrastructure Projects and the Government recognising many of these issues.[45] Take the National Grid's Norwich to Tilbury scheme – a project to transport power generated by East Anglia's shiny new offshore wind turbines inland to consumers[46] – which is not slated to be fully operational until 2031 and faces local opposition to the installation of overhead transmission lines, despite the much higher costs of long-distance undersea or underground transmission.[47]

The UK must be able to build again if it is to grow, contain housing costs and decarbonise. That will require a new approach to planning. Local authorities should be required to have up-to-date plans (six in ten in England do not), with a zone-based approach that includes designated growth areas and those plans

---

43 Department for Energy Security and Net Zero, Powering Up Britain, 2023.

44 National Grid, 2022/23 Half Year Results Statement, 2023.

45 Department for Energy Security and Net Zero, Powering Up Britain, 2023.

46 National Grid, About Norwich to Tilbury, https://www.nationalgrid.com/electricity-transmission/network-and-infrastructure/infrastructure-projects/norwich-to-tilbury/about, accessed 16 October 2023.

47 D Grimmer, Norwich to Tilbury pylon plan not affected by wind farm halt, Eastern Daily Press, July 2023; R Millard, This English village shows how a pylon backlash threatens the green energy shift, Financial Times August 2023.

must be binding: businesses submitting applications consistent with them would be automatically approved. While planning for housing development should take place at the local level, subject to meeting nationally set housing targets, decision-making for business developments should take place at a wider geographical level where the benefits, not just the costs, can be recognised. The scrappy patchwork of planning responsibility across combined authorities and vaguer strategic regions, such as the Oxford to Cambridge corridor, do not give potential commercial investors clarity on who is calling the shots.[48]

We need to invest more not less in the UK's education and workforce

Ensuring that workers have the right skills is essential to building a fairer and more productive economy, but not everyone in Britain sees it that way. When it comes to raising business investment everyone agrees the appropriate question is how to do it? (and the answer, as we have outlined earlier in this chapter, is to increase firms' desire and ability to invest). But when it comes to investing in human capital the question that dominates debates is do we already have too much?[49] Announcements that the destination of almost two-fifths of school leavers is higher education are met by comments that we are overeducated in the UK.[50] We are not. This debate is often dominated by fears of a brain drain from poorer places, but in reality young people from the most-deprived areas are two-and-a-half times less likely to leave their home area upon reaching adulthood than their peers in the least-deprived quintile.[51]

One important factor is the sectors that are the key to the UK's future prosperity are precisely those that require a more advanced skillset. The UK's high-performing and fast-growing sectors (such as finance and business, creative industries and life sciences, which collectively accounted for 18 per cent of employment in 2022) employ 1.7 times as many graduates as a share of their workforce as the rest of the economy, as shown in Figure 39.[52] And while analytical and personal skills have generally become more important across all sectors since the 2010s, they are particularly so in these key sectors.

48 P Brandily et al., Beyond Boosterism: Realigning the policy ecosystem to unleash private investment for sustainable growth, Resolution Foundation, June 2023.

49 G Roberts, Are too many students going to university? Record number have been accepted into their first choice, Sky News, August 2021.

50 R Bolton, Higher education student numbers, House of Commons Library, February 2023.

51 L Judge & D Tomlinson, All over the place: Perspectives on local economic prosperity, The Resolution Foundation, June 2022.

52 The share of these sectors' workforce with degrees is 65 per cent compared with 39 per cent in the rest of the economy. R Costa et al., Learning to grow: How to situate a skills strategy in an economic strategy, Resolution Foundation, October 2023.

Figure 39: Strategic growth sectors need more graduates

Proportion of workers aged 18-64 by their highest qualification, for strategic sectors and the rest of the economy: UK, 2011-2019

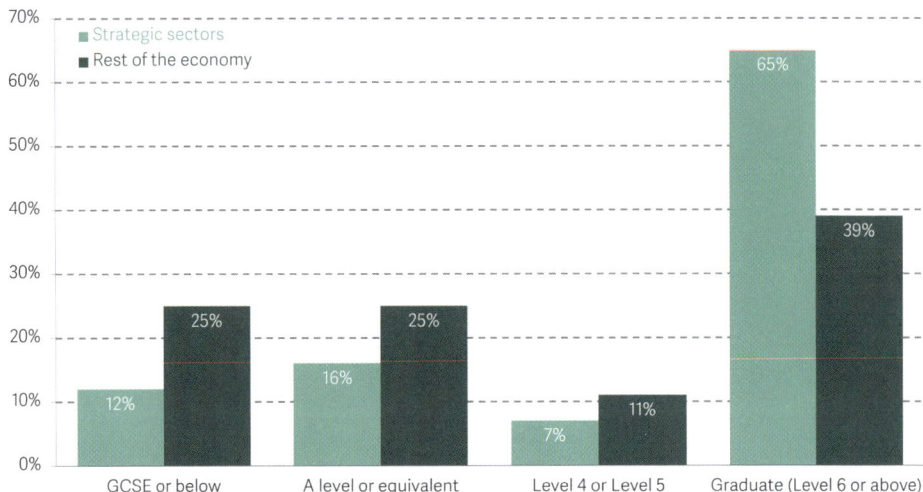

Notes: Strategic sectors are: financial and business services, the creative and cultural sectors and life sciences industries.
Source: Analysis of ONS, Labour Force Survey.

The call for fewer graduates is inconsistent with any economic strategy in which growing these key sectors play a central role. As discussed in the previous chapter, it also risks some of the national benefits of making a success of our second cities being lost in zero-sum competition for the existing stock of graduates, although skilled migration may offer some relief (see Box 19).

But this is just one reason for anticipating the number going to university is more likely to grow than shrink, in Britain as in many other countries. Others include the surge in the birth rate in the first decade of the millennium, and a wider range of groups and communities moving towards the participation rates of affluent families.

Box 19: The post-Brexit migration system supports a skilled worker strategy

Post-Brexit, the UK has had the opportunity to design a new immigration system outside EU free movement rules. The centrepiece of this new system is the Skilled Work Visa, which prioritises skilled work and workers and does not discriminate by country of origin. Under this new system, skill and salary thresholds enable non-UK workers to qualify for most high- and middle-skill jobs.[53] This new skill bias may have already supported some sectors' productivity.[54] This broad approach is correct, as one part of a strategy to build a higher-skilled workforce. For the UK, attracting top international talent and skilled labour is an important pillar of an economic strategy, in combination with developing more home-grown proficiency.[55] Being open to this type of migration is also a prerequisite for enhancing services trade, a clear objective for the UK.

But the narrow focus on the number of undergraduates misses the areas in which it is most obvious that the UK's problem is not being too highly educated. The share of workers qualified at sub-degree level – at Level 4 and 5 such as a higher national certificate (HNC) or a higher national diploma (HND) – is dramatically lower than it should be given the sectoral and occupational make-up of the UK economy. This point is worth labouring. It is not the familiar lament that the UK's industrial and educational outcomes do not more closely resemble a country like, say, Germany. Rather, it is highlighting that, given the UK's own industrial strengths, our workforce is massively skewed towards those with lower-level qualifications with far too many achieving at most, upper secondary qualifications. Given our economy's job make-up, the share of workers qualified at Level 4 and 5 (currently 11 per cent) should be more than twice as high; equally, the share who

---

53 K Henehan, If fewer workers migrate to Britain, our own will need greater mobility: Migration policy can complement an economic strategy, but it can't stand in for one, Resolution Foundation, February 2022.

54 H Nam & J Portes, Migration and Productivity in the UK: An Analysis of Employee Payroll Data, IZA Institute of Labour Economics Discussion Series, September 2023.

55 S Bhalotia, et al., Trading Up, The role of post-Brexit trade approach in the UK's economic strategy, Resolution Foundation, June 2023.

have peaked at Level 3 or below (A level equivalent or GCSE equivalent) should be dramatically lower as shown in Figure 40. Achieving this should be the focus of a new economic strategy.[56]

Figure 40: Shortages of intermediate and advanced skills are widespread in the UK economy

Gap between expected and actual level of education in the rest of the economy: UK, 2011-2019

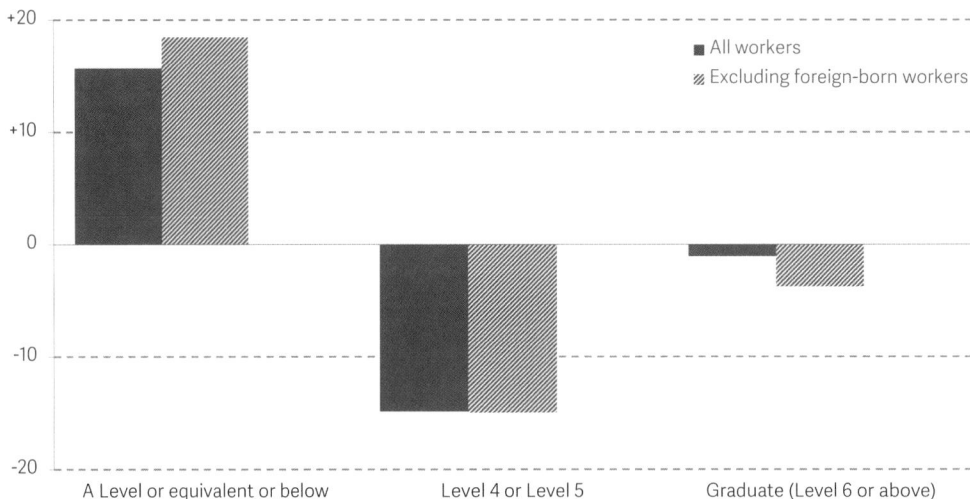

Notes: This chart plots the difference between the share of workers outside of the strategic sectors with a given level of education and the share expected to possess a given level of qualification given the underlying occupational composition (according to the US-based O*NET data). Positive values indicate an excess of workers with that level of education. The shaded bars indicate what the difference would look like if we excluded foreign-born workers from the computation of workers' actual qualifications.
Source: Analysis of ONS, Labour Force Survey linked to O*NET (US Department of Labor).

The dearth of such sub-degree level qualifications reflects a systemic failure. As we show in Chapter 6, large inequalities of educational outcomes see too few students achieve good Level 3 qualifications, blocking a wider pipeline that could go on to further technical study. Then too often clear, high-quality pathways to Level 4 and 5 qualifications aren't available. There are far too few well-established qualifications recognised by employers and students, with a few notable exceptions in nursing and engineering.[57] This is clear when we look at not only

---

56 R Costa et al., Learning to grow: How to situate a skills strategy in an economic strategy, Resolution Foundation, October 2023.

57 C. Hupkau, S. McNally, J. Ruiz-Valenzuela & G. Ventura, Post-Compulsory Education in England: Choices and Implications, National Institute Economic Review 240, May 2017; J Britton et al., Post-18 Education: Who is Taking Different Routes and How Much do they Earn?, CVER Briefing Note 013, September 2020.

the low numbers with such qualifications, but also the variable returns to them despite a positive wage differential on average. [58]

The scale of the necessary upskilling, together with the demographic bulge, represents both a major opportunity and a challenge for the HE and FE sectors.[59] The objective should not be to make existing universities ever larger: innovation in provision with new forms of sub-degree provision are required, just as we need new institutions able to serve so-called 'cold-spots' that lack a university such as in Blackpool and Hartlepool, building on recent successes in Lincoln, Chester and Worcester.[60]

More learners at Levels 4 and 5 will require more than just the right qualifications and institutions: the level of support for learners is crucial. The government's new Lifelong Loan Entitlement will apply to all non-apprentice students at Levels 4 and 5 as well as to degree students, but the student support system this broadens access to has flaws that will be particularly off-putting to precisely the types of young people that we most need to attract. The share of families eligible for the full level of maintenance loan support has withered (the parental earnings threshold below which students are eligible for has been frozen at £25,000 for 15 years). As a start, the real value of these thresholds should be immediately restored, and there is a strong case for introducing means-tested maintenance grants for those studying a first Level 4 and 5 qualification, particularly in priority sectors.[61]

The argument that the UK has too much education also ignores what is happening to a key route through which we continue to develop skills in our working life: training. British firms are doing far less of it – the average number of days an employee spent in training fell by 18 per cent (from 7.8 to 6.4 days) between 2011 and 2017.[62] Despite employers benefitting from an up-skilled workforce, they are

58 H Espinoza et al., Post-18 Education: Who is Taking Different Routes and How Much do they Earn?, Center for Vocational Education Research, September 2020.

59 A 10 per cent increase in the number of universities in a region is associated with about 0.4 per cent higher GDP per capita. A Valero & J Van Reenen, The economic impact of universities: evidence from across the globe, Economics of Education Review, Volume 68, February 2019.

60 D Willetts, How higher education can boost people-powered growth, Resolution Foundation, October 2023; A McNeil & D Soskice, Relational...., IFS Deaton Review of Inequalities, December 2022.

61 In a recent blog, Nicholas Barr argues for some restoration of the teaching grant, not increasing fees and reforms to parameters of the loan system (interest rates, time for repayment, and changing the income thresholds for repayment of loans). See: N Barr, A fairer way to finance tertiary education, LSE Politics and Policy, June 2023.

62 J Li, A Valero & G Ventura, Trends in job-related training and policies for building future skills into the recovery, LSE Centre for Vocational Education Research, December 2020.

less inclined to invest, because of the risk that workers, once trained, will move firms.[63] As skills requirements have become less firm-specific, this barrier to training may have grown.[64]

Figure 41: Worker training participation has fallen across the board

Proportion of employees receiving off-the-job training in the past four weeks, by hourly pay quartile: UK

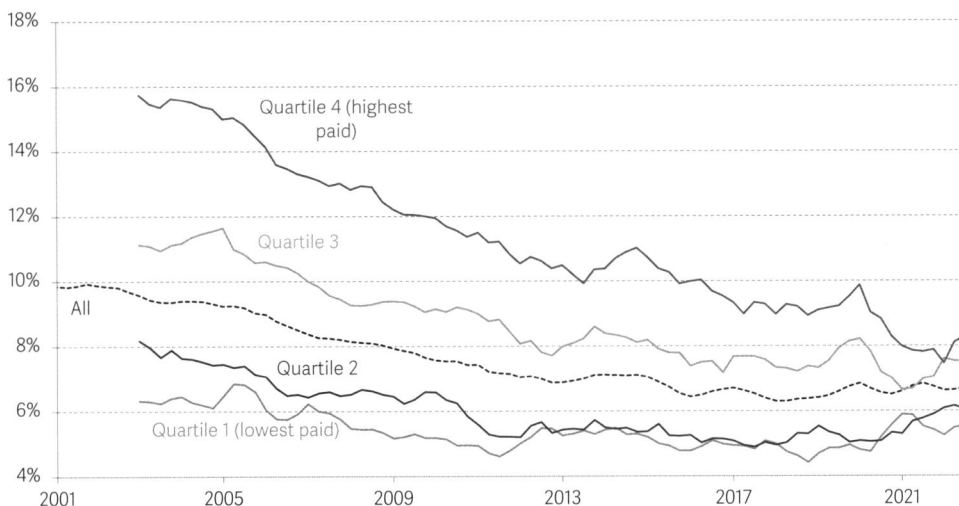

Notes: Four-quarter rolling averages. Latest data point is Q4 2022. Excludes full-time students. The pay measure used here is adjusted using the pay imputation method used by the ONS to correct for known issues in the LFS pay data. Pay data only available from 2002 due to variables used in the pay imputation not being in the data in earlier periods. Source: Analysis of ONS, Labour Force Survey.

Overcoming these concerns requires government to require or incentivise firms to train their workers, such as through the Apprenticeship Levy or via 'human capital tax credits' of the kinds that we see in Austria and various US states.[65]

So despite the popular wisdom that too many people have degrees the reverse is true when our education and training systems are taken as a whole. If we are to make Britain richer and fairer, we need more education not less. At this point we have put together a long list of things that Britain needs to invest in, across

---

63 For example, see: H Slaughter, Labour Market Outlook Q1 2023, Resolution Foundation, April 2023; G.S. Becker, Human Capital: A Theoretical and Empirical Analysis, with Special Reference to Education. University of Chicago Press, Chicago. 1964.

64 J Li, A Valero & G Ventura, Trends in job-related training and policies for building future skills into the recovery. Centre for Vocational Education Research Discussion Paper No. 33, December 2020.

65 A Fitzpayne & E. Pollack, Working Training Tax Credit: Promoting Employer Investments in the Workforce, Aspen Initiative. Future of Work Initiative, August 2018.

public and private sectors, to support our workforce's skills and our nation's green transition. But a tricky question remains, how does our stagnation nation fund its transformation into an investment nation?

A strategy for higher investment needs to wrestle with how it is resourced

Higher investment means more productive workers and a bigger economy. In time it means higher living standards, not to mention a greener and more sustainable economy. But only in time.

An economic strategy clear about the need for higher investment needs to be equally clear about the trade-offs involved, and how they can be navigated. The two options in a broadly fully employed economy are to fund higher investment through higher domestic savings or from overseas (a higher current account deficit), as Box 20 explores.

Box 20: Funding investment might require lower consumption today

When all potential workers are employed, the amount that the economy can produce is more or less fixed in the short run. Using more workers to make or install investment goods – such as heat pumps – means having fewer workers available to wait tables. In other words, there can be a trade off in the short run between investment and consumption. Investment goods, like machine tools for example, could be imported, but those imports will need to be financed by foreign debt or a reduction in imports for consumption. So higher investment is crucial, but it takes real resources – often requiring lower consumption today – to make it happen. A higher-investment economic strategy therefore needs to recognise that pressure on consumption, and answer difficult questions about whose consumption falls and on what.

The reforms discussed above will make the UK more attractive for foreign direct investment (FDI) and other forms of external financing, but there are strong resilience arguments, for the economy as a whole and individual households, for higher investment being accompanied by higher domestic savings given how much we already borrow from abroad and how little we save at home.[66]

The UK's current account deficit is already large and persistent – averaging 4 per cent of GDP over the last decade. The UK is very reliant on "the kindness of strangers".[67] Moreover, countries with higher investment do generally have higher domestic savings, in part because capital is not fully internationally mobile, with some 'home bias'.[68] The UK's national savings rate is extremely low, the third lowest in the OECD. British households in aggregate save so little that, after we account for their investment in housing, almost nothing is available to finance investment by British business.

The consequence of low savings for households, particularly in an unequal society, is widespread precarity despite high levels of illiquid housing wealth. Over two fifths (41 per cent) of families had savings of less than one month's income in 2018-2020.[69] Beyond the lack of rainy-day funds, the vast majority (over 80 per cent) are not saving enough to have an acceptable standard of living in retirement.[70]

A recent policy success – indeed the only policy to materially raise UK households' savings in decades – tells us what a plausible route to higher household savings rates will look like. The introduction of auto-enrolment into pensions saving from 2012 has seen the share of workers saving for a pension rise from 47 per cent in 2012 to 77 per cent in 2019. The next phase in its development should be a levelling up of the minimum contributions by both employers and employees to 6 percentage points (from 3 and 5 per cent respectively), representing a 50 per cent increase in total. A capped amount of these savings should be made available for everyday contingencies – tackling precarity for individuals as we underpin higher investment for the economy as a whole.[71]

---

66 M Ward, Foreign Direct Investment (FDI) Statistics, House of Commons Library, June 2023.

67 M Carney, A Fine Balance - speech by Mark Carney, Bank of England, June 2017.

68 N Apergis and C Tsoumas, A survey of the Feldstein-Horioka puzzle: What has been done and where we stand, Research in Economics, June 2009.

69 M Broome & J Leslie, Arrears fears: The distribution of UK household wealth and the impact on families, Resolution Foundation, July 2022.

70 N Cominetti & F Odamtten, Living Pensions: An assessment of whether workers' pension saving meets a 'living pension' benchmark , Resolution Foundation, July 2022.

71 P Brandily et al., Beyond Boosterism: Realigning the policy ecosystem to unleash private investment for sustainable growth, Resolution Foundation, June 2023.

Of course savings behaviour of individuals is just one of many elements shaping savings and consumption patterns for the economy as a whole. The levels and nature of tax, and choices about relative prices of different goods and services, matter hugely too and are powerful levers in ensuring that it is not lower-income households whose consumption is squeezed by a shift to a higher investment economy. We turn to both in chapters 7 and 8.

Investment and growth need to be underpinned by a sustainable macroeconomic framework

Economic stability, not just the policy stability addressed above, helps underpin higher investment.[72] This requires a strong, and sustainable, macroeconomic policy framework that gives policymakers the tools to stabilise the economy in a downturn. Today's framework – centred around the 2 per cent inflation target shepherded by the Bank of England, which has the primary responsibility for stabilising the economy – faces significant challenges.

The focus today is rightly on tackling high inflation, with the Bank engaging in the largest rate rises in more than three decades. While the judgements on the scale and duration of rate rises required is hard, the Bank certainly has the tools to prevent inflation becoming entrenched. What is far less clear is whether today's framework provides enough room for manoeuvre when it comes to the opposite problem, a downturn.

Constraints on interest rates being cut significantly because of their already low level (the zero lower bound constraint reflects the challenges of cutting interest rates below zero), alongside crises requiring targeted support such as with energy bills, left fiscal policy bearing much of the burden of responding to the repeated 'once-in-a lifetime' economic shocks of the past 15 years. The result is a trebling of public sector net debt, from 36 to around 100 per cent of GDP, an unprecedented peace-time rise with debt ratcheting up in each crisis but not falling between them.[73]

Today's level of UK debt appears sustainable, but its trajectory is not. Crisis induced ratchets up in debt, even if smaller than recently experienced because higher interest rates let monetary policy take more of the strain, are large. When

---

72 Nicholas Bloom, The Impact of Uncertainty Shocks, Econometrica 77(3), 2009.

73 S Pittaway & J Smith, Built to Last: Towards a sustainable macroeconomic policy framework for the UK, Resolution Foundation, October 2023.

combined with the Government's (and Labour opposition's) focus on holding debt stable or slightly falling during good times, this would see debt rise to 140 per cent of GDP over the next 50 years (see Figure 42), leaving the debt interest bill at a level not sustained for more than 70 years.

Figure 42: The path forward is more uncertain than ever

Long-term projections for public sector net debt as a share of GDP: UK

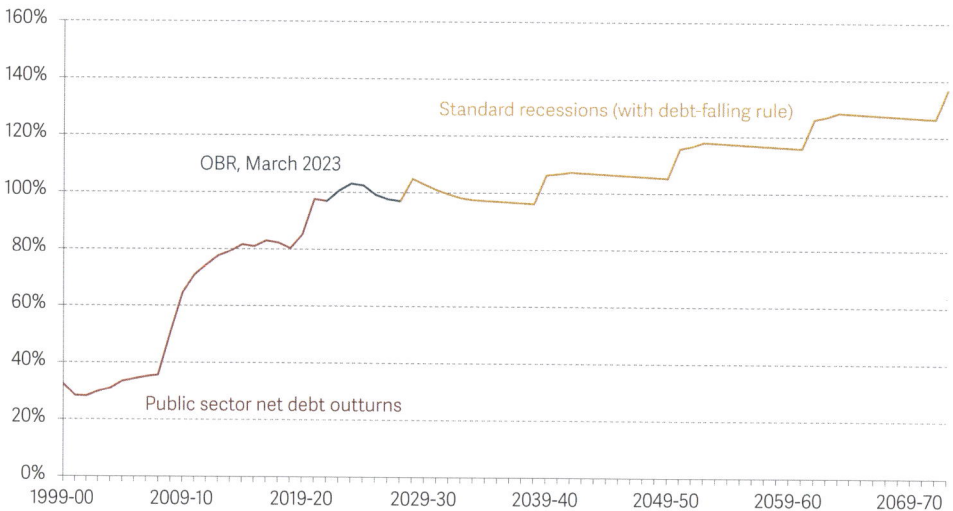

Notes: Projections are constructed over a 50-year horizon using the OBR's March 2023 forecast as the starting point, extrapolated out using the OBR's long-term economic and policy determinants. Following shocks we allow a period of two years to elapse before returning to a debt-falling rule for which the debt-to-GDP ratio is assumed to fall at a rate of 0.25 percentage points each year.
Source: Analysis of OBR, Public finances databank – February 2023 (EFO edition), Economic and fiscal outlook – March 2023 & Fiscal risks and sustainability – July 2023.

Worse, if we find ourselves in a world in which a return to low interest rates means monetary policy is once again marooned at the lower bound, and fiscal policy has to do the heavy lifting in supporting the economy in a downturn, then debt would be on track to nearly double over the coming half century (reaching around 190 per cent of GDP). Preventing that rise within our current macroeconomic policy framework would require the Treasury to run a 3 per cent primary surplus in three out of every four years, something only achieved three times in the last 50 years.[74] This is totally implausible.

---

74 S Pittaway & J Smith, Built to Last: Towards a sustainable macroeconomic policy framework for the UK, Resolution Foundation, October 2023.

So although these problems are not today's problems, they are not ones that we should continue to ignore. We need to reset Britain's approach to monetary and fiscal policy. To reduce the pressure on fiscal policy to support the economy in a downturn, the scope for the Bank of England to cut interest rates without hitting the zero lower bound should be increased. In the first instance that should include preparing for negative interest rates of up to -1 per cent, building on the experience of other European economies such as Denmark and Switzerland, which have cut rates as low as -0.75 per cent.[75] If we return to a low-interest rate world this will still leave the Bank of England too little room for manoeuvre, so in that scenario the inflation target should also be raised to 3 per cent. This should be introduced carefully, only after the current 2 per cent target has been hit, and ideally in coordination with other advanced economies. A higher inflation target means higher nominal interest rates, making hitting the zero lower bound from a once-a-decade event into a once-a-century one.

On the fiscal policy side, the ramping up of spending in downturns has so far come without us developing the tools to do it well. For example, the Energy Price Guarantee provided large amounts of unnecessary support to high-income households because no more targeted policy option was available. The Treasury should be building a flexible payments infrastructure to target support as required by very different types of crises, integrating the data held across different parts and levels of government (for example on individual incomes and household characteristics such as size). To prepare for a future energy shock, this should include links to energy firms' data. Building such a system would be a very cost-effective policy, with savings running into many billions of pounds from avoiding the more expensive universal support deployed recently. Higher levels of sustained public investment will also make it possible to ramp up infrastructure construction in a downturn – a particularly effective form of fiscal stimulus.[76]

---

75 To make negative rates as effective as possible, the Bank of England and the Prudential Regulatory Authority should work with banks to ensure their operational readiness for negative rates, building on previous work during the pandemic when cutting into negative territory was under active consideration. The impact on bank lending can also be reduced by following other central banks by implementing negative rates via a tiered structure, where negative rates only apply to central bank reserves above a certain threshold. This would limit the overall impact on bank profit margins and therefore the extent to which negative rates restrict the flow of credit to the real economy.

76 S Pittaway & J Smith, Built to Last: Towards a sustainable macroeconomic policy framework for the UK, Resolution Foundation, October 2023.

Resetting our macroeconomic framework in this way would leave governments needing to run primary budget surpluses of 1 rather than 3 per cent of GDP in good times, to repair the public finances after rightly supporting the economy during bad times. That is tough but achievable (towards the end of the 20th century, the UK ran a surplus of 1 per cent or more in three out of five years).

From faster growth to shared gains

This chapter has set out an ambitious plan for getting Britain investing again, while facing up to the macroeconomic challenges which come from that and from the lessons of our recent turbulent past. It's a credible strategy for ending the UK's relative economic decline that is honest about the trade-offs involved. But it is far from the end of a renewed economic strategy for the UK. Because the task is to get inequality down as well as growth up. It is to a hard-headed approach to achieving the former objective that the next chapter turns.

Chapter Six

Good work

Chapter summary

- We must be just as serious about reducing inequality as boosting growth. Good jobs must be a central objective of a new economic strategy, not a hoped for by-product of it.

- Successes need to be built on. The poorest half of households experienced two-thirds of the job growth in the decade after the financial crisis while the minimum wage has seen the lowest earners consistency receive the fastest pay rises for over two decades. The pace of minimum wage rises should be maintained, on a path to reach 73 per cent of median pay (£14 on current forecasts) by 2029, but a good work agenda must be more than a one-trick pony.

- We must also raise the floor on standards, offering lower earners more of the security, flexibility or control that higher earners take for granted: half of shift workers receive less than a week's notice of their working schedules and Statutory Sick Pay leaves many living on just £44 if they are sick for a week.

- Higher standards are only meaningful if they are enforced. 900,000 workers miss out on paid holiday because we have too many enforcement agencies (six, overseen by seven government departments) with too few boots on the grounds (just 0.29 labour market inspectors per 10,000 workers).

- Antiquated restrictions on unions should be modernised, but we cannot rely on union renaissance or tight labour market to remedy poor conditions in the most problematic sectors. 'Good Work Agreements' should be established, bringing together workers and employers to solve sector specific challenges. First up should be social care, where a predominately women (77 per cent) workforce is often illegally underpaid.

- While politicians are distracted debating whether too many people go to university, the reality is we need more education not less: almost a third of young people are not undertaking any education by age 18 – compared to just one in five in France and Germany.

- Unless more homes are built and housing support linked to rent levels, rising housing costs risk eating up many of the gains from growth: The share of income families dedicate to housing has doubled since 1980.

If the recommendations of the last two chapters were implemented, and steady British productivity growth resumed, then over time we should start to see rising national income and increasing average pay. Our challenges, from resuscitating public services to accelerating the green transition, would be easier to navigate, and improving living standards would be a lived reality rather than a distant memory.

But, crucially, ensuring that the promise of rising living standards is fulfilled for all our citizens requires something more: we must be equally serious about Britain's stubbornly high inequality as we are about its anaemic growth. For poorer and indeed middle-income families today, it is not just the lacklustre rise in our total output, but also the skewed way in which that output is shared, that produces stagnation, not to mention structurally disadvantaging certain groups.[1]

We need a broad fairness strategy

Discussions about how to reduce inequality often set two strategies up in tension: should we focus on changing what happens in the labour market or wider market economy (so-called 'pre-distribution'), or on picking up the pieces afterwards, by levelling incomes through taxes and benefits ('redistribution')?[2] This book's argument is that this debate is a distraction – it is imperative to act on both fronts at once.

It's not hard to see the flaw in staking everything on changing who earns what in the labour market: a significant swathe of the country will never receive the majority of their income in the form of pay (as a result of old age, ill health and caring responsibilities). Even when pensioners are excluded, 11 million people live in households where earnings constitute less than half of income.[3] Higher employment or a higher minimum wage simply can't fix everything.

Others may jump from this reality to the conclusion that the only sure way to bear down on inequality is via redistribution, with the state directly raising taxes on higher incomes and transfers to those on lower incomes. But this is equally awry, requiring implausible increases in tax and spending.

---

1   As we discussed in Chapter 1, the risks of being towards the bottom of the income distribution are far from equally shared with, for example, some ethnic minority groups and single people with disabilities over-represented.

2   See, for example: P Coy, How Democrats Lost Voters With a 'Compensate Losers' Strategy, New York Times, November 2023.

3   M Brewer et al., Sharing the benefits: Can Britain secure broadly shared prosperity?, Resolution Foundation, July 2023.

So to make a serious dent in inequality, we need a two-pronged approach. First, employment – good jobs, with decent pay and conditions, are the bedrock of widely-shared prosperity and should be the norm everywhere. This is not a by-product of a successful economic strategy but a central objective for it, and the focus of the current chapter. Work is an important source of meaning and contribution for people, as well as a source of income.[4] And second, we must ensure rewards and sacrifices are fairly shared, including via our tax and benefit systems, as set out in Chapter 7.

> "I am an active participant in society because of the work I do, my job... me and my company actively participate in the economy."
>
> Participant, Paisley focus group

Moving on these twin fronts simultaneously is challenging, but tackling our position as the most unequal large country in Europe was never going to be amenable to a single fix. And, as we shall show, if improvements in the world of work are combined with a stronger safety net, the effects could be transformative.

Lower-income households are the main winners from higher employment

It is important to start by recognising both what has worked, as well as what is missing, from Britain's approach to improving work. Successes need to be built on, as well as problems addressed.

In recent decades there have been two major achievements in terms of jobs. Both are important in their own right and play an important role in leaning against inequality.

The first is securing a high employment rate. To the extent that worklessness is concentrated towards the bottom of the income distribution, the greatest scope for raising participation will also be found there. And as Figure 43 illustrates, over the long jobs recovery since the financial crisis, the employment rate has risen by a substantial average of 6 percentage points across the lower half of income brackets, while not budging at all among the top half. Indeed, the poorest half of households experienced two-thirds of the jobs growth in the decade after the financial crisis.[5]

---

4   K Handscomb, L Judge & H Slaughter, Listen up: Individual experiences of work, consumption and society, Resolution Foundation, May 2022.

5   M Brewer et al., Sharing the benefits: Can Britain secure broadly shared prosperity?, Resolution Foundation, July 2023.

Figure 43: Recent jobs growth has been bottom-heavy

Change in working-age employment rate by income decile after housing costs: UK, 2009-10 to 2019-20

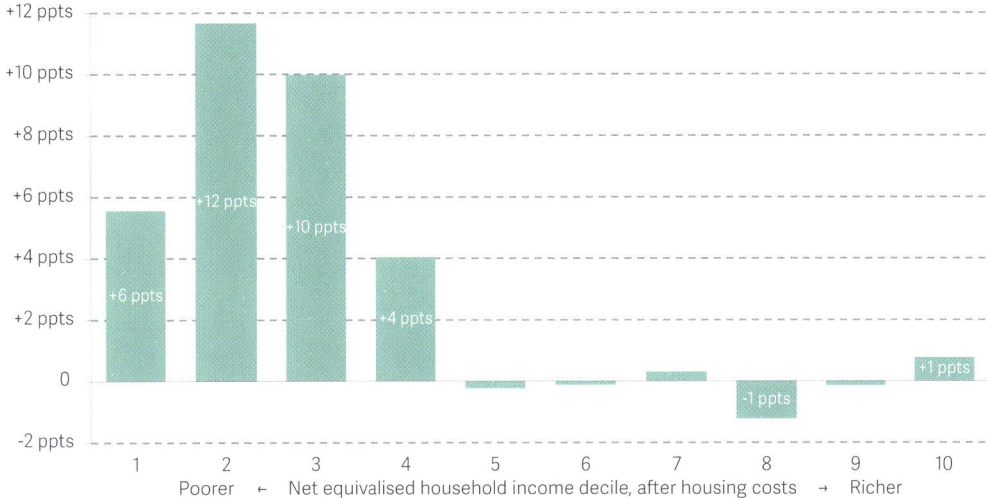

Source: Analysis of DWP, Households Below Average Income; DWP, Family Resources Survey.

The fact that Britain's flexible labour market has been effective at raising employment levels during the 2010s, with big income gains for poorer families, must not be forgotten or taken for granted. Indeed, the task is to repeat it, albeit without rerunning the income squeeze that left some – in particular women in couples – scrambling to work more to compensate.[6] In the context of stronger economic growth, targeted labour market policies focused on three groups – older workers, mothers with young children and the growing number of people who are sick or disabled – offer a plausible path to continuing employment growth, albeit at a slower rate than seen over the past decade.

This confidence in part reflects various underlying trends and established policy commitments. For example, consider older workers. The State Pension age is set to rise to (at least) 67 by 2028, increasing the expectation and need for many in their mid-60s to work for longer. Meanwhile, the fraction of 50-something homeowners who own outright – a predictor of early retirement – has fallen by

---

6   T Bell & L Gardiner, *Feel poor, work more: Explaining the UK's record employment*, Resolution Foundation, November 2019.

over 2 percentage points in the past decade. And as the long expansion of higher education steadily makes itself felt up the age distribution, we can expect a rising proportion of older graduates to increase overall participation.[7]

But additional policies will be needed to bolster these trends.[8] While it has been popular to focus on increases to the State Pension age, which affect the retirement prospects of those on lower incomes the most, reforms to the private pensions regime could nudge better-off groups into working longer. In particular, we recommend: loosening the rules of some final-salary-type pensions, which punish those who re-enter work for a spell; raising the age (set to rise from 55, but only to 57 in 2028) at which private pensions can be enjoyed with full tax perks; and lowering the cap on tax-free lump sums, which can encourage early retirement.

To boost the participation of parents, particularly mothers, we suggest a three-pronged approach.[9] Over the short term, there is a need to refine childcare support for lower-income households.[10] Over the medium term, as commitments to extend the availability of 'free hours' of childcare to children as young as nine months become a reality,[11] the goal should be to move to a universal childcare model with government support funding childcare provision directly.[12] This would disentangle support from Universal Credit, improve work incentives and simplify a complex system. Looking beyond childcare, a separate 'work allowance' in Universal Credit for second earners in couples should be introduced, allowing them to take a first step into work without large reductions in benefit entitlement. At present, second earners in couples (who we know are more sensitive to financial work incentives) have a much lower incentive to enter employment than the first earner.

---

7   L Murphy & G Thwaites, Post-pandemic participation: Exploring labour force participation in the UK, from the Covid-19 pandemic to the decade ahead, Resolution Foundation, February 2023.

8   Full details of the following recommendations on boosting workforce participation can be found in: L Murphy & G Thwaites, Post-pandemic participation: Exploring labour force participation in the UK, from the Covid-19 pandemic to the decade ahead, Resolution Foundation, February 2023.

9   There is evidence that having children creates long-lasting gender gaps in earnings by harming women's career prospects (but not men's). For example, see: H Kleven, C Landais & J E Sogaard, Children and Gender Inequality: Evidence from Denmark, NBER Working Paper 24219, September 2018.

10 The complexity of support on offer is itself a barrier to some entering work. For example, low-income families have to choose between claiming childcare support within Universal Credit or via tax-free childcare, but it is often impossible to know which would be most financially beneficial, while within Universal Credit, childcare support is administratively confusing on a month-to-month basis.

11 Department for Education, Budget 2023: Everything you need to know about childcare support, March 2023.

12 The exact approach to doing so is beyond the scope of the Economy 2030 Inquiry.

"By the time we were paying for childcare...I was earning about 50 pence an hour. And you just think, it's not worth it."

Participant, Sunderland focus group

Perhaps the most pressing drag on employment today is the worrying ill-health of parts of the workforce, with some alarming trends in reported long-term sickness and disability, particularly since the pandemic.[13] The most important priority is to support the underlying health of the British population, but within the sphere of economic policy the fundamental challenge here is to prevent people with health conditions from having to leave work in the first place. Improving people's attachment to work will be more effective than encouraging people to return to work after a long period of worklessness; people out of work due to long-term sickness or disability are four times as likely to re-enter work after a few months than they are after a break of over two years. Building on the success of maternity policy, there should be a new 'right to return' period, during which employers must keep jobs open for people who are away from work due to ill-health or disability.

In sum, even after the long years of jobs growth, there are still large parts of the population for whom barriers to work drag employment rates down. There is no reason that why smart policies cannot clear those barriers. By deploying them and allowing for underlying demographic trends, our expectation – which we will spell out in our projections in Chapter 9 – is that it would be realistic for the employment rate to continue to rise, though at half the rate of the 2010s.

Raising the wage floor

The second major success of the last decade is raising the pay floor. The UK's minimum wage has been gradually transformed from a comparatively modest outlawing of the very lowest pay rates on introduction (it was worth just 46 per cent of median pay in 1999) to a far more ambitious policy driving up pay for the UK's lowest earners (it is set to stand at 66 per cent of median pay by spring 2024). This has been achieved without adverse employment effects becoming apparent.[14]

Figure 44 sets out the change that the minimum wage has brought to the pattern of pay rises in Britain. In the two decades running up to the introduction of the wage floor, pay growth was far stronger for higher than middle or lower earners. But, in the two decades since, that pattern has been entirely reversed, with pay

---

13 L Murphy & G Thwaites, Post-pandemic participation: Exploring labour force participation in the UK, from the Covid-19 pandemic to the decade ahead, Resolution Foundation, February 2023.

14 Low Pay Commission, Low Pay Commission Report 2022, January 2023.

growth consistently strongest for lower earners, especially since big increases in the rate were instigated under the so-called National Living Wage from 2015.[15]

Figure 44: The minimum wage changed the pattern of wage growth in favour of low earners

Annualised growth in real hourly pay across the distribution in selected periods: GB

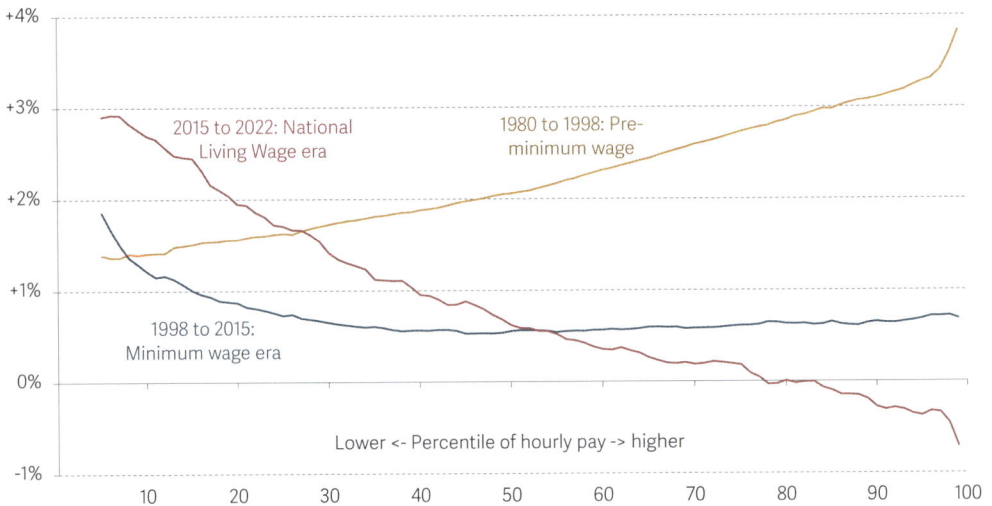

Notes: Pay is gross hourly pay, adjusted for CPI inflation.
Source: Analysis of ONS, Annual Survey of Hours and Earnings and New Earnings Survey Panel Dataset.

The fast-rising wage floor has closed wage gaps between places, and particularly benefitted younger workers and women.[16] In 1997, women were more than twice as likely to be low-paid as men. Twenty five years on, the gender low pay gap had narrowed, with women being just 1.4 times as likely to be low-paid as men in 2022 (although of course there is further to go to reach parity).[17]

There is a strong case for building on this success and aiming higher. Can this be done without destroying a significant number of jobs? This is reasonable question – we shouldn't assume that past success can be carried on indefinitely – but based on the evidence to date it is reasonable to aim to continue with the current pace

15 Detailed analysis, and our full proposals on the minimum wage, are in: N Cominetti et al., Low Pay Britain 2023: Improving low-paid work through higher minimum standards, Resolution Foundation, April 2023.

16 S Clarke, Mapping gaps: Geographic inequality in productivity and living standards, Resolution Foundation, July 2019.

17 N Cominetti et al., Low Pay Britain 2022: Low pay and insecurity in the UK labour market, Resolution Foundation, May 2022; N Cominetti et al., Low Pay Britain 2023: Improving low-paid work through higher minimum standards, Resolution Foundation, April 2023.

of increases in the years ahead. This would mean setting a new ambition for the minimum wage to reach 73 per cent of median pay (£14 on current forecasts) by 2029. Achieving this would give the UK one of the highest minimum wages in the world.

> [What would a better deal look like?] "A realistic minimum wage [that reflects the cost of living]."
>
> Participant, Sunderland focus group

The upward climb of the wage floor above 70 per cent of typical wages is inevitably riskier than previous increases from a far lower base, so we need the Low Pay Commission to remain vigilant to the danger of significant employment effects. And there are real trade-offs of raising wages. Higher prices are a likely result in sectors such as hospitality, retail and care, a subject that we return to in Chapter 8. But these are not the only dangers. Bigger in some ways is the risk that celebrating the success of the minimum wage blinds us to the total lack of progress in driving wider improvements to the world of work. A good work agenda must be more than a one-trick pony.

It is time for a good work agenda to go beyond the minimum wage

A warning of the dangers of focusing on just one problem – low hourly pay – rather than on job quality in the round comes if we look at what has happened to job satisfaction for the lowest earners. Exactly as the minimum wage has ramped up this century, their job satisfaction has, as Figure 45 sets out, fallen, even as it has remained broadly flat overall.[18] The job is very much not done on providing good work when insecurity affects a large swathe of Britain's workforce.[19] A tight labour market provides a helpful tailwind but, as recent experience shows, cannot be relied upon to drive up standards sufficiently.[20]

---

18 K Shah & D Tomlinson, Work experiences: Changes in the subjective experience of work, Resolution Foundation, May 2021. Similar results hold when using hourly earnings, although the decline for the lowest quartile is smaller in magnitude.

19 Unless otherwise stated below, evidence on the challenges faced by workers or proposals for change can be found in: N Cominetti et al., Low Pay Britain 2023: Improving low-paid work through higher minimum standards, Resolution Foundation, April 2023.

20 Periods of record labour market tightness have been accompanied by record levels of some forms of insecure work. See, for example: S Clarke & N Cominetti, Setting the record straight: How record employment has changed the UK, Resolution Foundation, January 2019.

Figure 45: Job satisfaction has fallen among low earners

Proportion of employees who are "mostly" or "completely" satisfied with their present job overall, for all employees and employees in the bottom monthly earnings quartile: GB/UK

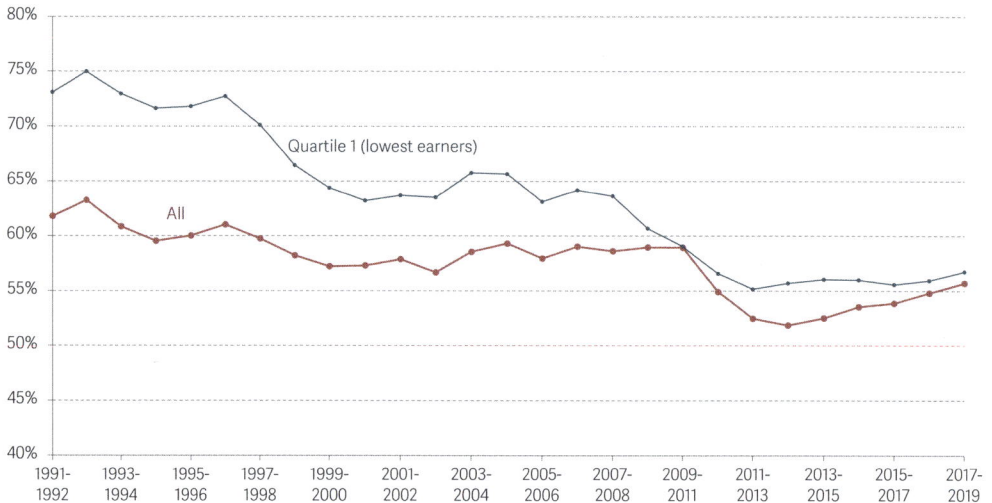

Notes: Combines responses from 18 waves of the British Household Panel Survey prior to 2009 with responses from 10 waves of the UK Household Longitudinal Study from 2009 onwards. Results are averaged over two years/waves. Survey covers Great Britain from 1991-2000, and the UK from 2001 onwards.
Source: Analysis of British Household Panel Survey; UK Household Longitudinal Study (Understanding Society).

In addition to low hourly pay, insecurity over working hours is a marked feature of too many jobs in Britain. There are forms of hiring – zero hours contracts being just one example – which leave people with almost no certainty over what money they have coming in or when they will be expected to work: half of shift workers in Britain receive less than a week's notice of their working schedules.[21]

This is just one example of the world of work for lower earners not offering the security, flexibility or control that higher earners take for granted: low earners are four times as likely as high earners to experience volatility in their hours or pay, or to be working fewer hours than they would like. This is not what good work looks like. So workers should have a new right to a contract enshrining minimum hours that reflect their usual work pattern, and employers should be required to provide two weeks' advance notice of shifts, with compensation for any late changes.

21 J Richardson, The insecurity complex: Low paid workers and the growth of insecure work, Living Wage Foundation, July 2021.

Wider measures to improve security for workers should include a reduction from two years to one in the service required to enjoy protections against unfair dismissal (as was the case until 2011).

Other forms of insecurity relate to whether you know that you will have breathing space if for some reason, most obviously sickness, you cannot work for a spell. Four-in-five of those earning over £60,000 per year would be paid in full if they were too sick to work for a week. That compares to one-in-five of those earning under £20,000, who are much more likely to be reliant on the UK's meagre Statutory Sick Pay (SSP) and receive just £44 compensation for a week's lost earnings due to sickness. The result is that illness is bad for the financial, as well as physical, health of low-paid workers in a way that most higher earners never experience.

Improving the level of SSP is best achieved by replacing today's low flat rate with a new system paying 65 per cent of usual earnings (in line with typical levels seen across the OECD) and reducing the number of 'waiting days' in which no sick pay is due from three to one. Extending sick pay to the lowest earners by removing the wage floor for entitlement (currently £123 per week) would protect the 1.6 million workers ineligible for any Statutory Sick Pay at all.

Such problems are most acute among the low paid, but it would be wrong to think of poor job quality as something that only blights the lives of the least-well-off Britons. Indeed, Britain's lowest-paid workers are themselves spread out fairly evenly among the bottom two-thirds of households when we look at total incomes. Making jobs better is a true national challenge.[22]

That said, there are imbalances in the extent to which different demographic groups bear the brunt of 'bad' jobs. There are large differences between ethnic groups: 22 per cent of Black workers report being on an insecure contract or experiencing volatile pay, against 13 per cent of White workers. Disability also matters: workers with a disability are roughly 20 per cent more likely than workers without a disability to express low job satisfaction, report a lack of autonomy at work, or to have an insecure job with volatile pay.[23]

Given our goal of pushing against Britain's stubbornly high income inequality, it is also worth highlighting an important feedback loop between the low quality of many jobs and the low number of hours often worked in them. In our focus groups,

22 N Cominetti et al., Low Pay Britain 2022: Low pay and insecurity in the UK labour market, Resolution Foundation, May 2022.
23 N Cominetti et al, Low Pay Britain 2023: Improving low-paid work through higher minimum standards, Resolution Foundation, April 2023.

participants told us that low-paid work often feels stressful and unfulfilling, with some putting in as few hours as they needed to cover their (often deliberately reduced) outgoings as a result.[24] To quote one young woman working part time:

> "If I had a job that I actually liked going to, then I'd increase my hours straight away."

Participant, Coventry focus group

This worker is far from alone in drawing a connection between job quality and the hours that she was prepared to put in. Low-paid workers as a whole now work considerably shorter hours than higher earners; for men at least, this represents a break from the historical pattern. Back in 1979, it was low-skilled, low-paid men who worked the longest hours – but by 2009 this pattern had flipped, with the most-educated men actually working longer. It seems more than plausible that this may be related to the declining experience of work at the bottom of the wage scale.[25]

This matters for overall inequality. While the minimum wage has made a meaningful dent in hourly wage inequality, the pay gap continues to be greatly magnified in the distribution of weekly earnings. In 2019, the ratio of earnings between the top (90th percentile) and bottom (10th percentile) earnings brackets was 3.4 on hourly wages but 6.3 on weekly earnings. Bad jobs, then, beget unequal hours – locking in unequal incomes.[26]

Rights are only meaningful if they are enforced

After raising the floor on standards, we also need to enforce it.[27] As things stand, non-compliance with labour market law is widespread: in 2022, 334,000 employees received less than the minimum wage they were entitled to;[28] some 900,000 workers reported they have no paid holiday despite this being a 'day one' entitlement; and a staggering 1.8 million workers said they do not get a payslip, a

---

24 L Murphy, Constrained choices: Understanding the prevalence of part-time work among low-paid workers in the UK, Resolution Foundation, November 2022.

25 L Murphy, Constrained choices: Understanding the prevalence of part-time work among low-paid workers in the UK, Resolution Foundation, November 2022.

26 N Cominetti et al., Low Pay Britain 2023: Improving low-paid work through higher minimum standards, Resolution Foundation, April 2023.

27 Unless otherwise indicated, the facts cited in the text below come from: L Judge & H Slaughter, Enforce for good: Effectively enforcing labour market rights in the 2020s and beyond, Resolution Foundation, April 2023, which also contains full details on our proposals for improving the labour market enforcement system.

28 Low Pay Commission, Compliance and enforcement of the National Minimum Wage, September 2023.

legal right that lets people check their pay is correct. All these problems are worse at the bottom end of the labour market: receiving no paid holiday is six times more common among the lowest than the highest paid. Worse, an increasing number of the lowest earners are largely outside employment protections: the share of the lowest earners who are self-employed rose from 15 to 23 per cent in the two decades pre-pandemic.[29]

These worrying signs reflect a labour market enforcement regime that is not fit for purpose. We have a sprawling patchwork of enforcement agencies – currently spread across six core bodies plus local councils, and overseen by seven government departments – leaving workers confused about where to turn. There are too many bodies, but they have too few boots on the ground and far too weak powers to fine unscrupulous employers in a way that would act as a real deterrent. The UK has just 0.29 labour market inspectors per 10,000 workers, less than a third of the 1 per 10,000 benchmark set by the International Labour Organisation. This puts the onus on workers to protect their own rights by bringing cases to employment tribunals, something low-paid workers – the very group most at risk of having their rights breached – are the least likely to do.

We need a new approach, because failing to enforce labour market rights undermines living standards by leaving workers short-changed, but also undermines productivity by allowing low-margin firms to survive just by exploiting an unlawful edge over their compliant peers.

The starting point must be a new Single Enforcement Body,[30] properly resourced and able to impose penalties that meaningfully deter non-compliance: a flagrant breach of an employment right should be liable for a penalty worth four times the arrears owed to the worker, bringing the UK more into line with international best practice. To ensure the pressure is not just on the most vulnerable workers to raise issues, worker and business bodies should be able to make a 'super-complaint' to flag systemic problems.[31] But we should also recognise that many cases, including for discrimination, will continue to be routed through employment tribunals, which themselves need greater enforcement powers. Extraordinarily, as things stand, an estimated 51 per cent of employment tribunal awards are not paid out.

---

29 G Giupponi & S Machin, Labour market inequality, IFS Deaton Review of Inequalities, March 2022.

30 Such a body was proposed in the 2019 Conservative Manifesto.

31 This should be modelled on the Competition and Markets Authority (CMA) which allows 'super-complaints' to protect consumer rights.

In the world of work, power and institutions matter

Designating and enforcing specific minimum entitlements is crucial, but our quest for good work cannot end there. Across the board, we should seek to foster conditions that make it more likely that labour standards surpass the bare legal minimum.

This means grappling with the subtler, but pervasive, question of power in the labour market.[32] The latest evidence suggests that wages could be between 15 and 25 per cent lower than they would be in a competitive labour market where employers did not enjoy their current imbalance of power over workers.[33] These estimates are imprecise – a wage markdown of 15 per cent would suggest an average worker today is losing out on over £100 a week[34] – but the conclusion from them is not: power matters.

The challenges a lack of worker power poses cannot all be simply addressed with national minimum standards. Many are not amenable to one-size-fits-all resolutions, with both problems and the circumstances that constrain the solutions varying greatly across workplaces and sectors. Instead, the direct experience and knowledge of workers and managers needs to be brought to bear, through structured dialogue in effective labour market institutions – some tried and tested, some new and experimental.[35]

Trade unions remain important, representing over 6 million workers, participating in national organisations and shaping local workplaces. But over the past four decades, union membership has fallen dramatically, from 52 per cent in 1980 to 22 per cent in 2022. As unions have declined, employers and managers have

---

32 In the labour market, firms' profits and workers' wages partly reflect power differences in bargaining between employers and workers.

33 Some indirect estimates based upon how quickly workers leave firms with low wages in the US – a labour market with a lower (and falling) labour share, a lower minimum wage, and less collective bargaining than the UK – suggest that wages could be between 15 and 25 per cent lower than they would be otherwise because of employer power over workers. See: M Langella & A Manning, Marshall Lecture 2020: The Measure of Monopsony, Journal of the European Economic Association 19(6), December 2021. Recent evidence from the UK focusing on a large multi-establishment corporation suggests a similar markdown of around 18 per cent. See: N Datta, The measure of monopsony: the labour supply elasticity to the firm and its constituents, CEP Discussion Paper No. 1930, July 2023.

34 This is updated from: U Altunbuken et al., Power plays: The balance of employer and worker power in the UK labour market, Resolution Foundation, July 2022. Average weekly pay (excluding bonuses and arrears) was £617 in July 2023. If employers are marking down pay by 15 per cent, average weekly earnings would be £726 in the absence of employer power over workers – that is, average wages would be £109 a week higher. Source: Office for National Statistics, AWE: Whole Economy Level (£): Seasonally Adjusted Regular Pay Excluding Arrears, September 2023.

35 Our full analysis and proposals on labour market institutions can be found in: C McCurdy, H Slaughter & G Kelly, Putting good work on the table: Reforming labour market institutions to improve pay and conditions, Resolution Foundation, September 2023.

increasingly assumed a dominant role in determining work conditions: in non-unionised private sector workplaces, there has been near-universal adoption of unilateral wage-setting by management.[36]

From the 1980s onwards, aggregate union decline was compounded by restrictive legislation and subtler policy changes. The professed goal was to modernise the industrial relations system and level the playing field between employers and unions. But that is not where we have ended up. Instead, the pitch is slanted against employees seeking to organise with, for example, requirements to demonstrate a very high level of support prior to union recognition that are not matched in other areas of democratic life. And the imposition of antiquated paper-based balloting procedures is nothing short of bizarre this far into the 21st century.

Such details matter more than might be imagined. It is widely understood that structural changes like deindustrialisation and the drift towards self-employment played a big part in the decline of trade unions, but this misses out on exactly how the process unfolded. In particular, the big change has not been 'de-recognition' in established unionised workplaces, but rather a failure to organise in newer firms.[37] This suggests it might be useful to focus on how unions get their crucial 'first foot in the door'.

With all this in mind, we recommend three reforms to provide a genuinely level playing field. To ensure workers understand their options, unions should be given a right to enter workplaces to raise awareness among employees. Second, union-recognition requirements under the Employment Relations Act 1999 should be adjusted, bringing them more in line with other aspects of democratic life: instead of the current requirement that 40 per cent of workers must actively vote in favour of recognition, we recommend a simple majority vote with a turnout threshold (also of 40 per cent). And finally, voting in such ballots should be more inclusive, with online voting available rather than banned.

---

36 U Altunbuken et al., Power plays: The balance of employer and worker power in the UK labour market, Resolution Foundation, July 2022.

37 Comparing establishments with 25+ employees created before and after 1980 reveals that, by 2011, there was a huge, 30-percentage-point gap in unionisation between the pre- and post-1980 vintage. U Altunbuken et al., Power plays: The balance of employer and worker power in the UK labour market, Resolution Foundation, July 2022.

Such modernising moves would help unions gain a footing in newer establishments, but changes are likely to be modest in scale and, crucially, unlikely to be large in those parts of the economy where low pay and poor conditions are most rife (even when unions were a bigger part of British economic life, they did not have large memberships in the lowest-paying industries).[38]

Addressing deep-rooted challenges in some sectors requires institutional innovation

Some of the gravest problems in the world of work are industry-specific. Domiciliary care workers, for instance, often don't get paid for the time they spend travelling between clients.[39] Meanwhile, participatory research has highlighted the high risk of harassment faced by cleaners working on the premises of other businesses.[40]

These are systematic yet sector-specific problems that we cannot ignore if we are serious about the quality of working life across Britain. National employment law is too blunt a tool to address all of them, and the fact that these issues have persisted through historically high rates of employment should dispel any illusion that a tight labour market alone will be the cure. Instead, now is the time for some well-calibrated institutional innovation.

Other relatively liberal labour markets around the world have either long had sectoral bodies (e.g. Ireland and Australia) or have more recently attempted to develop them (e.g. New Zealand). We should learn from these approaches, but also recognise that some problems are particular to us – any new institutions need to be rooted in the UK's own contemporary challenges and regulatory approach, rather than imported wholesale from abroad.

We propose 'Good Work Agreements' (GWAs) in problem sectors: a framework to bring together workers and employers to collaboratively solve problems about the quality of work in specific pockets of the economy, setting minimum standards or ways of working that would have to be adopted sector-wide. Box 21 explains how they would work.

---

38 C McCurdy, H Slaughter & G Kelly, Putting good work on the table: Reforming labour market institutions to improve pay and conditions, Resolution Foundation, September 2023.

39 N Cominetti, Who cares? The experience of social care workers, and the enforcement of employment rights in the sector, Resolution Foundation, January 2023.

40 M Åhlberg, E Paesani & L Granada, "If I Could Change Anything About My Work…" Participatory Research With Cleaners In The UK, Focus on Labour Exploitation, January 2021.

Box 21: Good Work Agreements

Our proposals for Good Work Agreements (GWAs) – collaborations between workers and employers that seek to resolve sector-specific problems – are intentionally pragmatic. But they nonetheless embody a serious ambition to raise standards in the workplace.[41]

First, we propose that worker or employer representatives could apply for the government to set up a GWA in sectors with material problems with labour standards. We envisage they would have a special focus on four areas: training and progression; sector-specific health and safety issues; pay (where there is justification for a floor above the National Living Wage); and wider terms and conditions, including contractual arrangements such as shift patterns and provision of basic materials.

The right place to start is in social care, where the Government should immediately set up a trailblazer GWA to enhance protections for the 1.7 million workers. For a predominantly female workforce (77 per cent), this would address urgent issues such as poor pay – likely unlawfully low for domiciliary care workers, once travel time is factored in – inadequate training, and unsafe conditions, all of which have fed an acute shortage of workers and poor standards for the people who rely on them.[42] GWAs in the warehousing and cleaning sectors are the obvious next steps, delivering higher standards for 200,000 and 500,000 workers respectively.

Because the initiative for and the leadership of GWAs would come from worker and employer representatives within the relevant sector itself, they should provide a natural forum to resolve disagreements. But an independent representative will be required to chair the negotiations and, if need be, break through deadlocks. The Government will also need to sign-off on the agreements that emerge at the end of the bargaining process, since there may be wider

---

41 Our full proposals on Good Work Agreements can be found in: C McCurdy, H Slaughter & G Kelly, Putting good work on the table: Reforming labour market institutions to improve pay and conditions, Resolution Foundation, September 2023.

42 In addition, the social care workforce is disproportionately from Black and other minority ethnic backgrounds – the share of social care workers who are Black is 2.5 times that of the workforce as a whole. So addressing poor working conditions in this sector would begin to push back against the entrenched inequalities in job quality mentioned earlier in this chapter.

public-interest and potential public-spending considerations. Once implemented, GWAs should be enforced in the same way as other labour market rights and, as always with innovative reforms, it will be vital to learn from experience as they are steadily rolled out.

So a higher minimum wage and employment; a raised and reinforced floor on workplace standards; new sectoral institutions to govern standards across the most problematic sectors – this is what a good work agenda looks like. It would be reinforced by some of the reforms proposed in earlier chapters. For example, adding representative workers to company boards with the principal aim of boosting investment (as set out in Chapter 5) would plausibly also boost corporate concern with job quality.[43]

The combined impact of this good work agenda should help ensure that resumed pay growth, not to mention improved job quality, will disproportionately flow to those at the lower end of the jobs market. The same also needs to be true for improvements to the skills of the British workforce.

Better jobs need better skills

The last chapter made the 'growth' argument for investing in human capital, setting out the major skills upgrade that Britain needs, with more workers attaining higher-level qualifications. But there is an equally strong 'fairness' argument to make. Raising the prospects of millions of workers who are poorly served by our existing education and training system will not only enable them to earn more, progress further in their careers and lead more fulfilling lives – it will affect the distribution of reward across society.

The UK performs relatively well when it comes to school attainment at age 16 and has, despite challenges, a world-class university system. But provision for those not following an academic route is patchy at best, and a disgrace at worst: under-funding is endemic, 'second chances' are scant and (as shown in Chapter 5) employer training is in steady decline. It is a national scandal that almost a third of the UK's young people are still not undertaking any education by age 18 – compared to just one-in-five in France and Germany, as Figure 46 shows. And too often, these young people are leaving the education system with a low level

---

43 A study from Finland found small positive effects of worker representation on some measures of job quality (as well as improved firm survival and productivity). See: J Harju, S Jäger & B Schoefer, Voice at work, NBER Working Paper 28522, March 2021.

of basic skills: we are the only OECD country where the literacy and numeracy of 16-24-year-olds is no higher than that of 55-65-year-olds, an alarming sign of generation-on-generation progress grinding to a halt.[44]

Figure 46: Britain has a drop-out problem

Proportion of young people in full-time or part-time education, by age and country: UK, France and Germany, 2019

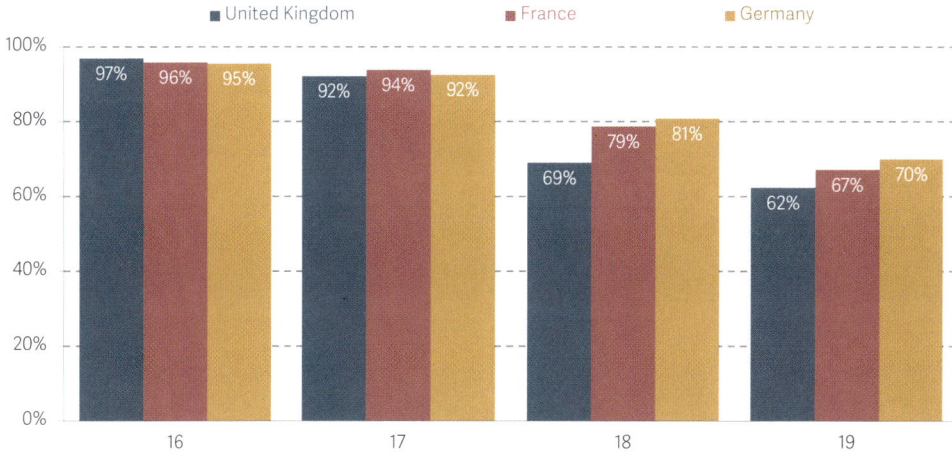

Source: Analysis of OECD Indicators, Education at a Glance.

Our poor post-16 performance for those not on the university track is a longstanding problem that has been compounded by recent deep cuts to spending on education and training.[45] For under-18s, there has been a real cut in further education (FE) funding per student of 12 per cent since 2012, so that it is now lower than in secondary schools and only just higher than in primary schools.[46] Things are at least as bad for those aged 18 and over taking part in FE or apprenticeships, where total funding is capped and has been severely reduced in the past decade (by 22 per cent in real terms).

44 OECD, Skills Matter: Additional Results from the Survey of Adult Skills, November 2019.

45 Our analysis of, and recommendations for, the further education and apprenticeship systems can be found in: R Layard, S McNally & G Ventura, Applying the Robbins Principle to Further Education and Apprenticeships, Resolution Foundation, October 2023.

46 The funding of sixth forms has fallen by 28 per cent between 2010-11 and 2019-20. See: E Drayton et al., Annual report on education spending in England: 2022, Institute for Fiscal Studies, August 2022.

Young people have also been increasingly overlooked in apprenticeship provision, which has been skewed towards older workers, despite the higher returns for young workers. As Figure 47 shows, in the decade since 2011/12, apprenticeship starts for under-19s have fallen 40 per cent while those for 19-24-year-olds have fallen 34 per cent.[47]

Figure 47: Trading down: the slide in youth apprenticeships

Annual number of apprenticeships starts, by age group: England

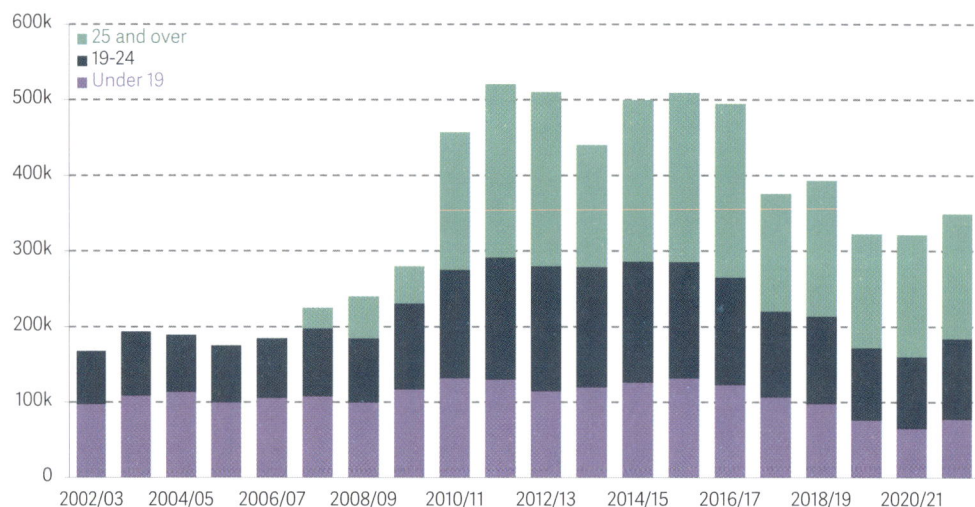

Source: Analysis of DfE, Apprenticeships and Traineeships data.

The UK's failure in this area translates into a big hit to wages for the lowest-skilled workers in the UK, who are paid far less relative to those with tertiary-level qualifications (such as degrees) than is the case in peer countries. Those whose highest qualification is a GCSE equivalent or below take home just two-fifths (42 per cent) of the earnings of their more-qualified peers – whereas in France and Germany they earn three-fifths of their tertiary-educated counterparts (62 per cent and 60 per cent respectively).[48] We explore the direct returns for workers who undertake further education and training in more detail in Box 22.

47 One concerning explanation for this is that the increase in older workers doing apprenticeships reflects existing employees doing continuous professional development that would previously have been funded directly by employers. See: R Layard, S McNally & G Ventura, Applying the Robbins Principle to Further Education and Apprenticeships, Resolution Foundation, October 2023.

48 OECD, Education at a Glance, September 2019.

Box 22: The large rewards of further education and training

The logical flipside of big wage penalties for the lowest-skilled British workers is high pay premiums for those who do progress in education and training. Level 3 qualifications (such as BTECs and NVQ 3s) exert strong earnings effects, ranging between 22 per cent to 32 per cent. Level 3 apprenticeships likewise achieve solid wage returns, especially for younger adults (16 per cent for those aged 18-24, though this drops to 6 per cent for those aged 25 and above).[49] There are also positive, albeit smaller, returns to Level 2 qualifications. So expanding the relevant traineeships and pre-apprenticeship courses is worthwhile in itself – as well as creating a vital ladder for young people to reach education and training at Level 3 and above.[50]

All told, then, instead of being grounds for despair, the UK's disappointing record on FE and training might usefully be regarded as evidence of the major rewards to be gained from putting things right.

Wasting the nation's talent in this way is iniquitous and keeps up high wage inequality across the generations. A sustained drive guided by clear priorities is needed to put this right. The centrepiece of reform should be a new 'apprentice guarantee', with the Government committing to fund sufficient apprenticeship places for all qualified young people. To this end, two-thirds of the revenue from the Apprenticeship Levy should be ring-fenced for workers aged under-25, to make clear that its primary role is to support the young. On its own, this would allow for an additional 63,000 apprenticeship starts per year – an increase of over a third on current levels.[51] The cap on the number of publicly supported apprenticeships in small businesses (which means only 41 per cent of apprentices are in firms with fewer than 250 workers, compared with 61 per cent of all employees) should

---

49 Taking part in further education or an apprenticeship at Level 3 also provides positive employment effects of between 3 and 4 percentage points.

50 See, for example: Department for Business, Innovation and Skills, Intermediate and low level vocational qualifications: economic returns, September 2011.

51 Re-directing funds in this way would should facilitate this growth at little or no extra overall cost, since these apprenticeships tend to be at lower levels than the higher-level apprenticeships that are typically undertaken by older groups, and so are cheaper to deliver.

be removed. Merely returning numbers in these firms to where they were in the mid-2010s would represent a doubling of places – an extra 124,000 apprenticeship starts a year, at an upfront cost of £1.5 billion.

More broadly, the role of FE institutions in increasing the quantity of, and reducing the inequality in, educational provision needs to be recognised. The Lifetime Skills Guarantee now makes further education free up to Level 3, but this does not guarantee that enough places will be there for those who want them because funding of further education for those aged over 18 is also capped.[52] This contrasts with the demand-led approach in higher education, where funding largely flows automatically with each student being taught. Over time, further education beyond 18 should move to a demand-led model, engendering a more dynamic system – with providers knowing they would be rewarded for attracting students to an approved course.[53]

To help fund the upfront costs of these proposals (where revenue from the Apprenticeship Levy would not be sufficient), alternative funding models could be considered. For example, degree apprenticeship funding could move to a fee-and-loan-based model, similar to the one already in place for university education.[54]

Improving prospects for young people poorly served by current options for education and training is a massive undertaking. It is also an inherently long-term investment. But get it right and the rewards should be huge, allowing Britain to steadily improve the skill level of – and close the skills gaps among – the rising generations moving into the labour market. Higher earnings and more fulfilling careers would result. But, as with all earnings growth, a large chunk of that success risks being eaten up by housing costs unless the biggest cost facing households is also front and centre in a new economic strategy.

The homes front

It is impossible to ignore the signs of acute pressure within the nation's housing system today. As Figure 48 shows, the share of income that families dedicate to their housing costs has trended upwards over the last 40 years: in 1980, the

---

52 Under the Lifetime Skills Guarantee, adults aged 19 and over who do not already have a Level 3 qualification (A level of equivalent) are able to study a full Level 3 qualification for free. See: HM Government, Major expansion of post-18 education and training to level up and prepare workers for post-COVID economy, September 2020.

53 The trade-offs in terms of costs here are real. Given the scale of need it is likely that moving to a demand-led approach would cost a further £1.5 billion.

54 For further discussion, see: D Willetts, How higher education can boost people-powered growth, Resolution Foundation, October 2023.

average family spent 9 per cent of their income on housing costs; in 2021 that figure stood at 17 per cent.

But as always, the average conceals as much as it reveals. Today, the poorest families spend around 34 per cent of their income on housing costs – twice as high as the 17 per cent they spent in 1980. In contrast, the highest-income families have seen this ratio rise much more modestly, from 5 per cent in 1980 to around 8 per cent in 2021. And other warning lights are flashing to suggest rising housing stress among vulnerable families: in early 2023, for example, there were over 100,000 households in temporary accommodation in England, the highest number on record, including nearly 65,000 households with children.[55]

Figure 48: Rising housing costs have hammered poorer families' living standards over time

Housing cost to income ratio among working-age family units, gross of housing benefit, by income quintile: GB / UK

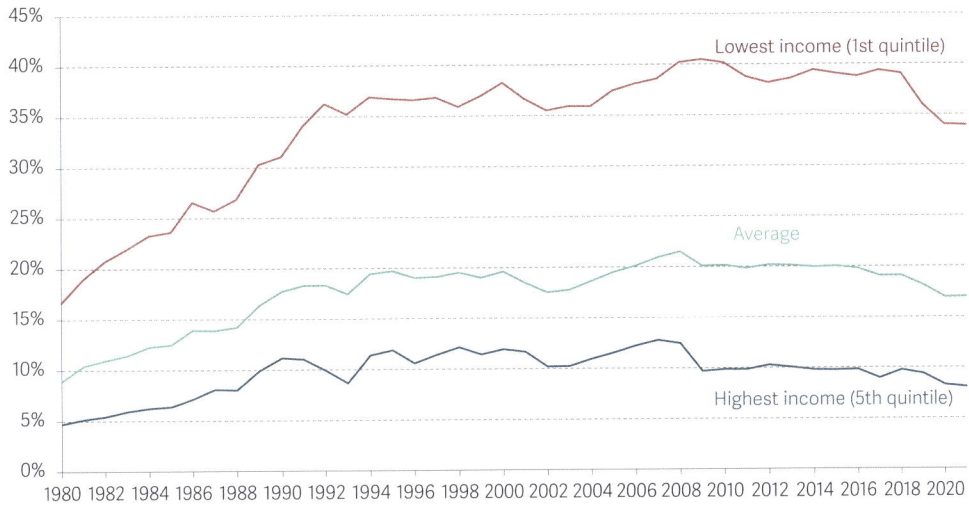

Notes: Family units are defined as any single adults or couples and their dependent children. Working-age family units are defined as those where the head of the family unit is less than 60 years old. Housing costs are calculated gross of housing benefit such that housing benefit is included in both income and housing costs. Income and housing costs are assumed to be shared equally between family units within each household. Data is for Great Britain only between 1994 and 2001. Income quintiles are calculated on a family unit basis.
Source: Analysis of IFS (1980-1993) and DWP (1994-2021), Households Below Average Income.

55 DLUHC, Statutory homelessness live tables, October 2023 update.

The starkly different housing experiences of lower- and higher-income families have been an important upward pressure on the inequality of disposable incomes. Why have experiences diverged so much? Two long-term trends are the root explanation. First, younger lower-income families have increasingly been both locked out of property ownership (because of rising house prices) and unlikely to secure a home in the social-rented sector (the UK's social housing stock is high by international standards, but it has shrunk given the failure to replenish social housing stock that has been sold off). So they fall back on private rentals, where costs are high and quality often low. At the other end of the spectrum, until recently, most higher-income home owners were seeing their housing costs flatline or even fall, thanks to the long period of rock-bottom interest rates (although things have obviously taken a different turn as interest rates have risen recently).[56]

Second, although low interest rates are the single biggest driver of rising house prices over recent decades, the country's failure to build sufficient homes to match growing demand has also pushed up housing costs over time. As illustrated in Figure 49, the number of homes relative to inhabitants in the UK is low compared to most other OECD countries, and has barely risen over the past ten years, in contrast to the increases seen in France and Italy. Moreover, the shortfall of UK housing against UK housing need is even more pronounced for affordable tenure types, with the building of homes for social rent falling from an average of over 40,000 homes per year over the 1990s, to just 8,000 per year over the past decade.[57]

Expanding housing supply needs to be part of any renewed economic strategy, with the 300,000 homes a year target included in the 2019 Conservative Manifesto and more recently adopted by the Labour Party providing a good starting point.[58] Achieving this will require significant reform of a planning system, as noted in Chapter 5, that has for decades frustrated efforts to build at scale. Reform is also needed to ensure that whatever the tenure, the housing offer is a good one. Action to drive up standards in the private rented sector is particularly important given that security and quality of provision is typically lower there.[59]

---

56 Over 54 per cent of those in the top income quintile are home owners according to DLUHC: English Housing Survey 2021-22, December 2022.

57 DLUHC, Table 1000: additional affordable homes provided by type of scheme, England, June 2023 update.

58 Conservative Party, Conservative Party Manifesto 2019, 2019; Labour Party, Keir Starmer's speech at Labour Conference, October 2023.

59 The recent Renters (Reform) Bill is clearly a step in the right direction. See: W Wilson, H Cromarty & C Barton, Renters (Reform) Bill 2022-23, House of Commons Library, October 2023.

Figure 49: The UK lacks houses – and has stopped building

Housing stock per 1,000 inhabitants aged 20+: UK and selected OECD countries, 1990, 2010 and 2020

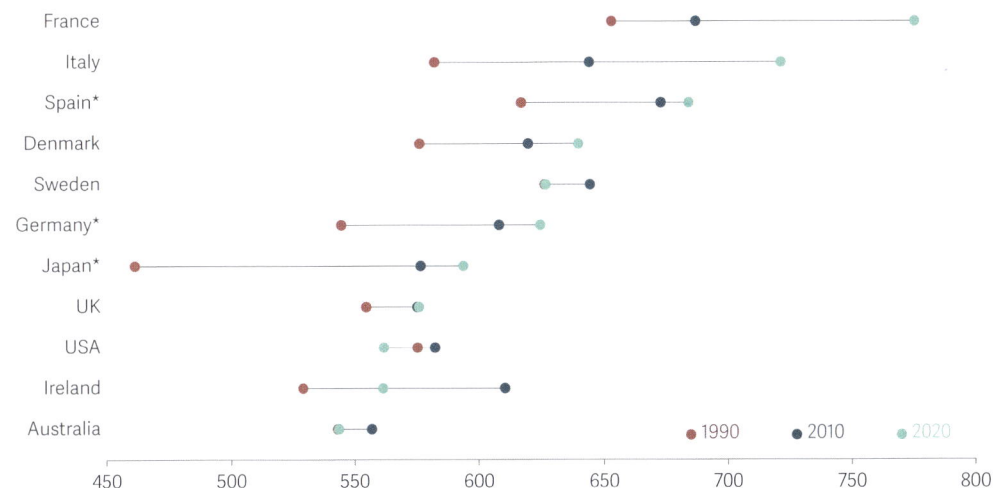

Notes: Countries with asterisks are those for which 2018 is used in place of 2020 due to data availability. Population estimates in 2020 may be affected by the impact of the pandemic.
Source: Analysis of OECD, Total housing stock in OECD and EU countries, selected years; UN, Historical population data.

Any strategy aiming to raise growth rates in the UK needs to grapple with the fact that growth at a national and local level often translates into higher housing costs. To the extent that workers have extra pay, they have more capacity to bid against each other in securing a home if those homes remain in short supply. The link between high growth and high rents is evident, with faster rent rises in higher-productivity parts of England: when a local economy succeeds, rent rises can accelerate. [60] There are obvious consequences for those city-regions that we have – in Chapter 4 – identified as the most plausible engines for restored nationwide prosperity. Building at sufficient scale (at both market and sub-market price points) in burgeoning areas is essential if rising housing costs are not to lock out potential workers who would otherwise move to growing areas, or to impoverish and eventually price out existing poorer residents.

There are also nationwide implications. Assuming Britain as a whole returns to having reasonable growth, then we must soften the consequences of higher

---

60 M Brewer et al., Sharing the benefits: Can Britain secure broadly shared prosperity?, Resolution Foundation, July 2023.

housing costs for many to ensure this translates into rising living standards for all. This is especially true of those who do not benefit from that rising prosperity but who see their housing costs rising in response to it. A key mechanism for doing this is through housing support in the benefit system. Box 23 explains what needs to be done.[61]

Box 23: Housing support in the benefit system

The primary method through which low-income families (whether working or not) are supported with private rents is via the Local Housing Allowance (LHA). This sets the maximum entitlement that families receive through legacy Housing Benefit or the housing element of Universal Credit, taking account of their location and family size.

However, the real value of LHA has been eroded in recent years; today, levels of support are frozen in line with 2019 rents. By early 2023, the system failed to cover the rents of over 900,000 households affected by the LHA through Universal Credit, equivalent to 60 per cent of all such claimants.[62] Looking at the problem another way, only 5 per cent of private rented properties listed on Zoopla today are affordable for Housing Benefit recipients.[63] Poorer people are having to top-up housing support out of low general incomes simply to cover the rent.

Beyond placing an inevitable immediate squeeze on living standards, the LHA freeze excludes ever-more claimants from areas of rising economic prosperity. Restoring an automatic link between housing support and the actual cost of housing is therefore essential both for facilitating mobility and controlling inequality. Restoring LHA to the value of the 30th centile of local rents, then pegging it to changes in those rents, would counteract the regressive tilt of rising housing costs across the income distribution.[64]

---

61 For further details, see: M Brewer et al., Sharing the benefits: Can Britain secure broadly shared prosperity?, Resolution Foundation, July 2023.

62 DWP, Households on Universal Credit, Stat-Xplore, accessed October 2023.

63 T Waters & T Wernham, Housing quality and affordability for lower-income households, Institute for Fiscal Studies, June 2023.

64 M Brewer et al., Sharing the benefits: Can Britain secure broadly shared prosperity?, Resolution Foundation, July 2023.

Even if we make good work more widely available, and control rising housing costs, it will not represent a comprehensive fairness agenda. Ultimately, for the millions of households for whom wages will never represent all of their income, the benefits system has a special role in ensuring the proceeds of growth are fairly shared. And in an era in which the quantity of tax is up, it is ever more important that we pay attention to its quality. It is to these questions about the state's direct role in setting policy to ensure rewards and sacrifices are fairly shared that we next turn.

Chapter Seven

Shared rewards, fair sacrifices

Chapter summary

- Markets, however fair, and jobs, however good, cannot ensure that growth automatically boosts the living standards of the whole population. We have an obligation to pensioners, and the 11 million people of working age for whom earnings make up less than half of their income, very often because of caring responsibilities or disabilities.

- The basic level of benefits in the UK are low. In theory they rise in line with prices but in practice we haven't even managed that: benefit levels have failed to keep pace with prices in 10 of the past 15 years, with wider benefits cuts reducing the incomes of poorest fifth by just under £3,000 a year.

- Any economic strategy that claims to be serious about reducing inequality will need to change tack; social security benefits must grow in line with wages rather than prices. The costs are real, but over half of them can be covered by uprating pensions on the same basis as working age benefits, rather than via the 'triple lock'.

- The state of public services, needs of our ageing population, and the net zero transition mean higher taxes are here to stay. This is why politicians declaring their low-tax 'instincts' have raised taxes to their highest levels since the 1940s; having averaged 33 per cent of GDP in the first two decades of this century, the tax take is now on course to rise by over 4 per cent of GDP (£4,200 per household) by 2027-28.

- Taxes are up, but their quality is not. The burden cannot continue to fall disproportionately on employees. We must tax incomes consistently whatever its source and wealth should take more of the strain.

- Fairness debates need to keep pace with the net zero transition. Road charging for electric vehicles would prevent motoring taxes falling on poorer households yet to switch to EVs. With the disposable income of poorer homeowners averaging £9,100, and the cost of insulating leaky homes over £8,000, major government intervention will be required if the costs of insulating homes and installing heat pumps are to be fairly borne.

Returning the UK economy to robust growth, plus a good work agenda that more fairly shares the rewards through the labour market, would represent significant steps forward. But markets alone cannot ensure the living standards gains from growth are realised for the whole population. This is the job of the social security system, but it is not fulfilling that role today.

Nor are benefits the only way in which the state makes big decisions about how rewards, and sacrifices, are shared. Choices over tax, and how the net zero transition happens, have big impacts on households' living standards. They are fundamental to how fair the UK is, and is perceived to be.

Our social security system is a recipe for rising inequality

As we have argued, while productivity growth is indispensable for rising wages and living standards, it is also an insufficient guarantor of truly shared prosperity. Even in a high-employment society, substantial numbers of people will inevitably not work and earn, either at all, or enough to provide an adequate income. There are 11 million individuals in working-age households where earnings make up less than half of household income, with benefits dominating the remainder. Almost half of these are in working households, while the majority of the other half are in households with someone who is long-term sick or disabled. Less than 1 million are traditionally unemployed. These families are disproportionately poor, with the lowest income fifth of households getting barely more than half of their income (55 per cent) from working, compared to the overwhelming majority (94 per cent) among the richest fifth (Figure 50).[1]

This tells us what growth will not do: when growth drives rising wages but doesn't feed through into other forms of income, there is a real danger that poorer households' living standards will drift away from those of the rest of the population. This growing 'prosperity gap' would be a direct result of the UK's approach to benefit income, which is supposed to have a default of rising in line with prices (generally slower-growing) rather than (generally faster-growing) wages. That is the worrying theory, but even worse is the practice, where benefit levels have failed to keep pace with prices in 10 of the past 15 years,[2] leaving the basic level of benefits at just £85 per week – only 14 per cent of average pay and its lowest level on record.[3]

---

1   M Brewer et al., Sharing the benefits: Can Britain secure broadly shared prosperity?, Resolution Foundation, July 2023.

2   L Judge & L Murphy, Rates of change: The impact of a below-inflation uprating on working-age benefits, Resolution Foundation, October 2023.

3   Weekly average pay was £621 in September 2023, and the weekly standard allowance for UC was £85.

Figure 50: The poorest fifth of households only get half their income from working

Proportion of income by source for non-pensioner households by income quintile: 2019-20, UK

■ Labour income share   ■ Benefit income share

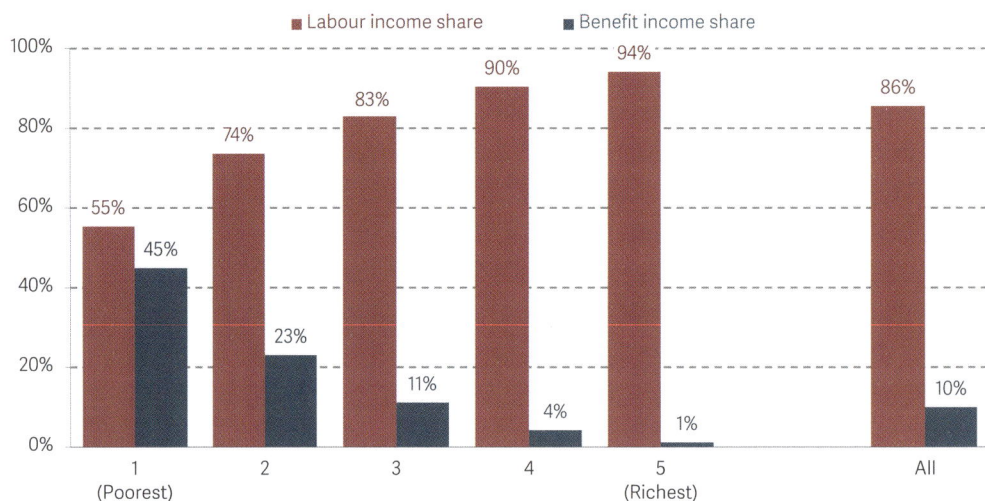

	1 (Poorest)	2	3	4	5 (Richest)	All
Labour income share	55%	74%	83%	90%	94%	86%
Benefit income share	45%	23%	11%	4%	1%	10%

Notes: Other sources of income not included, so totals do not sum to 100 per cent. Income shown is as a proportion of before housing cost income, by income quintile, with the income quintiles having been calculated using after housing cost income.
Source: Analysis of DWP, Households Below Average Income.

Figure 51 shows the staggering impact of benefit policy changes made since 2010. The dark red bars set out the impact of a wide range of cuts including a run of decisions to freeze benefit levels or uprate them by less than inflation (which has reduced incomes of poorest fifth by £2,800 a year). The lighter red bar show these cuts came on top of a technical decision to use CPI over RPI inflation for the indexation of benefits (which has reduced incomes of poorest fifth by a further £2,700 a year).

The sheer scale of these benefit cuts explains why income inequality did not fall during the 2010s, despite the pro-poor employment growth and a fast-rising minimum wage celebrated in the last chapter. And still worse, our social security system has not been able to prevent a more-than-doubling of destitution since 2017 alone, rising to 3.8 million people (including around a million children) experiencing destitution in 2022.[4] We need a definite change of direction when it comes to social security.

---

4   S Fitzpatrick et al., Destitution in the UK 2023, Joseph Rowntree Foundation, October 2023.

Figure 51: Benefit cuts have hit the poor hardest

Impact of benefit policy changes made between May 2010 and October 2023, by vigintile of equivalised household income after housing costs, in 2027-28

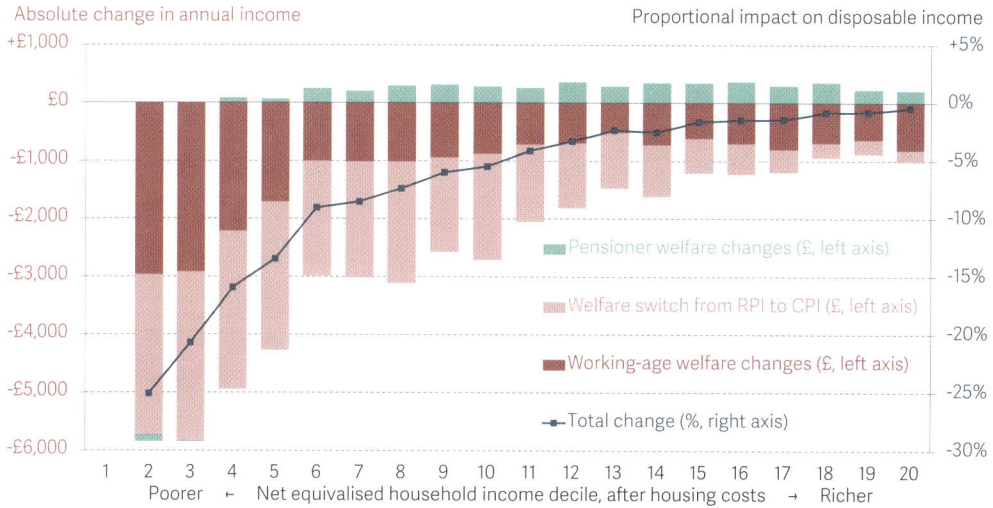

Notes: Policies include but are not limited to benefit freezes and under-indexations; the two-child limit and family element abolition; child benefit means-testing; the benefit cap; cuts to Council Tax Support; the freeze in Local Housing Allowances since 2020; reductions in the UC taper rate; changes in UC work allowances; the State Pension triple lock; changes to Pension Credit age rules; and the switch from RPI/Rossi to CPI uprating (including interactions with other policies). Full roll-out of UC is assumed. Scottish Government policy changes are not included.
Source: RF analysis of DWP, Family Resources Survey using the IPPR tax-benefit model.

Simply getting back into the habit of benefits rising in line with prices will not cut it, after years of deliberately choosing incredibly low levels of basic income protection in our social security system (with spending priority instead given to the extra costs of children and housing).[5] That would see the basic rate of unemployment benefit fall from 14 per cent of earnings in 2025-26 to 12 per cent in 2035-36 and 10 per cent in 2045-46, down from 17 per cent in 2000-01.[6] This is an approach that, far from acting as a bulwark against inequality, almost guarantees inequality will rise if strong growth returns. It means further disconnecting the living standards of poorer households from the rest of the population, when already over a quarter (27 per cent) of people in families where someone is disabled are in poverty (compared to 19 per cent of those in families in which no

---

5   M Brewer et al., Social Insecurity: Assessing trends in social security to prepare for the decade of change ahead, Resolution Foundation, January 2022.

6   This now takes the form of the Universal Credit standard allowance.

one has a disability) and 42 per cent of children in families with three or more children are in poverty, up from one-third in 2012-13.[7] Any economic strategy that claims to be serious about reducing inequality and financial hardship will need to take a different approach.

Benefit levels should, and can, keep pace with wages

Ultimately social security benefits must grow in line with wages rather than prices via a 'smoothed' earnings link.[8] This would be a big change, but it is also an unavoidable component of any plausible economic strategy that aims to see rising prosperity and falling inequality in Britain. [9]

In the context of old age, the argument for ensuring pensioners can share in rising prosperity long after they have exited the labour market has prevailed. The State Pension has been linked to economic growth via an earnings link (later gold-plated via the 'triple lock' that sees pensions rise each year in line with whichever is the highest out of earnings, inflation or 2.5 per cent) and, partly as a result, pensioners, so often through history among the poorest in society, are now less likely than the rest of the population to live in poverty.[10]

The UK's own recent social policy history, therefore, shows us that this sort of change can be made, and for by far the biggest group of benefit claimants. Looking further afield underlines that it is, in principle, perfectly possible to extend the approach to the working-age population: New Zealand has recently joined Germany, Belgium and the Netherlands in uprating some or all working-age benefits with reference to earnings or national income.

The major difference that earnings-uprating of non-pensioner benefits would make to household incomes and inequality is set out in Chapter 9. But first there are two important practical questions about this approach that need to be answered.

7   Department for Work and Pensions, Households below average income: for financial years ending 1995 to 2022, March 2023.

8   One of the practical challenges with an earnings link has been made more salient by the recent cost of living crisis – namely, what happens when pay lags behind prices. Pegging benefits to earnings in these circumstances would obviously make the poor poorer. This problem can be fixed by a 'smoothed' earnings link, where benefits rise with price inflation in years when prices rise faster than pay, but is then temporarily held down so that uprating still tracks earnings in the long-run, rather than outpacing them.

9   For full details on our proposed approach to ensuring the social security system delivers the benefits of growth to those who cannot work, see: M Brewer et al., Sharing the benefits: Can Britain secure broadly shared prosperity?, Resolution Foundation, July 2023.

10 See Section 5 of: P Bourquin, M Brewer & T Wernham, Trends in income and wealth inequalities, IFS Deaton Review of Inequalities, November 2022.

The first of these is work incentives. Would higher benefits in real terms deter people from moving into employment or seeking additional hours? That isn't likely. The starting point is one where Britain's main benefits replace a proportion of wages that is exceptionally low, by both international and historical standards.[11] Indexing benefits to earnings represents nothing more than a commitment to ensure that this so-called 'replacement rate' does not sink further. Indeed, when combined with our proposals for the minimum wage to continue rising faster than wages and wider improvements to the quality of work, this is a package to strengthen work incentives for those moving into low-wage work. Cutting out-of-work benefits is not the only way to improve work incentives.

A particularly instructive international comparison is Denmark, which – like the UK – has liberal rules on hiring and firing, yet provides more generous benefits, and achieves similarly high overall employment. Box 24 explains how Denmark shows us that it is possible to strike a better balance between flexibility and security than the UK does today.

Box 24: The Danish model – flexible and secure[12]

The economic debate is sometimes pitched as if countries have to make a choice between dynamism and security. The argument is that you can have Anglo-Saxon flexibility for employers and the associated anxiety for workers, or continental protections that make hiring so cumbersome it comes at the expense of some people having no jobs at all.

But Danish 'flexicurity' provides a ready-made example of a third way, marrying a labour market with UK-style flexibilities with more generous benefits that offer meaningful protection when jobs disappear. The recent record of the Danish labour market is stellar – not only has unemployment stayed low, but overall employment has risen. And, crucially, job mobility rates have remained high, suggesting that it may have found a form of protection that encourages workers to take a leap, rather than locking them in post.

What lessons can the UK learn? Essentially, that ours is not the only path to a vibrant jobs market: as

---

11 M Brewer et al., Social Insecurity: Assessing trends in social security to prepare for the decade of change ahead, Resolution Foundation, January 2022.

12 The evidence in this box draws on an externally commissioned essay as part of the Economy 2030 Inquiry. See: A Ilsøe & T Pernille Larsen, Flexicurity and the future of work: Lessons from Denmark, Resolution Foundation, June 2023.

shown in Table 1 the employment, unemployment and job-to-job mobility rates look remarkably similar in Denmark and the UK. Both countries are near the top of the OECD league table when it comes to the ease of hiring and firing measured by so-called "external numerical flexibility," a gauge of employers' freedom to vary the size and composition of their workforce. And yet when it comes to the generosity of income security the two countries look vastly different. The 87 per cent of Danish workers signed up to an unemployment insurance scheme are offered up to 90 per cent of previous earnings for up to two years, with a cap of just under €2,600 a month. This results in unemployment benefits replacing, on average, around 57 per cent of former earnings, vastly higher than the average UK equivalent of 35 per cent even after factoring in top-up benefits for things like housing.[13]

In addition, Denmark spends considerably more than the UK and other peers on intensive support and training to help workers find jobs or move roles (measured here by Active Labour Market Spending as a share of GDP). Where well-executed, such schemes ensure workers are not just more willing to consider a move, but more capable of going through with it.

Table 1: Similarities and differences between Denmark and the UK

Markers of labour market flexibility and income security

	Denmark	UK
External numerical flexibility	EPL: 1.5	EPL: 1.4
Unemp. benefit: replacement rate	57%	35%
Unemp. benefit: coverage	87%	100%
Active Labour Market spend (% GDP)	1.2%	0.3%
Employment rate	77%	76%

Notes: EPL: Employment Protection Legislation Indicator. Low value means easy legal access to hiring and firing. High value means less easy legal access to hiring and firing (2019). Job-to-job mobility: share of employed who changed jobs within the last year (2019). Source: Eurostat/Labour Force Survey. Coverage rate: share of workers covered by the unemployment insurance (2020). Replacement rate: average replacement of former earnings via unemployment benefit including housing benefit/ Universal Credit in the UK (2022). ALMP expenditure (2018). Employment and unemployment rates (share of working population aged 15-64 years) (Q3 2022).
Source: Analysis of OECD; Danske A-kasser.

13   OECD, Benefits in unemployment, share of previous income (indicator), accessed on 07 July 2022.

The second major question about a benefit earnings link is: what will it cost? The slow power of a reformed indexation regime plays out cumulatively, over time. The potential issue is not affordability in the early years, where the effects and the cost are modest, but rather how the bill racks up over time. Figure 52 therefore concentrates on how costs evolve over the next two decades.

Figure 52: Rising benefits, dwindling burden

Working-age and pensioner welfare spending as a proportion of GDP: UK

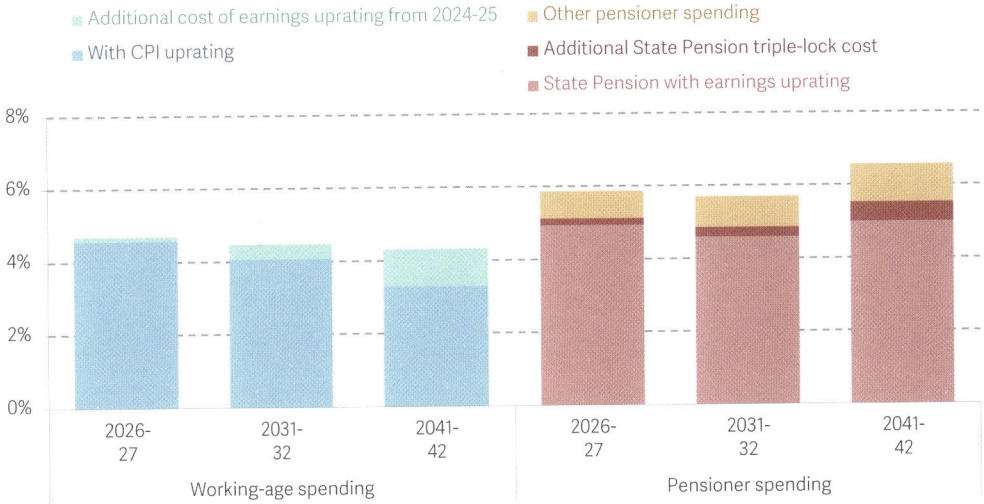

Notes: Categories are in line with those in the OBR Fiscal Risks and Sustainability report. Working-age spending includes spending directed at children. We assume the default OBR uprating is the triple lock for the State Pension, and CPI for all other welfare spending until 2026-27, and then by average earnings thereafter. We assume other pensioner spending remains unchanged compared to the original OBR projection. The cost estimate of earnings uprating includes restoring LHA rates to the 30th percentile of local rents and earnings-uprating the benefit cap.
Source: Analysis of OBR, Fiscal Risks and Sustainability report - July 2022; OBR, Economic and Fiscal Outlook - March 2023.

All else being equal, paying people higher benefits inevitably comes at a cost. But Figure 52 provides some reassurance: while pegging working-age benefits to earnings does cost more than inflation-uprating, the share of GDP devoted to them would still be on track to decline, from 4.6 per cent in 2026 to 4.2 per cent in 2041. Why? Well, if we peg benefits to general prosperity while the relative size of the working-age population declines in our ageing society, then the burden of paying for them should be expected to fall.

There are of course bigger pressures on another major part of the social security budget: pensions. A bigger pensioner population plus the 'triple lock' means outlays are due to increase from 5.9 per cent of GDP in 2026 to 6.6 per cent by 2041. Ultimately the State Pension and working-age benefits should be uprated under one consistent policy. Switching pensions to the same smoothed earnings link proposed for working-age benefits would gradually save 0.5 per cent of GDP compared to current plans by the 2040s, offsetting over half of the higher cost that comes from pegging working-age benefits to wages.[14]

A long-term earnings link is a vital part of our wider strategy. But it won't fix every problem of poverty: a couple of glaring holes in the safety net need fixing more directly.[15] Means-tested social security around the advanced world is based on a link between a family's needs and its entitlement. Two particular benefit cuts of the 2010s directly weaken that link in a manner incompatible with shared prosperity: the two-child limit and the benefit cap. Box 25 explains why the first needs to go, and the second needs – at the very least –adjusting for inflation.

Box 25: Poverty ratchets – two-child limit and benefit cap

The two-child limit and the benefit cap were introduced in the 2010s to limit the benefits that some families can receive, and thereby deliberately break the traditional link between entitlement and need. The two-child limit was introduced in 2017, and mostly prevents families from receiving child-related welfare benefits for any children after their first two.[16]

The two-child limit impoverishes children in large families, and since it only applies to those born after April 2017, it will represent an increasing blow right through to 2035, when the full cohort of all third and subsequent children up to 18 is finally covered. It already hits the poorest fifth by an average of £780 a year, a figure that will steadily rise

14 M Brewer et al., Sharing the benefits: Can Britain secure broadly shared prosperity?, Resolution Foundation, July 2023.

15 An overall assessment of the adequacy of benefit levels is outside the scope of the Economy 2030 Inquiry. But for other work in this area, see, for example: Trussell Trust & Joseph Rowntree Foundation, Guarantee our Essentials: reforming Universal Credit to ensure we can all afford the essentials in hard times, February 2023.

16 This excludes child benefit, and there are exceptions from the policy in certain circumstances, such as 'non-consensual' conception (the caveat sometimes described as the 'rape clause').

to £1,310 by 2035 without a change of direction (Figure 53).[17] This limit should be abolished: aside from the highly regressive impact, it has had minimal impacts on fertility, meaning that its primary impact has been to take income away from poorer families.[18] Meanwhile, the household benefit cap reduces entitlements relative to needs for specific groups, notably large families and renters in high-cost areas. The lack of any automatic adjustment for inflation deepens the selective hardship produced: the cap is now worth 15 per cent less in real terms than it was in November 2016. At an absolute minimum, it should be indexed to wages or some groups will be fated to sink into ever-deeper poverty.

Figure 53: *The two-child limit is making poor children poorer*

Impact of the current and a fully rolled out two-child limit on non-pensioner annual household incomes, by income vigintile: UK, 2023-24

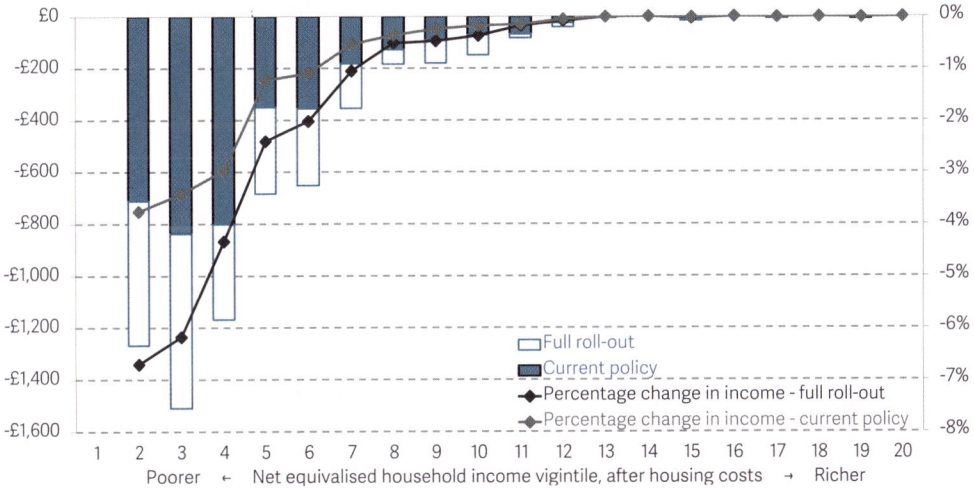

Notes: Counterfactual is if the two-child limit did not exist. The bottom vigintile is excluded from our analysis due to concerns about the reliability of data.
Source: Analysis of DWP, Family Resources Survey using the IPPR tax-benefit model.

17 M Brewer et al., Sharing the benefits: Can Britain secure broadly shared prosperity?, Resolution Foundation, July 2023.
18 M Reader, J Portes & R Patrick, Does Cutting Child Benefits Reduce Fertility in Larger Families? Evidence from the UK's Two-Child Limit, Benefit Changes and Larger Families Study, April 2022.

211

Taken together, this package of reforms would allow for overall social security spending as a share of GDP to remain contained at current levels, rebalance support more fairly across the age range, and drive sustained reductions in absolute poverty.[19] But it would still require funding to the tune of 0.6 per cent of GDP by 2039-40 relative to existing policy. And even if this one set of reforms is affordable, there is no escaping the fact that there are many other pressures on public spending.[20] Which leads us to another part of the distributional jigsaw for us to consider: the question of the smartest – and fairest – way to raise revenue.

Taxes are up, and likely to stay that way

The tax system bears a number of responsibilities. It must raise the revenue needed to meet the needs that society has decided to collectively provide for, and we have in this chapter added to the pressures by identifying urgent spending measures that need to be paid for. We have also been clear (as discussed in Chapter 5), that it is unlikely to be possible to fund sorely needed public investment entirely through borrowing: a (temporary) sacrifice in consumption from some will be required. The tax system is our key mechanism for ensuring this burden is shouldered by the right people. More widely, the tax system must lean into supporting growth while also leaning against Britain's high inequality.[21]

Given the high bar set by these objectives, it is particularly unfortunate that the quality of public discourse on tax is at a low ebb. Despite, or perhaps because of, the centrality of tax to British political debate, there is more wishful thinking about this subject than any other component of economic strategy. It has become the norm for politicians to declare their low tax 'instincts' while shrinking from spelling out anything the state should stop doing – sometimes at the same time as they are raising taxes.

The most immediate issues overwhelming easy tax-cutting rhetoric are the surging cost of servicing public debt as we enter an environment of far higher interest rates, and the Government's, not to mention the public's, wish to unwind the

---

19 This comes from the series shown in Figure 52 (note that the OBR's long-run projections of social security spending assume that working-age benefits will track earnings growth in the long run).

20 The cost of uprating working-age benefits by earnings and getting rid of the two-child limit and the benefit cap would cost 1.1 per cent of GDP by 2039-40, but converting the State Pension triple lock into an earnings link would save 0.5 per cent of GDP over this period.

21 All proposals in this section are from: M Broome, A Corlett & G Thwaites, Tax planning: How to match higher taxes with better taxes, Resolution Foundation, June 2023.

extremes of austerity for public service spending of the late 2010s.[22] The result is a sharp rise in the tax take, which is matching or exceeding the highest levels recorded since the 1940s (see Figure 54). Having averaged 33 per cent of GDP in the National Accounts in the first two decades of this century, the tax take is now most of the way to 38 per cent, where it is forecast to land in 2027-28. That is an increase equivalent to £4,200 per household.

Figure 54: The rising cost of government

Total taxes and spending as a proportion of GDP: UK

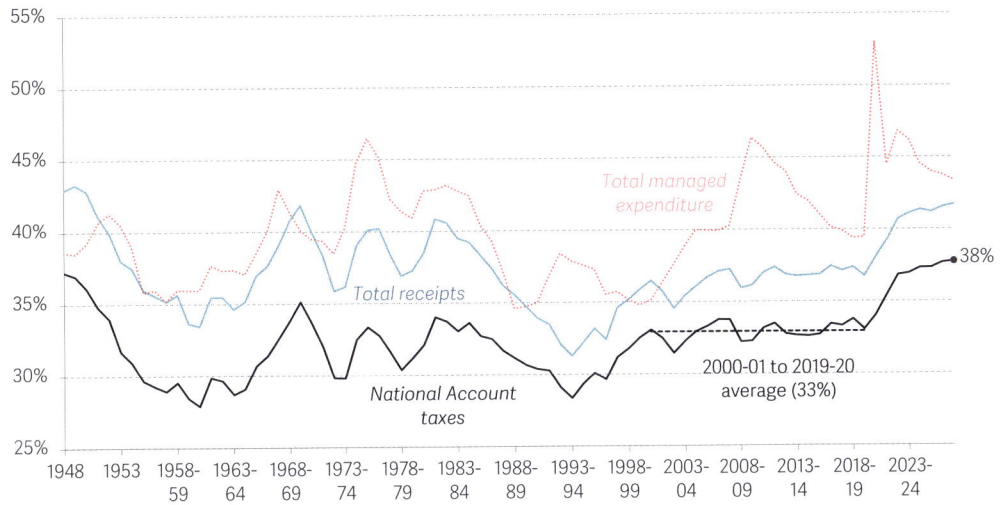

Notes: Final data point is for 2027-28.
Source: Analysis of OBR, Economic and Fiscal Outlook, March 2023.

The exact future level of tax and spending is uncertain, while different political choices can always be made. But a new economic strategy should plan on the basis that taxes remain at levels higher than we are used to. The current state of public services points in that direction.[23] Looking ahead, so does the demographic tide, with the number of people aged 65 and above increasing by 20 per cent during this decade.[24] Healthcare spending has been growing faster than other

---

22 In the OBR's Economic and Fiscal Outlook, March 2023, a 5-percentage-point rise in the tax to GDP ratio between 2019-20 and 2027-28 is accompanied by a 2 percentage point rise in debt interest spending and a 1 percentage point rise in day-to-day departmental spending as a share of GDP.

23 Institute for Government, Performance Tracker 2023, October 2023.

24 M Broome, Big welcomes and long goodbyes: The impact of demographic change in the 2020s, Resolution Foundation, June 2022.

spending throughout the 2010s and this is likely to continue.[25] Other major pressures come on top of this: answering new geopolitical realities (with a current 'aspiration' to raise defence spending to 2.5 per cent of GDP), and addressing the many new tasks that the state faces in getting to net zero. [26] For all the real pain involved in significant tax rises to date, there seems to be little public appetite for shrinking the state as yet.[27]

It is also clear that tried-and-tested approaches for managing pressures on spending without higher taxes are today unavailable or undesirable. For example, the doubling of outlays on health, education and social security spending in GDP between 1955-56 and 2019-20 was in large part funded by shrinking defence spending – from 8 per cent of GDP in 1955-56 down to the current 2 per cent. This cannot be repeated. Running down public sector investment, another common fix for the Treasury, is part of Britain's economic problem, not its solution.

Perspective is needed on the UK's tax take. We are not in danger of becoming a high tax nation by European standards. In the latest comparable data, taxes in Germany and France were 6 and 12 per cent of GDP higher than in the UK.[28] But we are on track to be a higher tax nation than we are used to. Indeed, these rising pressures on the state, together with our argument that higher public investment needs to be part funded by taxation at the same time as we move to a tighter fiscal policy (as set out in Chapter 5), mean that further net tax rises are needed.

The increase in the quantity of taxation has not been matched by an increase in its quality

The right reaction to taxes reaching a seven-decade high for these structural reasons is not to pretend a major tax-cutting era is just around the corner, as Liz Truss demonstrated, but to focus on a simpler, more efficient, fairer and more predictable tax system. We need better, not just more, taxes.

The cost of the tax cut rhetoric and tax rise reality mismatch is policy unmoored from a strategy, and poorly done as a result. Corporation Tax has been a great

---

25 K Shah, J Smith & D Tomlinson, Under pressure: Managing fiscal pressures in the 2020s, Resolution Foundation, February 2022.

26 The current Government has an 'aspiration' to raise defence spending to 2.5 per cent of GDP 'over the longer-term…as the fiscal and economic circumstances allow', though this is less ambitious than Liz Truss' ambition for defence spending to reach 3 per cent of GDP. See: M Chalmers, Security, defence and foreign affairs challenges facing the UK, UK in a Changing Europe, September 2023.

27 J Curtice & A Scholes, Role and responsibilities of government: Have public expectations changed?, British Social Attitudes 40, September 2023.

28 OECD, Global Revenue Statistics Database, accessed October 2023. The latest figures are for 2021.

source of policy uncertainty, rather than the stability that underpins business investment, going from a standard rate of 28 per cent in 2010 to 19 per cent in 2017, before rising back to 25 per cent in 2023. The existential challenge to Fuel Duty posed by electric vehicles has been ignored, while we have spent the last decade with a policy of raising it in line with inflation and a reality of that rise being cancelled every year. Instead of being reformed, Council Tax – an unfair, near-poll tax only weakly linked to three-decades-old property values – was cut in the 2010s but is now being increased to record highs relative to incomes, as a predictable result of unsustainable local government finances. A long-term political competition to be seen to lower Income Tax has led to repeated increases in National Insurance (NI), worsening the bias in the tax system against salaried employment, while the Income Tax personal tax allowance was greatly increased in the 2010s only to see its real-terms value slashed in the 2020s by threshold freezes.

This is what a mess, rather than a strategy, looks like. Given the scale of the pressures, this is a self-indulgence that we can no longer afford. As fiscal pressures intensify, falling back on large, stealthy revenue raisers twinned with a few eye-catching giveaways, while leaving damaging problems within our tax system unaddressed, is liable to produce ever-greater economic distortion and rising public resentment. The growth and fairness penalties from our incoherent tax system are rising with the higher tax take.

Different sources of income need to be consistently taxed

Reasonable people can disagree about how high the tax rates on income should be, but should agree they ought to be consistent across different forms of income. That is not what the UK's tax system does today, harming both efficiency and equity.

Capital gains, for example, are taxed at a maximum of 28 per cent, and often lower rates of zero or 10 per cent, compared to a top total tax rate (including National Insurance) on the highest earnings of 47 per cent (or 53.4 per cent once employer taxes are included).[29] And this 'top rate' is reached only via a bizarre route which levies a marginal rate of 67 per cent rate on some people just below the top (as the personal allowance is withdrawn, on earnings between £100,000 and £125,140), and hits some working parents (those in the £50,000-£60,000 wage bracket whose Child Benefit is withdrawn) with effective marginal rates of 80 or even 100 per cent, depending on their number of children.

---

29 Accounting for the impact of employer National Insurance (which may be passed on through lower wages), the top marginal tax rate for employees can be seen as 53.4 per cent, while the basic rate rises to 40.2 per cent.

So we propose a set of tax rises and cuts that would mean that incomes from employment, self-employment (for those on higher incomes), dividends, real capital gains and rents would all be subject to a similar schedule of marginal rates. More specifically, we propose:[30]

- Increasing the basic rate of tax on dividends from 8.75 to 20 per cent, while slightly reducing the higher rates, to align treatment with earnings.[31]

- Reforming Capital Gains Tax (CGT), so that it targets only real gains, made above inflation. That represents a tax cut, but at the same time marginal rates should be increased to match those facing employment income and dividends. Real gains on shares would be taxed in line with the new charges on dividends, implying a maximum CGT rate of 37 per cent (still below the 40 per cent rate established by Nigel Lawson in 1988, which prevailed for three decades). The tax rates for gains on real estate and other assets need to increase more for parity with wages: to a range of between 40 and 53 per cent.

- Given inflation indexing, the combined effect of those capital gains reforms alone would be a giveaway to landlords. We propose offsetting it by charging NI on rental income so that landlords pay the same tax on rental income as tenants pay on their earnings. We suggest eventual rates of 20 per cent for basic-rate taxpayers and 8 per cent for those with higher incomes.

- Increasing from 2 to 8 per cent the National Insurance charged on self-employed earnings above the higher-rate income tax threshold (around £50,000), helping to address a substantial distortion against employee posts in the current system that sees corporate lawyers and accountants paying less tax than identically paid bankers.[32]

---

30 Ideally, these proposals might be coupled with some reduction in the employer NI rate – a tax that is levied only on employee pay – but this would be expensive. Certainly, at the very least, increasing employer NI rates should not be seen as a good stealthy way to keep raising revenue.

31 The top dividend tax rate is 39.35 per cent, but if profits have already been taxed at the main Corporation Tax rate of 25 per cent then the effective rate is 54.5 per cent.

32 For true parity, NI rates for the more moderately-paid majority of self-employed individuals would also need to rise significantly, but other changes may be a higher priority for scarce political capital.

- To do away with the most punitive effective marginal rates, two distortionary income tax charges on the better-off – the clawing-back of Child Benefit at £50,000 and of the personal allowance at £100,000 – should be abolished.[33] At the same time the threshold for the additional (45 per cent) rate should be reduced from £125,140 to £100,000.

- Finally, special cases where effective tax rates are zero should be limited or ended: with reform of non-dom taxation, and the end of forgiveness of tax due on capital gains upon death or upon leaving the UK.

Under these reforms, effective marginal rates for employees would be unchanged or lower, but the economy would now have the benefit of a simpler system, with the highest effective rates levelled down and the lowest rates available to high earners levelled up. Crucially, higher incomes would now be taxed at similar rates irrespective of whether they came from employment, self-employment, (real-terms) capital gains or rents. This is a reform package that is both efficient and fair.

Our tax system cannot ignore the rise of wealth

Above and beyond the need to rationalise taxes on the flow of income, taxation needs to grapple with the stock of wealth. Although we must wait to assess the full – and potentially significant – effect of newly raised interest rates in reducing overall levels of wealth, the big story of the last 40 years has been of private wealth racing ahead of income, rising from around three times to more than seven times of GDP. One might have imagined that as wealth increased, tax on wealth would increase in rough proportion. Figure 55 reveals nothing of the sort has happened. Instead, wealth taxes remain roughly where they were 15 or even 35 years ago, at somewhere around 3 per cent of GDP.[34]

---

33 This would make Child Benefit a universal benefit once again. See: M Brewer, K Handscomb & G Kelly, Inconsistent incentives: How the overlap between Universal Credit and the High Income Child Benefit Charge limits work incentives, Resolution Foundation, December 2022.

34 K Shah, Wealth on the eve of a crisis: Exploring the UK's pre-pandemic wealth distribution, Resolution Foundation, January 2022.

Figure 55: While wealth soared, wealth taxes stagnated

Total wealth and wealth taxes as a proportion of GDP: GB, 1965-2020

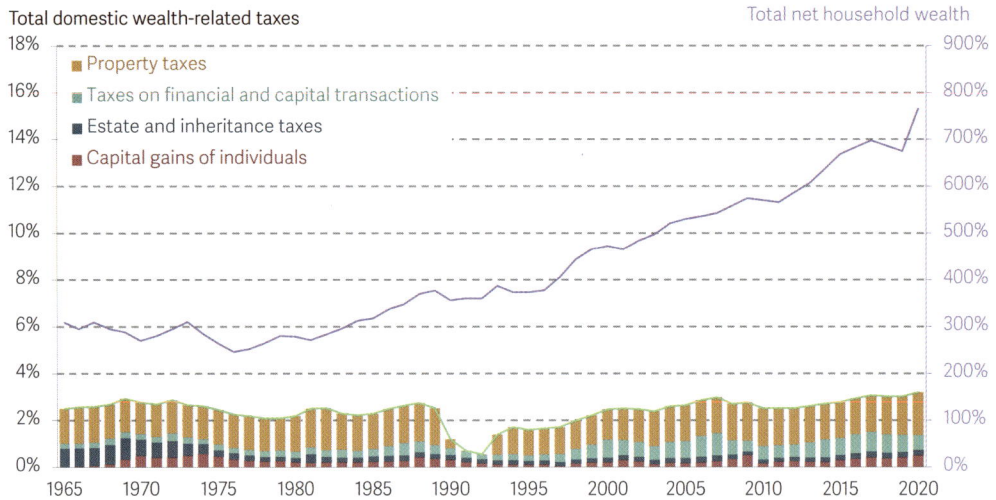

Notes: Estimated 2020 value calculated by multiplying the value of wealth as a proportion of GDP from the Wealth and Asset Survey by the growth rate in this value found between 2019 and 2020 in the National Accounts.
Source: Analysis of D Blake & J Orszag, Annual estimates of personal wealth holdings in the United Kingdom since 1948, Applied Financial Economics 9, 1999; ONS, UK National Accounts, ONS, Total Wealth, Wealth in Great Britain, ONS Gross Domestic Product at market prices; Current price: Seasonally adjusted £m; OECD, Details of Tax Revenue.

One possible reason for this discrepancy is that our current set of taxes on wealth are poorly designed and ill-placed to do more work. As well as the oddities of Council Tax already highlighted, we tax property through Stamp Duty, which invites socio-economic sclerosis by making it costly to move. We tax pension pots and contributions in an inconsistent manner, and approach bequests in a way that makes avoidance relatively easy for the richest and best-advised. As with taxing incomes, the discussion about wealth – especially if we need to tax more – must start with taxing better.

An obvious priority for reform in the taxation of property is a determined but carefully paced overhaul of Council Tax, not least to give local government and city-regions a better tax to work with, as we noted in Chapter 4. This would involve revaluations in every part of Great Britain followed by automatic annual updates, to end the absurdity of Scotland and England basing taxes on 1991 values.[35] On

---

35 Wales implemented a revaluation in 2005, and another is intended to take effect from 2025. Council tax does not operate in Northern Ireland, but its system of domestic rates is based on values from 2005.

the basis of these valuations, a straightforward, proportional property tax should be levied, ditching the British anomaly of relying on bands to set tax levels and bringing us in line with other countries. To avoid the political explosions that have doomed proposals for reform up until now, these reforms should be delivered without major overnight redistribution of tax burdens across councils, affecting only the distribution within council areas (requiring different local authorities to initially have different property tax rates).[36]

Stamp Duty should be cut for people's (main) homes, with a halving of rates and the cancellation of a planned reduction in the tax-free threshold, allowing the housing stock to be used more efficiently and helping workers move to better jobs.[37] Stamp Duty Land Tax should also be cut for businesses, so that premises and land can be allocated to their best uses. Halving the Stamp Duty rates would boost commercial transactions by an estimated 20 per cent, and could be funded by reducing the UK's unusually high and distortionary VAT registration threshold (see Chapter 8).

A close competitor to Council Tax for the least popular tax, is Inheritance Tax. An effective tax on bequests is even more important in a society that has seen such a large rise in wealth levels, creating patterns of winners and losers based to a great extent on luck – such as large swings in interest rates or being born to the right parents. But such a tax can cannot sustain public support when it is too easily avoided by the wealthy and well-advised. To rebuild its reputation, reliefs for business and agricultural property that are widely abused should be scrapped or tightly focused, pension pots included within an estate, and the complicated Residence Nil Rate Band abolished. These changes would make it possible to replace Inheritance Tax's high, flat rate of 40 per cent with a more popular banded structure, with rates of 20, 30 and 40 per cent.[38]

When it comes to the taxation of pensions, we can do better at focusing expensive tax reliefs on low and middle earners. The National Insurance treatment of pension contributions should be reformed, charging NI on employer contributions while

---

36 A separate, more gradual, convergence of tax rates can then be pursued via the local government finance settlement process.

37 Stamp Duty Land Tax is devolved and its equivalents should also be cut in Scotland and Wales.

38 In time, Inheritance Tax should be entirely replaced by a lifetime, recipient-based acquisitions tax similar to Ireland's.

introducing NI relief for employee contributions. This would help many lower earners build up their savings. The roughly £270,000 cap on tax-free lump sum withdrawals from pensions should gradually be reduced, based on date of birth.[39]

Taken together, these steps would tax the building and possession of wealth more rationally. Moreover, while these reforms comprise a mix of tax rises and tax cuts, in combination they would raise some revenue, and thereby go some way towards tilting the tax burden towards owners rather than earners.

Tax policy alone is not going to resolve the UK's low growth and high inequality woes. But the design of the tax system should be part of the answer rather than part of the problem. Altogether, this far-reaching package of tax changes would make income taxes fairer, see wealth take more of the strain, and remove barriers to dynamism. This package of tax rises and tax cuts would raise a net 0.6 per cent of GDP (or £17 billion in 2027-28) and, just as importantly, put the tax system on solid foundations should additional revenue be needed in future. The political challenges involved should not be discounted, but neither should the problems with the status quo or the prize for doing better, especially in a higher-tax world.

The net zero transition must be fair if it is to be sustainable

While fair taxes are always at the centre of political debates, the fair financing of the net zero transition is a novel, but increasingly important and contentious focus for the 2020s. This is the decade during which major disruption will be felt by people as consumers, as the tax base has to be tilted towards pollutants, and funds have to be raised for major investments in low-carbon infrastructure. If the costs for transition are not manageable for people of modest means, support will fall, jeopardising the whole project.

The top priority has to be protecting poorer households from large, upfront bills – a preeminent example being the immediate cost of improving the energy efficiency of our housing stock and then installing heat pumps.[40] Many homeowners are likely to be required to get their home up to an Energy Performance Certificate (EPC) C rating by 2035, but, after years of policy failures, efficiency installations in Britain's homes are running at around 10 per cent of the levels seen in the early

---

39 Specifically, this is the tax-free lump sum. See: HM Government, Tax when you get a pension: What's tax-free, accessed 31 October 2023.

40 For the detail of these proposals, and the data behind them, see: A Anis-Alavi et al., Hitting a brick wall: How the UK can upgrade its housing stock to reduce energy bills and cut carbon, Resolution Foundation, December 2022.

2010s.[41] To keep us on track for net zero this needs to change fast, with low-income property owners highly exposed: 72 per cent of them live in homes rated EPC band D (the average energy efficiency rating for UK homes) or below.[42]

The costs of improving a home to EPC C standard differ by property type, but for those unable to meet this standard without insulating walls, the cost is estimated at over £8,000 per household. Put that beside the average disposable income of poorer homeowners of around £9,100, and it is plain that such investment isn't going to happen without major government intervention.

The big difficulty is how that support should be targeted. Current support, for example for heat pump installations, is available to any households irrespective of their financial means[43] – but with a finite and unchanged budget that means a first come, first served approach will serve fewer homes and therefore not be able to cope with the scale of home upgrades required.[44] Instead, targeting is needed, but this is not straightforward. Trying to allocate funds purely on the basis of receipt of existing benefits will also fail to reach many of those who will need help: 2.3 million households in the poorest quintile don't receive benefits. And using Council Tax bands for eligibility will be equally far off the mark: an outright majority (59 per cent) of households within the top fifth of the income distribution live in modestly-valued homes (using the crude approximation of a Council Tax Band of D or less), implying that a lot of subsidies paid on this alternative basis would go to families who could in fact pay for themselves.

Instead, we propose a new form of assessment, which – like the reformed system now used for social care – takes some account of both income and wealth. The details will be important, including for how those with property wealth but few liquid assets can get support upfront that is repaid later. But the principle is straightforward. An indicative threshold for having home improvement costs covered might be household income of less than £30,000 and total assets worth less than £100,000. Imposing an upper threshold on assets of £250,000 could save

---

41 A Corlett & J Marshall, Shrinking footprints: The impacts of the net zero transition on households and consumption, Resolution Foundation, May 2022.

42 Properties are rated on how efficient a property is, with bands from A to G. The most efficient homes are in band A, and the least efficient are in band G. The Government has set a target of all homes reaching an EPC C rating by 2035.

43 GOV.UK, Apply for the Boiler Upgrade Scheme: Check if you're eligible, accessed 9 November 2023.

44 Climate Change Committee, CCC assessment of recent announcements and developments on net zero, October 2023.

public funds, by ensuring that half of homeowners had to pay all their own home improvement costs. For those in between, support would be covered on a sliding scale.[45]

Shielding poorer households from unaffordable decarbonisation costs is essential to a successful transition. Our proposed approach is comparable to that in the National Infrastructure Commission's most recent five-yearly assessment of the UK's infrastructure needs, which recommended that lower-income households receive targeted support to make their homes more efficient and are shielded from the upfront costs of installing a heat pump.[46]

As well as these subsidies, a host of specific tax reforms will be required to support a green transition, both to secure the revenue base and to ensure efficiency and fairness.[47] In particular, we must urgently establish a per-mile 'Road Duty' system for Electric Vehicles (EVs), with the purposes of replacing around £25 billion in Fuel Duty revenue that will otherwise vanish, while ensuring that the burden of motoring taxes does not become unduly concentrated on those yet to switch to electric.[48] A per mile charge of 6p (plus VAT) would be equivalent in cost to Fuel Duty and should be levied on EV drivers, implemented via in-vehicle GPS-linked systems that councils can also deploy for smooth congestion charging. By 2039-40 this policy will by itself – relative to inaction – improve the public finances by around 0.7 per cent of GDP, while, crucially, ensuring that EV driving remains cheaper than driving a non-electric car. If we add to this the net tax rises of 0.6 per cent of GDP set out earlier in this chapter, it amounts to a significant increase in revenues of 1.3 per cent of GDP by the end of the next decade.

Securing the gains

Renewed growth is the first pre-condition for ending stagnation. Without it we are stuck as a nation. But also crucial is the broader set of reforms, set out in this chapter and Chapter 6, that would extend certain positive developments of the last decade (rising employment and a higher wage floor), restart progress where it has stalled (on having a tax strategy or improving the world of work beyond hourly pay rates), and mark an abrupt about-turn when we've been headed in the wrong

---

45 A Anis-Alavi et al., Hitting a brick wall: How the UK can upgrade its housing stock to reduce energy bills and cut carbon, Resolution Foundation, December 2022.

46 National Infrastructure Commission, Second National Infrastructure Assessment, October 2023.

47 For the detail of these proposals, and the data behind them, see: A Corlett & J Marshall, Where the rubber hits the road: Reforming vehicle taxes, Resolution Foundation, June 2023.

48 We should also extend up-front Vehicle Excise Duty to cover EVs, which will – by 2035 at the latest, on current plans – be the only new vehicles available.

direction (as on benefits). In combination, these steps would ensure that the gains from restored growth would reach every group in society and every part of our country. Without them inequality would rise, but with them it would fall.

The potential rewards go far beyond materially higher incomes. A fairer Britain would have less hardship and division, and more opportunity and cohesion. A country more at ease with itself, able to embrace change and look to the future is a tremendous prize.

This is crucial because the truth is that neither a single period of restored growth, nor the immediate impact of any particular package of progressive reform can lock in the change that the country needs. That is why the motivation for the new economic strategy proposed in this book is more ambitious: to set the economy moving in a new direction so that – over time – further progress that feels unimaginable today is achieved. It is to these tasks of embracing, and steering, change that we now turn.

Chapter Eight

Steering change

Chapter summary

- The goal of a new economic strategy is not a somewhat richer, somewhat fairer, version of the UK's stagnant status quo, but a more enduring shift in direction; economic change will have to be embraced and steered.

- Despite popular claims that change is speeding up, it is slowing down; the reallocation of labour between sectors is at its lowest level in over 90 years. That matters. Higher productivity sectors growing and lower productivity ones shrinking used to add 0.4 percentage points per year to growth in the pre-financial crisis decade.

- For the UK, the size of high value tradable sectors servicing global demand is far from set in stone. Small changes make a big difference; halving the pace of decline in our share of global service exports between 2005 and 2018 would have meant an extra 585,000 people working in these growth-critical fields.

- If some sectors grow others will have to shrink. Hospitality represents a higher share of consumption in the UK than anywhere else in Europe, because it is relatively cheap. Improving conditions for workers in this and other lower productivity sectors will over time change that. Better pay for low earners in hospitality, paid for by higher prices that most affect better off households, will create a more equal UK.

- Shifting resources from low to high performing firms is much more important to raising national productivity than the current focus on supporting the 'long tail' of firms to improve. But our tax system discourages growth by favouring small firms over large. Support should be focused on young, rather than small, firms, and competitive pressures fostered via greater trade-openness and pincering poor performers between higher investing competitors and rising labour standards.

- Hiring and firing is easy in the UK, but dynamic labour markets require more than that; the proportion of workers switching jobs each quarter declined by 25 per cent between 2000 and 2019. The missing ingredient is empowered workers, willing and able to take risks. Greater protection against income falls if a new job doesn't work out and stronger rights at work would make taking a leap for a new job more of a promise, and less of a threat.

The goal for a renewed economic strategy for Britain is not merely a somewhat richer, somewhat fairer, version of the UK's stagnant status quo. Instead it is a more enduring shift in direction, requiring economic change itself to be centre stage, with considerations of its pace, nature and drivers knitted into the fabric of the strategy. The scale of our ambitions to raise growth, tame inequality and complete the net zero transition are such that they can only be achieved – and sustained – if the process of structural change within our economy is accelerated and steered towards those ends. Setting out how that can be done is the task of this chapter.

Thinking hard about economic change, rather than panicking about too much of it

We are not used to thinking about economic change. British policy debates tend to focus on specific policies aimed at improving things for particular workers, firms or sectors. The role of structural economic change – as workers shift jobs, entire sectors emerge or fade, or firms grow or fail – is too often overlooked. When we do talk about change, it is often only superficially, whether claiming that change is always accelerating but out of our hands as technology develops, or pointing at a few eye-catching high-tech industries and suggesting that these need to grow.

Taking a longer look in the rear-view mirror makes clear the dominant role of slow-burn economic dynamics. The gradual movement of the workforce from the land, first into the factories and then to offices, has unlocked a 12-fold increase in real wages since the industrial revolution.[1] This is why thinking about shifting structures is intuitive for economic historians in a way it is not for policy professionals. But the very long view of the economic historian has dangers too, focused on the biggest shifts seen across countries, but ignoring smaller or more contingent adjustments that are still material to countries' different economic paths.

While the presence of economic change is inevitable, policy can influence its pace and direction. Getting this right requires, first of all, a clear understanding of the path we are currently on. Second, it means identifying the parts of our economic structure that can and should change, and those that we are either stuck with or have no reason to alter. Third, it involves developing policies that will shape market-led change while protecting the people and places that might otherwise lose out from it. Finally, and most importantly, is the need to guard against wishful

---

1   Bank of England, A millennium of macroeconomic data, (accessed 22nd October 2023).

thinking. Favouring a particular economic direction or goal – whether higher pay or increased productivity – is a different thing to pinpointing mechanisms that can plausibly bring it about. The current UK approach to economic policy falls woefully short on all these counts, starting with profound misperceptions about the pace of economic change.

Declining dynamism in Britain

Newspaper headlines often suggest that the UK economy is at the mercy of a tsunami of accelerating change.[2] The reality is very different. Structural change in the economy – the growth and shrinking of the different industries in which we all work – is currently at its lowest level in over 90 years, as Figure 56 shows. Regardless of exactly how sectors are defined the 'reallocation' of the workforce has slowed very substantially – between a third and a half – since the 1980s.[3]

This slowdown matters. Over time, the overall shift of workers has generally been from lower to higher productivity industries. This has been a tailwind for our economic performance, contributing 0.4 percentage points per year to growth in the pre-financial crisis decade. For example, the share of total hours worked in agriculture, with productivity levels less than half the economy wide average, fell by around one-third in that period. But in the decade that followed, the contribution to growth from this kind of industrial reallocation across the economy fell to zero. Had that slowdown been avoided it would – on its own – have resulted in average wages being £1,400 higher today.[4] Britain today isn't wrestling with the consequences of ever faster change, but rather the fall-out of a big slow down.

---

2   For one of many examples see: S Greenhouse, US experts warn AI likely to kill off jobs – and widen wealth inequality, The Guardian, February 2023.

3   R Davies et al., Ready for change: How and why to make the UK economy more dynamic, Resolution Foundation, September 2023.

4   R Davies et al., Ready for change: How and why to make the UK economy more dynamic, Resolution Foundation, September 2023.

Figure 56: A dive in dynamism over the last generation

Sectoral reallocation in the 10 years to date shown, expressed as a percentage of total employment: UK

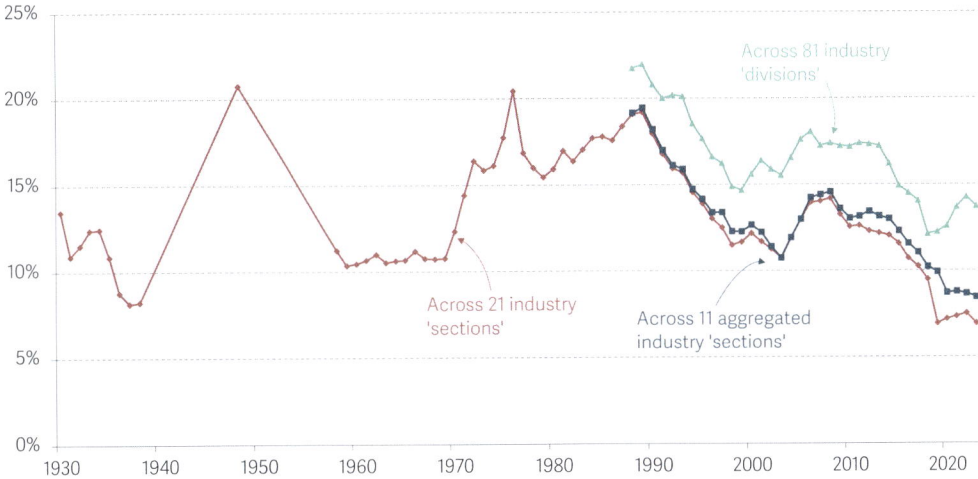

Notes: Sectoral reallocation is measured as the weighted average, across sectors, of the absolute change in employment share compared to a decade ago, based on a measure used in the US by G Chodorow-Reich & J Wieland, Secular Labor Reallocation and Business Cycles, Journal of Political Economy 128(6), April 2020. Red line uses SIC 2007 sections but some have been condensed for consistency with long-run data; the blue line uses the full set of industry sections in SIC 2007, for which Workforce Jobs data is available from 1978 onwards.
Source: Analysis of ONS, Workforce Jobs; Bank of England, Millennium of Macroeconomic Data.

Choosing the high road

The direction of change matters, not just the volume. Disruption that leaves workers being shunted out of one set of low-productivity firms into another achieves nothing but increased insecurity. Not only did change slow in the post-crisis, pre-pandemic period, but the little dynamism that we did see was less likely to boost the best firms than before.[5]

So the task is to identify and steer change towards the core objectives of the strategy – higher growth and better jobs, with the benefits felt by ordinary households throughout the country – as well as the other pressing needs of the country, from the net zero transition to providing care for a growing elderly

5   The responsiveness of resource allocation to productivity differences across firms fell by 30 per cent in the post-crisis period. See R Davies et al., Ready for change: How and why to make the UK economy more dynamic, Resolution Foundation, September 2023.

population. As we have highlighted throughout this book, we must avoid wishful thinking. The desired change must be possible, the mechanisms to secure it must be plausible, and the potential disruption planned for and managed. In a market economy like the UK's, change and reallocation are driven in large part by the price mechanism and the role of economic policy is, in no small part, to shape the decisions taken by workers and firms.

Technology has been the central driver of economic change throughout human history, from the domestication of crops and livestock, through the harnessing of fossil energy and electricity, to the invention of the integrated circuit. But in each of these cases, technological progress happened in the context of social and economic forces. For example, one (albeit contested) cause of the Industrial Revolution in England may have been that relatively high wages encouraged the adoption of labour-saving machines.[6]

Government shapes this context. A new wave of research is documenting the pivotal role that it played in the process of industrialisation.[7] This has been especially true in times of war and heightened concern about national security, something that regrettably has increased salience today.[8] Similarly, trade unions, empowered by enabling legislation, may have encouraged the development and adoption of technologies that made workers more productive in the early 20th century, in contrast to the ones that put their predecessors out of work a hundred years previously.[9] Today, we see the cost of renewable energy and electric vehicles plummeting, with prices driven down in markets shaped by the objective of net zero, backed by an array of taxes, subsidies and regulation around the world.

As well as steering technology, governments can shape change for particular geographic areas, for example Germany's qualified success in supporting the convergence of living standards between East and West.[10] We showed in Chapter 4 how a number of post-industrial cities have turned around their economic trajectory. In Lille, Pittsburgh and Bilbao, for example, there been a strategic focus on building more competitive economies but also on making the urban areas attractive places to live.

---

6   R Allen, The high wage economy and the industrial revolution: a restatement, Economic History Review 68, February 2015.

7   R Juhász & C Steinwender, Industrial policy and the Great Divergence, National Bureau of Economic Research, September 2023.

8   J Abbate, Inventing the Internet, Cambridge, MA: MIT Press, July 2000.

9   D Acemoglu & S Johnson, Power and Progress: Our Thousand-Year Struggle Over Technology and Prosperity, Basic books, May 2023.

10 K Enenkel & F Rosel, German reunification: Lessons from the German approach to closing regional divides, Resolution Foundation, December 2022.

We need humility, though, when applying these lessons to contemporary Britain. The UK is a middle-sized country whose borders are highly porous to technologies developed elsewhere. This openness is hugely beneficial, enabling the UK to benefit from the world's research and development, but it will constrain attempts to steer technological change. Moreover, since exiting the EU, Britain no longer has direct influence on globally relevant product and technology standards. When it comes to economic geography, the UK is too small to have 'a global city in every region'[11] even if, as Chapter 4 set out, there are solid grounds for thinking that a high-voltage, sustained investment agenda would over time transform the productive capacity of our biggest conurbations outside London.

What these different debates on steering structural change make clear is the need to take account of the path that the economy is currently on, shaped by an understanding of the constraints, as well as opportunities, we face. In learning from strategic initiatives overseas, such as the Inflation Reduction Act in the US, we must, as discussed in Chapter 4, take care to translate their lessons to the British context, rather than assuming we can transplant them wholesale.

In sum, economic change is ubiquitous and often beneficial, though sometimes disruptive. And it can be shaped, subject to constraints of technology, history, geography and the fundamentals of a market economy. The next questions are what we want to achieve with economic change and how.

The how and the what of structural change

In an economy like the UK's, the gradual process of economic change mostly results from disparate decisions taken by workers and private firms in response to price signals and regulation. To achieve beneficial economic change, the UK does not need a dirigiste 'master plan', but it does require government to set and stick to a long-term strategy to influence the allocation of resources to meet key policy objectives, through the price mechanism and by adjusting taxes, spending, regulations and place-based policies. Margaret Thatcher was the most recent British politician to combine a diverse set of policies in pursuit of a strategic view of the economy, as Box 26 sets out. What the UK needs today is a strategy of similar clarity and scale but of a different nature: to harness change in the pursuit of inclusive growth.

---

11 HM Government, Levelling Up the United Kingdom, February 2022.

Box 26: Margaret Thatcher's economic strategy

It is worth looking back at the last prime minister to have reset the direction of economic policy – albeit controversially – and made that change stick. When Margaret Thatcher took power in 1979, many pointed to the UK's stubborn industrial conflict as an immutable gravitational force. In the 1960s and 1970s several attempts had been made to set the frequently bitter interaction between workers and managers in a new framework, but to no avail: days lost to industrial action peaked at just short of 30 million in 1979. The temptation to prop up so-called 'lame duck' businesses was also held up as a reason why economic sclerosis was a given, and decline inevitable.

Margaret Thatcher disagreed. Her administration ruthlessly steered Britain towards a more dynamic, and in practice unequal, economy. All sorts of policy levers were pulled towards this end: financial deregulation, such as the Big Bang of 1986; a staunchly disinflationary macroeconomic regime (whose basic consistency was sometimes obscured by different, and baffling, forms of monetarism); allowing the exchange rate to rise to the point that it made huge swathes of manufacturing uncompetitive; and tolerating previously unthinkable, geographically concentrated, rates of unemployment at a very high cost to people and communities. Incremental but remorseless restrictions on union power were used to forge a less organised, less regulated labour market. Taxes were redirected away from top incomes, and shifted onto consumption. Restrictions on social security benefits ramped up the pressure on the workless to accept new posts. Crucially, the European Single Market, which Mrs Thatcher helped to create, brought bracing winds of competition that did for some old firms, but at the same time created vast new opportunities for rising companies.

Thatcherism wrought a whirlwind of change – with greater job mobility across sectors and income growth – as well as rapidly increasing poverty and surging inequality. To supporters, who had bemoaned what they saw as the artificially 'telescoped' earnings wrought by 1970s incomes policies, these widening differentials were a desirable spur to individual ambition and industry. But many others warned that they entrenched disadvantage in some communities, and the widening gaps would create lasting problems, some of which we still confront in Britain today. The new inequality of the 1980s endured, and – at the top end – developed further in the years that followed.

The Thatcher era changed the 'facts on the ground' in Britain.[12] It created new parameters within which much of the British economy continues to operate more than three decades after she left office – from the formidably strong services sector and liberal labour market, to the high inequality between households and places. In seeking growth that 'goes with the grain' of the UK as it is, we have made proposals that would harness the strengths and tackle the many weaknesses bequeathed by those years. Even the many opposed to the economic strategy of that time can learn lessons from it. They were years that showed that given a clarity of purpose, it is possible to reshape an economy in line with changed priorities.

Even desirable change will – as it always does – throw up surprises and create losers. The way to make progress inclusive is not to pretend there will not be some dislocation, but to pay close attention to potential costs, especially if concentrated on particular groups or places. Managing these must be at the core of an economic strategy, not an afterthought.

Our discussion now turns to the specifics of change, at the level of sectors, firms and then workers. At each level British economic policy needs, first, to think differently about underlying change, and then to steer developments in a more productive and fairer direction:

At the level of sectors or industries, we must dispatch with the notion that it is somehow improper to take a view on the shape of our economy that reflects choices about what we consume as a nation, or how much carbon we emit, as much as the shape reflects those forces of technology and globalisation over which we have less direct control. The task is to build capacity – in terms of people and places – for higher-productivity tradable activity, while improving conditions for workers across our domestically focused non-tradable sectors in particular. The latter will have the effect of raising relative prices in these sectors, which in turn should gradually reduce their relative size compared to the current trajectory. If

---

12 J Muellbauer and D Soskice, The Thatcher Legacy: Lessons for the future of the UK economy, Resolution Foundation, November 2022

done cautiously, as part of a wider strategy that helps workers adjust, this kind of incremental, structural change is welcome. It is a feature, not a bug, of improving labour market conditions.

At the level of firms, discussions of raising productivity have focused exclusively on helping existing firms improve, but not enough on ensuring good, well-run companies can grow. That requires freeing up the land, labour and capital too often stuck in the hands of badly-run outfits. This will release more resources either for growing firms in the same sector or to move into other, rising, high-productivity industries.

At the worker level, we need to recognise that a dynamic labour market is a key mechanism through which reallocation between sectors and firms takes place. Dynamism is about far more than the right to hire and fire: it is about having more skilled and empowered workers, able to take the risk of moving to a new role, and equipped to progress in their careers.

The UK would benefit from a bigger role for higher paying, and smaller role for lower paying, sectors

Around the world, pressing challenges from the net zero transition to rising geopolitical tensions are prompting governments to take more of a hands-on view regarding the composition of their economy. Motivations focus on greater resilience of supply chains, particularly of raw materials or manufactured goods.[13] But there are wider reasons to consider the evolving balance of sectors from the point of view of our twin over-riding concerns: higher growth and lower inequality.

This is difficult. Our choices are constrained by geography, history, technology and international economic forces. It is, particularly for politicians, far easier to identify a sector that it would be nice to expand, with resources of capital and labour flowing in, than it is to grapple with which sectors might play a smaller role in our economy as a result.

Chapter 4 made the case that a higher-productivity Britain requires greater capacity to produce and sell high-value services, while protecting existing high-value manufacturing. This requires the right trade policy so UK firms can connect with growing demand, and more places and workers equipped to meet their needs. Figure 57 spells out the value of this approach, highlighting the steep productivity

---

13 For example, see European Commission, Critical Raw Materials Act: ensuring secure and sustainable supply chains for EU's green and digital future, March 2023; The White House, FACT SHEET: Biden- Harris Administration Announces Supply Chain Disruptions Task Force to Address Short-Term Supply Chain Discontinuities, June 2021.

gradient across sectors. Shifting a greater proportion of your workforce into sectors like ICT and business services can raise aggregate productivity without any sector becoming more productive.

Figure 57: A steep ladder: mapping productivity across sectors

Sector size and relative productivity in the UK: 2022

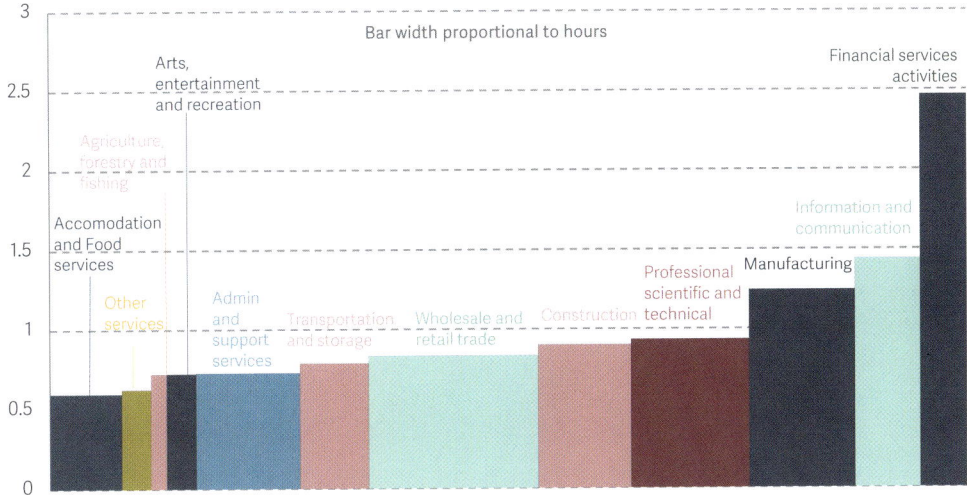

Notes: Notes: Width of bars represent the relative size of the sector (gross output in the baseline). Height represents relative productivity compared to average.
Source: ONS, Quarterly Output per hour worked by section-level industry aggregations, Chained volume measure (CVM), April 2023.

While there are limits to how large a part of your economy these sectors can become, we are not close to these limits. Global demand for these services is growing and the UK is a medium-sized economy for whom small changes in market share do not risk exhausting global demand.

A thought experiment illustrates the size of this prize. Despite our continuing strength in tradable services, our share of the growing global markets for them has reduced. Some reduction should be expected as more countries reach stages of development that see them competing to provide such services, but the exact size of that fall is far from pre-ordained. Between 2005 and 2018 our share of global service exports dropped from 8.8 to 7.2 per cent. If we had merely halved that reduction in market share, the result would be an extra 585,000 people working in these growth-critical fields today, worth a 1.5 per cent boost to GDP compared to a scenario where this group worked in non-exporting jobs.[14]

---

14 Source: Analysis of OECD, International Balanced International Trade in Services; OECD Trade in employment (TiM) 2021; OECD Trade in Value Added 2021; ONS Subregional Productivity June 2023 release.

This focus on higher-value sectors will not just benefit those already at the upper end of the pay range, such as accountants, architects or consultants. Pay in so-called strategic sectors spanning key services and parts of manufacturing[15] is consistently higher than in the rest of the economy, including for those with lower-level qualifications. Indeed, the premium going to those working in these sectors is of a similar size (around 30-40 per cent) for those with the very lowest qualifications as it is for university graduates.[16]

Figure 58: Growth sectors pay better across the skills range

Average weekly wages by workers' highest qualification, for the strategic sectors and the rest of the economy, in 2015 prices: UK, 2011-2019

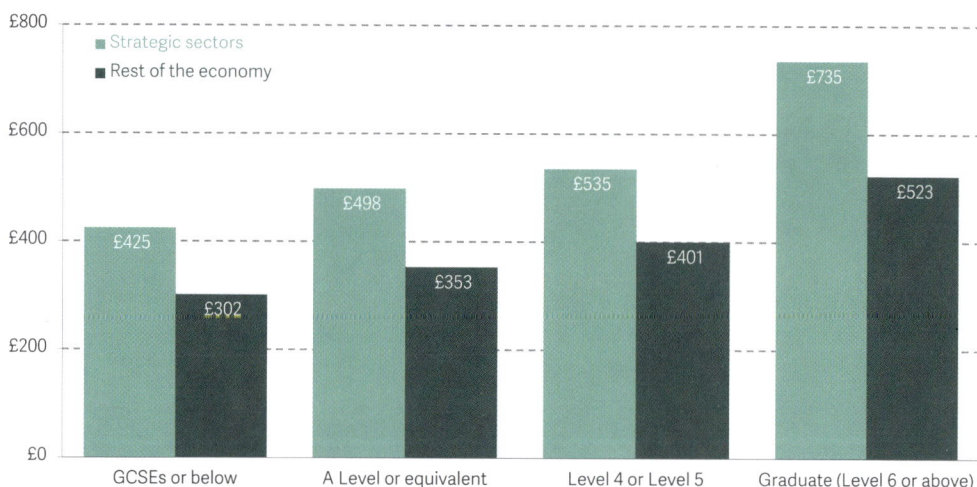

Notes: We obtain these estimates by performing augmented Mincerian regressions where the control for differences in workers' potential labour market experience and full-time employment status.
Source: Analysis of ONS, Labour Force Survey.

Not only do these sectors deliver higher wages across the board, they enable more sustained wage growth over a career, thanks to steeper returns to labour market experience. This is especially true for less qualified workers: those whose highest qualifications are GCSEs or below have average annual earnings growth of 1.3 per cent outside the strategic sectors, but 1.9 per cent within them.[17]

15 Strategic sectors are defined here as financial and business services, the creative and cultural sector, and life sciences. Life sciences includes pharmaceutical manufacturing, biotechnologies and manufacturing medical equipment.

16 R Costa et al., Learning to grow: How to situate a skills strategy in an economic strategy, Resolution Foundation, October 2023.

17 See R Costa et al., Learning to grow: How to situate a skills strategy in an economic strategy, Resolution Foundation, October 2023.

There is a common misconception that wages will only rise in a sector if productivity growth takes place in that sector. But, in the right circumstances, the benefits of productivity growth in one part of the economy are felt elsewhere. Take hairdressing – the quintessential example of an occupation in which the scope for productivity growth is very limited. Over the sweep of decades, hairdressers' real wages have risen despite the lack of productivity growth, in order to prevent too many workers leaving for other industries.[18] The circle has been squared by a rise in the relative price of haircuts (Figure 59).[19] In the end we do want our hair cut.

Figure 59: Real wages can keep pace even in occupations that do not experience productivity growth

Real median hourly pay for hairdressers and all workers and the real price of a haircut, 1997=100

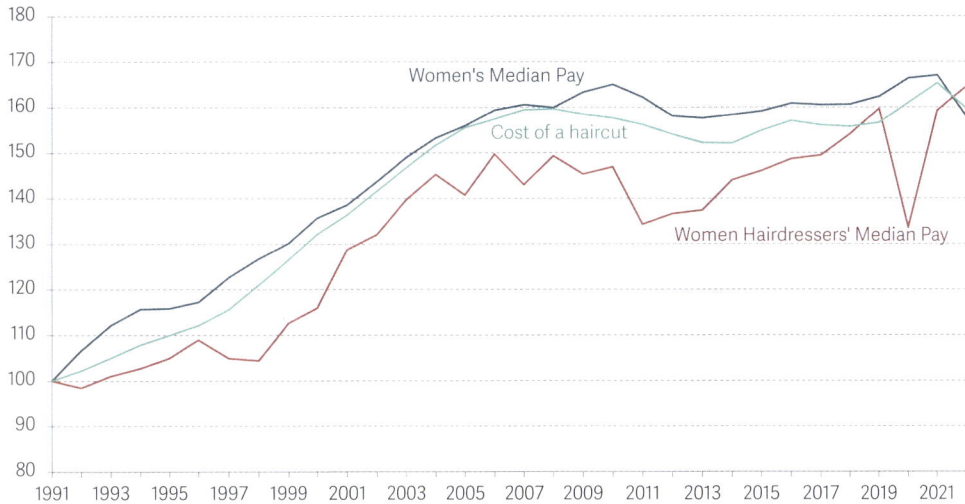

Notes: Wages are nominal hourly pay. Cost of a haircut is component 12.1.1 of the CPI ('Hairdressing and personal grooming establishments') All datapoints indexed to 1997=100. Source: ONS ASHE Survey 1997 onwards, ONS CPI data.

This tendency of low-productivity-growth services to rise in price is often referred to as a 'cost disease'. But it is a feature, not a bug, of a well-functioning market economy. It is the way that productivity growth in some industries spreads to benefit all.

18 The chart also shows that when aggregate real wages and productivity stagnated, hairdressers' wages flattened off too.

19 We see the same pattern across countries at different levels of development as we do comparing one country over time. The price of non-tradable services – and the real wages of those that produce them – tend to be lower in countries with lower aggregate productivity. Productivity growth is concentrated in tradable sectors and this causes the relative price of non-tradables to rise, as producers have to compete with higher wages available elsewhere. This is known as the Belassa-Samuelson effect.

What we buy shapes what we produce

The easy part of a story about sectoral change is identifying which sectors can grow. For that to happen others will have to be smaller, if not in absolute terms then at least as a share of employment. The UK has large amounts of labour allocated to certain lower-productivity, lower-paying sectors, as Figure 57 showed. Figure 60 shows that some change is underway. Employment in the retail sector (and its cousin wholesale) has been shrinking for many years, partly offset by rising numbers in warehousing – two sides of the decline of bricks-and-mortar shopping. Change like this is often effected by younger people not joining an industry, rather than mid-career workers leaving.[20]

Figure 60: Retail has shrunk over the past decade as hospitality has grown

Average annual employee jobs in selected sectors as a proportion of total sectors: GB

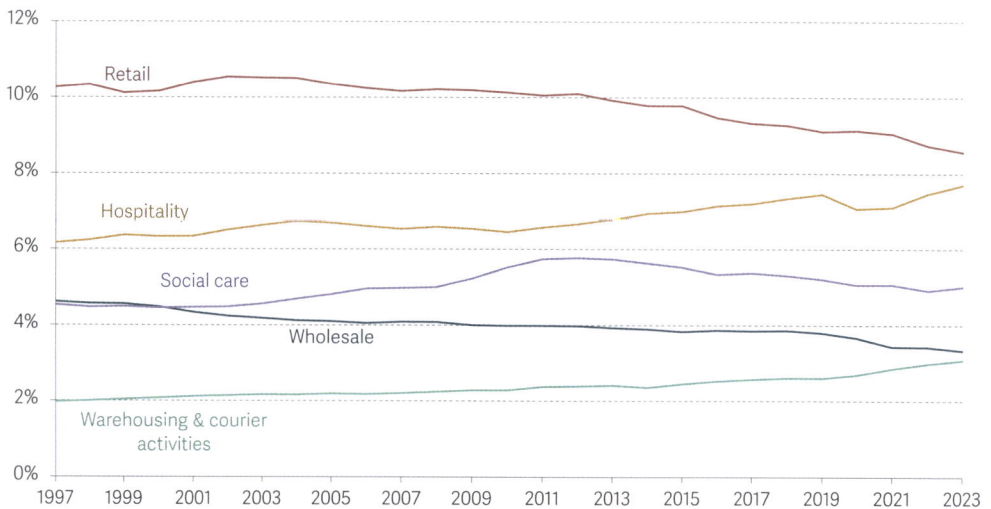

Source: Analysis of ONS, Workforce Jobs.

With an ageing population and growing care needs, it is likely and desirable that the social care sector will grow: the tight spending settlements of the 2010s held down employment in the sector by rationing the numbers receiving care.[21] The challenge is to ensure that the sector can provide good jobs for the growing number who will be working within it, a central focus of the Good Work Agreements and other labour standards measures proposed in Chapter 6.

20 N Cominetti et al., Changing jobs? Change in the UK labour market and the role of worker mobility, Resolution Foundation, January 2022.

21 H Alderwick et al., What should be done to fix the crisis in social care?: Five priorities for government, The Health Foundation, August 2019.

But what about hospitality, an industry that has got far larger over the last 15 years, accounting for over 60 per cent of total growth in all employment across the lower-paying sectors since 2008?[22] Restaurants, cafes and hotels are significant chunks of the 'everyday economy' and are – and will remain – crucial employers, not to mention a source of significant pleasure for many.

It is time to think harder about how such sectors fit into our economic strategy. The size of these non-tradable service sectors is driven, not by our share of global markets, but by patterns of domestic consumption – by the proportion of our family budgets we spend there – and by relative costs.

These things vary significantly across countries. As Figure 61 reveals, the proportion of total consumption that hospitality represents is higher in the UK than anywhere else in Europe. This in part explains why the sector's employment share is bigger than in France, despite tourism being a far smaller part of our economy.[23] The chart also suggests why this might be: in the UK hospitality is relatively cheap (compared to the price of other things) and there is a clear negative relationship between how much people pay for hospitality services, and how much each nation consumes.

It may feel odd to think about the size of various low-paying, low-productivity sectors as anything other than 'natural'. The reason they exist at this scale is, after all, to answer the choices made by firms and all of us as consumers, and those choices harden into familiar habits. But those choices are always conditioned by prices. And those prices are not fixed, but depend on things that policy can change. In particular, a substantial part of the cost of providing lower-productivity services is labour, the cost of which is in part shaped by the supply of low-skilled labour (influenced by demographics, migration, and the proportion of people the education system leaves with few skills) and regulations on pay and standards. Changes in these drive shifts in the cost of labour, the relative price of these bread-and-butter services, and in turn how much of them we consume.

---

22 Low-paying sectors defined here as retail, wholesale, warehousing, hospitality and social care.
23 Accommodation and food service activities are 5.4 per cent of UK employment in 2019, compared to 3.8 per cent in France, according to OECD data.

Figure 61: Pricier menus, fewer meals out

Hotels and restaurants as a share of resident consumption (2015) plotted against its prices relative to that of other goods and services within the economy (2019), by country

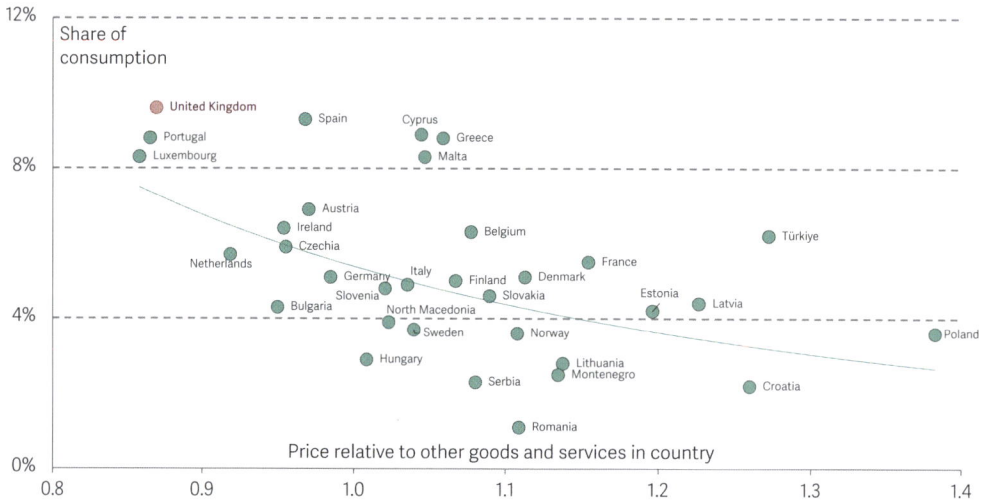

Source: Analysis of Eurostat.

This dynamic is one a serious economic strategy for the UK should embrace. Our focus on boosting the UK's skill mix, in particular tackling the outsized proportion of each cohort who enter the labour market with limited qualifications, aims to reduce the relative supply of low-skilled workers, as we at the same time raise the floor on the quality of work in ways that go beyond a higher minimum wage (see Chapter 6). As well as supporting more good jobs, this will heighten incentives to make better use of lower-paid labour, pushing up on productivity within these sectors.

But the experience of the minimum wage tells us that its effects will eventually be to raise somewhat the relative prices of things produced by low-wage workers.[24] The trade-offs here are real and need to be grappled with. Cross-country evidence indicates that, for a given level of productivity, higher wages in non-tradable

24 A Dube, Impacts of minimum wages: review of the international evidence, HM Treasury & Department for Business, Energy and Industrial Strategy, November 2019.

industries, paid for by higher prices, make an economy more equal.[25] Workers in lower-income households benefit most from improved conditions in the likes of hospitality, leisure and retail because that is where their employment is concentrated, while it is richer households, who spend a larger share of their budgets on such face-to-face services, who are most affected by the higher prices that follow, as Figure 62 sets out. This distributional outcome matters not just in its own terms but also given the wider question highlighted in Chapter 5 concerning whose consumption falls to fund the shift to a higher investment economic strategy.

Figure 62: Better pay and conditions in non-tradeable services would benefit low-income households, while any price effects would be mainly felt by higher-income households

Retail, leisure & hospitality as a share of consumption and employment, by after housing cost income quintile: UK, 2019-2020.

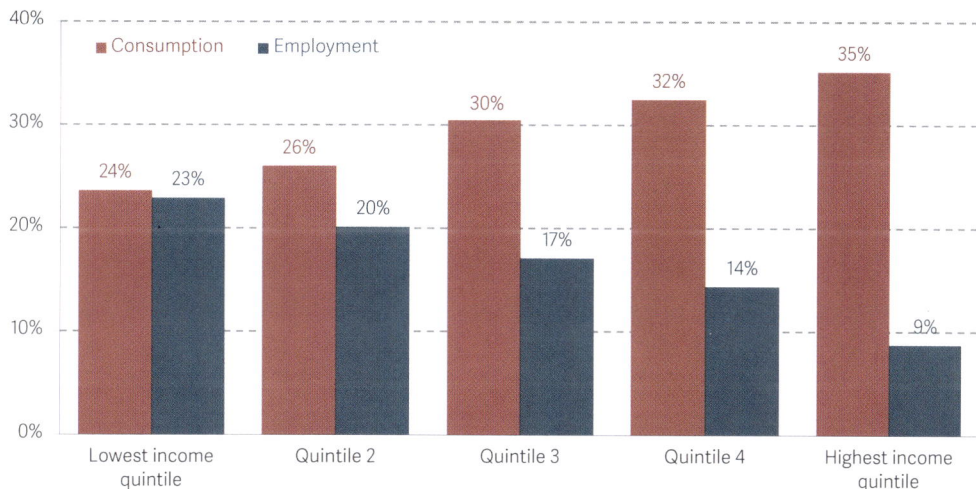

Source: Analysis of ONS, Living Costs and Food Survey; DWP, Family Resources Survey.

So lower-paying sectors would be expected gradually to become better employers, relatively more expensive and relatively smaller than they would otherwise be (while, to be clear, remaining among the biggest employers in our economy). When

25 We compare how expensive the cost of a given basket of goods is (i.e. how high the real exchange rate is) and how big the difference is between wages at the 10th and 50th percentiles of the wage distribution. If the price of tradable goods is similar across countries (because they are tradable) then the real exchange rate will be driven by differences in the price of non-tradable goods. We control for productivity (TFP) to strip out any effect from richer countries tending to be more or less equal, and because more productive countries tend to be more expensive. A 10 per cent increase in the real exchange rate reduces inequality by about 1/6th of a standard deviation.

combined with steps to increase the UK's capacity to grow higher value-added sectors, this would, over time, see a proportion of the British workforce – together with some share of land and capital – redeployed away from lower to higher-productivity, sectors. This is what a strategy that seeks to steer the process of change towards a higher-productivity and lower-inequality economy looks like.

The pace and nature of change matters

While the benefits of structural change are clear, we must remember that change can hurt too. Deindustrialisation hit some communities very hard. So there will be understandable doubts about whether more reallocation is truly desirable. In response it is worth noting that many other experiences of change look very different, including others that involved face-to-face services. The speed of change in such cases has generally been lower, without the pressure of shifts in international competition, and lacks the poisonous geographical concentration of the decline of manufacturing. Face-to-face services by their nature are spread throughout every community, with at least a quarter of private-sector jobs in non-tradable services in every travel to work area.[26] As an example, the decline of domestic service is considered in Box 27.

Box 27: The shrinking of British domestic services

The biggest-employing sector of all for women in the late 19th century was domestic service. Its growth, explosive into the mid-Victorian age, slowed after 1871. By the interwar years the traditional full-time "indoor" live-in maid had often gone in favour of a part-time "daily." By 1951, two-thirds of female servants were non-resident, and their total number – at 260,000 – was around 80 per cent down on a few decades before.[27] The dwindling of domestic service preceded the end of coal-fires and the widespread arrival of labour-saving appliances, so is best thought of instead as an adjustment to cheap labour becoming harder to come by, in part because of the new opportunities opening up in clerical work and elsewhere. Despite "can't get the staff" complaints in the letters pages of a certain class of magazine, this huge transition played out without any great social convulsion, and is now rightly

---

26 N Cominetti et al., Low Pay Britain 2023: Improving low-paid work through higher minimum standards, Resolution Foundation, April 2023.

27 S Todd, Domestic Service and Class Relations in Britain 1900-1950, Past and Present: A Journal of Historical Studies, Oxford University Press, May 2009.

understood as a positive thing: only in very unequal societies can many higher-income households have sufficient disposable income to command the entire labour of several lower earners.[28]

The pace of change is key. No one should be eager to rush into rapid structural change: few workers walk away from, say, a café on a Friday afternoon and into an accountant's office on the Monday. But a crucial channel for reallocation, especially when it comes to sectors with younger workforces,[29] is the choices made by the rising generation of workers, rather than the stereotype of older workers being made redundant.[30] This underlines, once again, the importance of improved educational opportunities, particularly for the young (see Chapter 6), to a strategy seeking to harness the progressive power of economic change.

In sum, the sectoral balance of our economy is always changing, even if that process has slowed down of late. No economic strategy can simply dictate the nature and scale of that change, but a strategy worth its name must engage with and seek to steer it. Stepping back, the approach that we have set out is a recipe for gradual but ultimately profound change. And yet described this way, it also risks sounding abstract. Economic change crystallises not at the generalised level of industries and sectors, but in the operations of individual firms and lives of individual workers – which we now consider in turn.

Firms in Britain have become less dynamic, imposing a high productivity penalty

A central case for the market economy is that it has powerful mechanisms for shifting resources – capital, labour, land – from firms that can't get the best out of them to those that can. This is important because productivity differs hugely across firms, with poor performers lagging a long way behind the best, as Figure

---

28 This was referred to as the 'servant problem'. See, for example, C Frederick, It works like a charm: Scientific management and the servant problem, The New Housekeeping series, Ladies Home Journal, December 1912.

29 Almost half – 47 per cent – of hospitality workers are aged under 30, compared to 23 per cent of the workforce as a whole. Source: ONS, Employment by age, industry and occupation, UK, 2010, 2015 and 2019, November 2020.

30 In the UK this is why manufacturing employment among workers in their 60s was actually higher in 2018-19 than 1994-95, despite manufacturing jobs being down 38 per cent. For more, see: C Covounidis et al., Obsolescence Rents: Teamsters, Truckers, and Impending Innovations Warwick University, November 2022.

63 illustrates.[31] And consistent with the disciplining effect of competition having weakened, productivity gaps between high and low performing firms have increased over time, particularly among larger firms.[32]

Figure 63: Inequality among British firms is stark – and rising

Estimated firm-level productivity (turnover per employee) by decile in selected sectors of the market economy: 2020

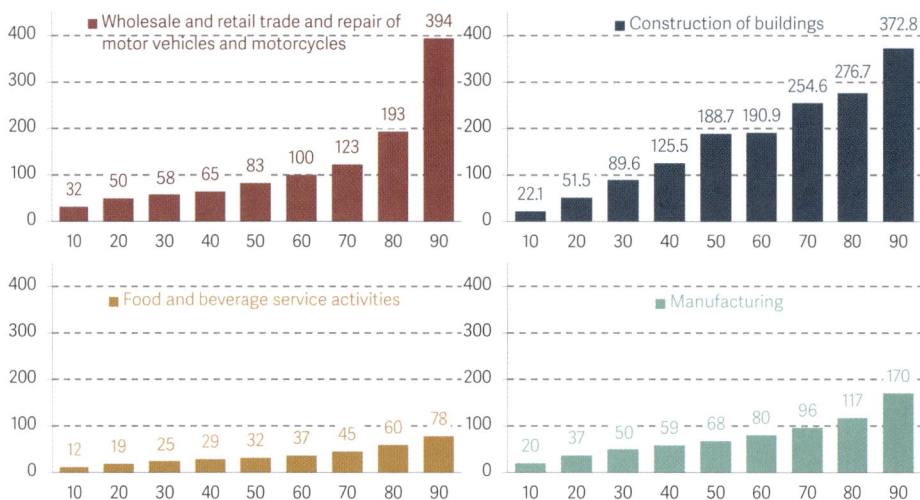

Notes: Deciles are estimated as the mean value in a band defined by the two neighbouring deciles.
Source: Analysis of ONS, Business Structure Database.

There are accordingly three ways to increase productivity at the national level. First, you can improve the best firms, either the current leaders or the ones with the most potential for innovation and growth. This way has received a good deal of policy attention, with a number of well-intentioned and, in some cases, effective schemes to support high-growth firms, including R&D tax credits and the relatively new British Business Bank. Innovation policy is important, not least because the UK's biggest firms are in strikingly 'old economy' lines of business (see Box 28).

---

31 See also: J De Loecker, T Obermeier & J Van Reenen, Firms and inequality, IFS Deaton Review of Inequalities, March 2022.

32 R Davies et al., Ready for change: How and why to make the UK economy more dynamic, Resolution Foundation, September 2023.

Box 28: *Britain's top five firms are dinosaurs in comparison to the top five in the US*

While the UK has some advantages in growth sectors, including digital, it is some time since those were translated into building new large companies. As Figure 64 shows, notwithstanding the importance of AstraZeneca, the UK-listed top five firms are much smaller, older and weighted more heavily towards banking and extraction than their technology focused counterparts in the US.[33] An economy fossilised in areas that were important for growth in a bygone era is not prioritising the future.

Figure 64: The UK stock market lacks large firms in the tech sector

Market capitalisation of five largest listed firms: US and UK, October 2023

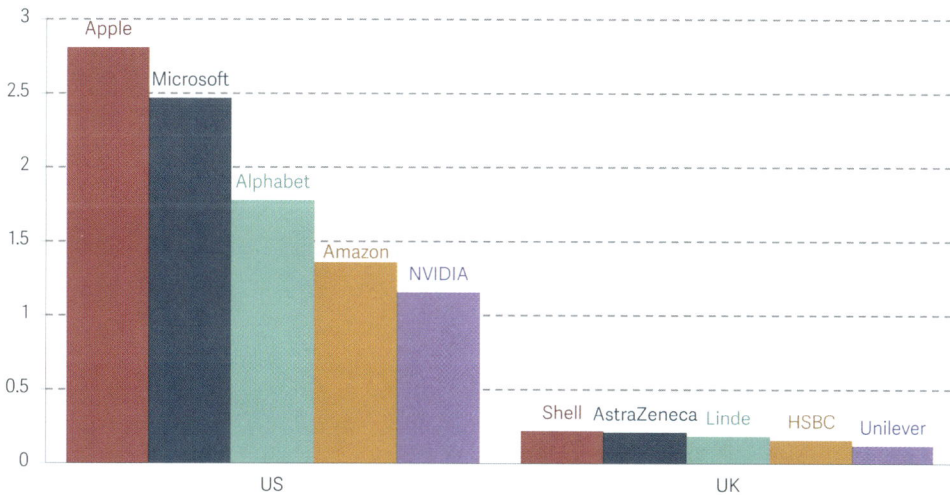

Notes: The Linde Group is listed in London but headquartered in Dublin.
Source: Analysis of October 2023 market capitalisation data, from: companiesmarketcap.com.

33 When interpreting this chart, it is important to note that the country a company is listed in is not necessarily where most of its value is added.

Second, you can improve the worst ones. The 'long tail' of underperforming firms has received a lot of policy attention.[34] But a focus on the 'long tail' catching up must confront the difficulties of reaching many firms with business support interventions (see Box 29 for an example of the challenges of a diffusion-focused strategy). Business support policies can make a difference to some companies,[35] but the need for them to be targeted on motivated firms means their aggregate impact risks being overstated.[36]

Box 29: Managers must be willing to learn for diffusion to be effective

The UK Government has placed diffusion centre-stage in its efforts to raise productivity, with a big focus on supporting small, low-productivity, businesses to improve.[37] But the evidence from attempts to do so is not encouraging, reflecting the reality that firms are often small precisely because their owners or managers are not focused on growth. Figure 65 shows what happened when over 12,000 firms who had completed the Management and Expectations Survey were asked if they would like feedback on how their management compared to others, with the intention of providing them with online coaching. A minority asked for feedback, while an even smaller minority of those actually visited the website signposted for the coaching. When we look at the fairly modest number making it over these hurdles (around 1,500), only a tiny fraction took the final step and registered for tuition. A grand total of 44 firms ultimately enlisted for coaching.

---

34 See, for example: Department for Business, Energy and Industrial Strategy, Business Basics Programme, January 2019; and www.bethebusiness.com.

35 Training, consulting and information provision interventions can have positive impacts though there are differences depending on programme design and intensity, see: See: D Scur et al., The World Management Survey at 18: lessons and the way forward, Oxford Review of Economic Policy, 2021.

36 J Phipps & R Fuller, Developing policies to promote SME digital adoption: a rapid evidence review, IGL Working Paper, November 2022.

37 HM Government, Business Productivity Review, November 2019.

Figure 65: Hard to help – most current firms turn down managerial coaching when offered

Actions by Management and Expectations Survey respondents

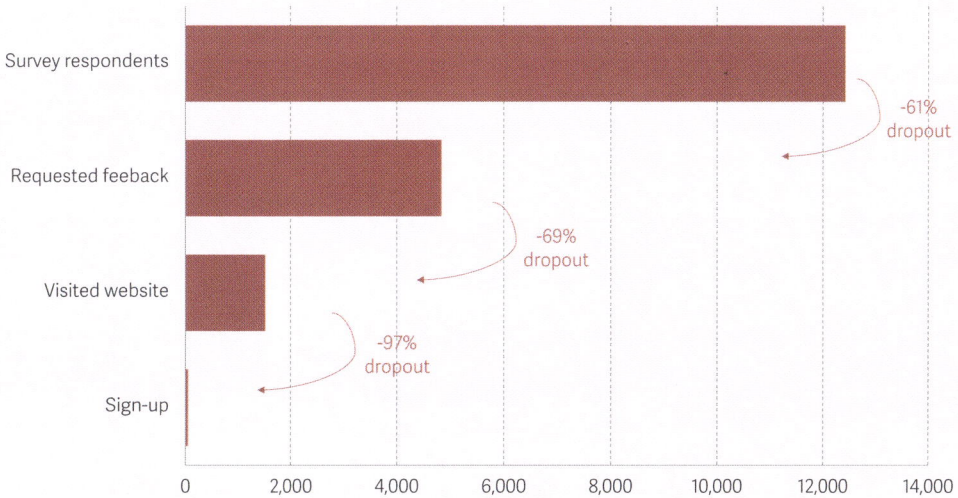

Notes: MES = Management and Expectations Survey
Source: Meng, C., Mizen, P., Riley, R. and Schneebacher, J. (2023) "Who wants to improve their management? Evidence from a failed experiment", ESCoE Discussion Paper 2023-22, London: ESCoE.

Third, you can shift resources from the worst firms to the best. This reallocation at the level of firms – some shrinking and others growing – raises the average productivity of the economy. Yet it is strangely absent from debates about Britain's productivity challenge.

It might be expected that the elevated economic turbulence of the last 15 years would have accelerated the waxing and waning of companies, as they adjust to repeated shocks. In fact, firms have been growing and shrinking less rather than more: the rate at which jobs were reallocated from closing or shrinking, to starting or growing, firms fell by one-fifth after 2008, as Figure 66 illustrates. That is a pretty substantial drop and can be seen within all the large sectors, including manufacturing, retail and construction. The impact of this firm-level stagnation accumulates over time and tots up to 7.5 million "missing moves". This is economically costly, representing a slower flow of labour from generally lower-productivity firms to generally higher-productivity ones. Moreover, the impact of this slowdown in moves has been compounded by a weakening in the tendency for the expanding firms to exhibit higher productivity.[38]

Figure 66: Job reallocation between firms has been falling

Annual churn in UK jobs attributable to firms hiring, firing, starting up or shutting down

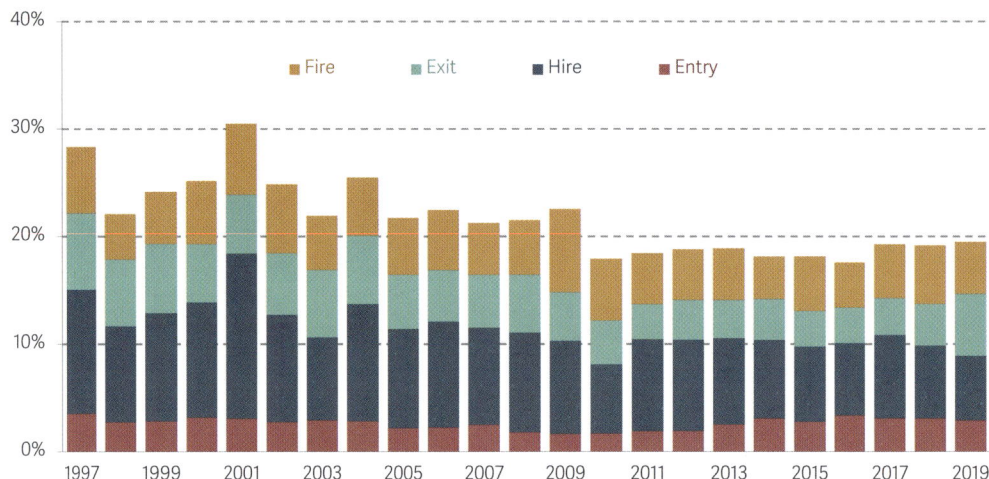

Notes: Rates are defined as total jobs created or destroyed in a particular period relative to the stock at the end of the previous period. Rates are percentages as a proportion of the total workforce. Non-market sectors (education, healthcare) and the financial and real-estate sectors are excluded.
Source: Analysis of ONS, Business Structure Database.

The upshot is that in parallel with – and plausibly because of – reduced redeployment between firms, the potential gains to be had from such redeployment have increased. We should focus on shifting resources from poor performers to good ones, rather than pinning our hopes on changing the performance of the former. Indeed, the potential gains from targeting the 'long tail' are sometimes overstated: raising the productivity of the least productive firms employing 40 per cent of workers by a huge 10 per cent would raise overall productivity by only 1.2 per cent. In contrast, transferring one-tenth of those

38 The sensitivity of net hiring to productivity fell by 30 per cent in the immediate aftermath of the financial crisis. See: R Davies et al., Ready for change: How and why to make the UK economy more dynamic, Resolution Foundation, September 2023.

workers into high-performing firms (assuming, for illustrative purposes, that could be done without affecting the productivity of those firms) would boost productivity by some 6 per cent.[39]

We all pay the price for poor firms – a smaller economy with lower tax revenues and higher costs – but workers in those firms pay a particularly high bill. They do so directly via lower wages, with the OECD suggesting they directly shoulder 15 per cent of productivity differences[40] and international evidence showing that most of the widening in wage inequality across workers is due to widening disparities in average wages between firms.[41] And surveys indicate workers in lower productivity firms are also more likely to report lower well-being,[42] while lower productivity firms with less structured management practices have also been less agile when it comes to enabling work-from-home or online sales since the pandemic.[43]

The slowing in firm dynamism has been common across many industrialised countries, suggesting that deep technological or demographic forces may be at play. But there are a number of other things that governments can do, or indeed stop doing, to get more resources to the best firms.

The Government needs to stop being a barrier to dynamism, while bad firms should be pincered between investing rivals and rising labour standards

The Government should lower barriers to change, even when they are not the cause of the slowdown in firm dynamism. Restrictive planning controls (including those preventing the change of land use) don't just prevent things getting built (see Chapter 4 and 5), but also hinder the economy from adapting. Planning should be reformed and both residential and non-residential Stamp Duty halved (see Chapter 7). This will make it easier for high-growth firms to find premises and co-locate in clusters, and cheaper for workers to relocate to them.[44]

---

39 J Oliveira-Cunha et al., Business time: How ready are UK firms for the decisive decade?, Resolution Foundation, November 2021.

40 C Criscuolo et al., The firm-level link between productivity dispersion and wage inequality: A symptom of low job mobility?, OECD, August 2021.

41 For a summary of the evidence, see: J De Loecker, T Obermeier & J Van Reenen, Firms and inequalities, IFS Deaton Review of Inequalities, March 2022. For an example of a specific study (from the US), see: J Song et al., Firming Up Inequality, The Quarterly Journal of Economics, February 2019.

42 C Krekel, G Ward & J De Neve, Employee Wellbeing, Productivity, and Firm Performance, Saïd Business School, March 2019.

43 ONS, Management Practices, homeworking and productivity during the coronavirus (Covid-19) pandemic, May 2021.

44 Halving non-residential Stamp Duty would be enough to boost transaction volumes by 20 per cent. M Broome et al., Tax Planning: How to match higher taxes with better taxes, Resolution Foundation, June 2023.

More broadly, the UK needs to rethink the types of firms it focuses support on. Our systems of tax and regulation explicitly favour small businesses at the expense of large ones, with lower Corporation Tax, employer National Insurance and Business Rates. As noted in Chapter 7, firms with turnover below £85,000 are not required to register for VAT, making their sales artificially cheaper to some customers. It also strongly favours the self-employed over employees. This approach, often defended as supporting smaller, growing firms, instead acts as a tax on growth. UK firms hold back from expanding and instead bunch below the VAT threshold,[45] consistent with evidence from France that having regulations that kick in when firms reach a certain size discourages business growth.[46] In a world where larger firms are on average more efficient than smaller ones this approach has high costs. Instead of favouring small firms, tax and regulatory policy should if anything prioritise young firms, which have far higher potential to grow and attract new staff.[47] For the VAT threshold specifically, the best outcome would be lowering it to the point where almost no business owner would consider the option of deliberately staying below that level of turnover.

Competition is a key driver of pressure on firms to sink or swim. Low productivity firms are able to survive in part because they face weak competition for customers or for the workers and capital tied up in their businesses. In practice, except for the very largest firms, the most important thing is the broader competitive environment, rather than competition policy itself. Policy must therefore act to strengthen the range of competitive pressures that force poorly performing firms to improve. Trade openness is an important source of such pressure in a medium-sized economy like the UK's and, as discussed in Chapter 2, this has gone backwards over recent years and must be addressed. Moreover, part of the intention of reforms set out in chapters 5 and 6 is to create two domestic sources of increased pressure, pincering poorly performing firms between higher-investing competitors and rising labour standards.

45 Office for Budget Responsibility, The impact of the frozen VAT registration threshold, in Economic and fiscal outlook, March 2023.

46 L Garicano, C Lelarge & J Van Reenen, Firm size distortions and the productivity distribution: Evidence from France, American Economic Review, November 2016.

47 J Haltiwanger, R S Jarmin & J Miranda, Who creates jobs? Small versus large versus young, Review of Economics and Statistics 95(2), May 2013.

Recent experience of raising labour market minimum standards, including the minimum wage in Germany, has seen it play a role in shifting labour out of low-wage, low-productivity firms and into employers whose higher productivity means they are in a position to pay their staff more.[48] But this must be about more than a higher minimum wage. Firms that are only able to operate by refusing to give their workers any certainty about the hours they work, illegally underpaying them because of weak enforcement, or relying on disguised self-employed labour in order to pay lower taxes (see Box 30), would all feel more competitive pressure as part of this economic strategy. The Good Work Agreements (set out in Chapter 6) would act as a mechanism for raising labour standards, putting upward pressure on low productivity firms and steering us towards the high road.

Box 30: Self-employment isn't the solution to a more dynamic economy

Britain has seen a surge in self-employed workers, such as freelancers, consultants and gig workers this century.[49] This increase has been particularly striking following the financial crisis where, until 2014, self-employment made a larger contribution to the growth in overall employment than the growth in employees.[50]

Some have credited this boom in self-employment to new technologies, but Britain's preferential tax treatment of these workers is a more convincing cause. After all, technological change has been common across developed economies but the huge growth in self-employment is very UK specific. Indeed, in most European countries solo self-employment has been flat or falling as a share of employment over the past 20 years, as shown in Figure 67.

---

48 C Dustmann et al., Reallocation effects of the minimum wage, Quarterly Journal of Economics, February 2022.

49 The number of self-employed workers increased from 3.5 million people in 1992 to around 5 million by the end of 2019, prior to the pandemic. This translates into the proportion of workers who are self-employed rising from 13.5 per cent in 1992 to 15.3 per cent by 2019.

50 Source: ONS, Trends in self-employment in the UK, February 2018.

Meanwhile the UK's tax system has a bias against the employed compared with the self-employed, who do not face equivalent national insurance contributions. A market income of £30,000 would attract over £2,000 less tax if structured as self-employment rather than employment in 2022-23, with this tax advantage estimated to cost HMRC £6 billion in 2022-23 alone.[51]

Figure 67: Self employment has grown faster in the UK than elsewhere

Index of self-employment as a proportion of total employment (2003 = 100)

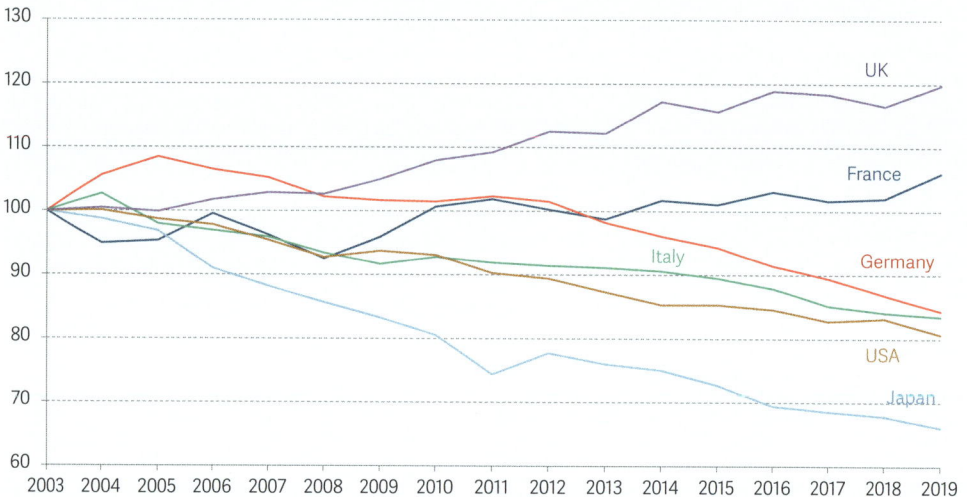

Source: Analysis of OECD, Self-employment rate (indicator).

An economic strategy that is clearsighted about economic change should recognise that survey evidence tells us that many people like the flexibility that self-employment brings. But that doesn't mean that we should accept the scale of tax-incentivised self-employment. Although it is popular for politicians to talk about all self-employed workers as entrepreneurs, the increase in this type of employment has been entirely about solo agents not those

---

51 The self-employed pay Class 4 National Insurance Contributions (NICs) at a lower main rate than the Class 1 NICs paid by employees, but also pay no equivalent of 'employer' NICs. This is not justified by any significant differences in social security entitlements. For example see: N Cominetti et al., Low pay Britain 2022: Low pay and insecurity in the UK labour market, Resolution Foundation, May 2022; A Corlett, Happy new tax year? National Insurance and Income Tax changes in 2022, Resolution Foundation, April 2022; M Broome, A Corlett & G Thwaites, Tax planning: How to match higher taxes with better taxes, Resolution Foundation, June 2023.

employing others.[52] In addition, the self-employed are, on average, lower paid than employees,[53] and have higher levels of insecurity, lacking many of the employment rights afforded employees.[54] Perhaps most concerningly, there has been a rise of 'false' or 'bogus' self-employment in recent years, whereby firms classify workers over whom they have considerable control as self-employed to side-step costs in the form of both tax and employment rights.[55]

Ultimately policy should ensure that those doing the same economic activity in different guises (such as the same work being done by an employee, a self-employed person or a business owner) are taxed at the same rate and afforded the same protections.

On the other side of this pincer movement, the package of reforms aiming to boost investment (see Chapter 5) will see low productivity outfits, who are likely to continue investing very little, face intensifying competition from rivals investing at higher rates than we see today. As those firms increasingly operate with more or higher-quality capital, they will stretch their lead over weaker performers. Periods in which countries engage in significant upgrading of production methods, with higher investment, have also seen higher levels of reallocation. It is not a coincidence that the late 1990s and early 2000s was the last time both were seen, as the IT revolution transformed how many firms operated. The need for significant investment and innovation to deliver the requirements of the green transition – which will necessitate the transformation of energy, transport and urban systems, and significant changes in production methods in some sectors (e.g. cement and steel) – may have a similar effect, as avenues for trying to run a company with little or no investment are closed off.

All told, this would be a much tougher environment for under-investing, low-paying firms. Over time, the goal is that their share of the workforce will steadily decline, as the share deployed in higher-investing, higher-productivity outfits increases. But these firm and sectoral changes require labour to adjust too – whether

---

52 G Giupponi & X Xu, What does the rise of self-employment tell us about the UK labour market?, IFS Deaton Review of Inequalities, November 2020.

53 A Teichgräber & J Van Reenan, Have productivity & pay decoupled in the UK?, CEP Discussion Paper, November 2021.

54 See Box 1 of: L Judge & H Slaughter, Enforce for good: Effectively enforcing labour market rights in the 2020s and beyond, Resolution Foundation, April 2023.

55 Citizens Advice, Neither one thing nor the other: how reducing bogus self-employment could benefit workers, business and the Exchequer, August 2015.

through existing workers moving jobs, or via changes in the flow of workers entering and leaving the labour market. It is the implications of economic change for workers that we turn to next.

Workers are moving jobs less, holding back their prospects

Traditionally, labour market dynamism has been seen as synonymous with labour market flexibility – with the assumption that all that matters is ease of hiring and firing. Britain's 'flexible' labour market has proven itself effective at generating a good quantity of work, with strong employment growth – as Chapter 6 underlined – being of disproportionate benefit to poorer households. A broadly flexible labour market also helps avoid a two-tier insider/outsider workforce of permanent (often older) and temporary (often younger) workers.[56] It is important to guard these advantages, which is why the standards-raising and security-bolstering protections in Chapter 6 have been carefully tailored to ensure they preserve what is, by international standards, a relatively flexible approach to hiring and firing.[57]

But it is equally clear that flexibility is not the same thing as dynamism. The notional flexibility of the UK labour market has gone hand-in-hand with an increasingly sclerotic reality. Despite managers' complaints about workers moving roles too often, fewer workers are moving jobs. In 2000, 3.2 per cent of workers moved jobs per quarter. In 2019, the rate of job mobility was 2.4 per cent, down 25 per cent.[58] Job-to-job moves picked up in the aftermath of the Covid-19 pandemic, reflecting pent-up demand for change among workers and post-pandemic economic restructuring for firms, but have been falling back again since the end of last year.[59]

Fewer job-to-job moves comes at a high price for all of us, in terms of lower productivity growth, as well as for the individual workers concerned. As Figure 68 shows, average wage rises are around four-fold higher for those who move jobs compared to those who do not, rising to nearly six-fold among those who switched not only their firm, but also their region or sector.

56 A Lindbeck & D Snower, Insiders versus outsiders, Journal of Economic Perspectives, Winter 2001.

57 OECD, OECD Indicators of Employment Protection, accessed 23 October 2023.

58 N Cominetti et al., Changing jobs?: Change in the UK labour market and the role of worker mobility, Resolution Foundation, January 2022.

59 T Bell et al., Understanding the labour market: pandemic not pandemonium: The labour market is normalising, not overheating, Resolution Foundation, June 2021; Office for National Statistics, X02: Labour Force Survey flows estimates, August 2023.

Figure 68: It pays to move on

Median annual growth in CPIH-adjusted hourly pay, 2005-20: GB

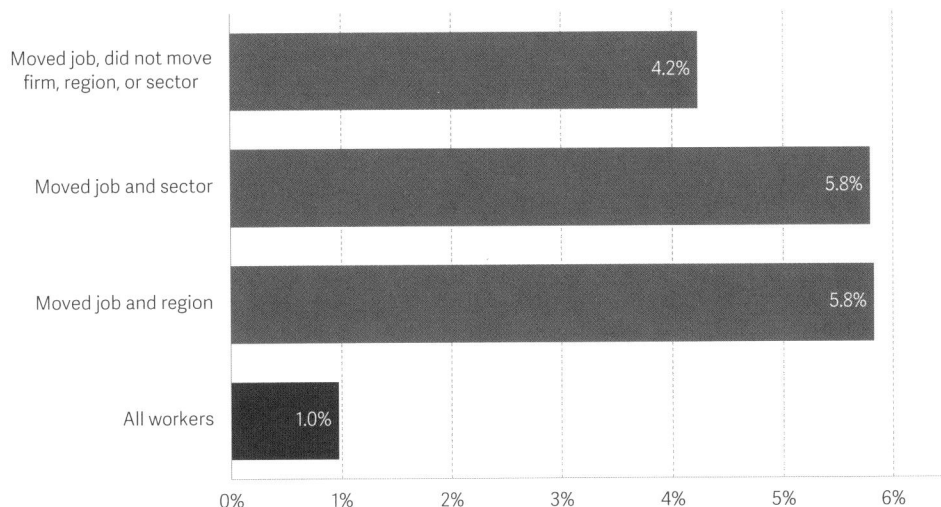

Source: Analysis of ONS, ASHE.

The prerequisite of a more dynamic labour market is confident workers

Focusing just on the freedom for employers to make changes risks missing a key component of a dynamic labour market: empowered workers with the confidence to make job moves. Those moves don't come without risks. While the generic risk is common – that a new role doesn't work out – what that means varies significantly between different kinds of workers.

Among mid and higher earners, the risk flows from the meanness of the UK's social security system that offers them little by way of income protection (relative to their established earnings) should a new role not work out, nor a breathing space in which to find a better match going forward. In contrast, lower earners might receive proportionately greater income protection from the benefits system, but risk losing important security and flexibility on moving from an established role. For both groups, we need to ensure that taking a leap for a new job is more of a promise – and less of a threat.

In the lower reaches of the earnings distribution, there are threats to job quality that go way beyond hourly wage rates. Especially in casual and part-time posts, all sorts of 'last in, first out' protocols, formal and informal, deter workers from taking a chance. Informally, a new joiner is less likely to get the same pick of the shifts that might be available to someone who is well-entrenched within a workplace. The resulting loss of control over hours could be impossible for someone with caring responsibilities, deterring them from seeking a change. As one hospitality worker recently told the Low Pay Commission, when shifts are uncertain:

> "You've got to work your way up again. Hope that you get a good, decent amount of hours."

Participant, Low Pay Commission focus group[60]

This tallies precisely with what we have found in our own focus group research. One young woman described the dangers of moving when:

> "They [management] are flexible once you've earned your stay there."

Participant, Coventry focus group

The measures in Chapter 6 to prevent short-notice allocation of hours and shifts being a widespread management tool aim to change this.

More generally – and indeed formally under British law – long spells have to be worked with a particular employer before rights such as protection against unfair dismissal and maternity pay are accrued. Widening the coverage of such protections, as proposed in Chapter 6, is sometimes caricatured as curtailing flexibility, but – from the workers' perspective – the result might well be to encourage dynamism.

Moving further up the pay scale, there is another distinctive problem in the UK that is more likely to inhibit dynamism: namely, the lack of meaningful income insurance when a job is lost. Across most OECD countries, the benefits received in the first instance in the event of redundancy often bear at least some relation to the wage previously earned. In the UK, by contrast, the basic rate of unemployment benefit has long been entirely flat-rate, and very low. Basic unemployment support is now worth just 14 per cent of average earnings, down from 24 per cent in 1980-1981, and replacement rates for a single earner on average wage in the event of unemployment are among the lowest in the OECD.[61] The UK has more top-up benefits for housing and the cost of disability than many other states, but the low basic coverage still makes job loss a trapdoor to a huge income

---

60 Quoted in S O'Connor: "Why don't people leave bad jobs?," Financial Times, 19 September 2023.

61 M Brewer & L Murphy, From safety net to springboard: Designing an unemployment insurance scheme to protect living standards and boost economic dynamism, Resolution Foundation, September 2023.

loss in a way that it simply isn't elsewhere: the typical worker in a just-above-average income family would see that family income drop in half in the event of unemployment, as Figure 69 shows.[62]

Figure 69: Replacement rates in the event of unemployment are higher for workers on low incomes than those on high incomes

Distribution of replacement rates in the event of unemployment within each decile of household income: UK, 2022-2023

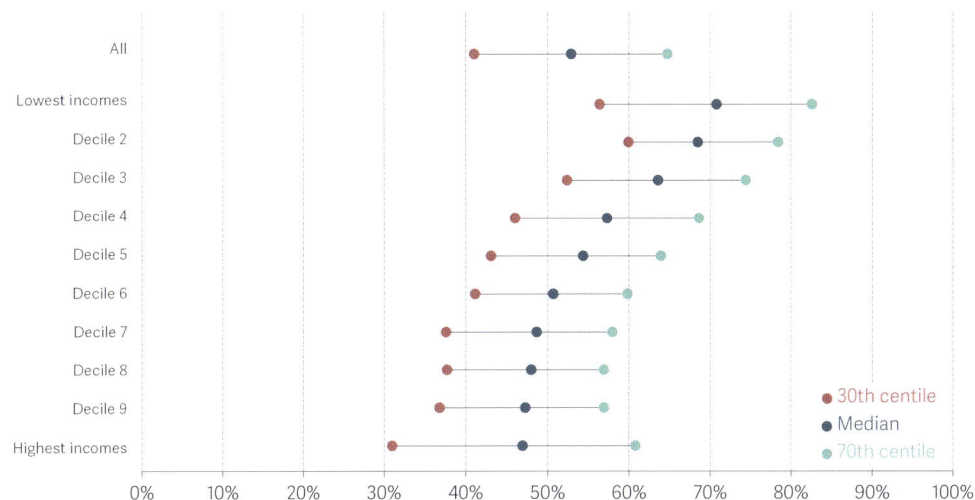

Notes: Household income measured after housing costs and equivalised. For details of modelling assumptions, see Annex 1 in: M Brewer et al., Social Insecurity: Assessing trends in social security to prepare for the decade of change ahead, Resolution Foundation, January 2022.
Source: Analysis of DWP, Family Resources Survey, using the IPPR Tax Benefit model.

Our qualitative research found that this lack of insurance weighed on workers when it came to taking labour market risks. Fear of a sudden collapse in income, which could render them unable to meet their obligations, and perhaps threaten their home, is a powerful deterrent.

> *"I'm the main earner of the house. … If I really wasn't happy, OK, I might look for other jobs, but I wouldn't just quit mine and walk... as [the] main breadwinner, no, I see it as my job to keep my salary coming in."*
>
> Participant, Chippenham focus group

---

62 M Brewer et al., Social Insecurity: Assessing trends in social security to prepare for the decade of change ahead, Resolution Foundation, January 2022.

So we propose new earnings-related Unemployment Insurance. Our preferred approach is to cover 65 per cent of previous wages for the first three months out of work, up to a cap of median earnings – currently £2,260 per month.[63] The objective is to increase security and improve job-search, while having careful regard to cost and work incentives. The limited duration means this will not lead to major changes to the incentive to work or public spending: it is projected to cost £0.4 billion in 2024-25.[64] But it will help overcome worker concerns over insecurity that may deter potentially attractive job moves. And it will also give them more time to find a good match if the worst does happen, rather than being rushed into accepting the first available post, with benefits for their future career trajectory, earnings and – consequently – the Exchequer too.

Such an approach to boosting labour market dynamisms draws not just from overseas, but from Britain's own history: the 1960s Wilson Government introduced reforms including statutory redundancy pay and earnings-related benefit supplements precisely to facilitate a more dynamic labour market.[65] An economic strategy with a central role for embracing certain kinds of economic change should include measures – such as Unemployment Insurance – that support workers who lose out to navigate the disruption involved.

Workers don't just need the confidence to move, they need the financial incentive to do so. When it comes to job moves that also require moving location, a new barrier comes into view: housing costs. Despite Britain's yawning regional gaps, the rate at which people have been moving to take up a new job has been falling, with the proportion of younger people switching both job and home down by one-third in the first two decades of this century. In part, this is for positive reasons: thankfully, there are fewer low employment hotspots in the UK today, so fewer people have to move to find any work at all. But declining geographic mobility also reflects the fact that rents and house prices have grown faster in areas where incomes have also grown at pace (see Figure 70), meaning the returns to moving

---

63 The duration of Unemployment Insurance should flex with the economic cycle, with governments able to increase the length of coverage in downturns to protect workers while they spend longer looking for work. This would also allow the unemployment insurance scheme to contribute to our reformed macroeconomic stabilisation toolkit discussed in Chapter 5.

64 M Brewer & L Murphy, From safety net to springboard: Designing an unemployment insurance scheme to protect living standards and boost economic dynamism, Resolution Foundation, September 2023.

65 J Micklewright, The Strange Case of British Earnings-Related Unemployment Benefit, Journal of Social Policy, 18(4), 527-548, 1989.

to more affluent areas have diminished because higher housing costs absorb much, or all, of the living standards gain. Given this, it is not surprising that, this century, a larger proportion of those changing address are relocating to lower-housing cost – and lower-productivity – areas.

Figure 70: Higher growth, higher rent

Average growth in median private rental price, by deciles of LA-specific growth in income per capita: English local authorities, 2011 to 2019

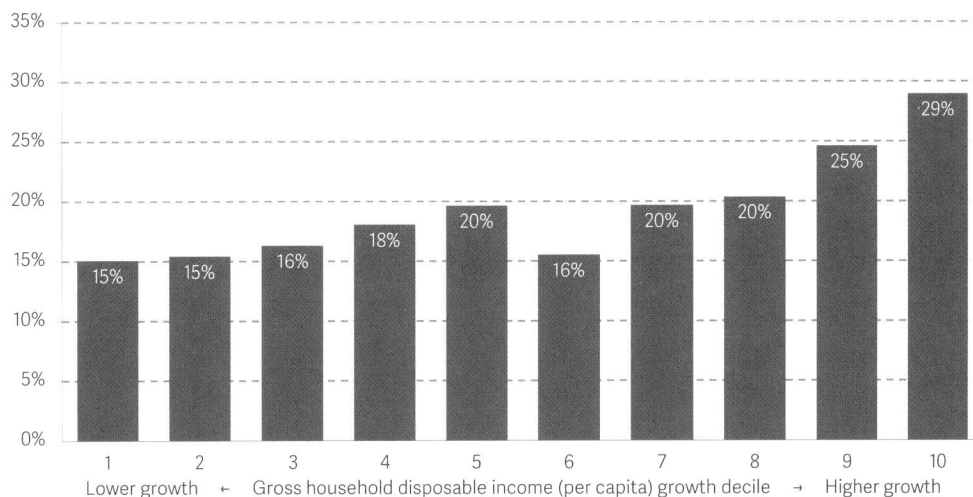

Notes: Analysis uses a GDHI cash measure derived using the methodology set out in Box 1 of L Judge & C McCurdy, Income Outcomes: Assessing income gaps between places across the UK, Resolution Foundation, June 2022.
Source: Analysis of ONS, Private rental market summary statistics; ONS, Gross Disposable Household Income.

One way of leaning against these forces is through lower transaction costs for moving, which should include halving residential Stamp Duty (currently a significant barrier). But the underlying driver of the problem is the concentration of service sector growth in and around London. Stronger regional cities, as discussed in Chapter 4, provide the plausible answer, giving more workers options to pursue their career somewhat closer to home, easing the dilemma too many face between 'get out and get ahead' or 'stay put and get stuck'. But this must be a complement, not an alternative, to greater housing supply, both in the South East and in these growing cities (where it will be required to ensure they remain within reach for aspiring workers even as local growth picks up).

Change takes time

Economic change is not an event, but a process which must unfold – and be steered – over time. That is good news in many ways: it should allow society to plan for change, and manage it rather than risk dislocation. Rising generations move into new lines of work, rather than older people having to give up jobs and the identity that comes with them. It gives time, too, to learn about what does, and does not, work.

The long-term nature of change demands two things in short supply: patience and persistence. Creating enduring institutions that help steer the direction of change, and which outlast individual policy makers or governing administrations, is vital. That thought has been at the back of our minds in settling on the recommendations made throughout this book. New trade agreements will lock down access to – and productivity-driving pressure from – overseas markets. Employee seats on boards together with the Good Work Agreement architecture will ensure workers' voices aren't just shaping decisions today, but tomorrow too. A rewired pensions architecture, in which large funds hold big stakes in firms will mark a fundamental shift in the wiring of British capitalism, and allow more financing to reach future generations of high growth-potential UK firms. Fiscal devolution will give our great cities far more ability to shape their destinies and help embed a long-term outlook about their future growth-trajectories.

In all these ways, the UK's economic governance needs to be recast to create a bias towards long-termism that has been so sorely missing. Even so, in a democracy, the way a timetable for change chimes with the electoral cycle will remain an important concern at the heart of power. To envisage how the reforms we have set out could play out and start to change the British economy, it is useful to reflect on examples of what might realistically be expected to happen when. Box 31 sketches a potential timeline. While some important changes – to taxes, benefits, employment standards and planning reform – could be put in place within five years, other reforms will take longer. And so more particularly will many of the key benefits that accumulate over time.

Box 31: A strategy in time

An unequal, stagnant nation will not become an investment nation overnight. Instead, the evolution would play out gradually, as our reforms – and the reaction to them – bed in. Here is a rough outline of how that journey might unfold:

Short-term: the first five years

These are immediate policy changes and new institutions that can be up and running in time to start making a bigger difference by 2030:

- New fiscal framework in place

- Public investment raised to 3 per cent of GDP, supporting the acceleration of the home heating transition

- 20-year growth plans set out for Greater Manchester and Birmingham

- Planning laws overhauled so local plans cover the whole country, with a new presumption that compliant developments happen

- Key planks of good work agenda legislated including new security on hours, a wage floor above 70 per cent of the median, and a revolution in enforcement

- New growth board in place to hold ministerial feet to the fire

- A new apprenticeship guarantee introduced, and further education invested in

- First new sectoral bodies for good work operating in social care, warehousing and cleaning

- Stronger earnings insurance for workers who lose their jobs

- Benefits uprated in line with wages, and poverty rates for large families cut substantially with abolition of Two Child Limit

- A fairer and more efficient tax system, treating different forms of income on the same basis

Medium-term – five to 10 years

Completion of the policy framework as the structural shift picks up pace:

- Britain's pension funds have been consolidated. A larger fraction of their investments are in directly held UK firms.

- Workers on boards of all companies with more than 200 employees

- More complicated tax changes fully phased-in: fiscal devolution, council tax revaluation, road pricing rolled out

- Sectoral deals established across further low-wage sectors

- New "UK protocol" to restore access to EU market for British goods

- New service trade deals signed with key advanced economies

Some of the returns to our strategy – such as the resurgent Greater Manchester and Birmingham we want to see – will take 20 years to play out. We say that knowing many politicians and commentators may feel this is far too long a timeline. But there is no getting away from the reality that the sort of deep change that we are talking about often takes a generation. The best political leaders on all sides have often invested in institutions and processes that pay rewards over a longer horizon. Think of the Low Pay Commission (now 25 years old) or the Pensions Commission. Both were instigated under a government of one stripe, but the reforms embodied in each have – with the implementation of auto-enrolment and the acceleration of increases in the minimum wage – been built on by a government of another complexion.

An economic strategy engaging with change will face opposition

A precondition for a more productive Britain is a more dynamic Britain. This is true, too, for a more equal Britain, with more people working in higher paid roles; as well as a greener Britain, as the net zero transition shifts how firms operate and we all live our lives. This chapter has set out how an economic strategy should seek to steer the process of change and the forces that can be marshalled to make this happen. But there are also forces that will resist change, that cannot be wished away.

While the status quo doesn't work for Britain as a whole, that doesn't mean changes to that status quo will be universally popular or that gravitational forces will not weigh against them. While low productivity firms hold up labour and capital that could be more fruitfully employed elsewhere, their owner managers are often happy to continue as things are. It is easy, of course, to point at others as barriers to change. But almost all of us will be to some extent – for example, as consumers of face-to-face services, where our habits and expectations have been shaped by ready access to relatively cheap and insecure labour. Pessimists will also point to strong incentives for politicians to support today's businesses (who have a voice) over their potential replacements (who don't). Likewise, in an ageing society the understandable impulse to 'hold on to what you've got' can seem more attractive than the disruption that comes with building a prosperous future.

These forces will need to be overcome, not once but repeatedly in the years ahead. Confidence that they can be comes from two sources. First, a widespread recognition, 15 years into relative decline, that the status quo is not working – and not working for the majority of Britons, not just those experiencing its most acute failings. And second, an understanding of the prize that economic change could bring about. Our final chapter returns to where we started and considers the size of that prize through the lens of the families and individuals who have been squeezed for so long.

Chapter Nine

The prize of ending
stagnation

Chapter summary

- Renewing the UK's economic strategy will be far from easy and some will question whether it will be worth it. Such fatalism misjudges the UK's catch-up potential.

- The UK does not need to equal American productivity or Scandinavian equality. If we matched the average income and inequality of peer economies like Australia, Canada, France, Germany and the Netherlands, the typical household would be 25 per cent (£8,300) better off, with income gains of 37 per cent for the poorest households. There is a lot to play for.

- The strategy outlined in this book could move us in that direction, boosting GDP by 7 per cent over 15 years. Raising growth alone would also raise inequality but our labour market, tax and benefit reforms shift the rewards decisively; the poorest households would see the fastest income gains. This is a new economic strategy capable of raising growth and cutting inequality.

- Typical incomes before housing costs for the working-age population would rise by 11 per cent (almost £4,000) more than they otherwise would; sufficient to overtake France and halve the income gap with the Netherlands and Germany. Relative poverty, rather than rising by 1.1 million as currently expected, would be cut by 1.3 million people. This would put Britain back into the pack of peer economies, but with a lot more work to do.

- Faster growth, combined with tax changes, would also raise revenues to the tune of 3 per cent of GDP to boost public investment, see debt falling, and support the rebuilding of public services.

- Change is politically, as well as economically, feasible. While some benefit from the status quo, there is an emerging majority for change. Middle income Brits, not just the poorest, have fallen behind. Older voters know the lack of growth threatens the funding of services they rely on. The comfortably off do not want to live in a nation where every town needs a food bank.

- This stagnant chapter of British life has gone on long enough. It is time to turn the page.

This book has argued that the UK requires a new economic strategy, one aimed squarely at raising living standards by tackling Britain's toxic combination of low growth and high inequality. It has set out what this should look like given the constraints, pressures and trade-offs involved. An agenda to build on our strengths and, above all, to invest our way to a more prosperous future has been outlined. Good jobs, as well as tax and benefit systems that fairly share reward and sacrifice, have also been put centre stage. So has the state's role in embracing and steering economic change. All of these elements are important, but none are easy.

Given the many economic and political challenges involved, some may be wondering: is success possible? Can a relatively small and mature economy, already wrestling with decarbonisation and ageing, really make a material difference to its economic trajectory? In this final chapter, we turn to what is at stake, assessing the scale of gains that this strategy could generate for the country and different groups within it, as well as some of the barriers that would need to be overcome. Our conclusion is that the prize from ending stagnation is large, plausible and well worth fighting for. Britain can do better than this.

The UK has plenty of catch-up potential

Those of a gloomy disposition may point to research suggesting that advances in technological progress have slowed, condemning the most advanced economies to much weaker growth than in previous eras.[1] A slowdown at the productivity frontier (currently the US) is of course relevant for the UK. If growth for the leader slows, in the fullness of time, the potential for growth for the laggards – including the UK – is lower too. But this 'slowdown' hypothesis is contested, and more pertinent to our prospects than this debate is our starting point. Because there is one silver lining to Britain's relative decline: we have a lot of catch-up potential. The pace of growth at the global frontier is not the binding constraint facing the UK today because we start well behind the vanguard. We have seen that productivity (measured by GDP per hour) is between 14 and 23 per cent higher in the US, Germany and France, leaving an awful lot of productivity 'catch-up' for the UK to aim at before we need to worry about the rate and power of inventions slowing down (if indeed that is happening).

To put the scale of potential catch-up growth into perspective, consider the single issue that has dominated economic policy discussions over the past seven

1   R Gordon, The Rise and Fall of American Growth: The US Standard of Living since the Civil War, Princeton University Press, August 2017; J Fernald & H Li, Is slow still the new normal for GDP growth?, Federal Reserve Bank of San Francisco, June 2019; T Philippon, Additive growth, NBER Working Papers 29950, April 2022.

years: Brexit. The UK's withdrawal from the EU is estimated by the OBR – as we reported in Chapter 2 – to represent a hit to output of 4 per cent of GDP.[2] This headwind is significant, but it is less than a quarter of the size of the UK's 18 per cent productivity gap on average with those nations at the frontier. Our economic challenges were there before Brexit, and plenty of scope for making progress remains in its wake.

The other dimension of the UK's stagnation is inequality. Just as catching up with the US's productivity levels is a very tall order – the last time Britain was at the productivity frontier was at the start of the 20th century – so, too, would be dragging UK income inequality down to the level of highly egalitarian Norway any time soon.[3] Again, though, there is a very long way to go before we have to worry about catching up with the real 'leaders.' Figure 71 shows where we stand in relation to the broad pack of OECD members: the UK has decidedly average household incomes but relatively high inequality.

Figure 71: Britain is only averagely rich but unusually divided

Gini coefficient and average household disposable income: OECD countries, 2019

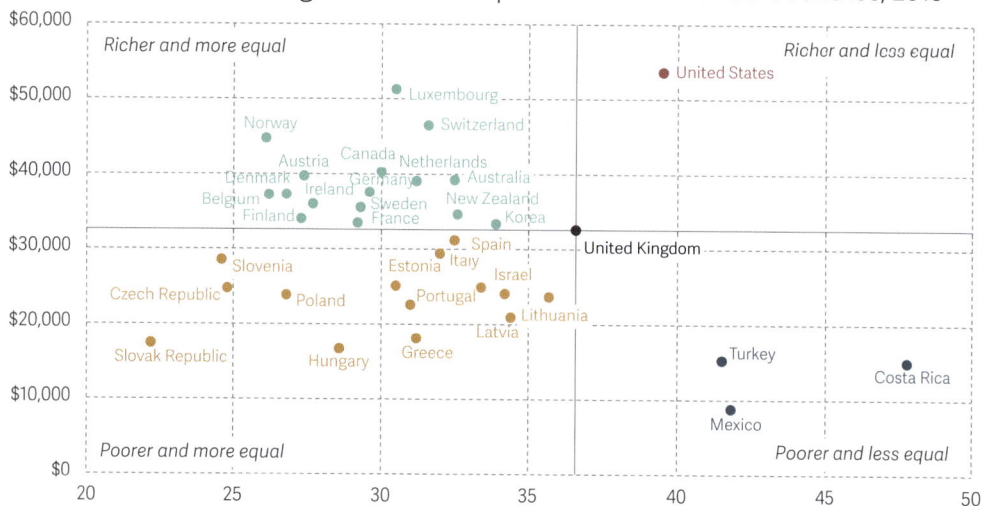

Notes: Income is equivalised and PPP adjusted.
Source: OECD, Income Distribution Database.

2   OBR, Brexit analysis, May 2022. According to the OBR, 0.4 per cent of the 4 per cent productivity hit is related to lower EU migration (which is partially compensated for by non-EU migration to the UK). The smaller working population implies that 3.6 per cent of the productivity reduction is equivalent to a fall in GDP per capita. The OBR estimates that two-fifths of the productivity effect had already taken place by January 2021, largely driven by falls in investment due to uncertainty post referendum.

3   A Bergeaud, G Cette & R Lecat, Productivity trends in advanced countries between 1890 and 2012, Review of Income and Wealth, September 2016.

The prize is large

If we put to one side the most prosperous and most equal advanced economies, we can instead identify a cluster of comparably sized nations with incomes that are both higher on average and more evenly distributed than the UK's. Indeed, there is a group of other medium-sized countries – Australia, Canada, France, Germany and the Netherlands – who many in the UK would think of as our natural peers. This cluster provides a useful guide as to where realistic ambition could take us, and gives us a sense of how much better life could be for millions of Britons if we could only find our way back into the middle of this pack, on both the growth and the inequality front.

There is a 16 per cent gap between average disposable incomes in the UK and those in our comparator set. Figure 72 allows us to think about fixing the growth and the equality problems in isolation – and then combining the two effects.[4] Raising average incomes to fill that 16 per cent gap, while holding inequality constant (shown on the left of the chart), would obviously have that same effect across rich and poor. By contrast, reducing inequality to the level in the comparison group would, in isolation, boost incomes for the poorest fifth of the country by 18 per cent while reducing them for the richest in society by 11 per cent. Now let's combine the two impacts – that is, closing the gap on growth and inequality. As Figure 72 shows, this would have huge effects at the bottom and middle of the income distribution, increasing incomes by 37 per cent among the poorest fifth of the country, and by 25 per cent for the middle, without reducing incomes at the top (indeed, they would still rise slightly).

Moving towards the richer and fairer norms seen across peer economies in this way would make a material difference to the living standards of low- and middle-income Britain. If we had the average income and inequality of Australia, Canada, France, Germany and the Netherlands, the typical household in Britain would be £8,300 better off. We are not arguing that this sort of gain would be easy to achieve, but illustrating the order of magnitude of the improvements that could be on offer. The size of the prize is enormous.

---

4   This analysis extends the international comparisons shown in: A Corlett, F Odamtten & L Try, The Living Standards Audit 2022, Resolution Foundation, July 2022.

Figure 72: Life could be transformed for low-and-middle income Britain

Effect of moving UK to the average inequality and income of Australia, Canada, France, Germany and the Netherlands, by income quintile: 2019

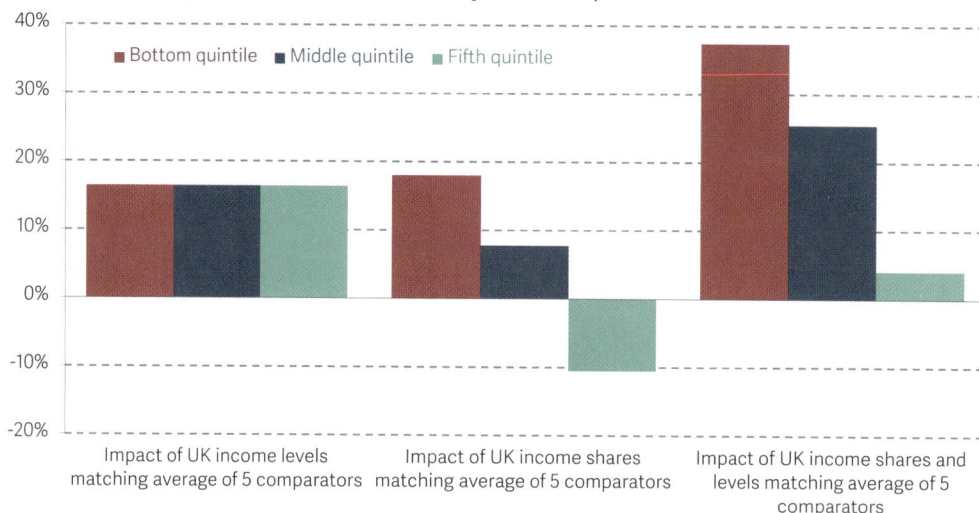

Notes: Impact on UK incomes for the first quintile, the middle quintile and the top quintile of matching average of five comparators mean income and inequality and then both together.
Source: Analysis of OECD, Income Distribution Database.

A better future for the UK does not need global growth to suddenly accelerate, or for Britain to achieve world-beating levels of productivity or equality. It just requires us to have the resolve to do what it takes to converge with countries that in many ways are not so different to us. The impact of Britain becoming more 'normal'? A transformation in living standards.

The economic strategy in this book would move us in the right direction

If progress on this scale is imaginable, would the new economic strategy outlined in this book move us towards it? To complement the 'top-down' analysis above, we now turn to a 'bottom-up' conservative assessment of the broad impact of our policy programme. We focus on the difference it might make over the coming 15 years: how much faster might the economy grow, and how much lower might inequality be, than would otherwise be the case? Our headline findings are that over 15 years:

- GDP per capita would be around 7 per cent higher, representing 0.4 percentage points faster annual growth than currently expected;

- Average wages would be boosted by about 5 per cent, with that boost skewed towards the lower paid;[5]

- Typical incomes before housing costs for the working-age population would rise by 11 per cent (almost £4,000) more than they otherwise would;

- Income inequality – rather than rising (the non-pensioner after housing costs Gini coefficient is expected to increase by 1.2 percentage points) would fall by 2.5 percentage points (an overall difference of 3.7 points) and;

- Relative poverty would be cut by 1.3 million people, rather than rising by 1.1 million.

We are on course for some growth, but a more unequal future

Forecasts for the UK economy point to huge uncertainty about growth from the mid-2020s onwards. As the country emerges from the biggest inflation shock for four decades, should we expect growth to return to the very weak levels of the past 15 years or partially recover towards the growth rates seen in the pre-financial crisis period? The Office for Budget Responsibility projects the UK's labour productivity to grow at an average rate of 1.3 per cent per year over the 15 years from 2024 – equal to the average of the past 30 years, but more than three times faster than the 0.4 per cent rate seen in the post-financial crisis, pre-pandemic period. The Bank of England is significantly more pessimistic, expecting future growth to be more like the recent past – it projects annual labour productivity growth of 0.6 per cent in the medium term.[6]

We take the average of these two 'official' views to generate a baseline for productivity growth of 0.9 per year. In the long run, we would then expect real wages to grow at around the same rate. Figure 73 shows what annual wage growth of 0.9 per cent would mean for income growth across working-age households over the next 15 years (the dark yellow bars).[7]

---

5   GDP would be boosted by more than wages because employment and average hours would also rise, with this increase again concentrated at the bottom of the wage distribution.

6   Bank of England, Monetary Policy Report, February 2023.

7   We model the impact of increasing all market incomes in line with productivity, with current tax and benefit policy. The uncertainty over supposedly 'known' trends – whether the rise of AI, geopolitical polarization or demographics – never mind of inevitable shocks – means this provides a useful baseline rather than a forecast for future levels of affluence or inequality.

Figure 73: If we continue on our current path the outlook for income growth over the next 15 years is grim for low-income households

Real change in net equivalised working-age household income (after housing costs) between 2024-25 and 2039-40, by income vigintile: UK

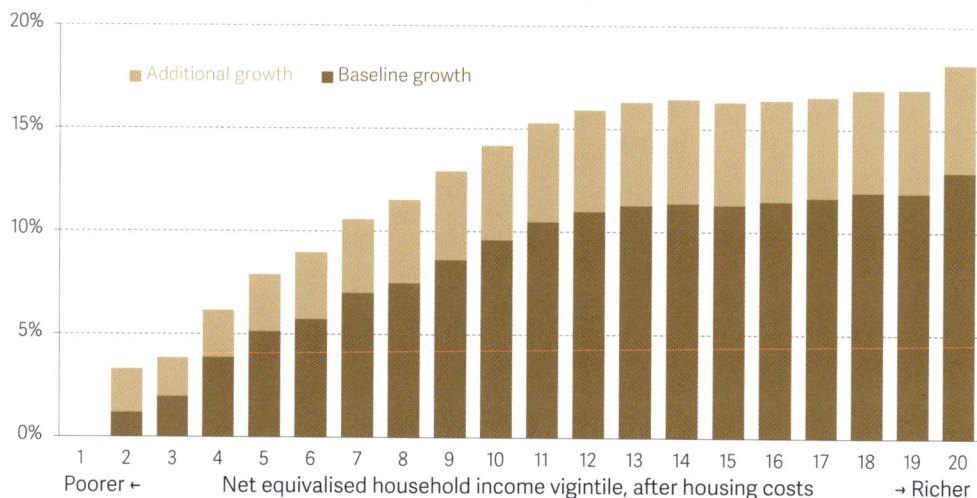

Notes: Detail of the scenario shown can be found in G Thwaites & L Try, Ending Stagnation: Technical Annex, Resolution Foundation, December 2023. We exclude the bottom 5 per cent due to concerns about the reliability of data for this group.
Source: Analysis of DWP, Family Resources Survey, using the IPPR Tax Benefit Model.

This highlights two problems: the level and distribution of expected income gains. The rate of income growth would be higher for the typical household than seen over the last terrible 15 years (0.7 per cent a year compared to 0.3 per cent) but would remain at half the levels seen in the decades before the financial crisis. The distribution problem is clearer still: growth alone is a recipe for rising earnings, but also rising inequality, with the top half seeing nearly twice the income gains of the bottom half.

We need to do better on both fronts. On growth, the agenda that we have set out in this book seeks to make a difference across all the main drivers: the quantity and quality of both capital and labour in our economy, and the efficiency with which these factors are used, as set out in Box 32.

Box 32: The building blocks of economic growth

Figure 73 above shows a conservative estimate of how our economic strategy might boost productivity growth, and therefore raise average wages and incomes (the light yellow bars). The chart below (Figure 74) show further income boosts from increased employment and hours. Together these impacts contribute to higher GDP than we would otherwise see, reflecting improvements to the quantity and quality of the following three elements:

Capital: boosting private and public investment will over time raise the amount of capital in the economy. Raising business investment halfway towards the average of France, Germany and the US would increase the capital stock by about 4 per cent, over 15 years.[8] A further boost would come from raising the public investment rate 0.8 percentage points of GDP to 3 per cent, close to the OECD average.[9]

Labour: a sharper focus on groups whose current employment rates are lower – mothers, older workers and those with a disability – will increase the quantity of labour, as will improved training and education, because workers with higher levels of education tend to work more. Moreover, better-skilled workers tend to earn and produce more, further raising the contribution of labour to economic growth.[10] Raising the productivity of our second cities will also raise employment rates for local non-graduates. Improvements in job quality will encourage low-hours, low-wage workers to put in more hours. Set against this, our measures to offer more support to job seekers will allow people to spend longer looking for a good job match, so the quality of their

---

8 We gauge the impact of business investment on growth using a standard 'production function' with typical estimates of how quickly capital depreciates and the size of the impact of extra capital on the supply capacity of the economy.

9 For the impact of public investment on GDP, we take an average of the approach adopted for private investment and the bigger impact implied by a survey of empirical estimates: P D Bom & J E Ligthart, What have we learned from three decades of research on the productivity of public capital?, Journal of Economic Surveys, 28/5, December 2014. Other studies have found bigger impacts still: A Abiad, D Furceri & P Topalova, The Macroeconomic Effects of Public Investment: Evidence from Advanced Economies, Journal of Macroeconomics, 50, 2016 and is based on IMF, Investment and Capital Stock Dataset: 1960-2021.

10 For both extra human capital and increased labour supply, we use the wage rates of the groups in question to quantify their relative contributions to growth.

labour can be better harnessed but at the price of a minor increase in the unemployment rate, as people flow from unemployment into work somewhat more slowly.

Efficiency: Lower trade costs from new trade agreements would enable the UK's best firms and industries to grow, raising overall efficiency in the economy. The agglomeration benefits of the likes of Birmingham and Greater Manchester being able to operate as larger cities, thanks to improved public transport and land use, will also increase efficiency. Planning reform will enable more activity to be located in the most productive parts of the country, although cutting the tax on investment may encourage more marginal investments to be made. Lastly, more business dynamism will improve resource allocation, putting resources in the hands of higher productivity sectors and managers that can get the best out of them, thereby boosting efficiency overall.

Taken together, we estimate that our programme could plausibly raise GDP by an additional 7 per cent over 15 years – a boost to annual growth of around 0.4 percentage points. Roughly two-fifths of this improvement would come from each of capital deepening and increased efficiency, and one-fifth from the higher quantity and quality of labour.[11] This increased growth would translate into an additional average wage rise of around 5 per cent over 15 years, sufficient to repair all of the damage done to relative wage levels in the UK compared to the G7 average between 2008 and 2022.[12] This growth boost would mean that Britain would be a country catching up rather than falling behind.

These are, nonetheless, conservative estimates in important respects. We assume the UK only closes half the private investment gap with France, Germany and the US, and make no explicit allowance for the reallocation of labour to more productive sectors. This sectoral reallocation has been a big source of growth in the past (contributing 0.4 percentage points to annual pre-financial crisis GDP growth); and is likely to be fostered by the trade, spatial, human-capital and labour-standards components of our strategy (see Chapter 8).

11 For itemised estimates of the impact of the key policies proposed in this report see G Thwaites & L Try, Ending Stagnation: Technical Annex, December 2023.

12 This is smaller than the rise in GDP for two reasons. First, part of the rise in GDP comes from increased labour supply rather than GDP per hour worked, so should not lead to a boost in wages. Indeed, higher labour supply will reduce wage rates unless the capital stock gets bigger. Second, increased human capital will raise average wages through a batting-average (i.e. compositional) effect rather than through higher wage rates for everyone. We also assume that the policy package does not change the share of labour compensation in the economy.

The focus on more and better jobs shifts gains towards the squeezed middle

Higher growth is essential to reversing the UK's relative decline and is the key precondition for a return to steady gains in living standards. But growth that boosts all market incomes (such as wages, dividends or rental income) at the same rate will increase inequality from the UK's already high levels (Figure 71). Lower-income households, far less reliant on market income, see little benefit. So next we turn to the impact of our agenda for bending the distribution of market incomes – the so-called 'pre-distribution' agenda outlined in Chapter 6 – as a result of more people moving into work and the spread of 'good jobs'.

Employment growth should be expected to boost incomes disproportionately in lower-income households, where a smaller share of adults is currently working. A plausible objective would be to raise the 16-64 employment rate by 1.5 percentage points.[13] This would represent good progress but is still a reasonable goal, representing only half the rate of improvement seen during the 2010s (as some of that growth was driven by people having to work more in response to stagnant incomes – an experience no one wants to repeat).[14]

Up until now we have assumed that wages rise equally for everyone, but the policy programme we have set out should see the biggest gains for those on lower pay. We can be confident that further increases in the minimum wage would continue the progressive hourly pay growth of the past two decades, and this should be reinforced by improvements to skills focused on low and middle earners, along with our wider reforms to industrial relations and corporate governance.

Taken together, faster growth in employment and wages among low-wage workers will skew the proceeds of growth so they are more widely shared. Figure 74 shows the extent of the progressive tilt: income gains are now projected to be more evenly shared across households, with incomes in the middle benefitting most from bottom-heavy wage growth, while poorer households are the main winners from higher employment. This pattern reflects people in poorer households having more scope to enter employment and those in middle-income households being more likely to work longish hours at lowish wages.

---

13 We also model reversing half of the fall in hours worked amongst lower-earning men this century, reflecting the improved quality of work available to them.

14 T Bell & L Gardiner, Feel poor, work more: Explaining the UK's record employment, Resolution Foundation, November 2019.

Figure 74: Predistribution shares growth more fairly but inequality still rises

Real change in net equivalised working-age household income (after housing costs) between 2024-2025 and 2039-2040, by income vigintile: UK

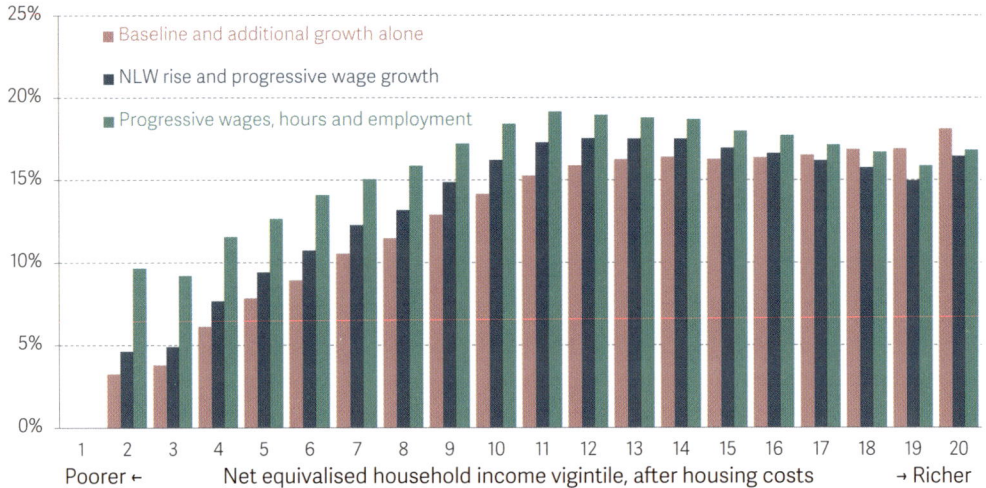

Notes: Detail on the scenarios shown can be found in G Thwaites and L Try, Ending Stagnation: Technical Annex, Resolution Foundation, December 2023. We exclude the bottom 5 per cent due to concerns about the reliability of data for this group.
Source: Analysis of DWP, Family Resources Survey, using the IPPR Tax Benefit Model.

This so-called pre-distribution agenda leads to much more widely shared growth, but it would still see those with the least falling even further behind the rest of society. Specifically, it does not do much for all those households who, for good reasons, will never receive significant income from the market economy – including large numbers with a disability. The many households whose income is a more even mix of benefits and wages, including many families with children, also continue to fall behind the rest of the population.[15] To overcome these challenges we must turn to the operation of the tax and benefit systems.

We can connect all households to the benefits of growth

Lifting the living standards of the poorest, and ensuring they keep up with the rising prosperity of the rest of society in an era of growth, inevitably requires changes in our tax and benefit systems. These are, after all, the key levers the state has for ensuring sacrifices and rewards are fairly and widely shared. Chapter

15 Low- and- middle income working households on Universal Credit will also gain less from earnings growth as they often face higher marginal tax rates, not just paying tax but seeing their benefits reduced by 55p for each extra £1 earnt.

7 showed us the regressive impact of the UK's current approach of pegging entitlements to, at best, prices: those on lower incomes fall ever-further behind over time as GDP, earnings and housing costs rise. Ensuring this doesn't happen requires us to increase social security entitlements in line with earnings. The impact of taking this approach, reversing some particularly punitive benefit cuts affecting larger families, and the broadly progressive reforms to the tax system (all detailed in Chapter 7), is set out in Figure 75.[16] The gains from growth are now widely shared and significantly tilted towards the bottom end of the distribution, resulting in steadily rising living standards for all alongside falling inequality.[17]

Figure 75: Tax and benefit reforms ensure that economic growth is shared and inequality falls

Real change in net equivalised working-age household income (after housing costs) between 2024-25 and 2039-40, by income vigintile: UK

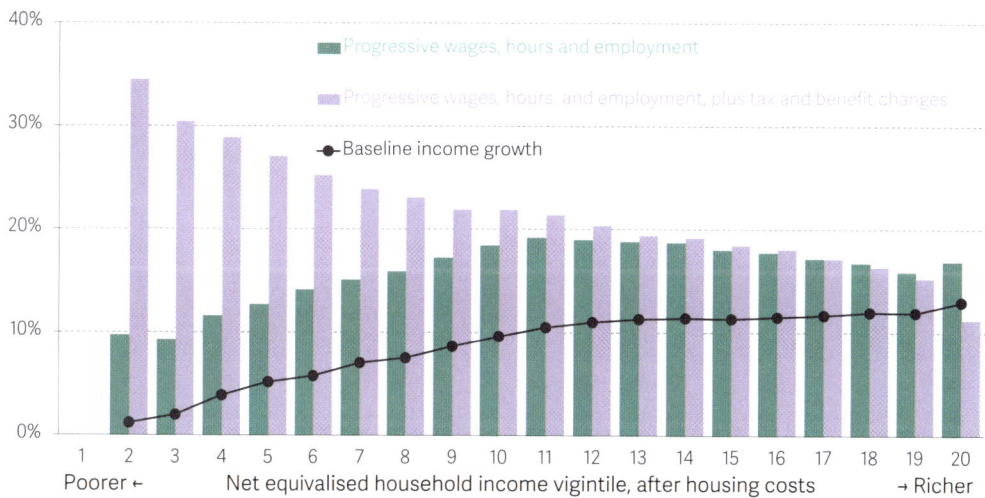

Notes: Detail on the scenarios shown can be found in G Thwaites and L Try, Ending Stagnation: Technical Annex, Resolution Foundation, December 2023. We exclude the bottom 5 per cent due to concerns about the reliability of data for this group. Source: Analysis of DWP, Family Resources Survey, using the IPPR Tax Benefit Model.

16 This chart shows the impact on the incomes of the working-age population. But having emphasised trade-offs throughout this book, it is important to note that the proposal to ensure both working-age benefits and the state pension rise in line with earnings means smaller income gains for pensioners than under the current triple lock policy. Even with this change, in 2039-40 the old basic state pension expressed as a fraction of average earnings would remain 12 percentage points higher than the basic rate of working-age benefits.

17 Figure 75 does not reflect the higher housing costs that 15 years of growth would bring about, which reduce income gains particularly for the lowest income groups (where one fifth of growth would be lost if real housing costs track earnings). As Chapter 6 set out, this is why uprating Local Housing Allowances – a key part of the benefit system – as well as increasing housing supply, is so vital. For the poorest, the impact of uprating Local Housing Allowances with local rents would, on its own, make up for about half of these extra housing costs arising from growth.

The full impact of our programme can be seen by comparing the purple bars and the black line in Figure 75. Household incomes for middle Britain grow more than twice as fast, compared to the baseline scenario, as stronger growth and the tilting of that growth towards low- and middle-income households combine to powerful effect. Raising living standards for those on low and middle incomes – the groups who have fallen behind peers in similar economies as seen in Chapter 1 – should be the strategic priority for Britain and this economic strategy delivers this priority. Relative poverty falls by 1.3 million over 15 years on the basis of our policy agenda, rather than rising by 1.1 million in the baseline scenario. Similarly, inequality (the Gini coefficient of non-pensioner after housing costs income) would fall by 2.5 percentage points, rather than increasing by 1.2 percentage points. Hidden within these charts are materially greater impacts on some groups, as discussed in Box 33.

Box 33: Who benefits?

Many of those who are structurally disadvantaged in 21st century Britain would see above average living standards gains. In particular our analysis indicates that over 15 years:

- The typical incomes of single parents would rise by 31 per cent, compared to 25 per cent for families with children and 24 per cent among other working-age households.

- Inequalities affecting some ethnic groups – including Bangladeshi and Pakistani households – would be reduced as they would experience the largest increases in typical incomes.

- Households including a person with a disability would see typical incomes increase by 26 per cent, compared to 24 per cent for other households. In contrast, in a 'baseline growth' scenario they would see only 4 per cent income growth, compared to 11 per cent for other households.

Turning from income to earnings we see that growth would, largely due to the minimum wage, be strongest for:

- Younger workers aged 18 to 24, whose earnings would rise nearly twice as fast as overall earnings.

- Women, whose earnings would be rising 20 per cent faster than men's earnings.

- Poorer areas, with Wales, the West Midlands, the North East and North West seeing the fastest earnings growth.

This represents a large, but plausible, shift of Britain back into the pack of peer economies

This modelling provides an indication that a higher investing Britain, intentionally aiming to share the rewards from higher prosperity, could make material progress. To consider what that might mean for the relative position of the UK, we can put the isolated impact of the package (ignoring the impact of baseline growth that we assume all countries would be seeing) into the context of the UK's deficits today with the group of peer economies we have focused on: Australia, Canada, France, Germany and the Netherlands. Boosting typical working-age household incomes by 11 per cent (around £4,000) would move the UK towards the middle of the pack of the peer economies we have focused on, overtaking the median income in France and approaching the Netherlands, while remaining materially below those in Canada and Australia (see Figure 11 in Chapter 1). On inequality, the 90:10 ratio would fall from 4.5 to 4.2, ending the situation where the UK is a clear outlier, with inequality falling below that in Australia and approaching that in Canada, but with France and the Netherlands remaining significantly more equal.[18] That amounts to a Britain back into the pack, but with lots more work to do.

These effects are large but plausible, as we argue in Box 34 below. They will become larger still if they become entrenched and are sustained beyond the 15 years that we have modelled. The growth effects of becoming a higher-investment nation would continue to build: only 60 per cent of the eventual impact on GDP of the higher rate of business investment would manifest within 15 years. Equally, thanks to improved educational opportunities, the rewards for young adults would be sustained over the decades of their unfolding careers, with the benefits slowly spreading their way across the whole workforce as new better-skilled cohorts replace older ones. And the shift to uprating working-age benefits in line with earnings would permanently tie the fortunes of lower-income Britain to rising national prosperity, meaning the whole of society would have a stake in a higher-growth future. These longer-term benefits all fall outside the scope of this 15-year modelling exercise but would result in further gains for Britain.

---

18 The 90:10 ratio is the ratio of the upper bound of the ninth decile (the 10 per cent of people with highest income) to that of the upper bound of the first decile (the 10 per cent of people with the lowest income). Source: Analysis of OECD, Income Distribution Database.

Box 34: How plausible is a 7 per cent boost to GDP?

The effects we are projecting for growth and inequality are substantial. But are they plausible? Do changes of this sort of magnitude lie within the historical experience of the UK and other similar nations?

Consider our projected boost to growth. One obvious yardstick to measure it against is current UK growth forecasts. Over the medium term the OBR projects potential per capita GDP to grow by a relatively upbeat 1.6 per cent over 2023-2025; the IMF projects a broadly similar 1.4 per cent over the same period; whereas the Bank of England's latest projections are far gloomier and point to annual per capita growth of 0.7 per cent.[19] The 0.9 percentage point range spanned by these three different official projections is roughly twice as large as the effect of our policy package (0.4 per cent a year faster annual growth). In other words, if the Bank of England forecast were the baseline, the effect of our package, while substantial, would take us only part of the way towards the OBR's far sunnier view of the world. Moreover, an acceleration of 0.4 percentage points on top of

the Bank of England's downbeat forecast of 0.7 per cent would only restore our growth rate to a decidedly average 1.1 per cent.

If we instead start with the more optimistic outlook – the OBR's projection of 1.6 per cent growth – and our programme were to boost this to 2 per cent, this would obviously mark a major improvement compared to recent stagnation. But even this would stay safely within historical British experience – since 1870, per capita growth has exceeded this rate in half of all years, and in two-thirds of those with positive growth.[20]

When it comes to the change in inequality, again, the scale of our projected impact looks plausible. It would also lie well within historical experience in the UK and other countries. For the OECD countries for which we have data, the typical fall in the Gini coefficient in the 15 years to 2019 was 2 percentage points – a similar order of magnitude to the one we are projecting. In the UK, the last decade or so is a particularly useful benchmark. During the 2010-2019 period the key

---

19 See Office of Budget Responsibility, Economic and fiscal outlook – March 2023, March 2023; IMF, World Economic Outlook, October 2023: Navigating Global Divergences, October 2023; Bank of England, Monetary Policy Report – February 2023, February 2023.

20 Based on analysis of Bank of England, A millennium of macroeconomic data and ONS data.

measure of inequality for (pre-tax) market incomes fell significantly (the Gini coefficient fell by 2.2 percentage points), whereas the Gini coefficient on (post-transfer) disposable incomes rose (by 0.9 percentage points) due to benefit cuts. This suggests that inequality could have fallen significantly in the UK, by a margin similar to the impact of our reforms, had changes in the tax and benefits system worked with, rather than pushed against, the gains arising from higher employment and minimum wage. Here, too, the order of magnitude of our programme feels ambitious but attainable.

Extra growth is an important part of easing the strain on the public finances

The additional growth our package generates will help with a broader challenge facing UK policy makers in the 2020s: how to reconcile deep pressures on both the public finances and public services with the urgent need to increase public investment. Any responsible government will need to grapple with this three-sided conundrum.

The combined effect of our economic strategy will be to free up resources for the government to the tune of 3 per cent of GDP over the 15-year period considered. Slightly more than half of this – around 1.7 percentage points – comes from the net benefits of faster economic growth on the public finances, with the remaining 1.3 percentage points coming from our package of tax reforms. We unpack these two components in turn, before turning to how they might be prioritised.

The additional 7 per cent boost to GDP we have projected from our strategy should lead to increased total tax revenues of around 7.5 per cent.[21] In isolation, that would generate a material improvement in the public finances, equivalent to 3 per cent of GDP. But faster growth has knock-on effects as large chunks of spending rise with it: public sector wages will need to keep up with those in the private sector in order to attract and retain workers. In addition, state pensions are already pegged to general prosperity, and we have extended that link to working-

---

21 This assumes that the broad tax richness of the UK economy remains unchanged and that future Chancellors do not choose to increase tax thresholds more than they otherwise would in response to faster growth (this is consistent with normal policy of raising them in line with inflation and with progressive average tax rates).

age benefits.[22] We estimate these knock-on effects of faster growth will raise spending by around 1.3 per cent of GDP. Revenues increase faster than spending because: some spending – for example that on goods and debt interest – will not automatically rise with faster growth; the economy grows faster than wages because of higher employment and hours worked; and average tax rates rise slightly as earnings growth outpaces indexing of tax thresholds. The net result, therefore, is that the government's overall budget balance should improve by around 1.7 per cent of GDP.

The tax package set out in Chapter 7 focused primarily on providing a more efficient, as well as fairer, system. But it also raises significant new revenue. On the same 15-year trajectory considered throughout this chapter it would bring in revenue amounting to around 1.3 per cent of GDP (£34 billion in today's prices), approximately half of which comes from the roll-out of Road Duty, to replace Fuel Duty (which is currently projected by the OBR to steadily disappear).

The total fiscal improvement of 3 per cent of GDP can be used to help meet three central objectives of this new economic strategy: increasing public investment, stabilising the public finances, and supporting public services. Around 0.8 percentage points is needed to boost the public investment rate to the 3 per cent of GDP target argued for in Chapter 5. This is a core part of the overall strategy. Another 1 percentage point is needed to run the tighter fiscal policy (aiming for a 1 per cent primary balance) required to avoid debt being on an upward trajectory over time, which we also made the case for in Chapter 5. This leaves over 1 percentage point of GDP to rebuild public services[23] struggling with the effects of austerity and the aftermath of Covid.[24]

It is worth emphasizing, again, that the fiscal outlook remains highly uncertain. No one can be at all confident about how much pressure debt interest payments will place on the public finances over the coming decade and a half. And reasonable people will disagree about the desired balance between additional tax rises and spending restraint. Our approach aims to provide an internally consistent framework for handling the competing and very real challenges facing the British state. Shifting to a higher investment future to support growth and deliver the

---

22 Here we are referring to the additional increase to benefits resulting from faster growth. We have suggested offsetting about half of the wider costs of uprating working age benefits with earnings by also uprating the state pensions in the same way, rather than current 'Triple Lock' approach.

23 It is important to note that these extra resources for public services are over and above the additional funds needed to reflect the impact of higher growth on public sector salaries, which have already been accounted for.

24 A small element of this be used to support the cost of uprating benefits in line with baseline growth.

net zero transition at the same time as repairing public services from the impact of austerity will be far from easy. It is likely to require higher taxes, even if we secure faster growth, while calls for major extensions of the state from the right (such as for defence spending to rise to 2.5 per cent of GDP) or the left (such as universal free social care provision) will likely have to remain aspirations.[25] But this framework brings out the big choices that society faces, including the balance between private and public consumption, and consumption today versus consumption tomorrow. It suggests that if we choose the right path it should be possible to make real progress on our three key goals. But are the required policy changes politically plausible?

A latent coalition for change means progress is achievable

We have argued that certain gravitational forces in UK politics, including short-termism and complacent contentment with the status quo in some parts of society, have reinforced the UK's stagnation. If that's right, it raises the question of why it would be possible to defy these pressures in future? If there are obstacles in the way, we need to understand them before we tackle them.

In particular, we need to consider the possibility of a "stagnation trap," where politics is consumed by battles over who gets to live off the wealth created in the past, instead of grappling with how to maximise what is earned in the future. Indeed, recent research shows that disappointing economic outcomes, of the kind experienced over the past decade, may erode confidence that society can work together to achieve greater prosperity, and instead fosters the zero-sum belief that gains for one group must inevitably come at the expense of another.[26] That sort of worldview obviously isn't going to help foster the sort of discourse that a healthy politics, and a new way forward on economics, requires.

The 40-year 'rise of wealth' relative to income which we highlighted in Chapter 1 (even as this partially unwinds due to the recent surge in interest rates) is another key feature of 21st century Britain. In an economy where houses are commonly worth more than many people earn in decades, we should not be surprised when some voters prefer planning restrictions to preserve the value of existing properties over the building of new homes. And this wealth is heavily concentrated among older cohorts, with high propensities to turn out and vote. The same forces can also shape the attitudes of the young too. Indeed, evidence suggests

---

25 See Cabinet Office, Integrated Review Refresh 2023: Responding to a more contested and volatile world, May 2023 and Labour Party, Towards the National Care Service, September 2019.

26 See Chinoy, S. et al., Zero-Sum Thinking and the Roots of U.S. Political Divides, September 2023.

a zero-sum outlook may be particularly prevalent among younger voters.[27] And with inheritances projected to double over the next two decades the current settlement has something to offer at least some of them – even if it involves very deferred gratification (the average age to inherit for people born in the 1970s is 62).[28] The wider point is that there are clear winners, as well as losers, from the UK's high inequality, and these winners are often powerful.

As well as active opposition to change there is also the inertia that flows from complacency. As we have shown in Chapter 1, well-off Brits already compare reasonably with those in, say, France and the Netherlands, so stagnation is a far less unpleasant experience at the top of society than in the bottom or the middle. For these more fortunate groups, there is likely to far less urgency about the need for change.

All these forces are very real. But pushing against them are a set of considerations that should make it possible to assemble a broad coalition of support for breaking with our current stagnation. Most importantly, while there will be opposition to change from some for whom the status quo works, the majority for whom it does not has grown too large to go unheard forever. Those on lower incomes have, of course, been hardest hit by the squeeze on benefit levels and a cost of living crisis focused on the cost of essentials. Low-income Brits are 26 per cent poorer than their German counterparts and 37 per cent poorer than their Dutch ones. But the pressure for change extends far wider. More than 60 per cent of Brits are at least 15 per cent poorer than their German counterparts. Older millennials (born in the early 1980s) have seen no income progress compared to the cohorts before them, earning less than Generation X (born in the 1970s) did at the same age. They are also much less likely to own a home than their parents, and – even if they make it – will achieve that goal later in life. The older half of Generation X is in their 50s, and rightly wondering why their wages peaked 15 years back.[29] The ability of rising wealth to compensate (some) for stagnant incomes depended on falling interest rates, a trend that could not persist for ever, and indeed has recently, and drastically, gone into reverse.[30]

27 J Burn-Murdoch, Are we destined for a zero-sum future?, Financial Times, September 2023.
28 L Gardiner, The Million Dollar Be-Question, Resolution Foundation, December 2017; P Bourquin et al., Inheritances and inequality within generations, Institute for Fiscal Studies, July 2020.
29 M Broome et al., An intergenerational audit for the UK: 2023, Resolution Foundation, November 2023.
30 M Broome et al., Peaked Interest?, Resolution Foundation, July 2023.

While older generations are insulated from some of these challenges, the idea that they are inevitably a block on change is overdone.[31] Concern about younger generations can be a powerful motivator for older voters too. Recent research has found, first, that many middle-aged and older voters are keenly aware of the diminished prospects for, and the financial strains on, younger relatives; and, secondly that this awareness fosters support for pro-growth policies in relation to skills, housing and more.[32] Even more directly, older people have a special interest in the quality of many public services, including the NHS. These services have to be paid for, something older voters are particularly supportive of, and they understand that growth can help foot the bills.[33]

In sum, the sheer depth and duration of stagnation has shaped a society in which it is increasingly clear to large swathes of the population that they have much to gain from faster and more fairly shared growth. And beyond any argument rooted in self-interest, the whole country is witness to the tsunami of hardship that too many have experienced. Many citizens living relatively comfortably themselves are nonetheless concerned about living in a nation where every town needs a food bank, and every city-centre has tents occupied by the homeless. The exceptional inequalities between regions and communities across the UK nag at the conscience of the country as a whole, ranking as a high concern for Conservative and Labour voters alike.[34] Likewise, the idea of dignity, decent standards – and fair rewards – at work is entirely in tune with public opinion. There is a reason both parties have vocally embraced the National Minimum Wage despite fewer than one in ten workers being on it.

For some time, leading politicians have – even if inchoately – seemed to sense that something needs to give. Well before Keir Starmer embraced higher GDP growth as a core mission for Labour, Theresa May acknowledged the need to do far more for those who were merely "just about managing" after the big squeeze of the early 2010s. Boris Johnson then pointedly turned away from austerity and vowed to spur growth specifically in those parts of the country where it had been too low for too long.

31 For evidence that older people did not cut back spending as much during the recent cost-of-living crisis, see Figure 4 in M Broome et al., Hoping and coping, Resolution Foundation, March 2023.

32 Some 17 per cent of the electorate are both over-forty and have young adult relatives that are struggling financially. Zack Grant et al, Family matters: How concerns for younger relatives bridge generational divides, RF and Nuffield Politics Research Centre, September 2023.

33 67 per cent of older people favour higher taxation and spending, compared to 43 per cent of younger people. See J Curtice et al., BSA 40: age differences, National Centre for Social Research, September 2023A

34 B Duffy et al., Unequal Britain: Attitudes to inequalities after Covid-19, King's College London, February 2021

Electoral politics is, of course, about much more than addressing major economic and social challenges: issues of the day, divisions within parties, and the coming and going of different leaders can all postpone a reckoning with them for a very long time. Nonetheless, the yearning for change that these otherwise starkly different politicians are seeking to tap into is well-grounded. Today six in ten Britons think the country is heading in the wrong direction, with far fewer – just 16 per cent – thinking it is heading in the right direction, as Figure 76 sets out.

Figure 76: The majority of British people think the country is heading in the wrong direction

Proportion of adults who think things in Great Britain are heading in the right direction or wrong direction

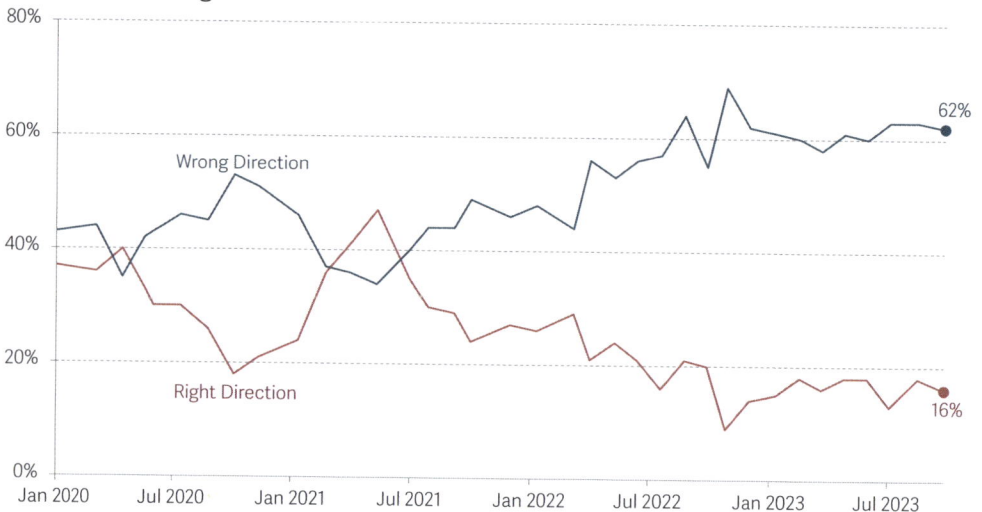

Notes: Data represents c.1000 nationally representative interviews, conducted online, with GB adults between January 2020 to September 2023 as part of the Ipsos Political Pulse series.
Source: Ipsos, Ipsos UK Political Pulse, September 2023.

All told, we do need to be mindful of the perils of a stagnation trap, but we should also take heart from the real and widespread desire across the nation to move on from a grim status quo. Britain can do better and, increasingly, it is evident that a large swath of the public are up for the challenge. Despite the political headwinds confronting those seeking to break out of stagnation, it is inherent in the promise of inclusive prosperity that a broad coalition could benefit – after all, an expanding pie, widely-shared, should create many more winners than losers.

Turning the page on stagnation

A year or two of weak growth may not register with ordinary people given how many other things affect their circumstances. But after 15 long years of stagnation the consequences have slowly but surely become impossible to miss – and the logic of change harder to resist. This report has shown that faster growth is achievable and that it can be used to secure higher living standards for all, with the biggest gains flowing to those who need them most. But for that to happen we need to summon the strategic focus that the UK's serious problems demand, bring rigour to bear in devising solutions, and then sustain the necessary change over the longer term.

In this chapter we've tried to quantify the scale of the improvement that we think is possible. But behind these numbers are a set of changes in the character of the British economy that would seek to reinforce our enduring strengths while remedying entrenched weaknesses. Above all, a nation that has got used to living off its past would instead mobilise and prioritise its resources to invest in a more prosperous and greener future. A growth model that is overwhelmingly dependent on London would be rebalanced with other key cities driving not only their own prosperity, but that of their regions and our nation. Post-Brexit trade strategy would move on from perpetually relitigating the division of a long-passed referendum to a new hard-headed assessment of where Britain's mid-21st century economic interests lie. A labour market model that has clear strengths, but generates far too much low-quality work, would be reformed so that its dynamism rests not just on flexibility for employers but meaningful security for Britain's workers. Our preoccupation with whether we have too many graduates would be replaced with an iron resolve to lift attainment at all levels, enabling millions of overlooked young people to build better careers. A tax system that too often undermines growth and reinforces unfairness would be made more efficient while raising the revenue needed to help stabilise our public finances and restore our public services. And our diminished social security system would be repaired and rewired to ensure that everyone enjoys the benefits of rising prosperity.

After these changes Britain would still have a recognisable, distinctively liberal, flexible, highly service-oriented economy. But it would be one that is looking to the future – not just embracing change, but having the self-confidence to steer it too. The scale and scope of this challenge should not daunt us. Economies can adapt and be shaped for the better. History teaches us that growth can speed up as well as slow down, and inequality can fall as well as rise. This stagnant chapter of British life has gone on long enough. It is time to turn the page.

The Commissioners

A small Commission of seven high-profile thinkers and doers provides The Economy 2030 Inquiry's strategic leadership and direction. Its membership is:

Baroness Minouche Shafik
President of Columbia University

Sir Clive Cowdery
Founder of the Resolution Foundation and Chairman of the Resolution Group

Adam Tooze
Kathryn and Shelby Cullom Davis Professor of History, Columbia University

Dani Rodrik
Ford Foundation Professor of International Political Economy at Harvard University

Dame Carolyn Fairbairn
Former Director-General of the Confederation of British Industry

Baroness Frances O'Grady
Former General Secretary of the Trades Union Congress

Lord Nicholas Stern
I G Patel Chair of Economics and Government, LSE

The Advisory Group

The Economy 2030 Inquiry is also overseen by an Advisory Group, who provide external input, challenge and advice. Its membership is:

Alex Beer, Nuffield Foundation

Alex Brazier, BlackRock

Chiara Criscuolo, OECD

Chris Colvin, Queen's University, Belfast

Darra Singh, EY

Deborah Cadman, Birmingham City Council

Gary Gillespie, Scottish Government

James Benford, HM Treasury

Jane Green, Nuffield College, University of Oxford

Jeromin Zettelmeyer, IMF and PIIE

Kate Bell, TUC

Kelly Beaver, Ipsos MORI

Pat Richie, Metro Dynamics

Rachel Ashworth, Cardiff Business School

Rain Newton-Smith, CBI

Rebecca Heaton, Lloyds Banking Group

Sushil Wadhwani, PGIM Wadhwani

The Economy 2030 Inquiry publications

All publications can be read at economy2030.resolutionfoundation.org.

1. The UK's decisive decade: The launch report of The Economy 2030 Inquiry
2. Levelling up and down Britain: How the labour market recovery varies across the country
3. Work experiences: Changes in the subjective experience of work
4. The Carbon Crunch: Turning targets into delivery
5. Trading places: Brexit and the path to longer-term improvements in living standards
6. Home is where the heat (pump) is: Assessing the Government's Heat and Buildings Strategy
7. Business time: How ready are UK firms for the decisive decade?
8. Begin again? Assessing the permanent implications of Covid-19 for the UK's labour market
9. More trade from a land down under: The significance of trade agreements with Australia and New Zealand
10. Social mobility in the time of Covid: Assessing the social mobility implications of Covid-19
11. Changing jobs? Change in the UK labour market and the role of worker mobility
12. Social Insecurity: Assessing trends in social security to prepare for the decade of change ahead
13. A presage to India: Assessing the UK's new Indo-Pacific trade focus
14. Under pressure: Managing fiscal pressures in the 2020s
15. Under new management: How immigration policy change will, and won't, affect the UK's path to becoming a high-wage, high-productivity economy
16. Shrinking footprints: The impacts of the net zero transition on households and consumption
17. Enduring strengths: Analysing the UK's current and potential economic strengths, and what they mean for its economic strategy, at the start of the decisive decade
18. Listen up: Individual experiences of work, consumption and society
19. Growing clean: Identifying and investing in sustainable growth opportunities across the UK
20. Low Pay Britain 2022: Low pay and insecurity in the UK labour market
21. Bouncebackability: The UK corporate sector's recovery from Covid-19
22. All over the place: Perspectives on local economic prosperity
23. Right where you left me? Analysis of the Covid-19 pandemic's impact on local economies in the UK
24. Big welcomes and long goodbyes: The impact of demographic change in the 2020s

25. Net zero jobs: The impact of the transition to net zero on the UK labour market
26. The Big Brexit: An assessment of the scale of change to come from Brexit
27. Income outcomes: Assessing income gaps between places across the UK
28. Bridging the Gap: What would it take to narrow the UK's productivity disparities?
29. Power plays: Assessing the impact of, and changes to, worker and firm power in the UK economy
30. Stagnation nation: Navigating a route to a fairer and more prosperous Britain
31. As good as it gets? The forces driving economic stagnation and what they mean for the decade ahead
32. Centralisation Nation: Britain's system of local government and its impact on the national economy
33. Adopt, adapt and improve: A brief look at the interplay between labour markets and technological change in the UK
34. Train in Vain? Skills, tasks, and training in the UK labour market
35. Hitting a brick wall: How the UK can upgrade its housing stock to reduce energy bills and cut carbon
36. Minding the (productivity and income) gaps: Decomposing and understanding differences in productivity and income across countries
37. Open for business?: UK trade performance since leaving the EU
38. Cutting the cuts: How the public sector can play its part in ending the UK's low investment rut
39. Low Pay Britain 2023: Improving low-paid work through higher minimum standards
40. Where the rubber hits the road: Reforming vehicle taxes
41. Trading Up: The role of the post-Brexit trade approach in the UK's economic strategy
42. Beyond Boosterism: Realigning the policy ecosystem to unleash private investment for sustainable growth
43. Tax planning: How to match higher taxes with better taxes
44. Sharing the benefits: Can Britain secure broadly shared prosperity?
45. Putting good work on the table: Reforming labour market institutions to improve pay and conditions
46. A tale of two cities (part 1): A plausible strategy for productivity growth in Birmingham and beyond
47. A tale of two cities (part 2): A plausible strategy for productivity growth in Greater Manchester and beyond
48. From safety net to springboard: Designing an unemployment insurance scheme to protect living standards and boost economic
49. Ready for change: How and why to make the UK economy more dynamic
50. Built to last: Towards a sustainable macroeconomic policy framework for the UK
51. Learning to grow: How to situate a skills strategy in an economic strategy
52. Talking trade-offs: Deliberations on a higher-productivity future in the Birmingham and Greater Manchester urban areas